AGRICULTURAL LAW

IN A NUTSHELL

By

DONALD B. PEDERSEN
Professor of Law
University of Arkansas
Fayetteville

KEITH G. MEYER
E.S. & Tom W. Hampton
Professor of Law
University of Kansas

COPYRIGHT © 1995 By WEST PUBLISHING CO.
610 Opperman Drive
P.O. Box 64526
St. Paul, MN 55164–0526
1–800–328–9352

ISBN 0–314–06454–0

TEXT IS PRINTED ON 10% POST
CONSUMER RECYCLED PAPER

PRINTED WITH
SOY INK

PREFACE

This Nutshell seeks to cover the basics of most law school survey courses in Agricultural Law. Also, we hope that selected chapters will be useful when the emphasis of a course or seminar is on a particular aspect of the discipline -- government regulation, resources management, or financing as examples.

When this Nutshell was in final editing, the United States Department of Agriculture was beginning the process of reorganizing pursuant to Pub. Law 103-354, approved by the President on Oct. 13, 1994. We point out these changes here, *and* in the text. The new Consolidated Farm Service Agency (CFSA) has taken over the programs of the Agricultural Stabilization and Conservation Service (ASCS) and the farmer loan programs of the Farmers Home Administration(FmHA). The Federal Crop Insurance Corporation (FCIC), while not abolished, is now operated as a subagency of CFSA. The new Rural Housing and Community Development Service (RHCDS) has taken over FmHA housing programs and certain other community loan programs. And, the new Natural Resources Conservation Service (NRCS) is successor to the Soil Conservation Service (SCS), except as to programs assigned to CFSA. USDA Secretary's Memo 1010-1 (Oct. 20, 1994).

Also part of the reorganization law is authorization to establish within the USDA an independent National Appeals Division, free from direction and control of any person other than the Secretary. The

PREFACE

Division will hear requests to review administrative decisions adverse to participants when rendered by the CFSA, RHCDS, NRCS, Commodity Credit Corporation (CCC) as well as the new Rural Utilities Service (RUS) or the new Rural Business and Cooperative Development Service (RBCDS).

We have omitted coverage of farm business and estate planning, including pertinent federal tax law. This subject requires its own Nutshell. We do touch on tax issues where important to an understanding of, *inter alia,* agricultural cooperatives, farm leases, grain sales and conservation easements.

It has been our good fortune to have had the help of numerous individuals in our writing and editing process. Special thanks go to Charles H. Carnes, Christopher R. Kelley, Mary Beth Matthews, Leslie S. Mead, John D. Reilly, and Julia R. Wilder. We are particularly grateful to Kelé Onyejekwe who reviewed almost all of the chapters. Problems that may remain are the sole responsibility of your authors.

It has been suggested that this Nutshell might be of interest to farmers and other nonlawyer agriculturalists. We welcome these readers, but stress that this book can never be a substitute for legal advise from a lawyer who is acquainted with the particular case. Note too that this Nutshell deals with areas of the law where change comes often.

Donald B. Pedersen, Fayetteville, Arkansas

Keith G. Meyer, Lawrence, Kansas

November, 1994

OUTLINE

PREFACE iii
TABLE OF CASES xvi

Chapter 1 Government and Agriculture
I. An Historical Perspective 1
II. Economic Regulation 5
    A. The Depression Era 5
    B. Farm Programs After the 1930s 11
    C. Contemporary Farm Programs 15
        1. Price Supports 15
        2. Income Supports 17
        3. Recourse Loans 20
        4. Supply Control and Soil Conservation 20
            a. Annual Programs 21
            b. Multiple Year Programs 22
        5. Marketing Orders 24
            a. Fruit, Tree Nut and Vegetable Orders 25
            b. Milk Marketing Orders 26
            c. State Marketing and Price Orders 28
        6. Assistance Programs 29
            a. Indemnity Programs 29
            b. Livestock Emergency Programs 29
            c. Crop Emergency and Insurance
               Programs 30
            d. Domestic Food Assistance Programs 32
        7. Issues in Administration of Programs 32

OUTLINE

D. Export Programs 37
III. Structure Issues 42
   B. General Concerns 42
   C. Anticorporate Farming Laws 45
   D. Restrictions on Non-resident Aliens 47
   E. State Finance Programs 48
   F. Federal Measures 49

Chapter 2   Financial Institutions and Programs
I. Introduction 51
II. The Farm Credit System 54
   A. The System Prior to 1985 55
   B. Funding the System 56
   C. Restructuring the System 57
   D. Borrowers' Rights 60
   E. Farm Credit System Litigation 64
      1. Federal Jurisdiction 64
      2. State Court Jurisdiction 65
III. Farmers Home Administration- Consolidated
      Farm Service Agency 68
   A. Farmer Program Loans 68
   B. Loan Servicing 71
   C. The Curry and Coleman Litigation 72
   D. FmHA/CFSA Farmer Borrower Rights 75
      1. Generally 75
      2. Primary Loan Servicing 76
      3. Preservation Loan Servicing 81
   E. Administrative Appeal and Review 83
   F. Guaranteed Loans 84
IV. Chapter 12 Bankruptcy 86
   A. Introduction... 86

OUTLINE

B. Overview and Selected Issues 87
C. Operational Financing 92
D. Chapter 12 Trustee 95

Chapter 3   Leases of Agricultural Land
I. Introduction 96
II. Types of Leases 96
III. Custom Farmers and Croppers 98
IV. The Lease Document 99
    A. Importance of Written Leases 99
    B. Enforceability of Leases 100
    C. Farm Lease Provisions 102
        1. In General 102
        2. Options to Purchase 104
V. Termination of Farm Tenancies 105
    A. Term of Years 106
    B. Periodic Tenancies 106
    C. Landlord's Right of Entry 108
    D. Land Preparation Costs 108
    E. Negotiating New Lease Terms 109
    F. Pastures 109
    G. Fall and Spring Planted Crops 110
        1. Lease Termination Law and Practice 110
        2. Confronting the Problem of
            Fox v. Flick 111
    H. Breach of Covenant or Making Waste 113
VI. Leasing From a Life Tenant 115
    A. Growing Crops 115
    B. Underlying Lease Terminates 117
VII. Tax Planning Considerations 118
VIII. Farm Program Payment Rules 119

OUTLINE

Chapter 4   Storage and Marketing of Crops
I.   Regulation of Warehouses and Grain Dealers 121
II. Law of Operations 123
  A. Generally 123
  B. Status of Parties Delivering Commodities 126
    1. Scale Ticket Holders 126
    2. Holders of Documents of Title 128
  C. Receipt Holders: No CommoditiesDelivered 129
  D. Warehouse Liability as Bailee 130
III. Producer Marketing Strategies 133
  A. Forward Contracting 133
    1. Cash Forward Contracts 133
    2. Price Later Contracts 135
    3. Deferred Payments Contracts 136
    4. Minimum Price Contracts 137
    5. Enforceability of Oral Cash Forward
       Contracts 138
      a. Confirmatory Memoranda 138
      b. Price Increases 143
      c. Casualty to Crop 143
  B. Commodity Futures Trading 145
    1. Commodity Exchanges 145
    2. The Futures Contract 146
    3. Who Trades in Futures and Why? 148
    4. Hedging Risks 150

Chapter 5   Crop and Livestock Financing
I.   Introduction 152
II. Secured Transactions 152
III. Scope of Article 9 153
  A. Generally 153

OUTLINE

    B. Land Contract Payments 154
    C. Standing Crops 155
    D. Leases of Equipment and Livestock 157
IV. Farm Products as Collateral 158
V. Attachment 163
    A. Value 163
    B. Rights in the Collateral 163
    C. Description of Collateral 165
        1. Generally 165
        2. Livestock Descriptions 166
        3. Crop Descriptions 167
        4. Proceeds 168
    D. Government Payments 170
VI. Perfection 174
    A. Farm Products 175
    B. Documents of Title 176
    C. General Intangibles, Accounts and
        Negotiable Instruments 177
    D. Financing Statement 177
VII. Priorities Under Article 9 177
    A. Generally 177
    B. Federal Agency Lenders 178
    C. Federal Farm Products Rule 179
        1. An Historical Perspective 179
        2. Federal Preemption 182
        3. Direct Notice to Buyers 184
        4. USDA Certified "Central Filing
        System"...187
        5. Multiple-Payee Checks and CCC 191
    D. Priority Between Secured Parties 192
    E. Production Supplier's Priority 193

OUTLINE

    F. Documents of Title 194
        1. Generally 194
        2. Non-Negotiable Documents 195
        3. Negotiable Warehouse Receipts 197
VIII. Assignments of Sale Proceeds 200
IX. Statutory Agricultural Liens 201
   A. Possessory Liens and UCC § 9-310 201
   B. Nonpossessory Liens 203
   C. Statutory Liens and § 1631 205

Chapter 6   Insolvent Warehouses and Buyers
I. Introduction 207
II. Shortages of Commingled Grain 208
   A. Status of Producer Bailors 208
   B. Status of Bailors Other Than Producers 210
   C. Overissue Warehouse Receipts 211
       1. § UCC 7-207(2) 211
       2. Receipts for Fungible Goods 212
       3. Holder by Due Negotiation 213
       4. Purchaser in Good Faith 213
       5. Without Notice of Claim or Defense 214
       6. Value 217
IIII. Remedies for Shorted Bailors 217
IV. Remedies for Unpaid Sellers 220
   A. Sales to Grain Dealers 220
   B. Unpaid Sellers and Secured Parties 225

Chapter 7 Animals
I. Breed Associations 229
   A. Basics 229
   B. Due Process Issues 230

OUTLINE

C. Antitrust Issues 231
II. Branding Laws 232
   A. In General 232
   B. Brands as Evidence of Ownership 234
   C. Bill of Sale Requirement & the UCC 235
III. Sales of Animals 236
   A. Generally 236
   B. Warranties 236
      1. Express Warranties 238
      2. Implied Warranties 240
IV. Packers and Stockyards Act 245
   A. Introduction 245
   B. Packers 246
      1. Activities Regulated 246
      2. Statutory Trust for Unpaid Cash
         Sellers...249
      3. Prompt Payment Rule 252
      4. Packer and Feedlot Operations 253
   C. Stockyards, Market Agencies and Dealers 254
      1. Stockyards 254
      2. Market Agencies and Dealers 256
      3. Unlawful Practices 258
      4. Reparation by Private Persons 260
   D. Live Poultry Dealers 261
      1. Terminology 262
      2. Unlawful Practices 263
      3. Prompt Payment Rule 265
      4. Statutory Trust for Unpaid Sellers 266
      5. Records Kept and Furnished 267
V. Communicable Animal Diseases 268
VI. Animal Patents 272

OUTLINE

Chapter 8   Agricultural Cooperatives
I.   Introduction 274
II. Formation of Cooperatives 276
III. Financial Structure 277
    A. Stock and Membership Purchases 278
    B. Patronage Based Financing 278
    C. Borrowed Capital 283
IV. Marketing Contracts 284
V. Taxation 287
    A. Generally 287
    B. Non-Exempt Cooperatives 289
    C. "Exempt" Cooperatives 292
VI. Securities 296
VII. Antitrust Laws 299
    A. Sherman Act 299
    B. Clayton Act 300
    C. Capper-Volstead Act 301
        1. Generally 301
        2. Cooperative Membership Structure 302
        3. Vertically Integrated Cooperatives 304
        4. Activities of Capper-Volstead
           Cooperatives 305
    D. Other Federal Statutes 308

Chapter 9   Agricultural Employment Law
I.   Background 309
II. Wage and Hour Laws 310
    A. The Agricultural Minimum Wage 310
    B. Employment and Joint-Employment Issues 311
    C. Agriculture Defined 313
    D. Overtime Pay 316

OUTLINE

   E. Remedies 316
III. Child Labor Laws 317
IV. Social Security 319
V. Unemployment Compensation 322
VI. Workers' Compensation 323
VII. Constitutional Issues 325
VIII.Job Services 326
IX. Migrant & Seasonal Agricultural Worker
      Protection Act 327
   A. Overview 327
   B. Regulated Persons 328
   C. Protected Individuals 329
   D. Worker Protection Requirements 330
   E. Joint Employment Doctrine 332
   F. Exemptions 333
   G. Determination of Contractor Registration 334
   H. MSPA Penalties and Remedies 334
X. Alien Farmworkers 335
XI. Occupational Safety & Health 339
   A. Generally 339
   B. Agricultural and Farming Operations 340
   C. OSHA Standards - Agricultural Operations 342
   D. Housing Conditions - OSHA 343
   E. Grain Warehouses - OSHA 343
   F. EPA Fieldworker Standard 343
XII. Farmworker Unions 346

Chapter 10   Farmland Preservation Law
I. A Farmland Conversion Crisis? 350
II. State and Local Laws 351
   A. Property Tax Relief 351

OUTLINE

    1. The Basics 351
    2. Constitutional Issues 353
    3. Who Benefits? Who Loses? 353
  B. Special Assessment Relief 355
  C. Right-to-Farm Statutes 356
    1. The Basics 356
    2. Construction of Right-to-Farm Statutes 358
  D. Agricultural Zoning 360
    1. Introduction 360
    2. Mutability of Agricultural Zoning 361
    3. Constitutional Issues 363
    4. Agricultural Zoning Techniques 368
  E. Agricultural Districts 369
    1. The Concept 369
    2. Selected Issues 370
  F. Severing of Development Rights 373
    1. Purchase of Development Rights 373
    2. Purchase of Agricultural Conservation
       Easements 375
    3. Transfer of Development Rights 375
    4. Donative Transfers 377
  G. Impact of State Programs 378
III. Federal Initiatives 380
  A. Farmland Protection Policy Act of 1981 380
  B. Other Federal Programs 381
  C. Federal Tax Policy 382

Chapter 11   Soil and Water Management
I. Soil Resources Law 383
  A. Soil Erosion 383
  B. Role of the States 384

OUTLINE

     1. As Forums for Litigation 384
     2. State Legislation 386
   C. Role of the Federal Government 389
     1. Prior to the 1985 Farm Bill 389
     2. Sodbuster & Conservation Compliance 392
     3. Conservation Reserve Program 393
     4. FmHA/CFSA Conservation Easements 395
     5. Surface Mining Control 395
II. Water Resources Law: An Agricultural
    Perspective 396
   A. Water Quality 396
     1. Generally 396
     2. Point Source Pollution 397
     3. Nonpoint Source Pollution 400
     4. Policy Alternatives 402
   B. Wetlands Preservation 405
     1. Swampbuster 405
     2. U.S. Army Corps § 404 Permits 407
     3. Wetlands Reserve Program 410
     4. Other Federal Laws 411
   C. Hazardous and Toxic Substances 411
   D. Allocation of Water Resources 412
     1. The Problem 412
     2. Rivers and Streams 413
     3. Groundwater 414
     4. Reclamation Projects 420
   E. Drainage 422
     1. Generally 422
     2. Common Law Drainage Principles 423
     1. Drainage Codes 425
INDEX 427

TABLE OF CASES

A. Gay Jensen Farms Co. v. Cargill, Inc., 309 N.W.2d 285 (Minn. 1981), *220*

Adams v. American Quarter Horse Ass'n, 583 S.W.2d 828 (Tex. Civ. App. 1979), *230*

Adams Fruit Co., Inc. v. Barrett, 494 U.S. 638, 100 S.Ct. 1384, 108 L.Ed.2d 585 (1990), *325, 335, 345*

Adrian v. Elmer, 178 Kan. 242, 284 P.2d 599 (1955), *239*

Alimenta (U.S.A.), Inc. v. Cargill, Inc., 861 F.2d 650 (11 Cir. 1988), *144*

Allen, Ex parte, 2 U.S.P.Q.2d (BNA) 1425 (Bd. Patent App. 1987), *273*

Allison v. Block, 723 F.2d 631 (8th Cir. 1983), *73-74*

American Indian Agricultural Credit Consortium v. Fort Pierre Livestock, Inc, 379 N.W.2d 318 (S.D. 1985), *167*

Anderson, U.S. v., 542 F.2d 516 (9th Cir. 1976), *70*

Appeal of Buckingham Developers, Inc., 61 Pa. Cmwlth 408, 433 A.2d 931 (1981), *363*

Applegate v. Commissioner, 92-2 USTC ¶ 623 (7th Cir. 1992), *137*

Appley Brothers v. U.S., 7 F.3d 720 (8th Cir. 1993), *220*

Arbogast and Bastian, Inc., In re, 42 B.R. 633 (Bankr. D. Pa. 1984), *250*

Arkansas Valley Industries, Inc. v. Freemand, 415 F.2d 713 (8th Cir. 1969), *264*

Asbury Hospital v. Cass Co., 326 U.S. 207, 66 S.Ct. 61, 90 L.Ed. 6 (1945), *46*

Aviles v. Kunkle, 765 F. Supp. 358 (S.D. Tex. 1991), *332*

Avoyelles Sportmen's League v. Alexander, 473 F. Supp. 525 (W.D. La. 1979), *409*

Azevedo v. Minister, 471 P.2d 661 (Nev. 1970), *139*

B. Rosenberg & Sons, Inc., v. St. James Sugar Coop, Inc., 447 F. Supp. 1 (E.D.La. 1976), affr'd 565 F.2d 1213 (5th Cir. 1977), *297*

Bamford v. Upper Republican Natural Resources District, 245 Neb. 299, 512 N.W.2d 642 (1994), *418*

Baskin v. State ex rel. Worker's Comp., 722 P.2d 151 (Wyo. 1986), *326*

TABLE OF CASES

Baugh Farms, Inc. v. Smith, 495 F.Supp. 40 (N.D. Miss. 1980), *133*

Bayside Enterprises, Inc. v. NLRB, 429 U.S. 298, 97 S.Ct. 576, 50 L.Ed.2d 494 (1977), *315, 340*

Becker v. McFadden., 221 Kan. 552, 561 P.2d 416 (1977), *109*

Beef Nebraska, Inc., v. U.S., 807 F.2d 712 (8th Cir. 1986), *252*

Beliz v. W.H. McLeod & Sons Packing Co., 765 F.2d 1317 (5th Cir. 1985), *312, 332*

Bell v. Vaughn, 46 Ariz. 515, 53 P.2d 61 (1935), *100*

Bennett, In re, 126 B.R. 869 (Bankr. N.D.Tex. 1991), *282*

Berens, In re, 41 B.R. 524 (Bankr. D.Minn. 1984), *94*

Berigan v. U.S., 257 F.2d 852 (8th Cir. 1958), *260*

Bisson, U.S. v., 839 F.2d 418 (8th Cir. 1988), *35*

Black Hills Packing Co. v. South Dakota Stockgrowers Ass'n, 397 F. Supp. 622 (D.S.D. 1975), *233*

Board of Education v. Board of Revision of Lake County, 57 Ohio St.2d 62, 11 O.O.3d 220, 386 N.E.2d 1113 (1979), *354*

Borden Co., United States v., 308 U.S. 188, 60 S.Ct. 182, 84 L.Ed. 181(1939), *306*

Boundary Drive Associates v. Shrewsbury Twp., 507 Pa. 481, 491 A.2d 86 (1985), *364*

Bracamontes v. Weyerhaeuser Co., 840 F.2d 271 (5th Cir. l988), *329*

Bradford v. Plains Cotton Cooperartive Ass'n, 539 F.2d 1249 (10th Cir. 1976), cert. denied, 429 U.S. 1042, 97 S.Ct. 743, 50 L.Ed. 754 (1977), *143*

Branch Banking & Trust Corp. v. Gill, 293 N.C. 164, 237 S.E.2d 21 (1977), *214, 217*

Brown v. Beckerdite, 174 Kan. 153, 254 P.2d 308 (1953), *109*

Bruhn's Freezer Meats of Chicago, Inc. v. USDA, 438 F.2d 1332 (8th Cir. 1971), *247*

Buckeye Production Credit Ass'n v. Farm Credit Adm'n, 997 F.2d 11 (4th Cir. 1993), *59*

Bueno v. Mattner, 829 F.2d 1380 (6th Cir. 1987), cert. denied 486 U.S. 1022, 108 S.Ct. 1994, 100 L.Ed.2d 226 (1988), *334*

Bunge Corp. v. Recker, 519 F.2d 449 (8th Cir. 1975), *144*

Burgmeier v. Farm Credit Bank of St. Paul, 499 N.W.2d 43 (Minn. Ct. App. 1993), *67*

Burt v. Arkansas Livesotck and Poultry Commission, 278 Ark. 236, 644 S.W.2d 587 (1983), *270*

TABLE OF CASES

Butler, v. U.S., 297 U.S. 1, 56 S.Ct. 312, 80 L.Ed. 477 (1936), *8*

Button Hook Cattle Co., Inc., In re, 747 F.2d 483 (8th Cir. 1984), *89*

Butz v. Butz, 13 Ill. App.3d 341, 299 N.E.2d 782 (1973), *104, 105*

Butz v. Glover Livestock Commission Co., 411 U.S. 182, 93 S.Ct. 1455, 36 L.Ed.2d 142 (1973), *259*

Cal-Almond, Inc. v. U.S. 30 Fed. Cl. 224 (Fed.Cl.Ct. 1994), *25*

Calderon v. Witvoet, 764 F. Supp. 536 (C.D. Ill. l991), *334*

California Agrarian Action Project, Inc. v. Regents of the University of California, 258 Cal.Rptr. 769, 210 Cal. App. 3d 1245, 53 Ed. Law Rep. 585 (1989), *50*

Cargill, Inc. v. Stafford, 553 F.2d 1222 (10th Cir. 1977), *139*

Carolinas Cotton Growers Ass'n, Inc. v. Arnette, 371 F. Supp. 65 (D.S.C. 1974), *286*

Carr v. Alta Verde Industries, Inc., 931 F.2d 1055 (5th Cir. 1991), *399*

Case-Swayne Co., Inc. v. Sunkist Growers, Inc., 389 U.S. 38 4, 88 S.Ct. 528, 19 L.Ed.2d 621 (1967), reh. denied 390 U.S. 930 (1968), *303*

Castillo v. Givens, 704 F.2d 181 (5th Cir. l983), cert. d eni ed 464 U.S. 850, 104 S.Ct. 160, 78 L.Ed.2d 147 (l983), *311*

CF Industries, Inc., v. C.I.R., 995 F.2d 101 (7th Cir. 1993), *290, 292*

Chamberlain v. Evans, 180 Mont. 511, 591 P.2d 237 (1979), *111*

Christiansen, U.S. v., 504 F. Supp. 364 (D. Nev. 1980), *233*

Chokecherry Hills Estates, Inc. v. Deuel County, 294 N.W.2d 654 (S.D. 1980), *367*

Coleman v. Block, 562 F. Supp. 1353 (D.N.D. 1983); 580 F.Supp 192 (D.N.D. 1983); 580 F. Supp. 194 (D.N.D. 1984); 632 F. Supp. 997 (D.N.D. 1986); 632 F. Supp. 1005 (D.N.D. 1986), *73, 74*

Coleman v. Lyng, 864 F.2d 604 (8th Cir. 1988), cert. denied 110 S.Ct. 364, 493 U.S. 953, 107 L.Ed.2d 351(1988), *75*

Coleman v. Sanderson Farms, Inc., 629 F.2d 1077 (5th C i r . l980), *43, 314, 315*

Collins, In re, 3 B.R. 144 (Bankr. D.S.C. 1980), *161*

Collins v. Day, 604 N.E.2d 647 (Ind. Ct. App. 1992), *326*

TABLE OF CASES

Colorado-Kansas Grain v. Reifschneider, 817 P.2d 637 (Colo. Ct. App. 1991), *141*

Colorado National Bank-Longmont v. Fegan, 827 P.2d 796 (Kan.App.1992), *164*

Colorado Springs PCA v. Farm Credit Admin., 967 F.2d 648 (D.C. Cir.1992), *58*

Coomes v. Drinkwalter, 181 Neb. 450, 149 N.W.2d 160(1967), *234*

Conway County Farmers Ass'n v. U.S., 588 F.2d 592 (8th Cir. 1978), *290*

Cooperative Grain & Supply Co. v. C.I.R., 407 F.2d 1158 (8th Cir. 1969), *293-94*

Cort v. Ash, 422 U.S. 66, 95 S.Ct. 2080, 46 L.Ed.2d 26 (1975), *64, 65, 327*

Cosner, In re, 3 B.R. 445 (Bankr. D.Or. 1980), *282*

Cotter and Co. v. U.S., 765 F.2d 1102 (Fed. Cir. 1985), *292*

County of Lake v. Cushman, 40 Ill.App.3d 1045, 353 N.E.2d 399(1976), *369*

Cox v. Cox, 289 So.2d 609 (Ala. 1974), *142*

Crookston Cattle Co. v. Minnesota Department of Natural Resources, 300 N.W.2d 769 (Minn. 1980), *416*

Cugnini v. Reynolds Cattle Co., 687 P.2d 962 (Colo. 1984), *236*

Curry v. Block, 541 F. Supp. 506 (S.D. Ga. 1982), affirmed 738 F.2d 1556 (11th Cir. 1984), *72, 73*

Darby v. Cisneros, ___ U.S. ___ , 113 S.Ct. 2539,125 L.Ed.2d 113 (1993), *35*

Darragh Co., Secretary v., 1980/93/A2 (OSHARC fiche number), 9 OSHA (BNA) 1205, l981 OSHD (CCH) ¶ 25,066 (l980), *340, 341*

Davenport, In re, 153 B.R. 551 (9th Cir. BAP 1993), *92*

Davis v. U.S., 427 F.2d 261 (5th Cir. 1970), *264*

De La Fuente v. Stokely-Van Camp, Inc., 713 F.2d 225 (7th Cir. l983), *327*

Decatur Cooperative Ass'n v. Urban, 219 Kan. 171, 547 P.2d 323 (1976), *142*

DeGraaf Daries, Inc., In re, 41 Agri. Dec. 388 (1982), *246*

Demeter, Inc. v. Werries, 676 F.Supp. 882 (C.D.Ill. 1988), *122*

Denton v. Moser, 241 N.W.2d 28 (Iowa 1976), *106*

TABLE OF CASES

Dexter, State v., 32 Wash.2d 551, 202 P.2d 906 (1949), *389*

Diamond v. Chakrabarty, 447 U.S. 303, 100 S.Ct. 2204, 65 L.Ed. 2d 144 (1980), *272-73*

D.K.M.B., Inc., In re, 95 B.R. 774 (Bankr. D. Colo. 1989), *251*

Doane v. Espy, 26 F.3d 783(7th Cir. 1994), 35

Doe v. Hodgson, 478 F.2d 537 (2d Cir. l973), cert. denied subnom Doe v. Brennan, 414 U.S. 1096, 94 S.Ct. 732, 38 L.Ed.2d 555 (l973), *326*

Dolan v. City of Tigard, ___ U.S. ___, 114 S.Ct. 2309, ___L.Ed.2d ___ (1994), *364*

Donaldson v. USDOL, 930 F.2d 339 (4th Cir. l991), *327*

Downie v. Abex Corp., 741 F.2d 1235 (10th Cir. 1984), *239*

Dunavant Enterprises, Inc. v. Ford, 294 So.2d 788 (Miss. 1974), *144*

Durand Milling Co., Inc., In re, 9 B.R. 669 (Bankr. E.D. Mich 1981), *127, 194*

Eastway v. Eisenga, 420 Mich. 410, 362 N.W.2d 684 (1 9 8 4), *326*

Empire Kosher Poultry, Inc. v. Hallowell, 816 F.2d 907 (3rd. Cir. 1987), *272*

Enders v. Wesley W. Hubbard and Sons, Inc., 95 Idaho 590, 513 P.2d 992 (1973), *114*

Esch v. Yeutter, 876 F.2d 976, 278 U.S.App.D.C. 98 (D .C.Ci r. 1989), affirming and mod. Esch v. Lyng, 665 F. Supp. 6 (D.D.C. 1987), *35, 36*

Evanenko v. Farmers Union Elevator, 191 N.W.2d 258 (N.D. 1971), *281*

Fairdale Farms, Inc. v. Yankee Milk, Inc., 715 F.2d 30 2nd Ci r. 1983), cert. denied 464 U.S. 1043, 104 S.Ct. 711, 79 L.Ed.2d 174 (1984), *306*

Fairview State Bank v. Edwards, 3 U.U.C. Rep. Serv.2d 1 6 76 (Okla. 1987), *169*

Farmers Elevator Mututal Insurance Co., People v., 74 Ill. App.2d 1, 220 N.E.2d 585 (1966), *130*

Farmers Reservoir & Irrigation Co. v. McComb, 337 U.S. 755, 69 S.Ct. 1274, 93 L.Ed. 1672 (1949), *313, 316, 321*

Farmers State Bank v. Webel, 113 Ill.App.3d 87, 68 Ill. Dec. 619, 446 N.E.2d 525 (1983), *163*

TABLE OF CASES

Farmland Service Cooperative v. Klein, 244 N.W.2d 86 (N eb. 1976), *142*

Federal Land Bank of St. Paul v. Overboe, 404 N.W.2d 445 (N.D. 1987), *62, 66, 67, 68*

Federal Land Bank of Spokane v. L.R. Ranch Co., 926 F.2d 859 (9th Cir. 1991), *67*

Federal Land Bank of Wichita v. Read, 237 Kan. 751, 703 P.2d 777 (1985), 62

Finley v. McClure, 222 Kan. 637, 567 P.2d 851 (1977), *116*

First English Evangelical Lutheran Church of Glendale v. County of Los Angeles, 482 U.S. 304, 107 S.Ct. 2378, 96 L.Ed.2d 250 (1987), *368*

First National Bank in Creston v. Francis, 342 N.W.2d 468 (Iowa 1984), *168*

First National Bank in Lenox v. Lamoni Livestock Sales Co., 417 N.W.2d 443 (Iowa 1987), *161*

Fishermen's Marketing Ass'n, Inc. v. Wilson, 279 Or. 259, 566 P.2d 897 (1977), *285*

Flaspohler v. Hoffman, 652 S.W.2d 703 (Mo. Ct. App.1983), *105*

Flores v. Rios, 1994 WL 518285 (6th Cir. 1994), *334*

Florida Peach Growers Ass'n, Inc., v. U.S., 489 F.2d 120 (5th Cir. l974), *343*

Fox v. Flick, 166 Kan. 533, 203 P.2d 186 (1949), *111, 112, 113*

Frank, In re, 27 B.R. 748 (Bankr. S.D.Ohio 1983), *94*

Frank Diehl Farms v. Secretary, 696 F.2d 1325 (11th Cir. l983), *343*

Frederickson v. Hackney, 159 Minn. 234, 198 N.W. 806 (1924), *238*

Fulkrod, In re, 973 F.2d 801 (9th Cir. 1992), *95*

Gage, In re, 159 B.R. 272 (Bankr. D.S.D. 1993), *91*

George, In re, 85 B.R. 133 (Bankr. D. Kan. 1988), affirmed 119 B.R. 800 (D.Kan. 1990), *173*

Georgia Turkey Farms, Inc. v. Hardigree, 187 Ga.App. 200, 369 S.E.2d 803 (1988), *281*

Gibson Products of Arizona, In re, 543 F.2d 652 (9th Cir. 1976), *181*

Gomez v. Florida State Employment Service, 417 F.2d 569 (5th Cir. l969), *327*

TABLE OF CASES

Goshen County Cooperative Beet Ass'n v. Pearson, 706 P.2d 1121 (Wyo. 1985), *285*

Gotham Provision Co., Inc., In re, 669 F.2d 1000 (5th Cir. 1982), cert. denied 459 U.S. 858, 103 S.Ct. 129, 74 L.Ed.2d 111(1982), *249, 250*

Great Plains Royalty Corp., In re, 471 F.2d 1261 (8th Cir. 1973), *282*

Griffin v. Federal Land Bank of Wichita, 902 F.2d 22 (10th Cir. 1990), *64, 65*

Grinnell Corp., United States v., 384 U.S. 563, 86 S.Ct. 1698, 16 L.Ed.2d 778 (1966), *307*

Gunkelman & Sons, Inc., State ex. rel. Public Service Commission v. , 219 N.W.2d 853 (N.D. 1974), *130, 211*

Gutierrez v. Glaser Crandall Co., 388 Mich. 654, 202 N.W.2d 786 (1972), *326*

Hadacheck v. Sebastian, 239 U.S. 394, 36 S.Ct. 143, 60 L.Ed. 348 (1915), *270*

Haddix & Sons, Inc., United States v., 415 F.2d 584 (6th Cir. 1969), *211*

Halls, In re, 4 U.C.C. Rep. Serv. 2d 1204 (Bankr. S.D. Iowa 1987), *173*

Harmon, In re, 11 B.R. 162 (Bankr. N.D. Tex. 1980), *249*

Harper v. Federal Land Bank of Spokane, 878 F.2d 1172 (9 th Cir. 1989), cert. denied 493 U.S. 1057, 110 S.Ct. 867, 107 L.Ed.2d 951 (1990), *64, 65, 66*

Hatley v. American Quarter Horse Ass'n, 552 F.2d 646 (5th Cir. 1977), *230, 231, 232*

Helmke v. Board of Adjustment, City of Ruthven, 418 N.W.2d 346 (Iowa 1988), *369*

Hemberger v. Hagemann, 210 P.2d 995 (Colo. 1949)(en bank), *111*

Herrin v. Opatut, 248 Ga. 140, 281 S.E.2d 575 (1981) *358*

Hiatt Grain & Feed, Inc. v. Bergland, 446 F. Supp. 457(D.C. Kan. 1978), affr'd 602 F.2d 929 (10th Cir. 1979), *284*

Hodel v. State of Indiana, 452 U.S. 314, 101 S.Ct. 2376, 69 L.Ed.2d 40 (1981), *395*

Hoffman v. Clark, 69 Ill.2d 402, 14 Ill. Dec. 269, 372 N.E.2d 74 (1977), *353*

Hoffman Homes, Inc., v. E.P.A., 961 F.2d 1310 (7th Cir. 1992), *408*

TABLE OF CASES

Hodgson v. Wittenburg, 464 F.2d 1219 (5th Cir. l972), *316*
Hogan v. Pelton, 210 Neb. 530, 315 N.W.2d 644 (1982), *113*
Holly Sugar Corp. v. Goshen County Cooperative Beet Growers Ass'n, 725 F.2d 564 (10th Cir. 1984), *287*
Hopewell Township Bd. of Supervisors v. Golla, 499 Pa. 246, 452 A.2d 1337 (1982), *364*
Horne v. Oller, 5 Kan.App.2d 263, 615 P.2d 791 (1980), *111*
Huckaby v. Walker, 141 Ark. 477, 217 S.W. 481 (1920), *111*

In re (see name of party)

Interco, Inc. v. Randustrial Corp., 533 S.W.2d 257 (Mo. Ct. App. 1976), *239*

Jacobson v. Aetna Casualty & Surety Co., 46 N.W.2d 868 (Minn. 1951), *160*
Jasik, In re, 727 F.2d 1379 (5th Cir. 1984), *89*
Jay Freeman Co, Inc., U.S. v., 473 F. Supp. 1265 (E.D.Ark. 1979), *247*
Jenkins v. Missouri Farmers Ass'n, Inc., 851 S.W.2d 542 (Mo. Ct. App. 1993), *206*
Jenson v. Haynes, 633 S.W.2d 154 (Mo. Ct. App. 1982), *145*
Julis Goldman's Egg City v. U.S., 697 F.2d 1051 (Fed. Cir. 1983) cert. denied, 464 U.S. 814, 104 S.Ct. 68, 78 L.Ed.2d 83 (1983), *271*
Just v. Marinette County, 56 Wis.2d 7, 201 N.W.2d 761 (1972), *367*

Kearney Convention Center, Inc. v. Buffalo Co. Bd. of Equalization, 216 Neb. 292, 344 N.W.2d 620 (1984), *353*
Kelly v. U.S., 202 F.2d 838 (10th Cir. 1953), *256*
Kimball Foods, Inc., U.S. v., 440 U.S. 715, 99 S.Ct. 1448, 59 L.Ed.2d 711 (1979), *178*
Kingfisher Cooperative Elevator Ass'n v. Commr., 84 T.C. 600 (1985), *295-96*
Kingsley, In re, 865 F.2d 975 (8th Cir. 1989), *171*
K.L. Smith Enters., Ltd., In re, 2 B.R. 280 (Bankr. D. Colo. 1980), *161, 162, 165-66*

TABLE OF CASES

Lake Region Packing Ass'n, Inc. v. Furze, 327 So.2d 212 (Fla. 1976), *281*

Land O'Lakes, Inc. v. U.S., 514 F.2d 134 (8th Cir. 1975), *295*

Larson v. Archer-Daniels-Midland Co., 226 Minn. 315, 32 N.W.2d 649 (1948), *99*

Laux v. Chopin Land Associates, Inc., 550 N.E.2d 100 (Ind. Ct. App. 1990), *357*

Lehndorff Geneva, Inc.v. Warren, 74 Wis.2d 369, 246 N.W.2d 815 (1976), *47*

Lilliard v. Farm Credit Services of Mid-America, ACA, 831 S.W.2d 626 (Ky. Ct. App. 1991) review dismissed (June 16, 1992), *66-67*

Logan Ranch, Karg Partnership v. Farm Credit Bank of Omaha, 238 Neb. 814, 472 N.W.2d 704 (1991), *63*

Louthan v. King County, 94 Wn2d 422, 617 P.2d 977 (1980), *374, 378*

Loveladies Harbor II, 21 Cl.Ct. 153 (Fed. Cl. Ct. 1990) affirmed 1994 WL 259489 (Fed. Cir. 1994), *410*

Lucas v. South Carolina Coastal Council, ___ U.S. ___, 112 S.Ct. 2886, 120 L.Ed2d 798 (1992), *366, 367, 376, 389, 409*

Luther, United States v., 225 F.2d 499 (10th Cir. 1955) *209, 210*

McReery Angus Farms v. American Angus Ass'n, 379 F. Supp. 1008 (S.D.Ill. 1974), *232*

McElwee v. DeVault, 225 Iowa 30, 120 N.W.2d 451(1963), *114*

McLaughlin v. Elsberry, Inc., 868 F.2d 1525 (11th Cir. 1988), *335*

McNary v. Haitian Refugee Center, Inc., 498 U.S. 479, 111 S.Ct. 888, 112 L.Ed.2d 1005 (1991), *338*

Maguire v. Haddad, 325 Mass. 590, 91 N.E.2d 769 (1950), *109*

Martin, In re, 761 F.2d 472 (8th Cir. 1985), *93*

Martinez v. Hauch, 838 F.Supp. 1209 (W.D.Mich. 1993), *334*

Marvin Properties, Inc., In re, 76 B.R. 150 (9th Cir. BAP 1987), affirmed 854 F.2d 1183 (9th Cir. 1988), *251*

Maryland & Virginia Milk Producers Ass'n v. United States, 362 U.S. 458, 80 S.Ct. 847, 4 L.Ed.2d 880 (1960), *307*

TABLE OF CASES

Mayville Feed & Grain, Inc., In re, 96 B.R. 755 (Bankr. E.D. Mich 1989), *127*

Mead, U.S. v., 426 F.2d 118 (9th Cir. 1970), *37*

Michigan Canners and Freezers Ass'n Inc. v. Agricultural Marketing and Bargaining Bd., 467 U.S. 461, 104 S.Ct. 2518, 81 L.Ed.2d 399 (1984), on remand 422 Mich. 862, 365 N.W.2d 760 (1985), *308*

Mid-America Dairymen, Inc, In re, CCH Fed. Sec. L. Rptr. ¶ 81,110 (March 3, 1977), *296-97*

Mid-States Sales Co., Inc., U.S. v., 336 F. Supp. 1099 (D. Neb. 1971), *167*

Minnesota Milk Producers Ass'n v. Yeutter, 851 F. Supp. 1389 (D.Minn. 1994), *27*

Mitchellville Co-op v. Indian Creek Corp., 469 N.W.2d 258 (Iowa Ct. App. 1991), *281-82*

Moore v. Hardy, 748 P.2d 477 (Mont. 1988), *111*

Morling v. Schmidt, 299 N.W.2d 480 (Iowa 1980), *109*

Mousel v. Daringer, 190 Neb. 77, 206 N.W.2d 579 (1973), *204*

Munger, In re, 495 F.2d 511 (9th Cir. 1974), *171*

National Ass'n of Farmworkers Organizations v. Marshall, 628 F.2d 604, 202 U.S. App. D.C. 317 (1980), *318*

National Broiler Marketing Ass'n v. U.S., 436 U.S. 816, 98 S.Ct. 2122, 56 L.Ed.2d 728 (1978), *304, 305*

National Grain & Feed Ass'n, Inc., v. OSHA, 903 F.2d 308 (5th Cir. 1990), *343*

National Livestock Credit Corp. v. First State Bank of Harrah, 503 P.2d 1283 (Okla. Ct. App. 1972), *165*

Natural Resources Defense Council v. Costle, 568 F.2d 1369 (D.C. Cir. 1977), *399*

Nelson v. Union Equity Cooperative Exchange, 548 S.W.2d 352 (Tex. 1977), *140*

Nelson, U.S. Through FmHA v., 969 F.2d 626 (8th Cir. 1992), *88*

Nevala v. McKay, 178 Mont. 327, 583 P.2d 1065 (1978), *105*

Newcomb, U.S. v., 682 F.2d 758 (8th Cir. 1982), *156*

Nollan v. California Coastal Commission, 483 U.S. 825, 107 S.Ct. 3141, 97 L.Ed.2d 677 (1987), *364*

North Dakota v. U.S., 460 U.S. 300, 103 S.Ct. 1095, 75 L.Ed.2d 77 (1983), *411*

TABLE OF CASES

Northern Calif. Supermarkets, Inc. v. Central Calif. L e t t u c e Producers Coop., 413 F.Supp. 984 (N.D. Cal. 1976), affr'd per curiam 580 F.2d 369 (9thCir. 1978), cert. denied 439 U.S. 1090, 99 S.Ct. 873, 59 L.Ed.2 57 (1979), *305*

Oakley, U.S. v., 483 F. Supp. 762 (E.D. Ark. 1980), *167*
Orengo Caraballo v. Reich, 11 F.3d 186 (D.C.Cir. 1993), *336*
Organized Migrants in Community Action v. Brennan, 520 F.2d 1161 (D.C.Cir. l975), *344*
Osteroos v. Norwest Bank Minot, N.A., 604 F. Supp. 848 (D. N.D. 1984), *172*
Otto v. Hahn, 209 Neb. 114, 306 N.W.2d 587 (l981), *326*
Overholt, In re, 125 B.R. 202 (Bankr. S.D. Ohio 1990), *95*
Oxford PCA v. Dye, 368 So.2d 241 (Miss. 1979), *160, 161*

Paullus v. Liedkie, 92 Idaho 323, 442 P.2d 733 (1968), *243*
Payne v. Federal Land Bank of Columbia, 916 F.2d 179 (4th Cir., 1990), *63, 65*
Pendoley v. Ferreira, 345 Mass. 309, 187 N.E.2d 142 (1963), *356*
Penn Central Transportation Co. v. City of New York, 438 U.S. 1094, 98 S.Ct. 2646, 57 L.Ed.2d 631 (1978), *272, 376, 377, 395*
Pennsylvania Agricultural Cooperative Marketing Ass'n v. Ezra Martin Co., 495 F. Supp. 565 (D.M.D. Pa. 1980), *251-52*

People v. _____(see opposing party)

Perdue Farms Inc., U.S. v., 680 F.2d 277 (2nd Cir. 1982), *263*
Peterson v. U.S. Department of Interior, 899 F.2d 799 (9th Cir. 1990) cert. denied 498 U.S. 1003, 111 S.Ct. 567, 112 L.Ed.2d 574, *422*
Peterson Farms I v. Madigan, 782 F.Supp. 1 (D.D.C. 1991), *35*
Pipkin v. Connolly, 167 Mont. 284, 538 P.2d 347 (1975), *104*
Pollock v. Pollock, 247 Iowa 20, 72 N.W.2d 483 (1955), *108*
Preseault v. ICC, 494 U.S. 1, 110 S.Ct. 914, 108 L.Ed.2d 1 (1990), *368, 396*
Preston v. U.S., 776 F.2d 754 (7th Cir. 1985), *210, 217*

TABLE OF CASES

Price Brothers Co. v. Philadelphia Gear Corp., 649 F.2d 416 (6th Cir. 1981), cert. denied 454 U.S. 1099, 102 S.Ct. 674, 70 L.Ed2d 641 (1981), *238*

Producers Cotton Oil Co. v. Amstar, 242 Cal. Rptr. 914, 197 Cal.App.3d 638 (1988), *201*

Production Credit Association of Worthington v. Van Iperen, 396 N.W.2d 35 (Minn. Ct. App. 1986), *67*

Puget Sound Plywood, Inc. v. CIR, 44 T.C. 305 (1965), acq., 1966-1 C.B. 3, *289*

Pure Milk Products Co-op v. National Farmers Organization, 64 Wis.2d 241, 219 N.W.2d 564 (1974); 90 Wis.2d 781, 280 N.W.2d 691 (1979); 105 Wis.2d 758, 317 N.W.2d 510 (Wis. Ct. App. 1981), *287*

Rauch, U.S. v., 717 F.2d 448 (8th Cir. 1983), *256*

Real v. Driscoll Strawberry Assoc., Inc., 603 F.2d 748 (9th Cir. 1979), *312*

Redd v. Federal Land Bank of St. Louis, 851 F.2d 219 (8th Cir. 1988), *64*

Reves v. Ernst & Young, 494 U.S. 56, 110 S.Ct. 945, 108 L.Ed.2d 47 (1990), *297, 298*

Rhodes v. Sigler, 27 Ill. App.3d 1, 325 N.E.2d 381 (1975), *101, 107*

Rice v. Santa Fe Elevator Corp., 331 U.S. 218, 67 S.Ct. 1146, 91 L.Ed. 1447 (1947), *122*

Richmond Produce Co., In re, 112 B.R. 364 (Bankr. N.D.Cal. 1990), *251*

Riverside Bayview Homes, Inc., U.S. v., 474 U.S. 121, 106 S.Ct. 455, 88 L.Ed.2d 419 (1985), *407*

Roberts, In re, 38 B.R. 128 (Bankr. Kan. 1984), *160, 168*

Robertson v. White, 635 F. Supp. 851(W.D. Ark. 1986), *299*

Romero v. Hodgson, 403 U.S. 901, 91 S.Ct. 2215, 19 L.Ed.2d 678 (1971), summarily affirming 319 F. Supp. 1201 (N.D. Cal. 1970), *326*

Rowley v. Yarnell, 22 F.3d 190 (8th Cir. 1994), *91*

Safeway Stores, Inc. v. Freeman, 369 F.2d 952 (D.C. Cir. 1966), *247*

Saltzman v. Farm Credit Services of Mid-America, ACA, 950 F.2d 466 (7th Cir. 1991), *64*

TABLE OF CASES

Samuels & Co., Inc., In re, 526 F.2d 1238 (5th Cir. 1976), cert. denied, 429 U.S. 834, 97 S.Ct. 98, 50 L.Ed.2d 99 (1976), *165, 226, 227, 228, 249*

Sanchez v. Grain Growers Ass'n of California, 126 Cal. App. 3d 665, 179 Cal. Rptr. 459 (1981), *282*

Saxbe v. Bustos, 419 U.S. 65, 95 S.Ct. 272, 42 L.Ed.2d 231 (1974), *336*

Schmaling, In re, 783 F.2d 680 (7th Cir. l986), *172*

Schultz v. Ramey, 64 N.M. 366, 328 P.2d 937 (1958), *113*

SEC v. W.J. Howey Co., 328 U.S. 293, 66 S.Ct. 1100, 90 L.Ed. 1244 (1946), *297*

S.G. Borello & Sons, Inc. v. Department of Industrial Relations, 769 P.2d 399, 256 Cal. Rptr. 543, 48 Cal.3d 341 (1989), *99*

Shatto v. McNulty, 509 N.E.2d 897 (Ind. Ct. App. 1987), *357*

Sheehan, In re, 38 B.R. 859 (Bankr. D.S.D. 1984), *93*

Smith, State v., 88 S.D. 76, 216 N.W.2d 149 (1974), *233*

Smith v. Great Basin Grain Co., 98 Idaho 266, 561 P.2d 1299 (1977), *220*

Smith v. U.S., 832 F.2d 774 (2d Cir. 1987), *168*

Soler v. G & U, Inc., 768 F. Supp. 452 (S.D.N.Y. 1991), *311*

Solomon Valley Feedlot, Inc. v. Butz, 557 F.2d 717 (10th Cir. 1977), *257*

Southeast Mississippi Livestock Farmers Ass'n, U.S. v. , 619 F.2d 435 (5th Cir. 1980), *166-67*

Sporhase v. Nebraska ex. rel. Douglas, 458 U.S. 941, 102 S.Ct. 3456, 73 L.Ed.2d 1254(1982) on remand 213 Neb. 484, 329 N.W.2d 855 (1983), *419*

State v. _____(see opposing party)

State of (see name of state)

Sterling Colorado Beef Co., In re, 39 Agric. Dec. 184 (1980), appeal dismissed, No. 80-1293 (10th Cir. 1980), *257*

Stoppel v. Mastin, 220 Kan. 667, 556 P.2d 394 (1976), *108*

Straley v. Osborne, 262 Md. 514, 278 A.2d 64 (1971), *105*

Stuber v. Sowder, 168 Kan. 467, 213 P.2d 989 (1950), *101*

Sun Oil Co. v. Whitaker, 483 S.W.2d 808 (Tex. 1972), *419*

Swift & Co. v. U.S., 393 F.2d 247 (7th Cir. 1968), *246*

Szabo v. Vinton Motors, 630 F.2d 1 (1st Cir. 1980), *223*

TABLE OF CASES

Teague v. Roper, 526 S.W.2d 291 (Tex. Ct. App. 1975), *100, 101*

Terrell v. Palomino Horse Breeders of America, 414 N.E.2d 332 (Ind. Ct. App. 1980), *231*

Terminal Grain Corp. v. Freeman, 270 N.W.2d 806 (S.D. 1978), *140*

Thurston v. Cache County, 626 P.2d 440 (Utah 1981), *365*

Torstenson v. Melcher, 195 Neb. 764, 241 N.W.2d 103 (1976), *239*

Treasure Vally Potato Bargaining Ass'n v. Ore-Ida F o o d s , Inc., 497 F.2d 203 (9th Cir. 1974), cert. denied 419 U.S. 999, 95 S.Ct. 314, 42 L.Ed. 273 (1974), *306*

United Housing Foundation v. Forman, 421 U.S. 837, 95 S. Ct. 2051, 44 L.Ed.2d 621 (1975), *296*

United Savings Association of Texas v. Timber of Inwood Forest Associates, Ltd., 484 U.S. 365, 108 S.Ct. 626, 98 L.Ed.2d 740 (1988), *90*

United States v. _____(see opposing party)

Vlases v. Montgomery Ward & Co., Inc., 377 F.2d 846 (3rd Cir. 1967), *242*

Volker, In re, 252 N.W.2d 400 (Iowa 1977), *168*

Walkington, In re, 62 B.R. 989 (Bankr. W.D. Mich. 1986), *160*

Wallman, In re, 71 B.R. 125 (Bankr. D. S.D. 1987), *95*

West Central Coop. v. U.S., 758 F.2d 1269 (8th Cir. 1985), cert. denied, 474 U.S. 100, 106 S.Ct. 375, 88 L.Ed.2d 368, *294*

West Lynn Creamery, Inc. v. Healy, ___ U.S.___, 114 S.Ct. 2205, ___ L.Ed.2d ___(1994), reversing 415 Mass. 8, 611 N.E.2d 239 (1993), *28*

West Montgomery County Citizens Ass'n v. MNCP&P Com'n, 309 Md. 183, 522 A.2d 1328 (1987), *376*

Western Farm Credit Bank v. Pratt, 860 P.2d 376 (Utah Ct. App. 1993), *67*

Western Farmers Ass'n, In re, 6 B.R. 432 (Bankr. W.D. Wa sh. 1980), *226*

TABLE OF CASES

Whitney Benefits, Inc. v. U.S., 18 Cl. Ct. 394 (1989), corrected, 20 Cl. Ct. 324 (1990), aff'd, 926 F.2d 1169 (Fed. Cir. 1991), cert. denied, ___ U.S. ___, 112 S.Ct. 406, 116 L.Ed.2d 354 (1991) *395*

Wickard v. Filburn, 317 U.S. 111, 63 S.Ct. 82, 87 L.Ed. 122 (1942), *8, 9*

Wiener v. Eastern Ark. Planting Co., 975 F.2d 1350 (8th Cir. 1992), *62*

Willcut v. Stout, 670 S.W.2d 158 (Mo. Ct. App. 1984), *99*

Williams v. Stander, 143 Colo. 469, 354 P.2d 492 (1960), *116*

Wilson v. County of McHenry, 92 Ill.App.3d 997, 48 Ill.Dec. 395, 416 N.E.2d 426 (1981) *365*

Women Involved in Farm Economics (WIFE) v. USDA, 876 F.2d 994 (D.C. Cir. 1989) cert. denied 493 U.S. 1019, 110 S.Ct. 717, 107 L.Ed.2d 737 (1990), *34*

Wood v. Trenchard, 550 P.2d 490 (Wyo. 1976) , *117*

Woodbury County Soil Conservation District v. Ortner, 279 N.W.2d 276 (Iowa 1979), *388*

Woodsmall v. Lyng, 816 F.2d 1241 (8th Cir. 1987), *84*

Yancey v. U.S., 915 F.2d 1534 (Fed. Cir. 1990), *272*

Young & Cooper v. Vestring, 214 Kan. 311, 521 P.2d 281 (1974), *239*

Zajac v. Federal Land Bank of St. Paul, 909 F.2d 1181 (8th Cir. 1990), *64, 65*

Ziegler v. Hendrickson, 528 P.2d 400 (Colo. Ct. App. 1974), *111*

CHAPTER ONE

GOVERNMENT AND AGRICULTURE
I. AN HISTORICAL PERSPECTIVE

Throughout American history there has been a tradition of government support for and involvement with agriculture. This survey begins with a few observations about developments in the late 18th century.

The critical role of the federal government in opening millions of acres of public lands to agricultural settlement and in funding necessary transportation systems provides our starting point. Following the Revolutionary War and the War of 1812, Congress granted tracts of public land to veterans, thus promoting settlement west of the Appalachian Mountains. The Ordinance of 1785 established a plan for disposing of western lands, and the Land Act of 1796 authorized the sale of single sections (640 acres). While the Land Law of 1820 discontinued extensions of credit, it did reduce the price per acre from $2 to $1.25. The Preemption Act of 1841 provided for the sale of previously settled public lands to original settlers ("squatters") at $1.25 per acre.

The first of a series of Homestead Acts was signed into law in 1862. U.S. patents for 160 acre tracts were given to homesteading farmers who complied with statutory requirements. Homesteading ended, for practical purposes, in 1935 with the closing of the public lands to settlement following passage of the Taylor Grazing Act of 1934.

In 1827 and 1828, Congress made land grants to Ohio, Indiana, Illinois and Alabama to fund the construction of canal systems. Every other section of land for a certain distance on each side of the canal route was granted in checkerboard fashion and the granted lands sold by the canal authority to finance construction. Not only did this open land to settlement, but construction of essential transportation systems was funded. Starting in the 1850s the same approach was used to finance the construction of thousands of miles of railroad track and to thereby open land west of the Mississippi River to agricultural settlement.

In 1839 Congress appropriated $1,000 to the Patent Office for collecting agricultural statistics, conducting agricultural studies, and distributing seeds. The United States Department of Agriculture (USDA) was created in 1862. In 1889 the powers of the Department were enlarged and it became the eighth executive department of the federal government. The Commissioner of Agriculture became the Secretary of Agriculture and agriculture became the only industry to have a direct voice at the Cabinet level.

In the middle of the 19th century Congress took steps to encourage states to establish colleges. The Morrill Act of 1862 authorized grants of federal public lands to states to fund the establishment of "land grant" colleges. In 1890, a second Morrill Act authorized separate land grant colleges for Blacks and 17 were established. The 1862 schools, and to a lesser extent the 1890 schools, became known as agricultural colleges. The primary charge to the 1890 schools was to train teachers.

Because 19th century agriculture had no corporate giants capable of sponsoring significant plant and animal science research, support developed for government funded agricultural experiment stations. The first station opened in Connecticut in 1875 and later that year the California Agricultural Experiment Station was founded at the University of California. It was not until the Hatch Act of 1887, however, that federal grants were authorized to support research. Hatch Act funds still flow to experiment stations.

The Cooperative Extension Service, a partnership of federal, state and local governments, was authorized in 1914 in the Smith-Lever Act. Today, extension professionals at the county level continue to provide practical education to the people in agriculture, home economics and other subjects.

In a further effort to promote agricultural settlement, Congress enacted the Reclamation Act of 1902 which authorized the great dam and canal systems that were to bring flourishing irrigated agriculture to the 17 western states. Designed to promote settlement of small farms, the Act required that a recipient of project water live on the farm, which was not to exceed 160 acres in size. The failure of the Bureau of Reclamation to enforce the acreage limit and the Congressional response 80 years later are discussed in Ch. 11 *infra.*

State and federal regulatory programs designed to protect farmers from sharp practices by buyers, warehouses, and shippers emerged in the latter part of the 19th and the early years of the 20th centuries. Illinois took the lead in the 1870s by enacting

"Granger Laws" designed to regulate rail rates and public commodity warehouses.

A sampling of federal laws regulating trade practices illustrates the scope of the concerns of the Congress: the first animal quarantine law in 1884; the Meat Inspection Act in 1890; the Pure Food and Drug Act and the Meat Inspection Act in 1906; the Federal Insecticide Act in 1911; the Seed Importation Law and the Plant Quarantine Act in 1912; the U.S. Warehouse Act and U.S. Grain Standards Act in 1916; the Packers and Stockyards Act in 1921; the Commodities Exchange Act in 1922: the Grain Futures Act in 1924; the Plant Patent Act and the Perishable Agricultural Commodities Act in 1930.

In these same years, other important pieces of agricultural legislation emerged from the Congress. Agricultural cooperatives were given important, but limited, exemptions from the federal antitrust laws, first in 1914 in § 6 of the Clayton Act, and then more significantly in 1922 in the Capper-Volstead Act. The Federal Farm Loan Act of 1916 authorized establishment of the 12 Farm Credit Banks, the beginnings of the Farm Credit System. In 1923, the Agricultural Credits Act authorized the 12 Federal Intermediate Credit Banks. By 1933, the structure of the Farm Credit System was in place with specialized banks and associations designed to meet the credit needs of producers and agricultural cooperatives.

This recital of developments should not be read to suggest that all was well for American agriculture prior to the Great Depression, soon to arrive in the 1930s. Boom and bust cycles were well known, droughts and insect infestations arrived and departed, and farmers were, as they are today, price takers, both in selling their products and buying their inputs. Yet, there had been good years for agricultural in the latter part of the 19th and the early part of the 20th centuries. The political climate was still favorable and farm families tended to be self sufficient, producing much of what was needed to sustain livestock and household.

However, agriculture was soon to be caught in the whirlwind of the Great Depression, the New Deal, World War II, and a complex world of economic regulation presided over by labyrinthine federal administrative agencies. And, farming was about to undergo great changes with unprecedented yields made possible by advances in plant breeding and increased reliance upon fertilizers and, eventually, pesticides. The lifestyles of farmers and ranchers would change too, as they were converted to many of the ways of their city brothers and sisters. Increases in spending for family goods and production inputs were to add complexity to the lives of agriculturalists whose cash flow was not always adequate to support such habits.

II. ECONOMIC REGULATION
A. The Depression Era

The impact of the Great Depression on federal farm policy is of monumental importance. Had it not been for the extraordinary distress experienced by agriculture during this period, the option of massive ongoing federal intervention might never have been explored. Prior to the 1930s, there had been relatively little economic regulation of agriculture. The New Deal legislative emphasis represented a shift from establishing infrastructure and regulating trade practices, to creating programs of economic regulation on a scale not previously imagined. The seriousness of the economic problems served to negate political opposition.

Gross farm income in 1932 was less than half of what it had been in 1929 and net income had fallen even more. A great disparity existed between the prices of farm products and the prices of goods usually bought by farmers. By 1932, agricultural land values had declined by at least 50%, farm exports had declined dramatically, and credit was virtually unavailable. Farm mortgage foreclosures had risen to record levels. Creditors went bankrupt when they could not collect their claims and city business people suffered because they could not sell their merchandise. The weakness of the rural economy threatened the entire national economic system.

Franklin Roosevelt, elected President in 1932, was determined to solve the agriculture problem. His administration assembled a group of bright young lawyers and economists, many from Eastern colleges, to draft the New Deal legislation. Farm legislation for the most part had to be prepared from scratch. The drafters faced harsh realities: commodity prices were depressed; stockpiles were in excess of domestic needs; tariffs to discourage imports seemed to provide no answer; voluntary efforts by farmers to reduce production had failed; farm tenancy was on the increase; and farmers were stuck as price takers when selling commodities and when buying farm inputs. Special challenges were presented because there was no single farm problem that could be expeditiously addressed. Rather, there were distinct problems in various farm sectors and in various regions of the United States.

The first major piece of New Deal farm legislation was the Agricultural Adjustment Act of 1933. It was designed to raise prices of certain basic commodities, but not fruits, vegetables and products of livestock. The goal was to achieve "parity" which meant restoring farmer purchasing power to the level of the 1909-14 period. While the concept of parity was an operative part of the 1933 Act, the term as such did not appear in farm legislation until the 1938 Act. The calculation of parity price was complex, involving ascertainment of the current price per unit (bushel, pound or bale) needed to buy a set quantity of goods (standard list) that the same unit would have purchased in the 1909-1914 base period. To achieve parity various mechanisms were devised to favorably impact market prices: production controls, benefit payments, loans, government purchases, and enforceable marketing agreements. Farmers could voluntarily contact to reduce production, and benefit payments would be forthcoming. The objective was to support farm income with higher prices and government checks. Money to pay benefits was to be raised by a tax on the first processing of agricultural commodities for domestic use.

Problems soon developed in the administration of the 1933 Act. Voluntary participation by farmers was inadequate, program violations occurred, and yields per acre were increased. At the same time soil erosion problems worsened. And, the period of the dust bowl was setting in, with the worst episode destined for 1936.

In 1936 important portions of the 1933 Act were declared unconstitutional in U.S. v. Butler (Hoosac Mills) (U.S.Sup.Ct.1936). The production control and processing tax provisions were invalidated. Also, the Act was found to invade reserved rights of the states given its stated purpose to regulate and control agriculture production, a local activity deemed to be beyond the scope of the Congressional power to regulate commerce. But see Wickard v. Filburn (U.S.Sup.Ct.1942), p. 9 *infra*. The Hoosac Mills decision did leave in place marketing agreement programs and measures for government purchase of surplus commodities with general revenues.

Congress then enacted the Soil Conservation and Domestic Allotment Act of 1936, a temporary effort to deal with the constitutional problems in Hoosac Mills. This Act included soil conservation programs designed to reduce planted acreage of soil depleting crops, to idle land, to promote planting of soil enriching crops, and to fund soil conservation measures. Also, there were programs to support farm prices and incomes, funded by general appropriations.

The 1933 and 1936 Acts reflect two underlying themes: *voluntary* farmer participation in farm programs; and, *decentralization* of administration -- the latter being the impetus for the role of county level offices of the Agricultural Stabilization and Conservation Service (ASCS) in administering farm programs. Today, these themes continue in federal farm programs, although many local offices have been consolidated given a smaller farm population and federal budget deficits. In October, 1994 the functions of ASCS were taken over by the new Consolidated Farm Service Agency (CFSA).

The Agricultural Adjustment Act of 1938, the Organic Act, provides the theoretical foundation for ongoing price and income support programs. The major themes -- enhancing farm income, stabilizing prices, assuring an adequate low cost safe food supply, and preserving resources for the future -- remain important in farm legislation of subsequent decades, including the Food Security Act of 1985 (1985 Act) and the Food, Agriculture Conservation and Trade Act of 1990 (1990 Act). Indeed, many of the provisions in contemporary farm bills are structured as amendments to the 1938 Act or the Agriculture Act of 1949.

The constraint in Hoosac Mills on the power of Congress to regulate agricultural commerce proved to be temporary. In Wickard v. Filburn (U.S.Sup.Ct. 1942) it was held that Congress has the power under the Commerce Clause of the Constitution to regulate agricultural production, even a crop grown for on-farm use and not destined to enter channels of interstate or intrastate commerce. Wickard held that unauthorized excess production by a farmer who voluntarily participates in a federal program impacts interstate commerce even when the program crop is fed to livestock on the farm. The constitutional foundation was thus laid for far reaching contemporary farm programs.

To understand the workings of several federal agriculture programs it is necessary to know about the role of the Commodity Credit Corporation (CCC), created by Executive Order in 1933. CCC, a federal corporation within USDA, is vested with powers that enable it, *inter alia*, to stabilize, support and protect farm income and prices. This is done with loans to farmers, purchases of commodities, payments to farmers, and development of domestic and foreign markets. Domestic CCC programs are administered by CFSA, successor to ASCS.

Specifically, CCC can make nonrecourse loans to farmers, a unique price support mechanism first introduced in 1933, and still in use today. A farmer who voluntarily signs up for the annual program for an eligible commodity can, at harvest, opt for a nonrecourse price support loan from the CCC, typically for nine months. This generates cash flow at harvest when spot prices usually bottom out. The farmer grants to the CCC a Uniform Commercial Code (UCC) Article 9 security interest in the commodity, which is stored either on the farm or in a public warehouse. A loan rate, expressed in dollars per unit, e.g. per bushel, determines the amount of money CCC is committed to loan for each unit of collateral. If cash prices remain at or below the loan rate, the farmer usually elects to forfeit the stored crop to CCC in full payment of the loan and interest.

Consider this contemporary illustration: Farmer signs up for the corn program for the particular year. The loan rate is $3.50. Farmer harvests 100 bushels of corn. The market price is $2, so farmer obtains a $3500 program loan. By the end of nine months, the farmer must decide whether to pay off the loan or forfeit the corn. If the market price is at or below the loan rate, the farmer will default on the loan and the CCC will take possession of the farmer's corn. The loan is non-recourse, which means that upon default the CCC must take the corn as full payment and cannot sue the farmer for the difference between the value of the corn and the unpaid principal and interest. However, if the cash price is $4.00 or $4.50, the farmer will pay off the loan plus interest, redeem the corn, and then sell it.

Because the CCC is effectively in the market to buy at the loan rate, that rate tends to be a floor below which the market price of the program commodity is not likely to fall except in the harvest glut or in times of projections of extraordinary overproduction. The price support function of farm program loans thus becomes evident. The loans also provide favorable short-term financing for participating farmers because interest charged, if the loan is paid off, is always below commercial rates.

Until the 1970s, loan rates and other support rates were set at some percentage of parity. Today, however, the concept of parity has all but vanished from farm legislation. Some farm organizations make it their business to remind us of just what parity could mean to today's farmers. A rate of 75% parity would indicate that the current price of the commodity would purchase 75% of what it would have brought in the period 1910-14 (*revised* base period). In August, 1994, wheat sold for $3.23 per bushel (100% of parity price would have been about $8.37) and corn sold for $2.12 per bushel (100% of parity would have been about $5.77).

B. Farm Programs After the 1930s

Since 1933 Congress has enacted at least 56 major pieces of legislation designed to impact agricultural prices and production. For six decades, the policy objectives of higher farm prices, higher farm income, soil conservation, and a secure and adequate food supply have been constant.

During World War II, the thrust of the farm programs shifted from restricting supplies to increasing production. CCC loan rates were set at levels high enough to encourage full use of agriculture resources. When the war ended loan levels were kept high in an effort to avoid a repeat of the disastrous decline in farm prices that followed World War I.

The 1950s brought surpluses. Congress enacted Public Law 480, the Food for Peace program, to encourage sale of surplus commodities for foreign currency, barter for strategic materials, and donations for emergency relief. See p. 40 *infra*. In 1956 the Soil Bank was created, a voluntary program that paid farmers to idle land. At its peak, 58 million acres were removed from production.

During the 1960s, the acreage reduction programs that had become the hallmark of farm programs were coupled with domestic surplus commodity disposal programs. An expanded school lunch program used surplus commodities and the reinstated Food Stamp program provided a way to supply the needy with inexpensive food.

The early and mid-1970s saw a surge in agricultural export demand. Exports rose from $7 billion in 1970 to $43.8 billion in 1981 fueled by a strong world economy, large purchases by the USSR, and crop shortfalls in major producing countries. Surplus stocks were quickly exhausted and crop prices soared. Livestock producers faced higher feed costs, and consumers encountered sharply increased food prices. The 1970s and 1980s brought a series of Presidential economic embargoes on export of certain commodities ostensibly to protect domestic supplies and to head off runaway prices. By the late 1970s grain stocks were again becoming burdensome, with high world prices spurring the increased production.

The domestic farm programs of the 1970s introduced three new mechanisms and limited the total farm program payments one "person" could receive in a year. One of the new concepts was the target price, a key factor in calculating the deficiency payments that serve as income support for producers of certain "basic" commodities. Target prices and deficiency payments are discussed at pp. 17-20 *infra*. The second was that support prices should not be determined in relation to parity, but by indexing production costs. Finally, under 1977 legislation, the Secretary was authorized to offer wheat and feed grain producers the option to extend the nonrecourse loan period from nine months to three to five years, to pay participating producers annual storage costs, and to waive or adjust interest rates. This Farmer-Owned-Reserve (FOR) program is still in use from time to time. See p. 22 *infra*.

The 1980s brought a new federal program designed to control production of commodities already in surplus. The program used commodity specific payment-in-kind (PIK) certificates. Under the 1983 PIK program, farmers who diverted wheat, corn, sorghum, rice or upland cotton acreage from the farm's base, received commodity specific PIK certificates stating the amount of payment-in-kind due from CCC stocks. Participating farmers thus could take physical delivery of a quantity of the actual commodity that otherwise would have been produced. Acreage withdrawn from production was placed in conserving uses, although grazing was permitted during certain months. The 1983 PIK program was designed to hold down production and to reduce bulging CCC inventories.

The response by farmers was more extensive than expected. The idling of 77 million acres in 1983 adversely affected sellers of agricultural inputs and also caused commodity prices to rise beyond expectations. Taxpayers were upset by allegations of abuse. For example, because the regular $50,000 payment limitation did not apply to in-kind payments, a corporate farm in California received about $6 million in corn for idling about one-half of company owned acres. This PIK program, with minor exceptions, was a one year exercise.

A different payment-in-kind program emerged in 1985 and must not be confused with the commodity specific 1983 PIK program. In the 1985 Act and again in the 1990 Act the Secretary was authorized to direct that a percentage of certain government payments to participating farmers be made in non-commodity specific certificates rather than by check. A cash market in these generic certificates exists, or holders can redeem them for commodities in CCC inventories. In some years, however, no program payments are made in generic certificates.

The 1980s brought a new crisis to agriculture, called by some the farm debt crisis of the 1980s. In 1981 the boom of the 1970s ended almost as dramatically as had the boom of the 1920s. The responses to this crisis by farmers, institutions and government are explored in Ch. 2 *infra*.

C. Contemporary Farm Programs

The 1985 Act provided assistance in one form or another to producers of most major agricultural commodities, including milo, wool, mohair, wheat, corn, oats, rye, grain sorghum, barley, upland cotton, extra-long cotton, staple cotton, rice, peanuts, soybeans, sugar, honey burley tobacco, and flu-cured tobacco. The 1985 Act, as amended, governed through FY 1989, including the 1990 crop season.

The Food, Agricultural Conservation and Trade Act of 1990 (1990 Act) extended -- with a few modifications -- the provisions of the 1985 Act for crop years 1991 through 1995. An examination of the 1990 Act confirms that commodity programs continue to be structured in large part as amendments to the Agricultural Adjustment Act of 1938 and the Agricultural Act of 1949. The 1990 Act continues the basics of economic regulation -- supporting farm income and controlling and managing commodity supplies. It also continues programs that enhance U.S. agricultural exports. Important soil conservation measures that serve both environmental and supply control functions are continued, with some modifications, in the 1990 Act.

1. Price Supports

Under the 1985 and 1990 Acts prices farmers receive for "basic" and "nonbasic" agricultural commodities are supported by a variety of devices, including CCC entry into the market to create a floor below which prices for program commodities should not go. See illustration pp. 10-11 *supra*. Production controls are also used from time to time at the Secretary's discretion for their price support effect.

"Basic" commodities are wheat, rice, peanuts, upland cotton, extra long staple cotton, soybeans and feedgrains (corn, grain sorghums, barley, oats). 7 USCA §§ 1441 - 1445k. "Nonbasic" commodities are dairy products, cottonseed, sugarcane, sugar beets, honey and oilseeds. Oilseeds are soybeans, sunflower seeds, canola, rapeseed, safflower, flax-seed and mustard seed. 7 USCA §§ 1446 - 1446i. Programs for wool and mohair terminate at the end of 1995. Fruits, vegetables, nuts, poultry and live-stock are not included in the programs for "basic" or "nonbasic" commodities.

Unadjusted dollar price support loan levels for "basic" and "nonbasic" commodities, other than dairy products, were set in the 1985 Act. Statutory formulas were used to adjust these rates downward for 1987, 1988 and 1990. The 1990 Act seeks to establish price support loan rates higher than those in the 1985 Act. This is accomplished by calculat-ing the basic price support rate at 85% of the preceding five year moving average market price, dropping the high and low price years. However, the Secretary, under the Findley Amendment, may reduce the support rate based on projections of ending stocks-to-use ratio for the market year. In other words, when the amount of unused production rises to a certain level, the Secretary can use his discretion to lower the price support loan rate to encourage competitive prices in world markets. Under the 1990 Act reductions are limited to 10%.

Two types of loans are used: nonrecourse and marketing. Nonrecourse loans were discussed at pp. 10-11 *supra*. Marketing loans are implemented at the discretion of the Secretary except as mandatory for oil seeds, upland cotton and rice. When the marketing loan program is in effect for a commodity in a particular year, farmers may pay back their nonrecourse CCC price support loans at the prevailing world market price or 70% of the loan price, whichever is higher. The marketing loan program is designed to promote exports through lower market prices, while protecting farmers by letting them pocket the difference between their loan and the lower payback figure.

The CCC has a line of credit from the Treasury to purchase commodities and loan money to farmers -- $25 billion in recent times. The CCC becomes a buyer when farmers choose to forfeit program commodities rather than repay price support loans. These purchases generate the government stocks that receive so much publicity.

Direct purchases of dairy products is a key element of the distinct program for these commodities -- a program that does not include price support loans. This price support program is carried out through direct CCC purchases of butter, cheese and non-fat dry milk. Raw milk, which is not capable of prolonged storage, is not purchased.

2. *Income Supports*

Income supports involve direct payments to farmers and include deficiency payments, marketing loans, loan deficiency payments, and disaster payments. The latter are discussed at pp. 29-31 *infra*.

Deficiency payments to individual farmers are a direct method of supporting farm incomes. For "basic" commodities, an annual target price is set by statute well above the loan rate. Farmers who timely enroll for a particular commodity and year are eligible to receive deficiency payments. April 15 is a typical final sign up date for the coming crop season. The payment rate for most target price crops is determined by subtracting from the target price a subtrahend that is the higher of either the national average loan rate, or the national weighted average market price received by producers in a set period during the first part of the marketing year. The deficiency payment is determined by multiplying the payment rate *times* the farm's established yield *times* the crop acreage base for the farm. For corn, grain sorghums, wheat, barley and oats the crop acreage base is the average of the acreage planted or treated by law as planted for the five preceding crop years. For upland cotton and rice a three year figure is used. Special rules apply to double cropping. When the weighted average market price moves well above the loan rate for a program commodity, deficiency payments are substantially reduced.

Consider these examples. Wheat farmer enrolls, complies with program rules, and has a wheat acreage base of 100 acres with an established yield of 40 bu. per acre. 1) Assuming a target price for wheat of $4.00, a loan rate of $2.00 and a national average price of $4.50, farmer will receive no deficiency payment since the national average price exceeded the target price. 2) Now assume a target price of $4.00, a loan rate $2.00, and a national average price $1.50. Farmer will receive a payment of $2.00 per bu. (target price minus the loan rate). The deficiency payment is $800 ($2.00 x 40 bu. x 100 acres). Had the loan rate been lowered by the Secretary, the payment rate would be more than $2.00 per bu.

Regular deficiency payments are subject to a $50,000 per "person" payment cap. When the adjusted loan rate has been reduced under the Findley Amendment, the portion of the deficiency payment attributable thereto (adjusted loan rate minus Findley Amendment reduction) is subject to a $250,000 overall payment cap.

Advance deficiency payments may be requested at sign-up -- 50% for 1993 program crops. In some years, one-half of advance payments are disbursed in cash at sign-up and the remaining one-half in May in generic commodity certificates. A percentage of the balance of the deficiency payment has in some years been paid in generic certificates, rather than by government check. These certificates can be sold, sometimes above face value, in the private market-place, or may be redeemed by the farmer for available CCC commodities. Exporters purchase certificates to access CCC stocks stored near ports.

Loan Deficiency Payments (LDP), when available for a commodity, allow producers who are eligible for price support loans to forgo the loans and take LDP. The LDP rate is the amount by which the loan rate exceeds the local posted price. The payment is calculated by multiplying this rate times the quantity of commodity that could have been placed under loan. This program is authorized for oilseeds, which are noticeably absent from the regular deficiency payment program.

At the discretion of the Secretary, wheat and feedgrain producers may elect to participate in an optional acreage diversion program known as 0/85. See, e.g., 7 USCA § 1444f(c)(1)(E)(feed grains).

Electing producers devote all or a portion of their wheat or feedgrain acreage to conserving uses and receive deficiency payments not to exceed 85% of the crop's permitted acreage. A discretionary deficiency payment protection clause allows a guaranteed level of payment under the 0-85 program, no matter how high market prices go. Also, the Secretary can allow farmers with failed plantings to come under the 0-85 program. There is a parallel program for upland cotton and rice, known as 50-85, under which the optional acreage diversion may not exceed 50% of the crop's permitted acreage. See, e.g. 7 USCA § 1441-2(c)(1)(D)(rice). No deficiency payment guarantee exists for upland cotton and rice.

3. Recourse Loans

Price support recourse loans are available to program participants when certain commodities do not meet quality standards for CCC nonrecourse loans. 7 USCA § 1444f(q) (high moisture feed grain). This gives producers cash flow and eliminates the need to market such commodities during the harvest glut. But, these loans must be repaid with interest at or before the end of the nine month loan period. Forfeiture to the CCC in satisfaction of the principal and interest is not an option.

4. Supply Control and Soil Conservation

Implementing devices available to the USDA to impose supply control include acreage allotments, marketing quotas, acreage set-asides, acreage reductions, cropland diversions, payment-in-kind (1983 type program), long-term conservation reserves, and farmer-owned reserves. Not all are in current use.

The 1985 and 1990 Acts also continue the tradition of soil conservation measures in farm bills, but with new elements. We now examine annual and multiple year supply control and soil conservation programs.

a. Annual Programs

The Secretary, as a condition to participation in price support and deficiency payment programs, may require that the farmer set-aside in conserving uses a percentage of the farm's base acreage for program crops. This set-aside program is not commodity specific and no "rental" payments are made to the farmer. Haying and grazing on set-aside acres may be authorized by the Secretary under emergency conditions.

Under the Acreage Reduction Program (ARP), the Secretary may require that the farmer not plant a percentage of the farm's base acres for a specific crop, as a condition for participating in the price support loan and deficiency payment program for that same crop. In other words, the ARP program is commodity specific. No rental payment is made for acreage that is taken out of production. In 1991 under ARP, 17.1 million acres were taken out of wheat, feedgrain, upland and ELS cotton, and rice production, and devoted to conserving uses.

The Secretary has discretion to activate the Paid Land Diversion Program (PLD) for a particular crop and year. 7 USCA § 1445j(b). This program offers payments to farmers who contract to place in conserving uses cropland acreage in excess of that taken out of production under ARP and the set-aside program. For example, for 1987 and 1988, feed grain producers were offered an optional PLD program with payments to be made in generic commodity certificates. PLD has not been used in the years following 1988.

b. Multiple Year Programs

The Farmer-Owned Reserve Program (FOR) authorizes extending the term of price support loans and the making of storage payments to farmers who continue to store their wheat or feed gain beyond the nine month loan period. 7 USCA § 1445e. Entry into FOR may be permitted if either the national bushel limit for the particular FOR commodity is not already in FOR, or the average market price for a 90 day period is 80% or less of the price support loan rate. If both tests are met, the Secretary must permit entry. Direct entry by a farmer with no price support loan is not permitted. A farmer may redeem grain from FOR storage at any time but no later than 27 months from the expiration of the initial nine month loan, unless the Secretary opts to extend for six months. Interest accrues on loans when the market price of the commodity exceeds 105% of the then current target price. Government storage payments cease when the market price equals or exceeds 95% of the current target price for 90 days. If there is an emergency need for the commodity, USDA will call loans early and require farmers to redeem.

The Secretary may establish national marketing quotas for tobacco, peanuts, and extra-long staple cotton. While these programs are distinct and vary considerably in detail, they share certain characteristics. Before being imposed, marketing quotas must be approved in a referendum open to all farmers who produce the commodity. For example, under the 1990 Act if two-thirds of peanut producers vote in favor of quotas, the system goes into place for five years. Upon approval, poundage marketing quotas are allocated to states and then to specific farms based on historical production data. Substantial penalties can be imposed on farmers who produce and market quantities over their quotas. Quota systems, like acreage limitation programs, are designed to support prices by limiting production.

Authorized in the 1985 Act, the Conservation Reserve Program (CRP) was designed to serve both production control and soil conservation functions. Farmers contracted with USDA to place cropland meeting specific soil erodability criteria in conserving uses for 10 years. A bidding process was used. Some 36.4 million acres were selected in 375,205 contracts. Farmers receive annual rental payments -- the national average being about $50 per acre. Payments to one "person" may not exceed $50,000 per year, exclusive of other payment caps. Farmers with CRP contracts can get grants up to 50% of the cost of establishing vegetative cover, including trees.

The 1990 Act added the Wetlands Reserve Program (WRP). Under WRP up to one million acres of converted wetlands may be enrolled in 30 year or permanent easements in return for government payments. See Ch. 11 *infra*.

Production control is inherent in the conservation compliance provisions of the 1985 Act. Producers must control soil erosion to acceptable levels on highly erodible cropland if eligibility is to be retained for price and income support programs, disaster payments, federal crop insurance, farmer program loans, CCC storage payments, and other benefits. The 1990 Act adds benefits for which a violator is ineligible. The first compliance step was Soil Conservation Service (SCS) approval of a conservation compliance plan for the entire farm by Dec. 31, 1989. Full implementation on-site was required by Dec. 31, 1994. By then the functions of SCS had been assumed by the new Natural Resources Conservation Service (NRCS). Stringent requirements limit conversion of fragile grasslands and wetlands. The Sodbuster and Swampbuster Programs also emerged in the 1985 Act. See Ch. 11 *infra*.

Congress, on occasion, has gone beyond field crops to control production in other areas. In 1986 under the Dairy Herd Termination Program, dairy producers were given an opportunity to terminate milk production and dispose of whole herds by selling for slaughter or by exporting live cows. To encourage participation, incentive payments were made over a five year period, beginning upon disposition of the herd. During the program -- April 1986 to Oct. 1987 -- 1,244,600 dairy cows were slaughtered. About 65,860 live cows were exported. To ease the impact on domestic beef markets, USDA purchased almost 453 million pounds of red meat.

5. Marketing Orders

Commodity specific federal marketing orders, authorized by the Agricultural Marketing Agreement Act of 1937 (AMAA), are used in the fruit, nut, vegetable and dairy sectors instead of price support loans, deficiency payments, acreage and other controls. 7 USCA §§ 601-14; 671-74. Marketing orders are instituted regionally by the Secretary after notice, hearing, and referendum approval, in most instances by two-thirds of producers by number or volume of production of the particular commodity. Once approved, they are binding on all handlers within the region. "Orderly marketing" is supposed to bring adequate supplies to consumers at stable prices.

a. Fruit, Tree Nut and Vegetable Orders

Fruit, tree nut and vegetable orders regulate the rate of flow to market, allocate market shares, and also require handlers to meet certain size, grade, maturity, container, and packaging requirements.

Federal citrus orders, as an example, do not directly control volume. Management of volume is accomplished during critical harvest periods by prorates and shipping holidays. During the harvest season, a maximum volume to be shipped is set and each packing house gets a prorata share. Shipping holidays also prevent excess buildup of wholesale and retail supplies by barring shipments following major holidays such as Christmas and Thanksgiving. Fruit and vegetable orders do not set minimum prices to be paid by handlers to producers.

Almond marketing orders survived a regulatory takings challenge in Cal-Almond, Inc. v. U.S. (Fed. Cl.Ct.1994). Under the orders a percentage of the almond crop must be placed in reserve for sale outside the open market for school lunches and animal feeds. Prices received by handlers were well below market. But the court looked to entire crops and saw no taking of all economic value. It also held that those in a business regulated for over 40 years do not have a property right to market free of regulation, and that the orders were reasonable.

b. Milk Marketing Orders

Regional federal milk marketing orders regulate marketing of fluid milk and provide for minimum prices that handlers must pay to producers for Grade A raw milk. One of the purposes of the minimum price mechanism is to assure that prices do not bottom out in the spring after calving when production exceeds demand. Handlers are processors, cooperatives and others who use fluid milk for various purposes. About 45% of Grade A milk is used for fluid consumption (Class I milk) and a higher price is paid for this milk than for Grade A milk used for manufacture of soft dairy products such as ice cream, cottage cheese or yogurt (Class II milk), or for Grade A milk used to make cheese, butter or dried milk (Class III milk). Handlers pay a uniform price for all Grade A milk into a producer settlement fund (pool). As to milk put to a higher value use, additional payments (assessments) must be made by the handler into the fund. Handlers who use Grade A milk for a lower valued use draw out of the fund (rebates). Then producers of Grade A milk in the marketing area are paid from the fund essentially the same "blend" price for their milk, regardless of its use.

Prices for the three Grade A Classes are extrapolated from a sampling of prices paid by handlers for unregulated Grade B milk in the Minnesota-Wisconsin (M-W) area. Grade B milk is used for essentially the same purposes as Grade A Class III milk. CCC price support purchases of butter, cheese and non-fat dry milk indirectly support the M-W sampling. Class III milk is priced nationally at the M-W price. Class II milk is priced nationally at about

10¢ per hwt. above the M-W price. For Class I milk, orders for regions east of the Rocky Mountains use differentials that push minimum prices higher and higher as one goes away from the M-W area -- a response to purportedly higher production costs in areas less hospitable to dairying. If production costs are lower in the Upper-Midwest, it is posited that in an unregulated market, northern dairies could produce enough Grade A milk to serve the fluid needs of most of the nation and at prices below the cost of production in some southern areas. The differentials that are added to prices paid in southern and other outlying regions are supposed to reflect this, but are not enough to cover the cost of transporting fluid milk from the Upper-Midwest to other markets. Thus, it is difficult for lower cost milk from northern areas to be sold profitably in other regions when minimum order prices are being paid there by local handlers. When demand exceeds local supply in southern and other areas, higher prices will be paid and milk will be bought and transported in from reserve areas. This system, it is argued, assures a national rather than a one region dairy industry.

However, these east of the Rocky Mountains milk marketing orders are being challenged as violative of AMAA and are alleged to have contributed to the sharp decline of dairying in the Upper-Midwest. Minnesota Milk Producers Ass'n v. Yeutter (D. Minn.1994). The gist of the challenge is that the Secretary, in a final decision issued on March 5, 1993 following administrative hearings, left the Class I differential system unchanged without engaging in the type of analysis arguably required by 7 USCA § 608c(18)(consideration of price and availability of feed, plus other local marketing and production factors). The court does explain that AMAA requires such analysis region by region and not on a national basis. Thus, the legality of the differential system as such is thus far intact. Rather, it is a question of whether the fixed dollar Class I differentials must be adjusted in Upper-Midwest regions if prices there are to reflect production costs, insure supply, and assure "a level of farm income adequate to maintain productive capacity sufficient to meet anticipated future needs . . .." *Id.*

c. State Marketing and Pricing Orders

Some states have their own marketing order laws. California, for example, has a state administered milk marketing program comparable with and operated in lieu of the federal program. Florida has a state citrus order that includes requirements in addition to those in the applicable federal orders.

Until invalidated in 1994, a Massachusetts state pricing order required each state licensed milk dealer to contribute to the Massachusetts Dairy Equalization Fund based on the amount of "Class I" milk it sold in Massachusetts. Fund monies were paid to Massachusetts dairy farmers on a volume of production basis, with no payments to out-of-state dairy farmers who sold to Massachusetts licensed dealers. A Commerce Clause challenge to the order prevailed in West Lynn Creamery, Inc. v. Healy (U.S.Sup.Ct.1994). The court held that the order, designed to aid a flagging Massachusetts dairy industry, imposed a discriminatory burden on interstate commerce as it disadvantaged out-of-state producers. The combination of a tax and a subsidy was deemed fatal, though either alone might not have violated the Commerce Clause. Local benefits did not outweigh the burden on interstate commerce.

6. Assistance Programs

a. Indemnity Programs

In certain cases of pesticide contamination, dairy farmers and beekeepers who suffer losses for which there is no legal recourse can apply for USDA indemnity payments. The 1990 Act continues the Dairy Indemnity Program through Sept. 9, 1995. 7 CFR pt. 760 (1994). Indemnity payments also are available to encourage owners of brucellosis infected animals to slaughter under the USDA's brucellosis eradication program.

b. Livestock Emergency Programs

Under the Emergency Feed Assistance Program (EFAP), CCC is authorized to sell stocks of feed grain and wheat at 50% of average market price to livestock producers who have lost their feed supply due to a natural disaster. 7 USCA § 1471d(a)(2). Under the Emergency Feed Program (EFP), the CCC is authorized to pay 50% of the cost of feed purchased for eligible livestock under emergency conditions. 7 USCA § 1471d(a)(4).

Widespread drought conditions in the summer of 1988 prompted passage by the Congress of the Disaster Assistance Act of 1988. Many provisions were temporary and applied only to farmers hurt by the drought or other natural disasters in 1988.

An ongoing aspect of the 1988 Act is the Emergency Livestock Feed Assistance Act of 1988 which reauthorized feed and water assistance to eligible producers with livestock in counties declared disaster areas, and in contiguous counties. 7 USCA § 1471 *et seq.* Livestock is defined to include poultry and fish used for food. Producers must meet eligibility requirements in the Act and CCC regulations. CFSA now administers the program. Eligible producers may elect between this program and EFAP and EFP benefits. 7 USCA §1471c(c). Assistance under the 1988 Act can include: sales by the CCC of feed grain stocks at reduced prices; donations of CCC feed grains; reimbursement of a percentage of transportation and handling costs as to CCC feed grains and purchased hay or forage; reimbursement for a percentage of the cost of feed purchased. Other assistance to eligible producers can include reimbursement of a percentage of the cost of wells, pipes and other water facilities.

Payments under the Emergency Livestock Feed Assistance program to one "person" may not exceed $50,000, a payment cap distinct from others discussed in this chapter, except to the extent that it was combined with the overall $100,000 cap for the Emergency Crop Loss Assistance Program under the Disaster Assistance Act of 1988. 7 USCA § 1471g.

These feed assistance programs are among the few federal programs designed to provide direct benefits to the livestock sector. Meat purchases during the Dairy Herd Termination Program, certain quotas limiting imports, and benefits from statutorily de-pressed feed grain prices provide indirect support.

c. Crop Emergency and Insurance Programs

An expanded federal crop insurance program now covers virtually all major crops and is available in over 3,000 agricultural counties. 7 USCA §§ 1506 - 1508a. But, such insurance is not always available in all locations where a particular crop is grown.

With the enactment of the Federal Crop Insurance Reform Act of 1994, P.L. No. 103-354, Congress has said no to future *ad hoc* crop disaster programs in the event of floods, droughts and other natural disasters. To encourage participation in crop insurance starting with 1995 crops, the new law makes catastrophic loss coverage a prerequisite to availability of federal programs such as deficiency payments, farmer program loans, NRCS (formerly SCS) programs, CRP and WRP. Catastrophic coverage will be available for a $50 fee per crop per county and will protect against loses over 50% at a payment rate of 60% of anticipated market value.

Farmers may voluntarily purchase from private crop insurance carriers buy-up coverage with higher yield and price protection levels. As to such policies, CFSA (successor to Federal Crop Insurance Corp.) administers federal subsidies and sets uniform policy provisions and procedures.

Under the new law, Congress has provided for a standing disaster program for crops that are not insurable. The program offers the same 50/60 catastrophic coverage described above, without a fee. For this program to be triggered there must be an areawide 35% loss of yield for the particular crop.

The 1994 law also introduces a requirement that a farmer's Social Security number be used for all federal crop insurance and farm program documentation. The goal is to create a database of all dealings with the federal government for every farmer.

d. Domestic Food Assistance Programs

In an effort to help low-income Americans and to dispose of surpluses, USDA administers several domestic food assistance programs. Included are the food stamp program, free school lunches and breakfasts, elderly food assistance, supplemental food programs for women, infants and children, child care meals and summer child feeding.

Under USDA's temporary emergency food assistance program, seven types of food are distributed: cheese, butter, non-fat dry milk, honey, corn meal, flour and rice. Occasionally, certain of these distributions are suspended due to low CCC inventories.

7. Issues in Administration of Programs

Because the CCC has no operating personnel, the actual administration of domestic programs is carried out by the personnel of the new Consolidated Farm Service Agency (CFSA)(successor to ASCS). In the past, most disputes between the former ASCS and producers involved issues about measurement of acreage allotments, base acreage, allotment transfers, and alleged excessive production. Today, the emphasis is on payment limitations problems.

There is evidence that the largest farmers have reaped the greatest benefits from income support programs. Arguably, this results in the expansion of large operations at the expense of others, particularly those of "average" size. Since 1970, Congress has experimented with various payment caps. Currently, the total of regular deficiency payments and land diversion payments that one "person" can receive shall not exceed $50,000. The programs affected are those for wheat, feedgrains, upland cotton, extra long staple (ELS) cotton and rice. 7 USCA § 1308(1)(A). Non-recourse price support loans do not have a cap.

A distinct cap of $75,000 exists for the total of "other payments." These payments are gains from marketing loan repayments, loan deficiency payments, and Findley deficiency payments. 7 USCA § 1308(1)(B). An overall cap of $250,000 takes into account payments governed by the $50,000 and $75,000 caps, plus payments for resource adjustment (excluding diversion payments), inventory reduction, and disasters (under one or more of the annual programs). § 1308(2)(A). Payments made under the Conservation Reserve Program (CRP) are subject to a separate $50,000 cap per person. Disaster payments sometimes have a distinct cap. See p. 31 *supra*.

As indicated, statutory limits focus on the amount of payments one "person" can lawfully receive in any given year. Complex regulations defining the term "person" appear at subpt. B of 7 CFR pt. 1497 (1994) and are explained in ASCS (now CFSA) Handbook 1-PL "Payment Limitations". One "person" may be an individual; or, an entity such as a corporation, association, limited partnership, trust, estate, or other eligible legal entity. A "person" cannot be a cooperative or a joint operation (joint venture or general partnership), though members may qualify. Further, a "person" must be "actively engaged in farming." Here there are strict tests as to contributions of land, capital, equipment, labor and management. Most annual determinations are based on the status of the individual or entity on March 1.

Given the per "person" payment caps, efforts are made to structure single agricultural enterprises to create more than one "person." If successful, such efforts result in increased disbursements under pertinent farm programs. Litigation has erupted as USDA has challenged multiple "person" claims of many agricultural enterprises. To curb efforts by particular producers to become many "persons", current rules permit a "person" to double the $50,000 limit, but only to the extent that payments are received from two or three entities in which the "person" holds a substantial beneficial interest.

In Women Involved in Farm Economics (WIFE) v. USDA (D.C.Cir.1990), the court held that the automatic treatment of married couples as one "person" for payment limitations purposes did not violate the due process or equal protection clauses of the U.S. Constitution. Because married couples are deemed to be financially interdependent, there is a rational basis for treating husband and wife as one. Pending the appeal, the regulation for the 1988 crop year was revised to provide that a husband and wife would be separate persons if each maintained separate farming operations prior to and after their marriage. Congress had already authorized this change, but effective for the 1989 crop year. The 1990 Act reinstated the restrictive rule, but added a new exemption. Effective for the 1991 crop year, the Secretary was given discretion to provide that each spouse may have one interest - it may be as an individual or it may be as a substantial beneficial interest in a "true entity."

Persons dissatisfied with CFSA (ASCS) determinations may obtain reconsideration or review pursuant to 7 CFR pt. 780 (1994). Administrative review can be pursued through local, state and national levels.

From Nov. 1991 until recently, the final administrative appeal decision at the national level was made by one of the following depending on the nature of the case: the Director of the ASCS National Appeals Division; the Administrator of the ASCS; or, the Secretary of Agriculture. Exhaustion of administrative remedies normally is required prior to judicial review. U.S. v. Bisson (8th Cir.1988). A decision of the U.S. Supreme Court limiting the exhaustion requirement appears to have little potential to impact USDA administrative matters. Darby v. Cisneros (1993) applies only when neither the statute nor agency rule specifically require exhaustion before judicial review. Government efforts to head off judicial review under 5 USCA § 701(a)(2) turn on assertions that "agency action is committed to agency discretion by law," or rather that there is no legal standard against which to measure agency action. Such circumstances are rare.

Charges of arbitrary and unreasonable agency action and denial of due process can be reviewed by a U.S. District Court as can charges that the agency acted contrary to statute or regulation. Doane v. Espy (7th Cir.1994)(ASCS administration of disaster program). In a payment limitations case the only question is the number of "persons" who may receive payment up to the cap. Peterson Farms I v. Madigan (D.D.C.1991). Such questions may also be reviewed in the Federal Claims Court.

Most suits seeking monetary awards against the U.S., other than in tort, must be litigated in the Federal Claims Court under the Tucker Act. Esch v. Yeutter (D.C.Cir.1989). Under 28 USCA § 1346(a)(2), Esch holds that U.S. District Courts do *not* have jurisdiction over claims against the U.S. exceeding $10,000 if "founded either upon the Constitution, or any act of Congress, or any regulation of an executive department, or upon any express or implied contract with the United States . . .." Such claims must be brought in the Claims Court where there is no such dollar limitation. 28 USCΛ § 1491. However, the Claims Court does not have exclusive jurisdiction over a suit merely because contract-related issues are raised. Where declaratory or injunctive relief may have importance apart from a mere determination of the monetary liability of the government, the equitable relief sought is paramount and a U.S. District Court may assume jurisdiction over the nonmonetary claims. Accordingly, the District Court will take jurisdiction over a claim alleging arbitrary agency action subject to review under Administrative Procedure Act § 702. This could lead to a declaration by the District Court of the number of lawful "persons" even though such a declaration may entitle plaintiffs to prospective relief from the government in the Claims Court.

The former ASCS review and appeal process was but one of several within USDA. The former SCS reviewed decisions about the sodbuster, swampbuster and conservation compliance programs and CRP. 7 CFR pt. 614 (1994). Adverse SCS decisions resulted in some cases in ineligibility for ASCS administered benefits. The National Appeals Staff of the former FmHA heard agency farmer loan program appeals. 7 CFR §§ 1900.51-.61(1994). All of these review processes are subsumed in a newly authorized single USDA National Appeals Division pursuant to P.L. 103-354. There remains a cadre of administrative law judges, who with the Judicial Officer of the USDA, review enforcement of some 17 regulatory programs including the Packers and Stockyard Act and the Perishable Agricultural Commodities Act.

Farmers who run afoul of federal farm program and conservation laws may be in jeopardy as to qualifying for benefits, be sued for refund of benefits paid by mistake as in U.S. v. Mead (9th Cir. 1970)(refund only, no penalties or double damages), or be sued under the False Claims Act or proceeded against administratively under the Program Fraud Civil Remedies Act of 1986, 31 USCA §§ 3801-3812; 7 CFR §§ 1.301-.346(1994)(refund, penalties, and damages for false, fictitious or fraudulent claim).

D. Export Programs

Because almost 20% of our agricultural production is exported, the future of American agriculture is tied to developments in global markets. Both the 1985 and the 1990 farm bills included programs designed to make U.S. agriculture more competitive in international markets. Agricultural issues have been a major concern of the U.S. in recent multilateral and bilateral trade negotiations.

The l985 Act reflects major concerns about the then current decline in U.S. agricultural exports and the attendant decline in the U.S. agricultural trade balance. Agriculture had been a bright spot in an overall negative trade balance. In the 1985 Act price support loan levels for major export commodities were lowered and scheduled for further reduction during the five year period ending with FY 1990. In addition, the Secretary was given authority under the Findley Amendment to further reduce price support loan levels for certain commodities by up to 20% -- creating the potential of lower market prices, but larger deficiency payments. Further, the Secretary was given the authority to engage the marketing loan program for certain export commodities, allowing farmers to repay price support loans at the lower of the world price or the loan rate. Loan proceeds not repaid were kept by farmers. The goal of all of this was to create lower support floors, push down domestic prices, and thus make U.S. commodities more price competitive in world markets.

The export promotion theme in the 1985 Act is further reflected in the Targeted Export Assistance Program (TEA). The CCC, with the administrative assistance of the USDA Foreign Agricultural Service (FAS), was authorized to allocate to eligible export- ers or associations generic certificates for surplus federal commodities. Typically, the certificates were sold by recipients to raise cash to help finance approved overseas market promotion as well as export product development efforts. In theory, the TEA program was supposed to counter the adverse effects of unfair foreign trade practices. Commodi- ties promoted included high-value products such as seafood, meat, horticultural products, soybeans, peanuts, chocolate, lentils and plywood. In the 1990 Act, TEA was replaced by the Market Promotion Program (MPP). 7 CFR pt. 1485 (1994). Annual funding for TEA and MPP has far exceeded that for the ongoing Cooperator Program, now over 35 years old, with its focus on promoting bulk commodities.

Under the Export Enhancement Program (EEP), private export sales of several commodities are eligible to be subsidized by payments that can be made in kind using CCC inventories. 7 CFR pt. 1494 (1994). CCC can award bonuses to certain U.S. exporters in the form of generic certificates redeemable for CCC owned commodities -- wheat as an example. The redeemed commodity can be made part of the export transaction, sweetening the deal. Or, certificates can be sold. In either case, the goal is to allow U.S. exporters to compete in foreign markets at prices at or below those offered by competitors, particularly merchants in the European Union (EU). The EU offers "restitution" payments to its exporters to offset internal market prices which, due to the price support features of the Common Agricultural Policy (CAP), usually far exceed world prices for commodities such as wheat. The Dairy Export Incentive Program for dairy products such as eggs and dried milk functions similarly to EEP.

The general sales manager (GSM) of the Foreign Agricultural Service administers CCC payment guarantee programs. 59 Fed. Reg. 52866 (1994)(to be codified at 7 CFR pt. 1493). Under the GSM-102 and GSM-103 programs, the CCC issues guarantees to U.S. exporters of certain agricultural commodities to cover possible nonpayment under letters of credit opened by foreign buyers in favor of U.S. sellers on CCC approved foreign banks. The GSM-102 program contemplates payment up to three years. The intermediate term GSM-103 program allows payment over three to 10 years. The goal is to encourage banks in the U.S. to buy the interests of sellers in letters of credit and, as assurance of payment, to take assignments of CCC guarantees. This gives private U.S. sellers immediate cash flow instead of payment over a period of years -- using time drafts to draw on letters of credit. CCC no longer engages in direct lending to foreign buyers under any GSM program.

Title I of P.L. 480 authorizes a concessional sales program designed to promote private exports of U.S. agricultural commodities and to foster economic development in recipient countries. The sales program, which has been in existence for many years, is aimed at less developed friendly nations. Credit is extended by the CCC for up to 40 years, with a 10 year grace period for the commencement of repayment. Under Title III, as amended in 1985, a debt incurred under Title I may be forgiven upon compliance by the importing nation with food-for-development programs and other projects agreed upon by the U.S. and recipient country.

Import fees and quotas can be imposed on certain agricultural products if their importation into the U.S. will interfere with domestic agricultural programs. Section 22 of the Agricultural Adjustment Act of 1933, 7 USCA § 624(f). For example, import quotas for sugar can be tightened in the face of increased domestic production of beet sugar, cane sugar and corn sweeteners. To avoid the setting of meat quotas the U.S. periodically negotiates with Australia and New Zealand to set voluntary limits on the amount of their meat that will enter U.S. markets.

The United States is a contracting party in the GATT, the General Agreement on Tariffs and Trade. Agricultural trade barriers, including trade distorting features of domestic farm programs, were priority topics in the Uruguay Round of GATT talks which came to a successful conclusion in early 1994. The GATT now calls for the gradual reduction by the contracting parties of agricultural trade distorting devices and protectionist barriers. Congress is expected to legislate consistent with GATT, not just as to a reduction of U.S. export subsidies, but as to features of domestic agricultural policy that distort international markets by artificially impacting prices and levels of production.

If it uses its "fast track" procedure, Congress will in one vote either pass implementing legislation to conform U.S. laws to the GATT agreement, or reject the Uruguay Round implementing legislation as submitted by the President. GATT agreements are not subjected to the U.S. treaty ratification process.

Under the Uruguay Round agreement, internal or domestic agricultural support is to be cut by 20% from a 1986-88 base period. No changes in existing U.S. deficiency payment laws or other support programs will be required to meet this goal over six years. A GATT member facing cuts has discretion in how to reduce total Aggregate Measure of Support (AMS). This is the sum of all commodity and sector specific AMSs. Permitted or "green box" domestic programs are exempt from reduction. These include conservation, crop insurance, disaster assistance and extension programs. Decoupled income support payments to farmers -- not based on current production levels -- are permitted.

As to export subsidies, the agreement requires a 21% reduction in volume and a 36% reduction in value over six years from a 1986-90 base period. U.S. programs such as EEP will be cut by about $370 million, but EU cuts will be much larger. The agreement should not impact the GSM-102 or GSM-

103 programs except to the extent that fees paid for guarantees may now be subsidized. Changes in P.L. 480 Title I are not foreseen.

Nontariff barriers are to be dealt with in two main ways. Quotas are to be converted to tariffs and then gradually reduced -- comprehensive tariffication. The U.S. will convert import protection for beef, cotton, sugar, peanuts, cheese, low fat dry milk, butter and other dairy products to tariffs and assure access through tariff-rate quotas. Similar actions by countries such as Korea and Japan will open major markets for some U.S. agricultural commodities.

Sanitary and phytosanitary measures are to be made transparent and science-based. Unjustified measures are not to be used to artificially restrict trade. However, under GATT a country may have science-based standards stricter than international standards. See, e.g., *Codex Alimentarius.*

The U.S. is involved in two western hemisphere free trade area agreements, the U.S./Canada Free Trade Agreement and NAFTA, the North American Free Trade Agreement. This has resulted in two bilateral agreements on agricultural market access, one with Canada and the other with Mexico. Canada has its own market access agreement with Mexico. The agreements on export subsidies and sanitary and phytosanitary measures are trilateral.

III. STRUCTURE ISSUES

A. General Concerns

Some argue that the current trend toward fewer and larger farms and an increased role for vertically integrated agriculture is a threat to traditional values, the rural infrastructure, and the future of family farms. Family farm, as used here, means a unit of production that can support one family without hired labor and with minimal or no off farm income.

While not defined in any known statute, the term vertical integration is used in cases and secondary sources. Consider this illustration: Poultry Corp. (P) has a production division where eggs from the P flock are hatched and the chicks inoculated and debeaked. P employees deliver chick to independently owned and operated farms. By contract, title to the chicks remains in P, but farmers care for them using P supplied feed and veterinary products. Farmers are not at risk if they follow P policies and are paid by P under a weight gain formula. P employees come to the contract farms to catch "grown-out" broilers and haul them to P processing division. The poultry products are marketed by P marketing division. This is a vertically integrated enterprise. P, the integrator, controls all aspects of production and marketing of the food product. See Coleman v. Sanderson Farms, Inc. (5th Cir.1980).

Vertical integration is not present in this example. Farmer (F) buys wheat seed and fertilizer from Co-op Elevator (Co-op). Later, F decides to market at Co-op where delivery is made and payment received. Co-op sells to a customer, Mill Co, which makes flour. Mill sells the flour to Jobber, Inc., which then sells to Grocery Chain Ltd. No business entity has the control associated with vertical integration. Even if F enters into a cash forward wheat marketing contract with Co-op, it cannot be said that Co-op has attained such control. The mere presence of a cooperative is not determinative of whether or not vertical integration is present. It is overall structure and control that must be examined, not the choice of business entity by one or more parties.

In some quarters the concern is not that business corporations, vertically integrated or not, will control production, but that it will come to dominated by a relatively small number of large family operations. The fear is that more small towns will die, farm related business will go bankrupt, schools will be consolidated, opportunities for beginning farmers will be limited, and control of the food and fiber supply will be vested in fewer and fewer persons. The other side of the argument is that economic realities demand fewer and larger farms and that it is not realistic to attempt to derail inexorable economic trends. Larger operations, it is said, will be well financed and better able to use new agricultural technology. Further, the argument goes, such farms will be more likely than traditional family farms to survive periodic boom and bust cycles. The national goal, it is argued, should be a strong industrialized agriculture and not the preservation of socioeconomic museums in the countryside.

In response to concerns about structural trends, some states have enacted, *inter alia,* anticorporate farming laws, restrictions on ownership and use of agricultural lands by nonresident aliens, programs to encourage alternative agriculture, and financing programs for beginning farmers. At the national level, CFSA as a successor to the Farmers Home Administration (FmHA) continues to play a role in financing family farmers who cannot get credit elsewhere. The Reclamation Act, as amended in 1982, continues to restrict farm size. See pp. 420-422 *infra.* Payment limitation law is designed in part to target federal support to family farms. Legal aspects of some of these programs are now explored.

B. Anticorporate Farming Laws

A number of states, clustered largely in the central part of the United States, have enacted anticorporate farming statutes. They are Iowa, Kansas, Minnesota, Missouri, North Dakota, Oklahoma, South Dakota and Wisconsin. In Nebraska, the stricture was added to the state constitution. Most of these restrictive schemes provide that corporations and other investment type entities shall not engaged in farming, nor shall they directly or indirectly own or otherwise acquire interests in agricultural land.

Anticorporate farming statutes tend to be riddled with exceptions. Most allow family farm corporations to operate freely. A typical definition of such a corporation requires that the stock be held by persons within a certain degree of kindred and that at least one shareholder be actively engaged in the farming operation. As a result, these statutes do not restrict the growth and size of family farm corporations. Most of the statutes do not bar authorized farm corporations, those with a limited number of unrelated shareholders (five, for example) and at least one shareholder actively engaged in farming. While limited partnerships are constrained under some statutes, general partnerships typically are not.

Exceptions for favored integrated corporate agricultural sectors are common. The vertically integrated poultry sector may be tolerated, while the same state may ban the vertically integrated hog industry.

Most of the state statutes sanction acquisition of agricultural land by general business corporations where there is a plan to convert it to nonagricultural use within a set number of years. In the interim, such corporations are constrained in their agricultural operations and must rent to a farm entity that is not restricted by the statute. Anticorporate farming statutes, given constitutional strictures, have grandfather clauses that allow preexisting corporate operations to continue. In some cases limited expansion is permitted.

All of the state regulatory schemes contemplate that corporations, pension trusts and other business entities will make loans secured by agricultural lands. In most states, however, title acquired upon foreclosure or by deed in-lieu-of foreclosure must be divested within a set number of years.

Penalties for violation of anticorporate farming statutes vary somewhat from state to state. Typically, the state's attorney general is authorized to pursue divestiture actions. If successful, the entity in violation is given a period of time to market the land. If divestiture by private sale does not occur, the land may be sold at public sale in the manner prescribed for the foreclosure of a mortgage.

Anticorporate farming statutes present a variety of constitutional questions. Their general viability was established in Asbury Hospital v. Cass Co. (U.S. Sup.Ct.1945) where it was held that corporate farming restrictions do not violate the privileges and immunities clause of Art. IV, § 2, nor the due process or equal protection clauses of the 14th Amendment. An exception for a favored agricultural sector could raise equal protection questions notwithstanding Asbury. Yet, few such challenges have been litigated, perhaps because the parties who could raise the issue get their way through legislation or by investing in hospitable states.

C. Restrictions on Non-resident Aliens

Beginning in the late 1970s there was a flurry of state and federal legislation regulating ownership and use of U.S. agricultural land by non-resident aliens. It is conceded that discrimination against non-resident aliens can be justified under the 14th Amendment by the rational basis test. Lehndorff Geneva, Inc. v. Warren (Wis.1976) held that statutes restricting non-resident alien ownership did not violate the equal protection clauses of the U.S. or Wisconsin Constitutions, nor any treaty between the U.S. and Germany. Similar restrictions on resident aliens would be difficult to sustain as the discrimination would have to be justified under the more demanding compelling governmental interest test.

Spurred on by rumors of increasing alien investment in U.S. agricultural land, Congress in 1978 passed the Agricultural Foreign Investment Disclosure Act. 7 USCA §§ 3501-3508. This Act does not bar non-resident aliens from acquiring U.S. agricultural land, but mandates that they submit annual reports of their holdings to the local CFSA (formerly ASCS) office. U.S. corporate owners also must report if 10% or more of their stock is owned by foreign investors. The data collected covers cropland, pasture land, forest land, and other agricultural holdings.

The principal non-resident alien investors are from Canada, Germany, France, United Kingdom, Switzerland, Mexico and the Netherlands Antilles.

These investors own 73% of the foreign total with Canada leading with 25% Direct investment from Arab oil countries has been minimal and Japanese investors hold just 3% of the foreign total. At the end of 1991, foreign interests owned 14.8 million acres, or slightly more than 1% of privately owned U.S. agricultural land. The figure has been about 1% since 1981. Forest land accounts for 49% of the total.

State statutes fall into two categories, those that require only disclosure and reporting, and those that impose a ban on ownership or leasing of agricultural lands by non-resident aliens. In disclose and report jurisdictions, failure to comply can lead to an order of divestiture or a monetary penalty, or both. In jurisdictions which prohibit owning or leasing, the transaction by which the fee simple or leasehold interest passes is not nullified. Instead, proceedings may be instituted to compel divestiture.

Finally, aliens not admitted into the U.S. for permanent residence, and entities owned by them are not eligible for certain federal farm program payments. There is an exception for those who provide land, capital and substantial personal labor to the farming operation. 7 CFR § 1498.4(a) (1994).

D. State Finance Programs

Financial barriers to entry into farming are real. The cost of land, stock and equipment is high. Low commodity prices and relatively high input costs make it difficult for a would be farmer to demonstrate a cash flow, sufficient after family living expenses, to make payments of principal and interest on loans for land, equipment, livestock and operating expenses. Some states have special financing programs that allow eligible beginning farmers to borrow at below market interest rates. Funding comes from general revenues or from sale of "aggie bonds". In response to the farm financial crisis of the 1980s many states instituted emergency programs for financially strapped farmers.

E. Federal Measures

The former Farmers Home Administration (FmHA), a USDA agency, had a tradition of making loans at favorable interest rates to eligible family farmers who could not obtain credit elsewhere. See Ch. 2 *infra*. After decades of support for beginning and lower income farmers, FmHA in the 1980s found itself holding many nonperforming loans. It's successor as to farmer loan programs, CFSA, has yet to deal with numerous delinquent borrowers. The future of CFSA farmer loan programs is quite uncertain. It should be noted that the rural housing programs of FmHA have been turned over in the 1994 reorganization of USDA to the Rural Housing and Community Development Service (RHCDS).

Since the enactment of the Reclamation Act of 1902, agriculture in 17 western states has benefitted from irrigation water supplied below cost from federal projects. A 160 acre limit on farm size was designed to promote family farms, but was largely ignored. A 960 acre limit was substituted in the Reclamation Reform Act of 1982. See Ch. 11 *infra*.

Advocates of payment caps on federal farm program payments justify their position in part by concerns about structural trends. See pp. 32-36 *supra*. But, it is doubtful that capping payments has impaired the growth of large agricultural operations.

Arguably federal milk marketing orders have had an impact on the structure of the national dairy sector. Indeed, this impact -- be it seen as positive or negative -- may be more palpable than that of most other federal programs. See pp. 26-28 *supra.*

Historically, it was said that marketing and supply cooperatives would enable smaller agricultural operations to prosper. Legislation to foster cooperatives is discussed in Ch. 8 *infra.* But large farms patronize cooperatives and any suggestion that laws favorable to cooperatives restrain the trend toward fewer and larger farms bears strict scrutiny. Also, many cooperatives have merged or consolidated and some have become massive multistate operations.

The California Agricultural Experiment Station won a case wherein the plaintiff sought an order requiring a decision making process designed to ensure that Hatch Act research funds, 7 USCA §§ 361a - 361i, be expended only after consideration of the needs of all statutory beneficiaries -- with particular attention to small family farmers. The specific controversy was about mechanization research and was pressed on behalf of farm laborers and others. The lower court ordered the Station to file reports for five years and retained jurisdiction to monitor compliance with a court imposed decision making and priority setting process. The appellate court reversed holding, *inter alia,* that to require the Station to use a court imposed decision making process would violate elementary rules of administrative law. California Agrarian Action Project, Inc. v. Regents of the University of California (Cal. Ct. App. 1989).

CHAPTER TWO

FINANCIAL INSTITUTIONS AND PROGRAMS
I. INTRODUCTION

In this century, farmers have gone through several periods of financial turmoil, the most severe being the Great Depression of the 1930s and the financial crisis of the 1980s. The following table summarizes the farm debt picture for recent years.

FARM DEBT BY LENDER IN BILLIONS OF DOLLARS								
YEARS	1982	1984	1986	1988	1990	1991	1992	93FF
Real Estate								
FCS	43.7	46.4	35.6	28.4	25.7	25.2	25.3	25.0
FmHA	08.3	09.5	09.7	08.9	07.6	07.0	06.4	05.9
Life Ins.	11.8	11.9	10.4	09.0	09.6	09.4	08.5	08.5
Banks	07.6	09.6	11.9	14.4	16.2	17.3	18.6	19.7
Individuals	29.3	28.4	22.7	16.9	15.0	15.6	16.6	17.1
TOTAL	101.8	106.7	90.4	77.6	74.1	74.6	75.6	76.2
Other								
Banks	34.3	37.6	29.7	28.3	31.3	32.8	32.9	35.4
FCS	20.6	18.1	10.3	08.8	09.8	10.2	10.3	10.5
FmHA	12.9	13.7	14.4	12.9	09.4	08.2	07.1	06.4
Individuals	19.1	17.6	12.1	11.8	12.7	12.9	13.2	14.2
TOTAL	86.9	87.1	66.6	61.7	63.2	64.3	63.6	66.6
ALL DEBT	188.9	193.8	157.0	139.3	137.3	138.9	139.2	142.8

Excludes: CCC commodity loans and storage facility loans; operator households. FCS = Farm Credit System; FmHA = Farmers Home Administration (now Consolidated Farm Service Agency); Life Ins. = Life Insurance Companies; Banks = Commercial Banks; Individuals = Individuals and Others; FF = forecast. SOURCE: USDA/ERS

The gradual decline in the farm debt load, starting in 1985, largely can be accounted for by repayments, liquidations, write-offs of bad loans, and a reduced demand for farm credit.

This chapter is about institutions and programs designed to facilitate lending and extensions of credit to farming operations. The main focus is on the Farm Credit System (FCS), the Farmers Home Administration (FmHA) and its successor as to farmer program loans, the Consolidated Farm Service Agency (CFSA), and financing of rehabilitation under Chapter 12 of the Bankruptcy Code.

For many decades, the Farm Credit System, through its various federally chartered private banks and associations, was the nation's leading supplier of agricultural loans. By the end of 1987, however, the System's share of outstanding farm debt had fallen to 27.5%, while the share of commercial banks had risen to 28.4%. FCS law is at II *infra*.

CFSA, successor to FmHA, farm real estate and operating loans at favorable rates to low-income and beginning family farmers who cannot obtain credit elsewhere. In recent years, FmHA and now CFSA have been making fewer loans, but have become more and more involved in guaranteeing loans made by other lenders, particularly commercial banks. FmHA/CFSA legal issues are discussed at III *infra*.

Life insurance companies held many of the farm mortgages foreclosed during the 1930s. Today, several major life insurance companies remain active in farm ownership lending, but rarely make operating loans. These lenders are affected by state laws on farm foreclosures and by farm bankruptcy law.

Operating credit commonly is extended to farmers by farm input merchants such as dealers in seed, fertilizer, pesticides, and fuel. While the total of this debt is not separately reflected, it is included with "individuals" in the table. Legal issues associated with extensions of unsecured credit to farmers are explored in Ch. 5 *infra.*

The table does not show that the Commodity Credit Corporation (CCC) makes loans secured by harvested crops to many producers. A farmer who signs up for a price support loan program can, at harvest, obtain a CCC non-recourse loan at a favorable interest rate. See pp. 10-11 *supra.* To include such loans in the table would skew the farm debt picture in a negative way by several billion dollars. In reality these loans are one way in which cash flows to farmers from "marketing". The law of collateralization of CCC loans is at Ch. 5 *infra.*

Family members and other private lenders have long participated in financing agriculture and for many years were the major source of real estate financing. Seller financed sales of farm real estate still occur, but with less frequency than in the past. In some localities it remains common for these sales to be structured using installment land contracts, rather than purchase money real estate mortgages.

As the farm financial crisis of the 1980s deepened, some 37 state legislatures responded with one or more enactments. The level of legislative activity ranged from calling for a farm crisis telephone hotline to the enactment of laws designed to infuse new money into agriculture at below market interest rates and to slow the pace of forced liquidations.

From a constitutional perspective, states can alter remedies available to existing creditors so long as the changes do not allow repudiation of debt, do not introduce unreasonable delays in enforcement, and do not impair security to the point that the terms of the loan become unacceptable to a rational lender.

Agricultural drainage and irrigation districts often finance projects by selling bonds in money markets. Funds to pay principal and interest on bonds are raised by special assessments levied on benefitted lands. Assessments usually are paid in installments, with annual interest on the unpaid balance.

Finally, the economic importance of vertically integrated agribusiness corporations must be noted. Their investment in processing, marketing and transportation systems, plus involvement in production contracts with farmers, is critical to the financial well-being of certain sectors of agriculture. The debt load of corporate integrators is not reflected in the table, nor is that of agricultural cooperatives

II. THE FARM CREDIT SYSTEM

The federally chartered banks and associations in the Farm Credit System (FCS or System) make long and short term loans for agricultural purposes to eligible farmers, ranchers, and cooperative associations. 12 USCA §§ 2001-2279g. Borrower eligibility requirements are statutory. System banks and associations are owned by borrowers pursuant to a cooperative model. While the mission of the System remains substantially unaltered, its institutional structure has undergone great change as mandated by amendments to the Farm Credit Act in 1985 and 1987.

A. The System Prior To 1985

The Farm Credit System traces its beginnings to the Federal Farm Loan Act of 1916 wherein Congress authorized the creation of 12 Federal Land Banks (FLBs). Within its geographic district, each FLB made long-term farm ownership loans secured by mortgages. Local Federal Land Bank Associations (FLBAs) processed loan applications for their FLB.

The Agricultural Credit Act of 1923 authorized the creation of 12 Federal Intermediate Credit Banks (FICB) the original mission of which was to discount short and intermediate term farm loan notes held by commercial banks. In 1956 the FICBs began to discount Production Credit Association (PCA) notes. FICBs never did make loans to farmers.

The Farm Credit Act of 1933 authorized the creation of local Production Credit Associations. PCAs were front line lenders and made loans to farmers for short and intermediate term operational purposes. The 1933 Act also authorized the third set of FCS institutions, the Central Bank for Cooperatives and the 12 district Banks for Cooperatives (BCs). Local associations were not created. The 12 BCs served agricultural cooperatives within their districts, but looked to the Central Bank as their correspondent bank.

The Farm Credit Administration (FCA) was created in 1933 to serve as the System's regulator and "home office." Thus, prior to its recent reorganization, the Farm Credit System consisted of the FCA overseeing operations within each of the System's 12 geographic districts. Three banks existed in each district, a Federal Land Bank (direct lender), a Federal Intermediate Credit Bank (discounted paper of PCAs and other agricultural lenders), and a Bank for Cooperatives (direct lender with the Central Bank for Cooperatives as correspondent bank). In each district a farm credit board made policy and served as the board of directors for the three banks. Typically, there were several FLBAs (loan processing only) and PCAs (direct lenders) in each district. As the farm financial crisis of the 1980s deepened, some associations, particularly PCAs, merged intradistrict or were liquidated.

B. Funding the System

The original capital for FCS came when the U.S. Treasury purchased stock in System institutions. The federal government was repaid and its stock retired by 1968. The stock of FCS institutions is now held entirely by its farmer and cooperative borrowers, and by institutions within the System.

Borrowers play an important role in capitalizing System institutions. Farmers must purchase Class B stock in the FCS banks or associations making their loans. Associations, in turn, purchase stock in their district Farm Credit Bank. Stock purchases by a borrower must equal a set percentage of the loan amount. Each holder of Class B stock has one vote in the election of the local association's board of directors. When a loan is repaid, borrower stock outstanding on Jan. 1, 1988 must be retired at par. Retirement of more recently issued stock is not tied to time of loan repayment, but is at the discretion of the directors. 12 CFR § 615.5420(a)(1)(1994).Lenders hold liens on this stock and in cases of default can retire it and apply the proceeds to the loans.

Today, the Federal Farm Credit Banks Funding Corporation raises loan funds for System institutions by selling bonds in national money markets. These bonds are not guaranteed by the federal government. In 1987 Congress authorized formation of the Farm Credit System Insurance Corporation (FCSIC). 12 USCA §§ 2277a - 2277a-14. Funded by premiums paid by System institutions, FCSIC protects FCS institutions, stockholders, and investors.

In spite of its status as an independent agency in the executive branch of the federal government, FCA operations are not funded by appropriations. Instead, annual operating monies are generated by payments from FCS banks. System institutions service their own debt and generate operating funds and reserves from interest paid on loans. They do not accept deposits from borrowers or the general public. There are no savings or checking accounts.

C. Restructuring the System

In the mid-1980s several FCS institutions sustained serious operating losses. The System as a whole lost $2.7 billion in 1985 and $1.9 billion in 1986. Congress responded in the Farm Credit Act Amendments of 1985 (1985 Amendments) and the Agricultural Credit Act of 1987 (1987 Act) by requiring restructuring of the System to achieve greater efficiency of operation and tighter regulation. The 1987 Act authorized a federal "bailout," discussed at pp. 58-59 *infra*. By 1988 the System showed a positive net income of $704 million and by 1994 annual net profit had reached $1 billion.

After the 1985 Amendments, the Farm Credit Administration (FCA) ceased being involved in day to day System operations. The 13 member Federal Farm Credit Board was replaced by the Farm Credit Administration Board which has strong regulatory powers. The new Board has the power to modify district boundaries, charter FCS institutions, approve mergers, promulgate regulations, and conduct examinations of member banks. It can issue cease and desist orders to FCS institutions engaged in unacceptable practices. The Board has three full-time members appointed by the President with the advice and consent of the Senate. The Chair serves as CEO of FCA. See 12 CFR pts. 600-07 (1994).

The Farm Credit Corporation of America (FCCA), a new entity authorized in 1985, has taken over the "home office" functions previously handled by FCA. FCCA serves as the System's pricing and policy coordinator advising on such matters as interest rates, credit and financial standards, loan restructuring guidelines, and personnel administration. It is not a regulator.

The 1987 Act required certain FCS institutions to merge, permitted the voluntary consolidation of others, and authorized the indirect infusion into the System of up to $4 billion in bailout funds. Two new entities were authorized to institute the bailout -- the Financial Assistance Corporation (FAC) and the Financial Assistance Board (FAB). Healthy FCS institutions were required to make a one time purchase of FAC stock ($177 million) to capitalize FAC and to provide a fund to be used before resorting to the government guarantee in events of default. Colorado Springs PCA v. Farm Credit Admin. (D.C.Cir.1992)(forced purchase of FAC stock not a taking). FAC issued and sold to investors federally guaranteed 15 year FAC bonds. It then purchased special preferred stock of those System institutions certified by FAB as financially distressed. In this way the "federal bailout" worked to move funds to ailing FCS institutions. These institutions will pay back by repurchasing their special stock over time. Just $1.26 billion of FAC bond debt was guaranteed by Treasury, far below the $4 billion limit. Federal funds were made available to help pay interest on the bonds for the first few years. By 1994 FCS had repaid most of these advances. The work of the FAB is done and it has been disbanded.

Within each of the 12 districts, the Federal Intermediate Credit Bank and the Federal Land Bank were required to merge by early July, 1988. Each resulting institution is known as a Farm Credit Bank, e.g., the Farm Credit Bank of St. Louis. Each Farm Credit Bank can decide whether or not to transfer direct lending authority for real estate loans to the FLBAs in its district. When this happens, the FLBAs become Federal Land Credit Associations (FLCAs).

PCAs and FLBAs may now merge intradistrict whereupon the district Farm Credit Bank must transfer its long term real estate lending authority to the merged entity. The new entities are known as Agricultural Credit Associations (ACAs). Mergers have resulted in Associations competing directly in some areas. Buckeye PCA v. Farm Credit Admin. (4th Cir.1993)(overchartering sanctioned under 87 Act).

The 1987 Act also required that the FCA propose a plan that could lead to voluntary mergers of the 12 existing districts into no less than six districts. In early 1992, the St. Paul and St. Louis FCBs merged to form Agribank, FCB, St. Paul, serving seven states. Agribank, FCB has since taken over the Louisville FCB and its four states, making the St. Paul based bank the largest financial institution in the System. The Spokane and Omaha FCBs are to merge in 1994 and as AgAmerica, FCB will serve eight states.

Ten of the 12 district Banks for Cooperatives merged with the Central Bank for Cooperatives to form the National Bank for Cooperatives, CoBank for short. Two BCs elected to retain their separate identities. All three banks can loan nationwide.

The Federal Agricultural Mortgage Corporation ("Farmer Mac") also emerges from the 1987 Act. 12 USCA §§ 2279aa - 2279bb-6. It oversees a new agricultural mortgage secondary market designed to enhance the availability of mortgage money to farmers and ranchers. Lenders who purchase stock in Farmer Mac can originate loans which they then sell to a certified pooler. The pooler in turn sells securities backed by the pool to investors. These investors are protected by a federal guarantee. See p. 62 *infra* (rights of borrowers).

D. Borrowers' Rights

Prior to the 1985 Amendments, FCS loan servicing regulations spoke of forbearance in default cases. Forbearance contemplates an effort to rehabilitate a farmer borrower and to avoid liquidation. Essentially the same requirements were codified in 1985. Each district board must have a written policy describing circumstances when restructuring of loans will be considered, setting forth criteria and providing for internal review. Restructuring can include deferral or rescheduling of payments of principal or interest, renewal or extension of a loan, a reduction in interest rate, a write-off of principal, and other actions.

At least 45 days before starting foreclosure, a FCS institution must notify the borrower of his or her right to apply for restructuring and to meet with the lender to consider the application. The notice must be accompanied by a copy of the restructuring policy and information sufficient to enable the borrower to apply. The borrower must support the proposed restructuring plan with adequate financial information and realistic repayment projections. When a borrowers plan meets the statutory criteria, restructuring is mandatory. The most critical of these criteria requires that the cost of restructuring be equal to or less than the cost to the lender of immediate foreclosure. 12 USCA § 2202a(e)(1).

The cost of foreclosure equals the lenders total investment minus the liquidation value of the loan. 12 USCA § 2202a(a)(2). To determine total invest-ment, these amounts are added: loan balance plus accrued interest; current real estate taxes; disposition costs; legal fees; insurance; and repair costs. The liquidation value includes the borrowers class B stock and the net present value of the appraised value of property subject to foreclosure.

The cost of restructuring is found by figuring the net present value of what the lender would receive absent default, and subtracting therefrom the net present value of payments under the proposed restructuring plan. 12 USCA § 2202a(e)(2). Net present value is a calculation that assigns a lower current value to dollars to be received in later years than the value of dollars to be received currently. If two or more restructuring alternatives are viable, the System lender must opt for the plan that results in least cost to itself. If the borrower's plan does not commit all income in excess of reasonable living and operating expenses, the lender will propose a plan that applies such income to repayment.

If a restructuring request is denied the borrower has seven days in which to request review by the bank's credit review committee. The borrower may request and pay for an independent appraisal of collateral. The borrower is notified in writing of an adverse decision and reasons therefor. This ends the bank's review process. Courts routinely decline to review "banking" decisions. See, e.g., Federal Land Bank of Wichita v. Read (Kan.1985). But cf. Federal Land Bank of St. Paul v. Overboe (N.D.1987).

If a loan is to be pooled for sale in the secondary market, Farmer Mac, the borrower must be informed in writing that certain restructuring rights will be waived. By refusing to allow the loan to be pooled, the borrower retains all restructuring rights. 12 USCA § 2279aa-9.

The 1987 Act added a right of first refusal to allow certain FCS borrowers to lease or repurchase real property taken through foreclosure or deed in lieu of foreclosure. 12 USCA § 2219a. Wiener v. Eastern Arkansas Planting Co. (8th Cir.1992)(right of first refusal applies only to transactions occurring after the effective date of the 1987 Act). A more generous right of first refusal in a state statute is not preempted. A System institution must give 15 days notice of its intent to sell acquired real estate and if a timely offer to buy at appraised value is forthcoming from the former borrower, the offer must be accepted. If an offer to purchase at less than appraised value is tendered, but rejected, the institution may not sell to a third party at or below the rejected figure or on "different terms" without reoffering to the former borrower. Similar rules govern leasing of land by former borrowers. See Logan Ranch, Karg Partnership v. Farm Credit Bank of Omaha (Neb.1991)

Problems have emerged in administering the statutory right of first refusal. There is no mechanism to challenge appraisals and there is uncertainty as to what constitute "different terms." Certain federal district courts and the 4th Circuit have required that the former borrower be given the opportunity to purchase before a public auction sale can go forward. Payne v. Federal Land Bank of Columbia (4th Cir.1990). In a public sale, a qualified bid from the previous borrower must be accepted if it matches the high bid. 12 CFR § 614.4522(e)(1994).

Since 1987, the Farm Credit Act bars FCS institutions from foreclosing on a loan because of the failure of the borrower to post additional collateral -- if the borrower has made all accrued payments of principal, interest and penalties on the outstanding loan. System institutions must participate in certified state farm loan mediation programs. Waiver of mediation may not be required as a condition for consideration of loan restructuring.

FCS loans generally are exempt from Truth-in-Lending Act disclosures. 15 USCA § 1603(1). However, details of variable rate notes must be disclosed. At borrower request, all tiers of interest rates offered by the lender must be disclosed. The borrower is entitled to a review to determine if the proper interest rate schedule was used and to be told what is required to qualify for a more favorable rate.

E. Farm Credit System Litigation

1. Federal Jurisdiction

Beginning in the 1980s, we find cases addressing the issue of availability of federal jurisdiction, particularly to enforce borrowers' rights set forth in the Farm Credit Act as amended. Perhaps there was a perception that decisions favorable to FCS borrowers would be more readily forthcoming from lifetime-tenured federal judges. Whatever the motivation, the law is well settled that no express or implied federal cause of action exists under the Farm Credit Act and its amendments. This means no federal cause of action for money damages under lender liability type facts, no federal cause of action allowing federal courts to play super-banker and administratively review decisions of bank officers and review committees, and no federal cause of action allowing injunctive relief to stop foreclosures where statutory borrower rights have not been fully afforded. Cort v. Ash (U.S.Sup.Ct.1975); Redd v. Federal Land Bank of St. Louis (8th Cir.1988); Harper v. Federal Land Bank of Spokane (9th Cir.1989); Zajac v. Federal Land Bank of St. Paul (8th Cir.1990); Griffin v. Federal Land Bank of Wichita (10th Cir.1990); Saltzman v. Farm Credit Services of Mid-America, ACA (7th Cir.1991)

The 9th Circuit in Harper applied Cort v. Ash as it sought to determine the intent of Congress under the 1987 Act. Harper agreed that one of the purposes of the 1987 Act was to provide rights to an especial class, but concluded that the overriding objective of the 1987 law was to assist the System as a whole and to minimize any adverse impact on the federal budget. Administrative remedies provided by the 1987 Act -- review by the credit committee of the System bank -- were deemed to be adequate and intended by Congress to be exclusive. In addition, Harper pointed to the power of the FCA to issue cease and desist orders to System banks that violate the Act or its regulations. It was also noted that Congress legislated in light of a line of cases finding no implied federal cause of action under the 1985 Act. Thus, the 9th Circuit concluded that none of the Cort tests supported plaintiff's position and the 7th, 8th, and 10th Circuits are in agreement.

In Payne v. Federal Land Bank of Columbia (1990), the 4th Circuit, without mentioning Cort, Harper, Griffin or Zajac, remanded so that an injunction could issue stopping a pending FCS sale until the plaintiffs were given their statutory right of first refusal. Here, however, federal jurisdiction seems to be predicated on a challenge to the validity of FCA regulations. Payne aside, the only way FCS borrower litigation is likely to come under the jurisdiction of federal courts is as bankruptcy litigation or on the basis of diversity. The latter is rare.

2. State Court Jurisdiction

In a borrower action against a System lender, state court jurisdiction is a given. This is consistent with the fact that the state law of mortgages and secured transactions governs in FCS cases. The question is whether there are state law causes of action that will allow a borrower to seek one or more of forms of relief discussed above. Given the Harper line of cases it is settled that the Farm Credit Act does not create a private state cause of action.

In a significant case, the North Dakota Supreme Court held that state courts can sometimes use their broad equity powers to enjoin System lenders from proceeding with foreclosures on real and personal property. Federal Land Bank of St. Paul v. Overboe (N.D.1987). The bank had not done a serious forbearance analysis, nor had it determined whether its borrower, with reamortization, rescheduling, deferral or other relief, might have been able to successfully restructure his debt. And, the bank had not made a determination as to whether in restructuring it would have remained adequately secured and have sustained an equal or greater recovery over time than in immediate liquidation. Overboe holds that state trial courts may use their broad equity powers to enjoin foreclosure until the System institution gives good faith consideration to a restructuring request and, in the event of a negative decision, affords informal review by its credit review committee.

Overboe is important because the cause of action does not rest on any federal statute or doctrine. Equitable arguments supporting injunctive relief include failure to afford borrowers their statutory rights and failure to follow established bank policy as mandated by the Farm Credit Act. In addition, there is the equitable win-win argument. The farmer wins if restructuring takes place, but so does the System institution when it avoids the cost of foreclosure, the need to take land into inventory, and reduced recovery in immediate liquidation. Overboe has been followed in Lilliard v. Farm Credit Services of Mid-America, ACA (Ky.Ct.App.1991); Federal Land Bank of Spokane v. L.R.Ranch Co. (9th Cir. 1991)(Montana law); Western Farm Credit Bank v. Pratt (Utah Ct.App.1993); Burgmeier v. Farm Credit Bank of St. Paul (Minn.Ct.App.1993).

In PCA of Worthington v. Van Iperen (Minn. App.1986), the court reminds borrowers that they can sue Farm Credit System institutions for money damages in state courts. Causes of action known to state law include negligence in the administration of statutes and regulations, fraud, breach of contract, and breach of fiduciary duty. Any fiduciary duty running from a System institution to its borrower must be founded in state law. If the dealings between lender and borrower do not go beyond those of the debtor-creditor relationship, there is ample authority that a fiduciary relationship does not result. However, where the bank or association takes on the role of financial advisor or broker, a court might find a fiduciary relationship. Also, if the lender begins to advise the borrower on loan servicing alternatives, a new level of responsibility arises and arguably a fiduciary duty to the borrower. The borrower's case for a fiduciary duty could be strengthened if courts would break with past cases and attach significance to the fact that the FCS borrower is not just a debtor, but also a member of the lender, a cooperative institution. Should a fiduciary duty be found, it is breached in the loan restructuring stage if the lender is dishonest, fails to make disclosures, fails to deal in good faith, or fails to abide by federal statutes and regulations.

Success on a breach of fiduciary duty theory can lead not only to a reinstatement of the loan, but to the recovery of actual monetary damages. A number of cases hold that punitive damages may not be recovered against FCS institutions, given their status as federal instrumentalities. These rulings do not apply to directors, officers, or employees, when sued for unlawful acts outside the scope of their authority.

Generally, these state law theories do not provide a basis for a borrower to seek judicial review of the decisions of the bank's Credit Review Committee. Courts generally have been loath to assume the role of super-banker. Only the Overboe case suggests the possibility of very narrow review of procedurally correct substantive decisions, where restructuring nevertheless may have been denied in an arbitrary, capricious, unreasonable or unconscionable manner.

In the final analysis, most FCS borrowers experiencing financial distress will have their futures determined in internal restructuring decisions by System lenders. When the behavior of the lender is particularly egregious, some avenues of relief may be available in state courts. When all else fails, bankruptcy relief can be considered. See IV *infra*.

III. FARMERS HOME ADMINISTRATION - CONSOLIDATED FARM SERVICE AGENCY

A. Farmer Program Loans

The former Farmers Home Administration (FmHA), a USDA agency, made a variety of farmer program, rural housing and rural development loans. In the Oct. 1994 reorganization of USDA the farmer program loans were moved to the Consolidated Farm Service Agency (CFSA) and the rural housing loans to RHCDS. Here, farmer program loans are the focus. "Insured" loans are made from funds generated in national money markets by the sale of government-backed debt instruments. Today, loans are not made using funds from the U.S. Treasury.

Recent CFSA/FmHA authorization levels show reduced direct lending to farmers and a new focus on issuing guarantees to eligible non-government lenders who make farm ownership and operating loans to eligible borrowers. Total 1995 authorization for farmer program loans is $1,192 million ($1,095 operating; $97 farm ownership), whereas the authorization for guaranteed loans is $3,693 million ($2,822 operating, $871 farm ownership). The basic farmer loan program law, the Consolidated Farm and Rural Development Act (CONACT), as amended in 1992, requires CFSA to target each year 25 percent in amount of its farm operating and ownership loans or guarantees to beginning farmers and ranchers. 7 USCA § 1994(b)(2). Down payment loans for land purchases are part of the program. *Id.*

While not created until 1946, the idea for FmHA can be traced to efforts during the Great Depression to combat increasing farm tenancy and to foster the survival of family farms. As in the past, farmer program loans require borrowers to submit to ongoing supervision of their farming operations. This involves the annual preparation by each borrower of a Farm and Home Plan that sets forth a plan of farm operations, establishes good record keeping, and provides for the regular release by FmHA of normal income security (proceeds from routine sales of crops and livestock subject to CFSA/FmHA security interests). The U.S. typically ties up all of the borrowers farm assets, both real and personal, with mortgages and security interests.

Routine releases of normal income security (crops and livestock) provide cash flow to the borrower to pay operating and family living expenses. Some borrowers must now attend training classes.

To qualify for farmer program loans, borrowers must be family farmers who are unable to obtain "credit elsewhere" from conventional lenders. 7 USCA §§ 1961(a), 1983(1). Eligibility to be a farmer program borrower is determined by the local county committee, with adverse decisions generally subject to administrative appeal, now in USDA's National Appeals Division. See p. 83 *infra*. The county supervisor makes the decisions on loan applications from eligible borrowers. Any negative decisions are appealable. A borrower who gains sufficient economic strength to obtain guaranteed financing is required to "graduate" from the direct farmer loan program to the CFSA/FmHA guaranteed loan program and eventually to conventional financing. U.S. v. Anderson (9th Cir.1976). 7 USCA §§ 1949, 1983(3), 1983a(f).

In amendments to CONACT in 1978, Congress abandoned *fixed* low interest rates for farm program loans and tied rates to cost of money to the agency. The result was higher, though still favorable, interest rates for farmer borrowers. A distinct FmHA, now CFSA, program was created for limited resource (LR) applicants, those who meet eligibility requirements but due to low income cannot pay regular agency interest rates. They may receive insured (but not guaranteed) loans at lower rates.

Federal law governs farmer program loans. While state law on mortgages and secured transactions is adopted as the applicable federal law, CFSA/FmHA borrowers have many unique rights emanating from federal statutes and regulations as such. Caveat: state law hostile to the goals of FmHA will not be used as the applicable federal law.

B. Loan Servicing

Loan servicing -- the process of restructuring debt to make it manageable -- has long been part of FmHA, now CFSA, farmer programs. Under 7 USCA § 1981(d) borrowers in financial difficulty may ask to be considered for these loan servicing actions: consolidation of existing operating loans with easier payment terms; rescheduling of operating loans at the lower of the original or current regular interest rate; reamortization of real estate loans at the lower of the original or current interest rate; subordination of U.S. liens to liens of other creditors to help keep such creditors under control; liquidation of a portion of farm assets and restructuring remaining debt. Low income borrowers can ask to be switched to LR status and thus to lower interest rates.

In 1978 Congress added 7 USCA § 1981a which provides in part:

> In addition to any other authority that the Secretary may have . . ., the Secretary may permit, at the request of the borrower, the deferral of principal and interest on any outstanding loan . . . and may forego foreclosure of any such loan, for such period as the Secretary deems necessary upon a showing by the borrower that due to circumstances beyond the borrower's control, the borrower is temporarily unable

> to continue making payments of such
> principal and interest when due without un-
> duly impairing the standard of living of the
> borrower.

This deferral provision added a new tool for loan servicing, although it did not authorize forgiveness of principal or interest. Interest accrues during deferral and when that period ends both deferred principal and interest must be repaid in installments over time. The authority of FmHA, now CFSA, to write-down and forgive debt was made clear when CONACT was amended in 1987. For a number of years, USDA took the position that FmHA was not required to activate the § 1981a deferral program.

C. The Curry and Coleman Litigation

The refusal of the Secretary to implement the deferral program and to adequately administer other loan servicing options set the stage for Curry v. Block (S.D.Ga.1982), the seminal case on farmer-borrower rights. The court reviewed the history of FmHA's long standing policy of aiding "the family farmer who cannot obtain credit from a different source," the design "to lift the living standards of lower echelon farmers," and the management supervision which the agency is obliged to provide and that the borrower must accept. Curry held that the farmer loan programs are predominantly social welfare legislation and placed a liberal, rather than a narrow interpretation on § 1981a. Thus, while the Secretary may have discretion under § 1981a as to whether a particular borrower meets standards for deferral relief, Curry held that those standards must be articulated in regulations and that the deferral program be activated. Notice to borrowers about the deferral and other loan servicing programs and how to use them is required. FmHA was enjoined from accelerating loans in Georgia pending compliance with Curry. The 11th Circuit affirmed in 1984.

Meanwhile, a major case was emerging in federal district court in North Dakota. In Coleman v. Block (D.N.D.1983), the court considered the applicability of § 1981a to adverse actions by FmHA that preceded acceleration. While Curry had focused on foreclosure actions, Coleman added a focus on adverse FmHA (now CFSA) practices that precede foreclosure, most significantly "freeze outs" -- the abrupt cutting off of releases of normal income security as planned in the borrower's Farm and Home Plan. Termination of cash flow from normal marketing of crops and livestock usually made the borrower's "voluntary" liquidation inevitable.

Coleman ordered USDA to implement § 1981a. It also mandated that FmHA (now CFSA) give notice to borrowers of the availability of deferral relief and other loan servicing options as well as a chance to pursue them before starting any type of adverse action, including: cutting off planned releases of normal income security under the borrower's Farm and Home Plan; canceling a deferral; accelerating notes; foreclosing on real estate or seizing chattels; pressuring borrowers to liquidate voluntarily; or otherwise seeking to realize on collateral.

Coleman was transformed into a national class action and an injunction was made permanent on Feb. 17, 1984, aiding as many as 250,000 FmHA farmer borrowers. The decision in Allison v. Block

(8th Cir.1983) was critical to the work of the court in Coleman in that it made clear that farmers had the right to injunctive relief

Several years of trials, motions and proceedings followed in Coleman as borrowers sought to compel FmHA to develop adequate procedures, notices, and regulations as required by federal court injunctions. There were intermittent periods when officials, erroneously believing the agency to be in compliance, took adverse action against some borrowers. In most of these cases, borrowers who gave deeds in lieu or were divested by foreclosure did not get a second chance to salvage their farms. A May, 1978 order in Coleman provided that the failure by borrowers to object to FmHA practices during the liquidation process constituted laches.

The agency practice of cutting off planned releases of normal income security was hard to stamp out. The original Coleman order had to be amended to make clear that the giving of notice to the borrower of intent to take adverse action, of loan servicing opportunities and of appeal rights must precede a cutoff of income security -- even where there is no current Farm and Home Plan. In August 1987, FmHA conceded continued release of normal income security while an administrative appeal is pending over disagreements about the contents of a new Farm and Home Plan. 52 Fed. Reg. 32119 (1987). And, any borrower who decides to pursue loan servicing can do so without having income from the farm cut off. Current law requires releases to continue until acceleration. 7 USCA § 1985(f)(2); 7 CFR § 1962.17(a)(1994).

The 8th Circuit denied government and farmer appeals in Coleman -- holding all issues in the case to be moot in light of rights given to borrowers in CONACT, as amended by the Agricultural Credit Act of 1987. Coleman v. Lyng (8th Cir.1988). The effect was a Nov. 1988 lifting of the moratorium -- with the protection of the 1987 Act in place.

D. FmHA/CFSA Farmer Borrower Rights

1. Generally

What follows is a summary of certain of the existing rights of FmHA, now CFSA, borrowers under CONACT, as amended. The agency can no longer require additional collateral if the borrower is current on principal and interest payments. However, borrowers are ineligible for debt restructuring if they have unencumbered assets not essential to farm or family and will not apply same to program loans.

Any farmer borrower who is at least 180 days delinquent on interest or principal must be sent by certified mail a notice detailing FmHA, now CFSA, loan servicing programs -- including debt write-down, eligibility requirements, application procedures, deadlines, forms, and appeal procedures. Information about preservation loan servicing also must be included. Such notice must also be given upon request and prior to any adverse action. See p. 73 *supra*. After notice, the borrower has 60 days to request loan servicing. In the ensuing consideration USDA is required to place the highest priority on the preservation of the borrower's farming operations.

When projecting future production based on past yields, FmHA, now CFSA, must make adjustments favorable to the borrower of depressed past figures if the farm was in an officially designated disaster area. 7 USCA § 1981e(a). Absent adjustments, agency practices had resulted in denial of loan servicing due to inadequate cash flow projections. However, USDA can use its own price projection sheets.

The pattern of fits and starts in proceeding against delinquent borrowers seems destined to continue. The Clinton Administration moratorium on FmHA, now CFSA, adverse actions apparently is to be lifted. Borrowers can, however, take the initiative in seeking loan servicing.

2. Primary Loan Servicing

FmHA, now CFSA, offers two programs of loan servicing -- primary loan servicing and preservation loan servicing. Primary loan servicing offers: *loan consolidation,* two or more of the same type of loans can be combined (e.g. operating with operating, ownership with ownership); *loan rescheduling,* operating loans secured by personal property can be extended to 15 years; *loan reamortization,* real estate loans can be extended to 40 years from date of original loan; *interest rate reduction,* if the current rate is lower than the original rate, it may be used (even more favorable interest rates in appropriate cases by switch to limited resource (LR) status); *loan deferral,* if the previously described programs are inadequate -- and subject to various conditions -- principal and interest payments on some or all loans may be deferred for up to five years; the Softwood Timber Program is a distinct deferral program; *debt write down,* if previously described programs do not generate a feasible plan, FmHA, now CFSA, subject to certain conditions, will write down (reduce) both principal and interest to the recovery value of loan collateral. The Conservation Easement Program is a distinct debt write-down program. Various combinations of primary loan servicing techniques can be approved.

Primary loan servicing has five phases. 7 CFR § 1951.901(1994). **Phase I** is available to a farmer borrower who is current on payments, but who needs relief to avoid becoming delinquent. Reamortization and rescheduling may be used.

Phase II is reached when a borrower cannot remain in business and pay regular interest rates on loans extended by reamortization and rescheduling. Lowering of interest rates and deferrals may now be considered to aid the effort to avoid delinquency.

Phase III is reached when the borrower is unable to restructure using the devices available under Phase I and II. Prior to becoming 180 days delinquent, the borrower may apply for debt write-down and offer to grant conservation easements to the U.S. When a loan is 180 days delinquent, FmHA, now CFSA, must send by certified mail its Notice of Availability of Primary and Preservation Loan Servicing Programs for Delinquent Farmer Program Borrowers. All primary programs may now be used in tandem and the principal issue is whether the agency will realize its best recovery by keeping the farmer farming or by compelling liquidation. Phase III will include mediation under a state program, or where unavailable, a creditors meeting to seek cooperation from other creditors where adjustment of their claims is essential to the formulation of a feasible restructuring plan.

When a feasible plan cannot be formulated, Phase III contemplates that a borrower who has acted in good faith as to the loan, be offered the opportunity to buy out the U.S. at the *net recovery value*. See p. 80 *infra*. The borrower has 90 days to execute the buyout. Under CONACT, a borrower who elects to buy out the U.S. must sign a 10 year recapture agreement -- a Net Recovery Buyout Recapture Agreement. If the former borrower sells the real estate within the 10 year period, any gain must be paid over to the U.S. The exact amount will be determined by subtracting from the fair market value at time of sale, the net recovery value. 7 CFR § 1951.913(1994). Certain family sales are excepted from recapture.

If Phase III fails, **Phase IV**, the liquidation phase, is triggered. Before acceleration the borrower is automatically considered for Preservation Loan Servicing Programs. Before and after acceleration, the borrower can apply for debt settlement. **Phase V** is the post-liquidation phase. See Preservation Loan Servicing at pp. 81-83 *infra*.

A farmer borrower who applies for primary loan servicing must meet eligibility requirements. 7 CFR § 1951.909(1994). First, the County Supervisor must find that the financial distress or delinquency resulted from circumstances beyond the borrower's control. Examples are loss of essential off-farm income due to unemployment or underemployment; illness, death or injury of farm operator; production losses due to natural disasters or uncontrollable disease or insect damage; or depressed commodity prices and high local operating expenses.

Second, it must be determined that the farmer borrower has acted in good faith in dealing with the U.S. Fraud, waste, or collateral conversion, if confirmed by a case specific opinion from the office of USDA General Counsel, are acts of bad faith.

Third, the County Supervisor must determine that a feasible plan of operation can be devised. 7 CFR § 1951.906(1994). Such a plan must generate cash flow sufficient to meet family living and farm operating expenses, and to service all debts including restructured loans made by the U.S. Since amended in 1990, CONACT says that cash flow should be 105% of the amount needed. 7 USCA § 2001(c)(3). However, debt restructuring is not necessarily to be denied if a farmer cannot achieve 105%, but 100% is an absolute minimum. However, the plan must project that the present value of payments under the plan be equal to or more than net recovery value to the government from immediate liquidation.

In earlier litigation it was established that FmHA, now CFSA, has discretion to administratively adopt certain eligibility criteria as to deferrals: showing of an attempt at voluntary debt settlement with other creditors; proof of payment of real estate taxes and property insurance premiums before experiencing the hardship; and demonstration of use of recommended and recognized successful farm production and financial management practices.

FmHA, now CFSA, uses a computer program known as DALR$ (Debt & Loan Restricting System) to test various combinations of primary loan servicing options. The goal is to ascertain the minimum level of debt servicing required to produce the required cash flow. In other words, DALR$ tests loan servicing options to ascertain the combination that will give the U.S. its best net recovery. Within 90 days of receipt of an application for Primary Loan Servicing, the County Supervisor must calculate both the net recovery value to the U.S. from immediate liquidation and the present value to the U.S. of payments after primary loan servicing.

Net recovery value from immediate liquidation is computed by subtracting from the current appraised value of collateral -- and certain noncollateralized nonessential assets -- the following: value of priority liens; property taxes; depreciation, management charges, and lost interest during the projected inventory period; expenses of sale including repairs; legal and administrative fees; and miscellaneous expenses. 7 CFR § 1951.909(f)(1994). Projected increases or decreases in the value of collateral while in inventory must be added or subtracted. Expected rents during inventory from a signed lease also must be added.

Restructuring will be approved only where the present value of serviced loans is equal to or more than net recovery value. 7 USCA § 2001(b)(4). The present value of serviced loans is the value of projected payments to the U.S. over the life of such loans, discounted at a rate no more than the discount rate on 90-day Treasury bills at the time of loan servicing actions. Present value is a calculation that assigns a lower current value to dollars received in later years than the value of dollars to be received at present. If the test is met, and the borrower meets all eligibility requirements, FmHA, now CFSA, must offer to restructure and the borrower has 45 days after written notice to accept or reject the plan.

Debt write-down is an attractive loan servicing feature for those who qualify and can be essential to creating a feasible restructuring plan in some cases. 7 CFR § 1951.909(e)(4)(1994). Principal and accumulated interest, subject to certain conditions, may be forgiven to the extent that it exceeds *net recovery value*. See p. 80 *supra*. The U.S. may require added collateral as a condition of debt write-down. There is a lifetime limit per borrower of $300,000. 7 USCA § 2001(p). But, write-downs in bankruptcy, debt settlement and for conservation easements do not count toward this limit. Only one write-down or net recovery buyout is permitted per borrower for loans made after Jan. 6, 1988. 7 USCA § 2001(n).

When debt write-down is approved, the borrower must sign a *shared appreciation agreement* if the loan is secured by real estate. 7 CFR § 1951.909(e)(4)(ix)(1994). If within four years after restructuring the loan is paid off, the farm sold, or the borrower quits farming, 75% of any increase in appraised value must be paid to the U.S. If any of these events occur during years five through nine, 50% of such increase must be paid to the U.S. At the end of year 10, the 50% payment must be made even if the farm has not been sold and the borrower remains an active operator. If the farmer cannot afford a lump sum payment at the end of 10 years, the recapture will be treated as a loan and amortized. There is no recapture if the property has not increased in value during the 10 year period.

3. Preservation Loan Servicing

Preservation loan servicing may afford relief when the owner anticipates losing or has lost the farm to the U.S. by foreclosure, voluntary conveyance or after abandonment in bankruptcy. 7 CFR § 1951. 911 (1994). Preservation programs are: homestead protection -- lease-back from the U.S. of farm home, outbuildings and a limited acreage for up to five years with option to purchase; and, farm lease-back/buy-back -- lease of entire farm with option to purchase.

FmHA, now CFSA, borrowers are either automatically considered for homestead protection or may make application to rent their farm residence, adjacent outbuildings and no more than 10 acres, all for family maintenance. The applicant must have received gross income from the farm "reasonably commensurate" with the size and location of the unit "considering local conditions", and must have earned 60% of gross annual income from farming for two of the preceding six years. The latter requirement will disqualify borrowers who have been forced to rely heavily on off-farm income. Subject to an absence of up to 12 months for reasons beyond his or her control, the borrower must have occupied the homestead continuously during the previous six years. The period of occupancy can be for up to five years at a reasonable rent. CONACT provides that the agency "shall" grant homestead protection if the borrower meets the criteria. Prior to expiration of the rental period, the borrower has a statutory first right to buy the homestead from the U.S. at its current market value.

The previous owner may apply to lease back the entire farm from CFSA inventory for one to five years. The lease may be cash rent or crop share. Eligibility requirements vary from those for homestead protection. All such leases contain an option to purchase exercisable during the term of the lease at the farm's market value at the time of exercise. Federal law does not preempt more generous state rights of first refusal. 7 USCA § 1985(e)(1)(E).

When a borrower liquidates, assets often will not generate enough to pay to the U.S. both principal and interest. Debt settlement is then a possibility. If the borrower has not obtained a discharge in bankruptcy, CFSA has authority to compromise, adjust, and charge off and cancel the deficiency.

E. Administrative Appeal & Review

•Denial of loan servicing requests and other adverse agency decisions are appealable in the new USDA National Appeals Division. Unsuccessful appeals are subject to administrative review. Most farmer program administrative decisions that directly and adversely affect program applicants and borrowers can be appealed. But see 7 CFR § 1900.55(a) (1994)(17 nonappealable decisions listed).

In 1987 Congress sought to remove the appearance of inherent bias in then existing FmHA hearing system -- present because of the use of agency operating personnel as hearing officers. It authorized a National Appeals Staff with a cadre of hearing officers who, while FmHA employees, had no duties other than hearing appeals. Hearing officers had the authority to reverse or modify decisions of FmHA officials who made "front line" decision. Review officers had authority to reverse or modify decisions of hearing officers. It was unclear whether the Administrator could override a National Appeals System result deemed adverse to FmHA.

Moving appeal and review to the National Appeals Decision should remove lingering concerns about pressure in the process from the Administrator.

Judicial review can follow upon exhaustion of administrative remedies, but triggers application of the narrow arbitrary and capricious standard. Some matters are committed to agency discretion and are not subject to judicial review. Woodsmall v. Lyng, (8th Cir.1987) (no standard in statute or regulation against which court can review FmHA finding of lack of creditworthiness).

F. Guaranteed Loans

FmHA, now CFSA, is authorized to guarantee certain loans made to farmers by commercial lenders. 7 USCA § 1929(h); 7 CFR pt. 1980 (1994). The guarantee is for up to 90% of the lender's exposure. Participation in the guarantee program on the part of lenders is voluntary. Loans that will be considered for guarantees are those for operating expenses, the purchase of land, equipment or livestock, and for soil and water conservation practices. Farmer borrower eligibility requirements are essentially the same as for loans made directly by the U.S.

The farmer will approach a commercial lender and apply for credit. Typically the farmer and the lender apply together for the guarantee. If it is forthcoming, CFSA and the lender will enter into an agreement where the terms of the guarantee are set out and the lender agrees, if circumstances require, to provide certain loan servicing options, including negotiating in good faith with the borrower if payment problems arise, allowing the borrower to cure defaults, and participating in mediation if a program is available. To obtain a CFSA guaranteed loan, the farmer borrower must demonstrate a positive cash flow. Projected income from the farm and off-farm employment must be adequate to pay operating and living expenses, meet payments on other obligations, pay the new loan, and generate a 10% reserve for contingencies.

If repayment problems arise, the lender, with CFSA approval, may agree to consolidate, re-schedule, reamortize, or defer guaranteed loans. For CFSA approval to be forthcoming, the farmer borrower must meet loan servicing eligibility re-quirements which track those outlined for farmer program loans made directly by the U.S.

When rescheduling, reamortization and sale of non-essential assets is not enough, a special interest rate buy-down program is authorized, but unfunded in recent FYs. The theory is that the interest rate on the guaranteed loan could be cut as much as 4% for as many as three years. The lender would absorb one-half of the cut and the FmHA, now CFSA, would pay to the lender the other one-half. The cut would have to result in a positive cash flow.

Congress, in 1987, added a new aspect to the guaranteed loan program -- debt write-down. When other loan servicing does not result in the required cash flow, and when the loan is delinquent, the borrower may request debt write-down sufficient to achieve positive cash flow. If a write-down would produce as much return for the lender as would immediate liquidation, CFSA must give its approval, assuming borrower has met eligibility rules. As part of its guarantee obligation, CFSA pays the lender

90% of the write-down amount. The write-down can be used in combination with other servicing devices. Borrowers who get a write-down must sign a *shared appreciation agreement* benefitting the U.S. and the bank prorata. Compare p. 81 *supra.*

A lender is obligated to notify the CFSA when a borrower under a guaranteed loan is 30 days late, is otherwise in default, or has failed to provide timely financial statements. The lender must then meet with the borrower and the county supervisor to explore possible remedial action. At the meeting the lender is obligated to negotiate in good faith to apply loan servicing devices to salvage the situation. Any proposed plan must be approved by CFSA. A negative decision by CFSA must be followed within 10 days by written notice of reasons to the borrower and lender. An administrative appeal is then possible, but only if the farmer and lender appeal together.

If a lender decides to liquidate a guaranteed loan, it must seek CFSA approval of its liquidation plan if the guarantee is to be preserved. The decision to liquidate is an adverse decision made by the private lender and not subject to administrative appeal.

IV. CHAPTER 12 BANKRUPTCY

A. Introduction

When most people think of bankruptcy they contemplate liquidation, "financial death," and a new start. This is straight bankruptcy. However, under the so-called Chapter proceeding of the Bankruptcy Code the objective is not to liquidate assets, but to financially rehabilitate the business, farm or consumer debtor. However, most farmers who are capable of rehabilitation will accomplish this in the restructuring and debt service programs of the Farm Credit System and CFSA. If the farm can not be saved under these programs outside of bankruptcy, it is not likely that it will be saved in a Chapter proceeding. But, Chapter 12 has a particular role to play when creditors of a family farmer, other than the U.S. and FCS, are being obstructionist and will not cooperate in an out-of-court workout. Ch. 12 proceedings, while complex and costly, can sometimes bring such creditors to bay and compel them to participate in a plan to save the farm. Of course, not all Ch. 12 proceedings are successful -- even if a rehabilitation plan has been confirmed by the Court.

B. Overview and Selected Issues

Bankruptcy proceedings, while statutory, are equitable in nature and involve notions of fresh start and rehabilitation. When a financially distressed farmer elects to liquidate assets and discharge debts, a petition under Ch. 7 of the Bankruptcy Code (Code) will be filed. If successful, the debtor will be discharged from personal liability on all prepetition debts. A farmer cannot be forced into Ch. 7 by an involuntary petition filed by creditors. When a debtor wants to rehabilitate and continue to farm, a Chapter 11, 12, or 13 petition will be filed. Creditors cannot instigate rehabilitation proceedings.

Chapter 11, designed for non-farm businesses, is the only rehabilitation option for farms with debt loads too large to restructure in Chapter 12 -- over $1.5 million. Chapter 13, amended in 1994, can be used by individual farmers if secured and unsecured debts do not exceed $750,000 and $250,000 respectively. Some farmers in financial trouble could qualify. However, the Family Farmer Bankruptcy Act of 1986, eff. Nov. 26, 1986, created Chapter 12 to provide a suitable vehicle for rehabilitation of these and certain other farmers. It was to have expired on Oct. 1, 1993, but was extended for five years.

If the farmer is an individual, or an individual and spouse, Ch. 12 may be available if the definition of "family farmer" at 11 USCA § 101(18) (Code) is met. At filing the debtor must be engaged in farming operations as an owner or operator. Aggregate debts must not exceed $1.5 million. Eighty percent of non-contingent, liquidated debts must have arisen from petitioner's farm operation. The 80% does not include debt on the farm residence unless it arose out of the farm operation. Also, the individual or married couple must have received more than 50% of gross income from such farming operation for the tax year immediately preceding the year of the Ch. 12 filing. Also, the "family farmer" must demonstrate a regular annual income to qualify for Ch. 12. Code § 109(f). That annual income must be sufficiently stable to enable the farmer to make required payments under the plan of rehabilitation. Special tests govern the availability of Ch. 12 to partnerships and corporations. Code § 101(18)(B).

A Ch. 12 bankruptcy is commenced by the filing of a petition and various schedules. The filing constitutes an "order for relief." The automatic stay of Code § 362 is engaged and creditors must cease all collection efforts. U.S. Through FmHA v. Nelson (8th Cir.1992)(impact of automatic stay on FmHA loan servicing efforts). The debtor has 90 days in which to file a plan of rehabilitation. Courts have narrow authority to extend the 90 day period.

Failure to file a timely plan will result in the case being dismissed and the farmer will be precluded from refiling any type of bankruptcy petition for 180 days. Code § 109(g). Contrast Ch. 11 where creditors may then file a liquidation plan, which if approved will result in the farm being liquidated even if the farmer objects. In re Button Hook Cattle Co., Inc. (8th Cir.1984); In re Jasik (5th Cir.1984).

When a Ch. 12 plan of rehabilitation is timely filed, the court must hold a confirmation hearing within 45 days. Ch. 12 plans contain many of the features of common law workout agreements -- extensions, compositions, composition-extensions, debt write-down, etc. Chapter proceedings have the advantage of compelling participation -- subject to statutory rules -- by recalcitrant creditors who would not agree to a negotiated workout. Unlike Ch. 11, creditors in a Ch. 12 case do not vote on the plan.

Confirmation occurs when the court makes independent findings that the plan complies with the Bankruptcy Code, that the filing fee has been paid, that the plan has been proposed in good faith, and that the plan is in the best interests of creditors. Also, the court must be persuaded that the debtor will be able to make all payments under the plan and to comply with the plan, the feasibility requirement. Unrealistic future cash flow projections based on "visionary" prices and production estimates have led to denial of confirmation in some Ch. 12 cases.

Immediately after the filing of a Ch. 12 petition secured creditors often ask the court to lift the automatic stay so that they can pursue foreclosure or other remedy without delay. As an alternative to a lifting of the stay, such creditors may demand "adequate protection." Where the collateral is land, an *under*secured creditor who is not allowed to foreclose can insist upon adequate protection, which likely would be payment of reasonable rent for the ensuing period up to plan confirmation. Code §1205(b)(3). For Ch.12, adequate protection is defined at Code § 1205, not at § 36l. Thus, the issue of adequate protection as an "indubitable equivalent" which haunted Ch. 11 has not impacted Ch. 12. Happily, the matter was in large part resolved in United Savings Association of Texas v. Timber of Inwood Forest Associates, Ltd. (U.S.Sup.Ct.1988), by disallowing lost opportunity costs (e.g., interest in addition to rent as an element of adequate protection in Ch. 11). Caveat: a fully secured creditor will not persuade the court to lift the automatic stay or to order adequate protection. Such a creditor, though stayed, will not suffer deterioration of position while the plan is being formulated and confirmed.

It remains unclear in Chapter 12 whether rental to an *under*secured creditor with a mortgage on farmland must actually be paid prior to plan confirmation, absent evidence of declining value. It would be consistent with the objective of Ch. 12 to time such payments to the farm's cash flow.

Many farmers have *under*secured creditors, those whose collateral will not cover their outstanding claims. In a Ch. 12 plan secured claims can be scaled down to the value of the collateral and the remaining indebtedness treated as unsecured. Valuation disputes have prompted litigation with almost all reported cases using actual fair market value of collateral as the test. One case applied the agricultural value to a farm that had a higher value for development. Secured claims will not be scaled down to liquidation value, where that value is less than fair market value.

In Ch. 12, unsecured creditors do not vote on the farmer-debtor's plan and need only be paid the present value of what they would have received had there been an immediate liquidation of the farm in Ch. 7. Code § 1225(a)(4). If a farmer has few unencumbered, non-exempt assets, this mandatory amount will be minimal. If unsecured creditors and *under*secured creditors (as to the unsecured portion of the claim) are dissatisfied, there is little that they can do. Once the Ch. 12 plan is confirmed, the creditors are bound. However, if an unsecured creditor objects to the plan, the farmer must pay into the plan *all* disposable income. Rowley v. Yarnell (8th Cir.1994)(as opposed to *projected*). Disposable income is income not reasonably necessary for the maintenance or support of the debtor and his dependents, and not reasonably necessary for the preservation and operation of the debtor's business. Failure to turn over disposable income, if required, allows the trustee or a creditor to move for dismissal. Code § 1208(c). This also can be the basis for objection to a Ch. 12 discharge. In re Gage (Bankr. D.S.D.1993)(burden of persuasion on trustee).

Questions have arisen as to the interplay of the Bankruptcy Code and provisions of the Farm Credit Act and CONACT. Generally, the restructuring provisions -- whether for the FCS or CFSA -- are held not to override provisions of the Code. Thus, creditors in bankruptcy will be able to take advantage of Code provisions, even if there are provisions more favorable to the debtor in the other Acts. CFSA regulations (formerly FmHA) for borrowers in bankruptcy are at 7 CFR § 1962.47 (1994). There is a split of authority as to whether a Ch. 12 plan can require forced redemption of debtor's stock in a FCS institution. In re Davenport (9th Cir.BAP 1993), the only Circuit case, answers yes, noting that as emergency legislation, Ch. 12 prevails if there is a conflict with the Farm Credit Act.

In Ch. 12, unsecured creditor's claims can be modified both in the amount to be paid and by extending the time for payment. Secured creditors are entitled to the present value of their allowed secured claims which will equal the value of the collateral or the debt, whichever is less. This amount cannot be modified. Code §§ 1222(b)(2), 1225(a) (5)(B), 506(a). But, the payment period can be modified. And, the plan can provide that existing defaults be paid over time on a schedule distinct from regular plan payments to the creditor.

There are two types of discharges in Ch. 12. A farmer who makes all plan payments will be entitled to a discharge under Code § 1228(a). Several types of debts are excepted from this discharge, including long-term debts, the final payments on which will be made after completion of the plan. A debtor may be eligible for a hardship discharge when plan payments, even if modified, cannot be completed due to circumstances beyond debtor's control. Hardship discharges are granted only if creditors get at least what they would have gotten in a Ch. 7 liquidation.

C. Operational Financing

It is hard to envision a Ch. 12 debtor who will not need to find financing to continue the farming operation during the term of the plan. There are two main methods of getting operating money: using cash collateral from the sale of farm products; and, borrowing new money from a third party lender.

It is not uncommon for Ch. 12 petitions to be filed in the spring after the farmer has been unable to secure needed financing. After filing, these Ch. 12 farmers will want to use proceeds from the sale of stored farm products to finance a new crop. Lenders with security interests in stored crops and their proceeds can be expected to resist. Section 363 of the Code allows the court to approve the sale of non-cash collateral in the ordinary course of business, but such sale will not obviate the security interest in proceeds. This cash collateral, cannot be used by the farmer without court approval including a finding of fact that there is adequate protection of the secured creditor's interest. While the Code does not specifically address this issue, some courts have allowed Ch. 12 farmers to use the cash collateral if the secured creditors are given a lien on the next crop and crop insurance is obtained. See, e.g., In re Sheehan (Bankr.D.S.D.1984).

The court in In Re Martin (8th Cir.1985) lists factors to be considered before requiring a creditor with a security interest in crop cash proceeds to accept a "roll over" lien on the next crop. First, the value of the secured party's interest in existing stored crops, the cash proceeds of which debtor wants to use to put in the next crop, must be determined. Second, several factors are to be considered in determining whether a replacement lien on the next crop will afford "adequate protection." Because federal crop insurance will not cover crop loss caused by failure of the farmer to use good husbandry, productivity of the land, professional reputation and health of the farmer, past crop yields, machinery condition, probability of repossession of machinery, potential of liens on new crop by other creditors, and any anticipated fluctuation in market price are to be taken into consideration in determining whether the value of the secured party's existing lien in stored crops and cash proceeds is sufficiently protected. The objective is to provide the secured party as nearly as possible with bargained for rights -- adequate protection.

Special problems are presented when a farmer debtor seeks to use proceeds to take up a new type of farming or to plant crops on rented land. In In re Frank (Bankr.S.D.Ohio 1983) a debtor asked to use proceeds from soybean and cattle sales to buy more cattle. The court refused, seeing no proof that the cattle operation would produce reasonable profits without jeopardizing the replacement lien. When the replacement lien was to be on future crops to be grown on rented land, the court in In Re Berens (Bankr.D.Minn.1984) refused to allow the use of proceeds from the crop just harvested. The court noted a potential conflict between the lessor's interest in the future crop and the replacement lien.

In the alternative, the Ch. 12 debtor might seek a new operating loan from a third party lender, or to obtain credit from an input merchant. These parties may be skeptical about loaning money or extending credit to a farmer in Ch. 12. However, there are angles to pursue. 1) The court can authorize a priority over all administrative expenses, but probably only to save existing collateral. Code § 364(c)

(1). 2) The court can authorize a lien on unencumbered assets. Code § 364(c)(2). Here it is important to remember that Code § 522(b) prevents an existing perfected security interest in crops and future crops from attaching to a crop planted after the filing of a bankruptcy petition, or to the proceeds thereof. In re Wallman (Bankr.D.S.D.1987). 3) A new junior lien on already encumbered assets can be authorized by the court where equity exists in such assets. Code § 364(c)(3). 4) The court can authorize new credit that is secured by a senior or equal lien on property already encumbered. This can be done only where adequate protection can be offered to the holder of the existing priority lien.

D. Chapter 12 Trustee

Chapter 12 does have a feature that is not present in Ch. 11 -- the assessment of a statutory trustee's fee. Trustees are rarely appointed in Ch. 11 cases, but are regularly appointed in Ch. 12 cases. While the trustee does not operate the farm in the typical Ch. 12, most payments under the plan are channeled through the trustee's office. The trustee's fee is assessed against handled funds and is not to exceed 10% of the first $450,000 in payments under the plan, and 3% of payments over that amount. The law imposing this cost has been criticized as inimical to the goals of Ch. 12. Payments on unmodified claims of secured creditors made during the duration of a Ch. 12 plan do not have to be routed through the trustee. But, as to unsecured claims and modified secured claims, direct payments bypassing the trustee are not permitted.   In re Fulkrod (9th Cir.1992). *Contra* In re Overholt (Bankr.S.D.Ohio 1990).

CHAPTER THREE

LEASES OF AGRICULTURAL LAND
I. INTRODUCTION

Leased land plays an important role in many agricultural operations. Each year some 40% of the nation's farmers and ranchers rent more than 400 million acres or about 40% of available crop, pasture and range land. The focus of this chapter is on leases of such land. We do not delve into issues peculiar to leases of dairy facilities, orchards, fish farm ponds, animal confinement facilities, or other specialized properties.

The farm lease is a contract as well as a conveyance of an interest in real property. The tenant, as grantee of a leasehold estate, has the right of exclusive possession and control of the land for the term of the lease, as well as the usual responsibilities of one in possession. Economic terms and enumerated rights and duties are the contract side of a lease. Local customs often give rise to expectations as to provisions that "should" be in a farm lease.

II. TYPES OF LEASES

The primary objective of a farm lease is to provide for a profitable enterprise with economic returns satisfactory to both landlord and tenant. Traditionally, two types of farm leases have dominated, *cash rent* and *crop-share rent*. Today, variations are in use as parties negotiate provisions designed to achieve sophisticated objectives.

The *cash rent lease* is characterized by an economic term that obligates the tenant to pay either a fixed dollar per acre or a set rent for the entire farm. This provides the landlord with a predictable return, freedom from involvement in the operation, and no risk as to crop yield or price. The cash rent tenant bears all of the economic risks because the full rent must be paid despite crop failure, falling prices, or increased production costs. The landlord does run two major risks, the first being nonpayment of rent. The second is that the tenant may take a short term view and use farming methods that reap gains at the expense of the land.

Cash rent tenants sometimes seek to negotiate flexible economic terms. Examples include: rent to be adjusted to reflect production conditions and/or changing market prices; rent to be calculated by multiplying a set number of bushels by a price fixed at a later date (bushel lease); and, rent as a fixed quantity of a specified crop to be delivered to the landlord by a set date (guaranteed bushel lease).

Under the standard *crop-share lease,* the landlord agrees to pay part of the cost of inputs such as seed, fertilizer, and chemicals. In some cases the landlord agrees to supply specific equipment. In return for the leasehold estate and such inputs and equipment, the landlord receives from the tenant a share of the crop. This share is the rent and ranges from one-fourth to one-half of the crop depending on local custom and the extent of the landlord's contributions. Such a lease gives the landlord an enhanced return if production and prices increase. The landlord, however, shares with the tenant the risk of crop failure and declining market prices.

In some crop-share leases the landlord retains significant control over field and other operational decisions. Such participation can have legal ramifications for the landlord as explained in VII and VIII *infra*. From the tenant's perspective, a crop-share lease spreads yield and price risks and requires less capital. However, if a bumper crop is produced or prices escalate, profits are shared. A crop-share lease may seem to have the characteristics of a partnership -- each party makes a contribution and each has an undivided interest in the output of the enterprise. The landlord in particular will not want to form a legal partnership given liability, tax, and estate planning consequences.

III. CUSTOM FARMERS & CROPPERS

There are agreements other than leases pursuant to which an owner allows another person to come upon his or her premises to conduct farming operations. The use of employees is an obvious example. Custom farming is sometimes carried out by a farm management company or by an individual who is retained as an independent contractor and paid x dollars per acre to prepare, plant, cultivate and harvest. Specialized custom services are provided by combine crews that follow the harvest each year from Texas to Canada. Farmers who engage such outfits deal with them as independent contractors, as is the case when farmers hire aerial spray operators.

Somewhere between the status of lessee and employee there exists the amorphous classification of cropper. When the landowner supplies the land and all of the inputs, controls the operation of the farm, and pays a portion of the crop to the person who actually raises and harvests the crop, that person is likely to be a cropper and not a tenant. Unlike a tenant who has an estate in land and control over the farming operation, a cropper has but a license to be on the land, no legal interest in the crops, and a mere contract right to be compensated in kind for his or her labor. While a tenant is entitled to proper notice of lease termination, a cropper has no interest in real property to terminate.

To determine the true status of the parties courts seek to ascertain the intention of the parties as evidenced, *inter alia,* by the terms of the written or oral contract, circumstances surrounding such agreement, actions of the parties, and type of farming operation. Usually, no single factor controls, not even the parties' characterization of the arrangement. However, granting exclusive possession of a farm has been held to conclusively establish a landlord-tenant relationship. Larson v. Archer-Daniels-Midland Co.(Minn.1948); Willcut v. Stout (Mo.Ct. App.1984). A cropper was found to be an employee, not an independent contractor, under the California Worker's Compensation Act. S.G. Borello & Sons v. Department of Indust. Relations (Cal. 1989)("share farmer" paid one-half of proceeds from sale of farm owner's cucumbers crop).

IV. THE LEASE DOCUMENT

A. Importance of Written Leases

Written farm leases tend to be the exception rather than the rule. Parties apparently do not want it to appear as though they do not trust each other. Yet, written leases are justified by sound business and legal considerations. If one party to the lease should die, a written lease can protect heirs as well as the surviving party. A written lease can allow for adjustments in its economic terms in unanticipated conditions. The written document also reduces the role of the "selective recall syndrome" if there is a falling out. After reading V. *infra,* the merits of well drafted lease termination clauses will be obvious. Finally, the sheer magnitude of many of the leases would seem to dictate a written agreement -- land worth hundreds of thousands of dollars and significant rental payments.

B. Enforceability of Leases

All states have statutes requiring a signed writing before most transactions involving interests in real property will be enforceable. While these Statutes of Fraud vary from state to state, oral farm leases for a period of one year are generally enforceable. Yet, in some states a one year oral farm lease to commence in the future is unenforceable, e.g. an oral promise made on June 1 to rent land for one year beginning on September 1 next. The other and more realistic rule recognizes that most farm leases are entered into before the lease term begins. As demonstrated in Bell v. Vaughn (Ariz.1935), this rule requires that the tenant take possession within one year of the making of the oral lease.

Part performance can work as an exception to the Statute of Frauds in most states. In Teague v. Roper (Tex.Ct.App.1975), tenant was already farming four tracts of Texas land when a five year oral lease covering same was allegedly made. The tenant leveled one tract for irrigation and installed underground pipe, greatly increasing productivity. The landlord sought to evict. The party asserting the existence of an oral lease must first prove that an agreement was in fact made. Only then does the question of part performance become relevant. In Texas, an oral lease is removed from the strictures of the Statute of Frauds when three things occur: payment of consideration whether it be in money, goods or services; possession by the lessee; and, the making by the lessee of valuable improvement to the land. Some states omit the need to show an improvement. When a tenant already in possession enters into an oral lease and then continues in possession with no change in amount of rent, a question of fact can arise as to whether possession and rent payments relate to the earlier agreement, or are unequivocally referable to the subsequent oral lease. In Teague, unequivocal reference to the new oral lease was found and as a result the tenant prevailed.

The court in Teague also concluded that while the improvements were made only on one tract, the lease was enforceable as to all four since they were one agricultural unit. Planting a crop can be a valuable improvement for purposes of part performance. In Stuber v. Sowder (Kan.1950), the court held that while sowing a crop such as wheat would not constitute a valuable improvement, planting alfalfa, a perennial crop, would. The distinction was drawn because alfalfa adds nitrogen to the soil.

Another Statute of Frauds issue is raised when the tenant takes possession of land for an *indefinite* time under an oral lease, but with annual rent payments. In Rhodes v. Sigler (Ill.Ct.App.1975) the court concluded that an enforceable year to year tenancy had been created and that it continued until terminated by proper notice.

C. Farm Lease Provisions

1. In General

Most states do not have legislation governing the rights and duties of farm tenants and landlords, although statutes exist in many states setting out rights and duties under residential leases. Where farm lease statutes do exist, they tend to be limited to matters such as termination of tenancies, assignment of leases, landlord's lien for rent, and duty to control noxious weeds. Where common law rules remain in effect they concern, *inter alia,* removable fixtures, permanent improvements, rights of entry for a landlord or new tenant, lease termination, rights of tenant to harvest crops after lease expiration, and liability for rent in cases of a natural disaster.

Among the most common of written farm lease provisions are these: rent; length and termination of tenancy; procedure for amending lease; landlord's right of entry after giving notice of termination; limits on subleasing and assignment by tenant; land use obligations including compliance with government conservation programs; participation in farm program payments; types of crops to be planted; pesticide use; general maintenance duties; insurance; control of weeds; improvements to land and buildings; and, responsibility for hired labor. Further provisions might cover: arbitration of disputes; rights in case of condemnation of all or part of the farm; duty of the tenant to show adequate operational financing by a set time each year; enumeration of acts of default -- including failure to farm in a defined manner; form of notice of default to tenant and right to cure; hunting and recreational rights; and, payment of attorney fees in cases of default.

Landlords want every assurance of payment of rent. Except when rent is to be paid up front, cash rent leases usually require that the tenant grant to the landlord a security interest in all crops. The landlord will perfect by filing a financing statement. The creation of a security interest is advised even if there is a statutory farm landlord's lien for rent. Under the Bankruptcy Code, a statutory lien for rent will be avoided by the trustee in tenant's bankruptcy. 11 USCA § 545. But, the perfected security interest will most likely survive in such bankruptcy. Under a crop-share lease rent is paid by delivery to the landlord of the agreed share of the crop. In states where the tenant remains the owner of the entire crop until the landlord's share is delivered, the landlord will want the protection of a perfected security interest. In states where the landlord is deemed to be the owner of her share of the crop while it is still in the hands of the tenant, an attempt to take a security interest could be inappropriate and an invitation to legal confusion.

Provisions peculiar to crop share leases include: method of crop splits (e.g. every other wagon load, hopper or row); responsibility for payment of input expenses; responsibility for reserving storage space in public warehouses; name under which crop will be stored -- on scale tickets, settlement sheets, and warehouse receipts; responsibility for selling the crop; and, when necessary for tax planning, requirement of material participation by the landlord.

2. Options to Purchase

Because farm tenants often want an opportunity to purchase leased land if it comes on the market, option to purchase clauses are common in written farm leases. Problems can develop, as in Pipkin v. Connolly (Mont. 1975), where the lease provided that the tenant recognized the landlord's right to sell the land, so long as the tenant was given the right to match a third party offer. The lease, drafted by the *tenant's* attorney, did not state whether it terminated or continued if the tenant failed to exercise the option and the property was sold to a third party. While recognizing the general rule that a lease continues upon sale of the underlying fee simple irrespective of any option to purchase, Pipkin held that the lease terminated when the land was sold to a third party following tenant's failure to match the offer. Two reasons were given: the lease, being ambiguous as to termination, should be construed against the drafter; and, the unusual clause giving landlord the right to sell must have been intended to have important meaning. Courts in other states are likely to hold that lease termination upon tenant's failure to exercise an option to purchase will occur only if the lease clearly so provides.

When a written lease for a term of years contains an option to purchase, an issue arises as to whether the option continues upon renewal or extension of the lease. If the tenant holds over with the consent of the landlord, a year to year tenancy usually results. The issue then is whether the terms of the holdover tenancy are exactly those in the original written lease. Butz v. Butz (Ill.Ct.App.1973), states that ". . . the former lease is no longer effective as a contract but its terms may be consulted in determining rent, costs and essential duties of both landlord and tenant under the tenancy from year to year." Butz goes on to say that an option to purchase -- or any other term not essential to a year to year farm lease -- does not survive the expiration of the written lease. But, at least one court holds that all of the terms of the original lease, including an option to purchase, continue to apply in a holdover unless contrary intent is shown. Straley v. Osborne (Md.1971).

Some statutes on farm lease holdovers provide: "the tenancy shall continue . . . upon the same terms and conditions as the original lease unless written notice for termination is given . . .." See, e.g., Iowa Code Ann. § 562.6. A similar statute did not deter the court in Nevala v. McKay (Mont.1978), from concluding that the right of first refusal in a lease for a term of years did not carry over into a holdover tenancy because it was a covenant separate from the lease. Controversy over survival of an option can be avoided by a provision in the original lease.

Caution dictates that a tenant record a lease containing an option to buy so that any prospective buyer of the fee will be on notice of the tenant's interest. The existence of crops on a tract of land provides no constructive notice of the existence of a lease. Flaspohler v. Hoffman (Mo.Ct.App.1983).

V. TERMINATION OF FARM TENANCIES

From the landlord's perspective lease termination becomes necessary when the landlord wants to personally take over the farm, install a new tenant, or change the terms of the existing lease. Termination rules vary depending upon type of tenancy, type of crops and the peculiarities of state law. We do not deal with tenancies at will or at sufferance.

A. Term of Years

A lease for a term of years is created when the written agreement between landlord and tenant fixes the dates upon which tenant's interest begins and ends. A lease "for three years beginning on Oct. 1, 1993," will terminate at midnight on September 30, 1996. Generally, any fixed or computable term creates a lease for a term of years, whether it be 10 months, one year, three years, or 40 months.

The common law rule, which has been codified in some states, is that neither party need give notice to effect the termination of a lease for a term of years. Such a lease simply expires on the fixed termination date unless the parties have by contract created a notice requirement. Caveat: in some states leases for a term of years are now subject to statutory termination rules. Denton v. Moser (Iowa 1976)

The duration of agricultural land tenancies is limited by statute or constitutional provision in some jurisdictions. See, e.g., Minn. Const. Art. 1, § 15 (21 years); Wis. Const. Art 1, § 14 (15 years); Cal. Civ. Code § 71 (51 years); Mont. Code. Ann. § 70-26-207 (10 years).

B. Periodic Tenancies

A periodic tenancy is one that renews itself from period to period, usually month to month or year to year, until proper notice of termination is given. Such a lease may be expressly created or may result when the tenant holds over with the assent of the landlord upon the expiration of a lease for a term of years. In the farm setting such holdovers typically result in year to year tenancies -- often running from March to March. Usually, the factor determinative of the period of a holdover tenancy is the pattern of rental payments under the original lease. Rhodes v. Sigler (Ill.Ct.App.1975). For farm leases, rent is almost always annual whether paid in cash or crop-share. Even when farm rent is paid in two or more installments during a year, the payments are almost always referable to an annual rent.

When express assent to a holdover is not forth-coming, acceptance by the landowner of rent establishes it. However, in agriculture rent might not fall due until many months after holdover. Thus, it is generally accepted that assent occurs by the land-lord's acquiescence as the tenant enters the fields and makes preparations for the next cropping season. But sometimes preparations cannot be started until long after the holdover. Yet, the farm tenant needs a prompt indication of the landlord's intent. Montana has defined assent as the failure by the landlord to demand possession of agricultural land within 60 days after the end of a term of years. Mont. Code Ann. § 70-27-108.

Under the common law, a year to year tenancy could be terminated only by notice given 6 months prior to the end of the period. Many states have shortened the notice period by statute with times ranging from one to four months. Some statutes have set the date upon which farm holdover periodic tenancies end by making all holdovers run from March 1 to March 1, regardless of the original lease term. In general, notice statutes are designed to protect tenants and are to be liberally constructed. In most states, only the landlord must give notice to terminate a periodic tenancy. Until timely notice is given, the tenant can continue farming. If the state statute makes both parties subject to the notice requirement and tenant vacates without giving timely notice, he or she will be liable for the rent for the next period. Pollock v. Pollock (Iowa 1955).

C. Landlords Right of Entry

Even when the landlord has given proper and timely notice of termination, a dispute can arise as to when the owner can enter and begin to prepare the land for the next crop. Absent a written or statutory provision allowing entry before the lease terminates, the tenant, pending expiration of the lease, has the power to prevent the landlord from working the land. However, when a landlord has a right to enter before the end of the lease, it has been held that a tenant will be liable if crop loss results from delaying access. Stoppel v. Mastin (Kan.1976).

D. Land Preparation Costs

Controversy can arise as to compensation due a tenant for land preparation done prior to receiving notice of lease termination. Under common law theories of unjust enrichment or quantum merit a tenant might be entitled to compensation for services rendered and supplies furnished. Kansas by statute requires that a tenant -- who in such circumstances performs customary tillage and/or applies fertilizer, herbicides or insecticides -- be paid reasonable value for services and supplies furnished. Kan. Stat. Ann § 58-2506a. The problem with both the common law and statutory rules is that they may work unfair results if the land was similarly prepared by the landlord prior to the time the tenant originally took possession. Again, this is matter of compensation is best resolved in the farm lease.

E. Negotiating New Lease Terms

Giving timely notice of termination is sometimes as important for changing lease terms as it is for changing tenants. Recall that upon holdover the *essential* terms and conditions of the original lease continue to govern. If new terms satisfactory to the landlord cannot be negotiated, the landlord will want to take over the operation or lease to a new tenant. Thus, the tenant, upon receiving notice of termination, may also be presented with a written proposal of new lease terms. The giving of proper notice to terminate clearly enhances the negotiating position of the landlord. However, notice of termination given under such circumstances might be held to be equivocal and thus ineffective to terminate the lease. Maguire v. Haddad (Mass.1950). Suggesting an alternative method of raising rent, one court held that the tenant is subject to increased rent if the landlord timely notifies the tenant during the lease term that rent will increase upon holdover and the tenant holds over without objecting. Becker v. Mc-Fadden (Kan.1977).

F. Pastures

In some states, courts have held that compliance with statutory notice rules is not required where the land is rented for grazing or pasture. Morling v. Schmidt (Iowa 1980)(notice required only if land under cultivation); Brown v. Beckerdite (Kan.1953) (agreement to pasture cattle did not create a landlord-tenant relationship).

G. Fall and Spring Planted Crops
1. Lease Termination Law and Practice

States with moderate climates may offer a choice of two distinct growing seasons within a 12 month period. Spring planted crops such as corn, soybeans, milo, spring wheat, oats and barley are planted from late April until late June and are harvested in the fall. Winter wheat, the typical fall planted crop, is harvested the following summer.

Double cropping is practiced in regions with particularly moderate climates, the Mississippi Delta as an example. There, after winter wheat is harvested in June, the farmer can immediately plant another crop such as soybeans for harvest in the fall. Unless the land is to stand fallow, the farmer can again plant winter wheat in the fall. Thus, there can be a crop in the ground on a leased farm virtually year round. On a leased farm in eastern Arkansas one field might be devoted to winter wheat and soybean double cropping, another exclusively to winter wheat, and yet another exclusively to a spring planted crop such as rice, corn, cotton or soybeans.

The law with respect to termination of farm leases can be treacherous. Absent a termination clause in a written lease, common law and statutory termination rules will apply. Existing rules were conceived in the days when spring planting dominated and tend to provide for notices that work termination at the end of the calendar year or on March 1. And, if a lease lawfully terminates when a fall planted crop is in the ground, case law suggests that the tenant loses the crop because the tenant is "not entitled to a crop sown but not maturing before the expiration of his lease." See, e.g., Fox v. Flick (Kan.1949); Huckaby v. Walker (Ark.1920). Under the Fox rule the former tenant not only has no right in the growing crop, but is not entitled to be paid for expenses of preparation and planting, unless the lease or a statute provides otherwise. Faced with this inequity, some courts permit the tenant to harvest the crop after termination, if termination was not the tenant's fault. Moore v. Hardy (Mont.1988)(tenant at fault); Ziegler v. Hendrikson (Colo.Ct.App. 1974)(landlord estopped); Hemberger v. Hageman (Colo.1949)(unjust enrichment).

When tenant's crop would normally mature and be harvested before the lease expires, there is some authority holding that the tenant remains entitled to such crop if weather conditions prevent harvest before the termination date. Horne v. Oller (Kan.Ct. App. 1980); Chamberlain v. Evans (Mont.1979).

2. Confronting the Problem of Fox v. Flick

Under Fox v. Flick (Kan.1949) a tenant is **not** entitled to the crop which he or she planted and tended, but had not harvested prior to lease termination. In an effort to change this outcome, the Kansas legislature enacted a statutory farm lease termination scheme for oral leases and holdovers, and for holdovers following the expiration of written leases silent as to method of terminating holdovers. Kan. Stat. Ann. § 58-2506.

The Kansas statute puts all oral farm leases and holdovers into a March 1 to March 1 time frame. These examples show in part how the statute works. If notice to terminate as to a spring planted field is given after 30 days before March 1, 1995, but 30 days before March 1, 1996, termination occurs on March 1, 1996. For a fall planted field it is essential to know the planting history. For example, if there is a 1995 harvest of a 1994 fall planted crop, notice given 30 days before March 1, 1996 terminates the lease at harvest of the fall 1995 planted crop. If there is to be no 1995 spring harvest because of no 1994 fall planting and notice is given before fall 1995 planting, the lease ends March 1, 1996. This notice ought to dissuade the tenant from planting a fall crop in 1995. However, since such notice might be given far in advance -- e.g., in March, 1995, and since the tenant is entitled to be in possession into the next calendar year, potential for misunderstanding exists. And, a befuddled tenant would lose a 1995 fall planted crop on March 1, 1996.

On lands heldover at the expiration of a written lease, the Kansas statute uses the time frame from the written lease in fixing termination notice rules for spring planted fields. Assuming a January 1 to January 1 lease, notice to terminate on January 1, 1996 is adequate if given 30 days before that date. The March 1 to March 1 time frame is used for fall planted fields. The rules are the same as those for oral leases and holdovers. If there was *no fall planted crop in 1994*, but the tenant plants a fall crop in 1995, the statute still allows March 1, 1996 term- ination if notice is given prior to planting in 1995. In this example the tenant, under Fox v. Flick, still loses the fall l995 planted crop.

It is fair to say that the Kansas statute, which is only partially described, is complex. And, a tenant can get buffaloed by these statutory lease termination rules as did the tenant in the late 1940s under the law reflected in Fox v. Flick. From the tenant's perspective, whether in Kansas or elsewhere, a well drafted lease termination clause reflecting the realities of fall planting or double cropping operations is the best way to head off the Fox v. Flick type problem.

H. Breach of Covenant or Making Waste

Absent a statute to the contrary, the general rule is that a tenancy cannot be terminated for tenant's breach of covenant or condition unless the lease contains a specific clause providing for forfeiture or right of re-entry. If a farm lease has no express covenant on farming practices, state law usually implies a covenant of good husbandry. In Schultz v. Ramey (N.M.1958), the court found an implied covenant which required the tenant to farm leased land in a proper and diligent manner. However, the remedy for breach of the implied covenant of good husbandry was held to be injunction and money damages, not lease termination. Accord, Hogan v. Pelton (Neb.1982).

Disputes about farming methods and soil and water management practices can result in efforts by the landlord to terminate a lease in the midst of a cropping season. If such termination is judicially sanctioned, or if it is stipulated as a remedy in the lease, an issue arises as to whether an aggrieved landlord must give to tenant notice of the specific wrongful act and a reasonable time to cure.

In normal circumstances a holdover or periodic tenancy will continue absent timely notice of termination. The rule is different when a default occurs under an the terms of the lease. See, e.g., Iowa Code

Ann. § 562.6. Where termination is an available remedy for breach of an express or implied covenant, the giving of notice would not appear to be required.

Suppose that a written lease specifies that the landowner has the option to re-enter and take control of the land upon any default not cured within a set number of days after written notice to the tenant about the default. The decision in Enders v. Wesley W. Hubbard and Sons, Inc. (Idaho 1973) suggests that a tenancy could be terminated in the middle of a crop year. On the other hand, in McElwee v. DeVault (Iowa 1963) the court said that it would sanction mid-year termination for breach of covenants only in the case of a flagrant violations. Failure of the tenant to control weeds and "volunteer" corn in bean fields, to work the ground at the appropriate time, to follow directions as to where to place manure, and to give up a significant off-farm job were not grounds to justify mid-year termination. But, these facts were held to justify termination of a three year lease at the end of the first year. Arguably, the giving of a notice of termination was immaterial under the facts.

Allegations of waste can result in litigation when the landowner seeks either lease termination and damages, or injunction and damages. The term waste has no precise definition and its occurrence is determined on a case-by-case basis with courts generally requiring a finding of permanent or substantial injury to the real estate. Money damages and injunction are the usual remedies. Statutes in some states provide for double or triple damages if the act of waste is malicious or wanton. Termination of a lease for waste is not a traditional remedy and needs to be sanctioned by statute or a specific lease clause. Statutes that allow lease termination for waste usually contain no notice of termination requirement.

VI. LEASING FROM A LIFE TENANT

It is not uncommon for the title to agricultural land to be divided between a life tenant and a remainderman. Whether the life tenant farms or leases out the land, problems often arise upon that life tenant's death. Issues arise concerning rights in growing crops; entitlement to rents if a cash rent lease is outstanding; and, possible automatic termination of a lessee's (undertenant's) unexpired right to farm the land.

A. Growing Crops

The common law *doctrine of emblements* was fashioned to resolve disputes over the right to cultivate and harvest certain types of growing crops upon termination of a life estate and with it the dependant tenancy of the person farming (undertenant). Emblements are annual crops such as wheat, corn, cotton, rice, potatoes and vegetables -- crops that are not spontaneous, but that result from human labor.

Absent a governing state statute, courts use the doctrine of emblements to determine the claims of the estate of the deceased life tenant, the remainderman, and the undertenant. An undertenant who claims rights to growing crops under the doctrine of emblements must establish: 1) that appropriate crops are growing; 2) that the crops were planted prior to the death of the life tenant by one who held the land subject to termination at an unascertainable time (e.g., death of the life tenant); and 3) that termination of the estate was not the fault of the person planting the crops. Thus, if a life tenant dies after having leased out the farm for cash or on crop-share, the lessee is entitled to all growing crops (cash rent lease) or the agreed share (crop share lease).

The estate of a deceased life tenant and the remainderman may make conflicting claims to the life tenant's "rent" under a crop-share lease where the life tenant died after planting, but before the lessee had harvested. The common law rule, as in Williams v. Stander (Colo.1960), is that the remainderman is entitled to the landlord's share of the growing crop on the theory that title to such crops is in the lessee, rent is not due until harvest, and upon harvest the remainderman has the present interest in the land. This is consistent with the reality that a lease is not just a contract, but also a conveyance of an interest in real property, the latter including ownership by the tenant of crops produced during the lease term.

Another approach is illustrated by Finley v. McClure (Kan.1977) where the court held that the controlling factors are whether the growing crops are personal property or real estate, and whether the life tenant has a property interest in the crops at planting. Citing Kansas statutes, the court held that when rent is payable by a share of the crop, the lessor (life tenant) is deemed to be an owner of that share and that unsevered annual crops are deemed to be personal assets for purposes of the administration of the deceased life tenant's estate. Kan. Stat. Ann. §§ 58-2525, 59-1206. So, in Finley the Kansas court held that the life tenant's estate was entitled to the crop share on the theory that a landlord's ownership interest in crops attaches upon planting and that growing crops are personal property.

Many states have changed the common law by enacting statutes governing apportionment of rent. Illinois, for example, provides that the life tenant's estate "may recover the proportion of rent which accrued before his or her [life tenant's] death, and the remainderman shall recover for the residue." Ill. Rev. Stat. ch. 110 § 9-217.

B. Underlying Lease Terminates

Under the common law, a leasehold interest granted by a life tenant terminates upon that person's death. This result does not ensue, however, if the remainderman has given written consent or otherwise ratifies continuation of the lease. And, the remainderman might be estopped from denying the continuance of the underlying lease. However, in Wood v. Trenchard (Wyo.1976), it was held that equitable estoppel is unavailable to a lessee who claims no actual knowledge of the life estate, assuming its existence could have been discovered in public real estate records.

It is possible that a holdover or periodic tenancy could result if the lessee remains in possession after the death of the life tenant and the remainderman assents. Assent may be established by the remainderman's acquiescence in activities of the tenant in preparing for the next crop or by accepting cash rent due from the past year without giving termination notice. As noted hereinbefore, Montana has defined assent as the failure by the landlord to demand possession of agricultural land within 60 days from the expiration of the term of years. Mont. Code Ann. 70-27-l08.

Generally, if the remainderman gives notice of termination to the tenant immediately upon the death of the life tenant, the remainderman will be entitled to possession, subject, however, to the doctrine of emblements. This assumes the absence of a statute granting greater protection to the tenant. Some states have changed the common law by statute to permit the undertenant, under certain circumstances, to farm the land for one more year. See, e.g., Iowa Code Ann. § 562.8; Minn. Stat. Ann. § 500.25. Varying rules are triggered under the Minnesota statute depending on the date of the death of the life tenant.

VII. TAX PLANNING CONSIDERATIONS

The economic terms of a farm lease can have legal impact beyond the lease transaction. By leasing out farmland without adequate planning, a retired farmer or rancher (lessor) may be precluded from drawing full Social Security benefits. More significantly, a farmer upon death may leave his or her estate unqualified to elect special use valuation for farm real estate under IRC § 2032A and/or deferred estate tax payment under IRC § 6l66. The special use value election can save on estate taxes by reducing the value of the decedent's gross estate by up to $750,000. Deferred payments can extend over a 15 year period at a favorable interest rate.

Adequate lifetime planning to preserve these elections involves careful decisions by the lessor, consistent with tax rules, as to whether to structure farm leases as a cash rent leases, crop-share leases, or material participation crop-share leases. Depending on the circumstances -- the most important being the identity of the tenant -- the wrong choices can be costly, particularly in terms of needlessly destroying the § 2032A election. And, valid elections by the estate can be undone in a set post-death period by inappropriate leasing transactions. These tax rules are complex and beyond the scope of this Nutshell.

VIII. FARM PROGRAM PAYMENT RULES

Economic terms in farm leases impact distribution of federal farm program payments. We begin with the term *producers,* those persons (individuals and entities) who share in the risk of producing crops, more particularly landlords, tenants, or sharecroppers. 7 CFR § 1413.3(1994). Payments due the operator or other producer on a farm will not be made until it is determined that there is full compliance with the lease contract and federal regulations. 7 CFR § 1413.101(a)(1994).

As to lands farmed by tenants or sharecroppers, it is required that producers provide to the ASCS, now CFSA, county committee a copy of the written lease or a statement of terms if the lease is oral. If the lease is determined to be a cash lease, the landlord is not eligible to receive disaster or deficiency payments for the leased tract. 7 CFR § 1413.111(v) (1994). Recall that the Consolidated Farm Service Agency (CFSA) took over the duties of the ASCS in Oct. 1994.

In the case of a crop share lease, program payments will not be approved if is determined that the landlord has not given tenants and sharecroppers on the farm a chance to participate in the program. 7

CFR § 1413.150(a)(1)(1994). Each producer must be given the chance to participate in proportion to such producer's interest in the program crop. 7 CFR § 1413.111(a)(1994). Beyond this, approval is to be denied if the number of tenants and sharecroppers on the farm is reduced below the number in the previous year ". . . in anticipation of or because of participating in the program." 7 CFR § 1413.150 (a)(2)(1994)(subject to exceptions). Approval also will be withheld if the tenant or sharecropper, as a prerequisite to entering into a lease or contract, is required to agree to lessened participation in the particular farm program. 7 CFR § 1413.150(a)(3) (1994). When the landlord concocts schemes for the purpose of depriving a tenant or sharecropper of program payments otherwise due, payments will not be approved. If payments are made before the scheme is discovered, such monies must be refunded to CCC. 7 CFR § 1413.150(4)(1994).

A different division of payment will be approved by the county committee if the division is "fair and equitable" and all producers who would otherwise share in it agree in writing. With the concurrence of a representative of the state committee, the county committee can approve a different division, even though not all of the affected producers agree. 7 CFR § 1413.111(b)(3)(1994).

CHAPTER FOUR

STORAGE AND MARKETING OF CROPS
I. REGULATION OF WAREHOUSES AND GRAIN DEALERS

Grain storage warehouses and grain dealers have key roles in marketing and distribution of fungible commodities. It is typical for a single facility to function simultaneously as a dealer buying and selling grain and as a public grain storage warehouse. In this chapter we use the term grain broadly and not in the narrow sense of cereal crops.

At harvest, most farmers do not sell grain on the spot market. To satisfy the need for immediate cash flow some farmers take out Commodity Credit Corporation price support loans, while others fall back on personal financial resources. In either case, the strategy is to wait to market until prices recover from harvest lows. Many producers have limited on farm storage space and thus use the storage services of public warehouses. Fungible commodities such as wheat, rice, sunflower seed, corn and soybeans are commingled in the warehouse with commodities of like kind and quality. Cotton is stored in identifiable bales. Highly perishable commodities, such as fresh vegetables and fruit, are not commingled and even with refrigeration cannot be stored for long.

Grain in storage in a warehouse is considered to be in interstate or foreign commerce. Pursuant to the Commerce Clause of the Constitution, Congress has the power to regulate all such facilities. However, Congress has not used its power to preempt the warehouse regulatory schemes found in at least 30 states.

In these states each warehouse can choose whether to apply for a state or a federal license. The U.S. Warehouse Act is the federal law regulating warehouse storage operations. 7 USCA §§ 241-273; 7 CFR pts. 735-743(1994). To obtain a federal license, an applicant must have, *inter alia,* a properly equipped warehouse, a good business reputation, and a minimum net worth. State licensing laws vary considerably, with some states having requirements more stringent than those at the federal level.

Conflicts can arise when a state attempts to impose its warehouse laws on a federally licensed warehouse. Section 29 of the federal act provides: ". . . the power, jurisdiction, and authority conferred upon the Secretary of Agriculture under this Act shall be exclusive with respect to all persons securing a license hereunder as long as said license remains in effect." The U.S. Supreme Court in Rice v. Santa Fe Elevator Corp. (1947) considered this language and held that a state cannot preempt any matter regulated by the federal act. This is so even if the federal regulation as to the particular activity is less stringent than that of the state.

When a warehouse or elevator facility buys and sells commodities, it acts as a dealer and engages in activities not regulated by the U.S. Warehouse Act or state laws on warehouses. While there is no federal licensing program for grain dealers, some of the states require licensing. In these states it is possible to have a facility that is federally licensed for storage operations and state licensed for grain dealer operations. See, e.g., Demeter, Inc. v. Werries (C.D.Ill. 1988).

II. LAW OF OPERATIONS

A. Generally

Upon delivery of grain to a warehouse, a farmer can select one of several strategies, including: sell for cash; sell on contract to receive payment in the future (deferred payment contract); sell with the price to be set and paid later (price later contract); or store the commodity. If the commodity is stored in a public warehouse, a warehouse receipt stating the number of bushels stored will be issued to the bailor in most instances. However, it is not uncommon, particularly as to some state licensed warehouses, for a scale ticket to be the only document received by the bailor.

Whenever grain moves into or out of a warehouse, it is weighed and a *scale (weight) ticket* is issued. The scale ticket issued upon delivery into the facility will state the date, the name of the deliverer, the type and gross weight of the commodity, and in some instances the moisture content. But most scale tickets do not state the number of bushels or the quality. Grain, to be accepted for storage, must be below a specified moisture content. Drying can cause shrinkage and the test weight of a bushel can vary according to the quality of the grain. Usually, it is after issuance of the scale ticket that the warehouse determines moisture content, quality, test weight, and presence of foreign matter.

While practices differ from facility to facility, almost all give the deliverer a short period of time following delivery in which to decide whether the grain will be sold or stored. Some facilities treat grain as sold if the depositor does not notify the warehouse to the contrary within a set period. Others use a reverse presumption and during this initial decision-making period consider the grain to be in open storage. It follows that if a warehouse receipt eventually issues, grain has been in open storage prior thereto. Caveat: the term open storage is also used to describe grain delivered to a warehouse to be stored there *or* at another site.

Federally licensed warehouses are required to issue *warehouse receipts* for stored grain, but some state licensed facilities do not issue them, except at the request of the bailor. State licensed warehouses are required in most jurisdictions to issue warehouse receipts upon request. Federally licensed warehouses must use sequentially numbered USDA supplied warehouse receipt forms. Many states have a similar procedure.

Generally, warehouse receipts are documents of title and represent ownership of the grain. Federal warehouse receipts must indicate the name of the warehouse, its location, the date the receipt was issued, the name of the person to whom redelivery is to be made, the storage charge (tariff), and a description of the agricultural commodity delivered, including quality and quantity. The receipt must be signed by the operator.

Most states that mandate issuance of warehouse receipts require essentially the same information. UCC §§ 7-202 and 7-201(2). Absent some contrary state law, Article 7 requirements apply to all state licensed warehouses and their activities. Section 7-202 leaves the form of the documents of title to the discretion of state regulatory agencies. Under UCC

§ 7-104 a warehouse receipt can be either negotiable or non-negotiable. The distinction is important in resolving certain commercial and financing disputes. However, a bailee's responsibilities to a bailor are the same regardless of whether the bailor holds a negotiable or non-negotiable receipt.

Warehouse *storage charges* vary. Some facilities set a minimum charge -- e.g. for corn, 14 cents minimum per bushel for the first 120 days, 3 cents a month per bushel thereafter. A farmer contemplating whether to sell or store will not only consider drying and shrinkage costs, but also the cost of storage. And, the loss of use of sale proceeds for the storage period and interest expense if money is borrowed in the interim will be factored in. Sometimes it can make economic sense for a farmer to sell in the spot market straight out of the field.

In addition to storing commodities of others, a warehouse almost always functions as a *grain dealer,* buying commodities from farmers and storing or selling them for its own account. When a grain dealer stores its own grain, the warehouse receipt will name the company as owner and the commodity will be considered company or store-owned. From a *daily position record* the warehouse manager can tell how much of a specific commodity is on hand and whether it belongs to patrons or is company owned.

Grain will not be accepted for storage unless it has been inspected, graded and weighed by a licensed person. The federal government and most states have grain standards and inspection requirements. Federal requirements are at 7 USCA §§71-87; §§ 1621-1632 and Federal Grain Inspection Service regulations are at 7 CFR pts. 800-02(1994). Federal grain standards address weight and measure, and type and quality. Sec 7 CFR pt. 810(1994)(barley, canola, flaxseed, rye, sunflower seed, oats, wheat, corn, sorghum, soybeans, triticale, mixed grains). Each commodity is divided into classes and for each class there are from two to five numerical grades. Corn, for example, is classed as yellow, white or mixed, with five numerical grades plus U.S. sample grade. Grade is determined by moisture content, damaged kernels, shrunken or broken kernels, smell, foreign material, purity of class, and test weight per bushel. Each grade has its own test weight.

B. Status Of Parties Delivering Commodities

The status of a farmer who has delivered grain to a warehouse is critical if the facility goes bankrupt. An unpaid seller is an unsecured creditor and typically recovers little or nothing. See Ch. 6 *infra*. A farmer storing grain is a bailor and is likely to fare better if at least part of the pertinent commingled mass is on hand when the warehouse is closed.

1. Scale Ticket Holders

Upon delivery a farmer always receives a scale (weight) ticket and can either sell or store the commodity. If the farmer also receives a warehouse receipt, the grain is stored and the farmer as bailor is the owner of a specific amount of a commodity of a certain quality. The farmer shares as a tenant-in-common in the commingled mass. Because all producers receive a scale ticket upon delivery, it may be difficult to distinguish a seller from a bailor when a warehouse receipt has not been issued. Courts and legislatures have struggled with this problem.

Bankruptcy judges in Michigan have confronted this issue. In In re Durand Milling Co., Inc. (Bankr. E.D.Mich.1981) farmers delivered grain and received scale tickets stating that "All Grain Considered STORED Unless Other Arrangements Have Been Made." The grain dealer failed to comply with the statute that required the issuance of warehouse receipts within 30 days of delivery. When the warehouse failed, the question of whether farmers were bailors was considered. The court in effect held that Michigan law supplies a rebuttable statutory presumption that one holding a scale ticket has a non-negotiable warehouse receipt. But, this issue was revisited in In re Mayville Feed & Grain, Inc. (Bankr.E.D.Mich.1989) where the farmer delivered grain and received a scale ticket that contained these clearly highlighted words, "NOT A STORAGE WAREHOUSE RECEIPT." The court rejected the bailment presumption indicating that the legislature had not clearly indicated a presumption in favor of bailment. It also noted that producers have the responsibility to protect their bailor status by obtaining warehouse receipts. Finally, Mayville rejected earlier court holdings that the intent of the parties controls, concluding that the state's comprehensive regulatory program for the establishment of ownership and payment rights governs.

If the scale ticket does not indicate storage, and the elevator does not issue a warehouse receipt or have a governing published policy, an issue arises as to whether to place the burden of proof of ownership on the person asserting bailment or on the party claiming sale. Durand and Mayville offer conflicting approaches. Under Bankruptcy Rule 3001(g), absent a contrary provision in federal or state warehouse laws, "a warehouse receipt, scale ticket, or similar document of the type routinely issued as evidence of title . . . shall constitute prima facie evidence of the validity and amount of a claim of ownership of a quantity of grain."

In a few states, legislators have sought by statute to clarify the status of delivered grain. For example, Missouri defines "storage grain" as: "[a]ll grain received at a [Missouri] licensed public warehouse unless: (1) Payment for the grain is made upon delivery . . . ; (2) At the time of delivery of the grain to the warehouseman, the purchase price is established, documented . . . and payment made within thirty days or the account is entered . . . onto a formal settlement sheet . . .." Mo. Rev. Stat. § 411.325(2). There is an additional section dealing with gain received at a warehouse not licensed under Missouri law. *Id*. at § 411.325(3). In Florida, delivery tickets must state whether the delivered grain is sold or stored. Fla. Stat. Ann. § 604.32(g).

If grain is to be stored in a public warehouse, the best strategy for the depositor is to obtain a warehouse receipt. This is important as an assurance of treatment as a bailor in case the warehouse fails, and as a prerequisite to the farmer's participation in a federal price support loan program. The CCC will not make a loan secured by grain stored in a public warehouse unless it has physical possession of a negotiable warehouse receipt endorsed to it.

2. Holders of Documents of Title

All states have enacted UCC Article 7 which covers documents of title such as warehouse receipts.

In some jurisdictions, Article 7 and the state's pre-existing and unrepealed general warehouse statute are inconsistent on certain points.

A warehouse receipt is a document of title under UCC § 1-201(15). Section 7-403(1) obligates the warehouseman to deliver the goods to the person entitled to them under the document. Section 7-403(4) provides: "[p]erson entitled under the document, means holder in the case of a negotiable document or the person to whom delivery is to be made by the terms of or pursuant to written instructions under a non-negotiable document." Unless scale tickets are treated as documents of title, holders arguably would not be entitled to grain under UCC § 7-403. Document of title for UCC purposes is defined in § 1-201(15) to include: ". . . warehouse receipt . . . and also any other document which in the regular course of business or financing is treated as adequately evidencing that the person in possession of it is entitled to receive . . . the goods it covers." While no reference to a scale ticket appears in UCC § 1-201(15), a scale ticket and/or settlement sheet representing a storage obligation can be treated as a document of title for purposes of § 7-403. A scale ticket, however, will rarely if ever be treated as a negotiable document of title. See UCC § 7-104.

C. Receipt Holders: No Commodities Delivered

Buyers who purchase grain from grain dealers do not always take immediate delivery. Sometimes they receive only a copy of the contract of purchase which obligates the dealer to deliver at a specified time. In such cases, buyers should also insist upon issuance of a warehouse receipt.

Non-UCC provisions in some state warehouse statutes provide that warehouse receipts shall be issued *only* upon actual delivery of grain to the warehouse. In People v. Farmers Elevator Mutual Insurance Co. (Ill.Ct.App.1966), the court read such a statute to mean that no warehouse receipt shall be issued for grain not in the warehouse, not that contemporaneous physical delivery is mandatory prior to the issuance of a valid warehouse receipt.

In State ex re. Public Service Commission v. Gunkleman & Sons, Inc. (N.D.1974), the court held that while a state warehouse statute technically required physical delivery as a prerequisite to the issuance of a valid warehouse receipt, the fact that the warehouse owned the commodities at the time of issuance -- together with UCC § 7-403(1), (4), compels the finding that the holder of the warehouse receipt was the owner of the commodities which it represented. A contrary reading would compel a buyer of company owned grain to load out the entire purchase, drive around the block and "deliver."

Gunkleman did not address issues associated with the issuance of a warehouse receipt to a buyer at a time when there is insufficient grain in the warehouse to satisfy all outstanding receipts. See Ch. 6 *infra.*

D. Warehouse Liability as Bailee

Liability issues arise when a warehouse cannot redeliver the same quantity and quality of commodities bailed, either because of damage to or conversion of the goods. Here we focus on Article 7 of the UCC, which deals only with the liability of warehouses in unintentional damage cases. Conversion is considered in Ch. 6 *infra.*

Absent an agreement to the contrary, the warehouse is not an insurer of bailed goods and is not liable for loss of or injury to stored commodities unless caused by its own negligence. Under § 7-204(1), liability flows from the violation of a duty to exercise such care as a "reasonably careful man would exercise under like circumstances . . .." As contemplated by the drafters of UCC § 7-204, each state has an option to impose a higher duty. While several states have exercised that option, such provisions tend to have limited application.

There is general agreement that in litigation a bailor must offer proof of: 1) delivery of a certain quantity and quality of the commodity; 2) a proper demand for its return; 3) payment of storage charges; and 4) failure of the warehouse to redeliver upon demand. See § 7-403(2), (3). Even under the UCC, courts have struggled with the issue of who has the ultimate burden of persuasion as to the warehouse's failure to act reasonably. The question is whether the bailor must prove negligence or the bailee freedom from same.

Section 7-403 articulates the warehouseman's duty to redeliver goods as well as legitimate excuses for failure to do so. With the bracketed language omitted it allocates the burden of proof or risk of nonpersuasion to the bailee. Section 7-403(1)(b) imposes the duty to redeliver bailed goods:

> . . . to a person entitled under the document . . . unless and to the extent that the bailee establishes any of the following: . . .

> (b) damage to or delay, loss or destruction
> of the goods for which the bailee is not
> liable [, but the burden of establishing
> negligence in such cases is on the person
> entitled under the document]; . . ..

The optional bracketed language places the risk of nonpersuasion on the bailor in negligence cases. At least 11 states have adopted the optional language and four more have adopted it with modification. Section 1-201(8) defines the "burden of establishing" in terms of "persuading" the trier of fact.

Section 7-403 does not discuss remedy. UCC § 1-103 preserves common law and equity principles when not displaced by the UCC, and § 1-106(2) provides that any obligation imposed by the UCC is enforceable by action unless otherwise specified. Thus, the bailor could sue to replevy the goods or to recover their value from the noncomplying bailee.

Article 7 is subject to the general rule of UCC § 1-102(3) that obligations of reasonable care may not be disclaimed by agreement. However, the parties may determine by agreement the standards by which performance of this obligation is to be measured, as long as the standards are not manifestly unreasonable. Course of dealing and usage of trade will also affect any agreement. Subject to this limitation and any imposed by regulatory statutes or agencies, Section 7-204(2) permits warehousemen to limit liability for loss or damage by including in the storage agreement or in the warehouse receipt the measure of liability per item or per unit of weight. This limitation does not apply when the warehouseman converts bailed property to its own use.

In accepting grain for drying and storage a warehouse cannot disclaim its duty to use reasonable care. But, can the warehouse disclaim an implied warranty as to the quality of the commodity once dried? This curious issue arose in Baugh Farms, Inc. v. Smith (N.D.Miss.1980). Because the warehouse was not a seller or lessor it is difficult to find the basis for an implied warranty. Yet, without offering any explanation as to its origin, the court assumed such a warranty to exist, and seeing no constraining public policy reasons, gave the disclaimer effect.

III. PRODUCER MARKETING STRATEGIES

Today's farmer has several options when deciding how to set a price for his or her farm products. For example, prior to harvest a farmer can enter into a cash forward contract with a buyer at a set price for a set quantity. Or, a farmer can fix his or her return by hedging in the commodity futures market instead of actually committing to delivery of the commodity. Strategies available after harvest include selling straight from the field on the spot market, forward contracting with a buyer, or storing the commodity for later sale. If available and if the farmer signed up, the CCC price support loan program provides immediate cash flow when the storage option is chosen. See pp. 10-11 *supra*.

A. Forward Contracting

1. Cash Forward Contracts

Crops can be priced preharvest, at harvest, or postharvest. The *cash forward contract* is probably the most popular preharvest price setting device. This type of contract involves an agreement between two parties for future delivery of a certain quantity of a designated commodity at a set price. Payment is due upon physical delivery.

A farmer who wants to guarantee a market or lock in a profit -- prior to harvest but after production costs are determined -- can do so by forward contracting early in the production season. Such a producer then faces output risk (low yield, low quality, or both) and the possibility of being unable to fill the contract. Thus, most producers cash forward contract only part of their anticipated production, unless there is strong evidence of an impending serious decline in the market. As harvest nears, the farmer may be willing to contract more of the crop.

Forward contracts are executed outside of a commodity exchange and, unlike standardized futures contracts, can be tailored to meet the farmer seller's specific needs as to quantity, quality, and place and time of delivery. But, forward contracts do involve risk of buyer insolvency, a risk not associated with futures contracts. Futures contracts are discussed at pp. 145-151 *infra.*

It is interesting to make the connection between an active commodity futures market and the ability of a farmer to obtain locally a firm price quote for a cash forward contract for a traded commodity on most business days. A farmer can estimate the offer he can expect by looking at the current futures price for the commodity for the contract that closes nearest the delivery date under the farmer's projected cash forward contract. and subtracting therefrom the local grain dealer's basis. Basis typically reflects the grain dealers transportation costs from the local market to the futures delivery point (terminal elevator), plus a handling charge and profit margin. See example at p. 149 *infra*. If the price the local grain dealer commits to in a cash forward contract is not figured from the futures price, it likely will be figured on the basis of the price the local dealer can itself get on forward contract with another merchant such as a processor or terminal elevator.

2. Price Later Contracts

Under a *price later contract* a farmer sells a specific quantity of grain, delivers it, and thus transfers title to the buyer. However, the price is set and paid in the future. A partial advance payment at the time of delivery is sometimes available. The producer will monitor price movement after delivery, waiting to "set" the price on a favorable day. There always is a final contract date when the price, if not previously fixed, must be set.

Various pricing formulas are used. One requires the farmer to accept the *cash price* posted by the elevator on a day and time selected in the future. Under a *fixed basis contract* the seller delivers the grain, transfers title, and agrees to a pricing formula tied to the commodity futures market, usually the price of a specific futures contract minus the basis as fixed on the day of delivery. The seller may have several months during which to choose when the price will be set. Example:

> Farmer sells corn on Oct. 1 and agrees to a 30¢ per bushel basis discount from the next July corn futures. If Farmer prices the contract on June 1, when the July corn futures contract is quoted at $3.46 per

bushel, the net selling price of $3.16 per bushel is established by subtracting from the futures price the 30¢ per bushel basis discount.

This type of pricing is best used when the cash price is strong relative to the futures price -- which means that the basis is narrow (relatively low).

Under a *service charge contract* the price formula uses whatever the local buyer is paying on the date chosen by producer. From that figure, the buyer deducts a service charge for each month the seller delays pricing. Usually, the service charge is at the same rate as the storage charge. The farmer elects the day to price and is paid the current local cash price minus accumulated service charges. The contract will set a deadline when pricing must occur.

A farmer using any one of the deferred pricing contracts hopes that the price of the commodity will go up and that the basis, if not fixed, will narrow. In exchange for the opportunity to capture possible price increases, the seller under a deferred payment contract risks market price decline, a widening of basis (except where fixed), market price increase insufficient to cover service charges (if assessed), temporary loss of use of proceeds, and buyer insolvency. As a general unsecured creditor prior to being paid, the seller is in an unenviable position if the buyer becomes bankrupt.

3. *Deferred Payment Contracts*

Deferred payment contracts contemplate current delivery, sale, and pricing of the commodity, with payment deferred until a later date. For tax reasons farmers sometimes want to defer realization of

income until the next tax year. Prior to the enactment of the Installment Sales Revision Act of 1980,
IRC § 453, a properly drafted deferred payment
contract did not trigger constructive receipt of income in the tax year in which the sale occurred, but
in which no money was received. IRC §§ 61, 451;
Treas. Reg. §§ 1.64-4 and 1.451-2. To effectively
defer income to a subsequent tax year the contract
had to be in writing, provide that the seller could not
receive or use any of the proceeds until the stated
date of deferred payment, and declare that the farmer could neither use the contract as security for a
loan, nor assign it or the proceeds therefrom.

Now, under IRC § 453, so long as the grain was
not considered to be in the farmer's inventory for
tax purposes, payments can be reported in installments as received if at least one payment is to be
received after the tax year of disposition. Applegate
v. Commissioner (7th Cir.1992). An unresolved
issue is whether a farmer can currently opt out of
installment sale reporting under IRC § 453 and rely
upon the pre-1980 deferral of income law. The IRS
should be expected to assert the negative, arguing
that regulations require recognition in the year of
disposition of the fair market value of the entire
installment obligation, Temp. Treas. Reg. § 15A.453
-1(d)(2), and that the use of the old deferral law
would allow an unintended loophole from alternative
minimum tax liability imposed on some post-1986
§ 453 installment sales. IRC § 56(a)(6).

4. Minimum Price Contracts

Minimum price contracts are a recent development
made possible by the establishment of the commodi-

ty options markets in 1984. They offer the producer a chance to assure a minimum price while retaining the opportunity to gain if the futures market rises. Many features of minimum price contracts are similar to those of cash forward contracts. For example, terms include a minimum cash price, a delivery time and place, discounts for grain quality deficiencies, penalties for nonperformance, and procedures should the buyer be unable to accept delivery due to transportation problems.

These contracts are attractive if there is a risk that the market might go down, but where it is likely that prices will strengthen. The agreed upon minimum price will be less than the price that the producer could contemporaneously tie down in a cash forward contract. In effect, the "cost" to the farmer under a minimum price contract is the buyer's cost to protect itself in the commodity options markets against price rises. The contract will specify how to determine any increase from the minimum price. One method is to set the final purchase price on a particular day at the higher of (a) the minimum price or (b) the price of a specific futures contract delivery month, less a predetermined basis. The day will be chosen by the seller, subject to a final day on which the contract must be priced.

5. Enforceability of Oral Cash Forward Contracts

a. Confirmatory Memoranda

Typically, a producer will telephone a buyer for a price quote and agree over the phone to sell a certain amount of product. The buyer will send a written confirmation to the producer asking that it be signed and returned within 10 days. Sometimes the confirmation is not signed by the producer. In cases where the price of the commodity has gone up substantially between the making of the alleged oral contract and the performance date, buyers have sued to enforce favorable contracts. As a defense, farmers assert the UCC statute of frauds which requires some "signed writing" if the deal is to be enforceable.

Contracts for the sale of goods are governed by UCC Article 2. Section 2-201(1) provides that any contract for the sale of goods over $500 is not enforceable "unless there is some writing sufficient to indicate that a contract for sale has been made between the parties and signed by the party against whom enforcement is sought . . .." An exception to this rule applies when both seller and buyer are "merchants." Under § 2-201(2) a merchant (e.g., farmer?) cannot assert the statute of frauds as a defense to an oral sale contract with another merchant (e.g., grain dealer) if written confirmation of the oral contract is received (e.g., by the farmer seller) within a reasonable time and is not objected to by the recipient within 10 days after receipt.

The duration of a reasonable time depends on the nature, purpose and circumstances of such action. UCC § 1-204(2). One month was unreasonable in Cargill, Inc. v. Stafford (10th Cir.1977)(40,000 bu. wheat). Written confirmation 10 weeks after an oral contract for the sale of hay was reasonable as a matter of law in Azevedo v. Minister (Nev.1970).

A written confirmation does not establish the terms of the oral contract of sale, but merely removes the statute of frauds defense. The confirmation need not set out all contract terms, except that it must identify the quantity. Of course, even if the farmer is held to be a merchant, the buyer cannot prevail unless the existence and terms of the alleged oral contract of sale are proved.

If the farmer is not a "merchant," the confirmation doctrine does not apply and the farmer can rely upon the statute of frauds defense. The dispositive issue is whether the farmer is a merchant. The UCC definition is at § 2-104 (1), (3):

> (1) "Merchant" means a person who deals in goods of the kind or otherwise by his occupation holds himself out as having knowledge or skill peculiar to the practices or goods involved in the transaction . . . (3) "Between merchants" means. . . any transaction with respect to which both parties are chargeable with the knowledge or skill of merchants.

Whether a farmer is a merchant is a much litigated issue. Courts are divided and the answer varies depending on the jurisdiction and the facts of the case. Illustrative of cases holding that a farmer is a merchant is Nelson v. Union Equity Cooperative Exchange (Tex.1977), where the court so classified Nelson, a farmer who sold cotton and wheat produced on his 1200 acre farm. Nelson had for the previous five years sold all of his production and had daily kept abreast of the current market prices and conditions by talking to grain dealers and listening to the radio. Arguably, Nelson was a typical or average farmer in southwestern Oklahoma. On the other hand, the court in Terminal Grain Corp. v. Freeman (S.D.1978), concluded that "the average

farmer . . . with no particular knowledge or experience in selling, buying, or dealing in future
commodity transactions, and who sells only the
crops he raises to local elevators for cash or who
places his grain in storage under one of the federal
loan programs is not a 'merchant.'"

The term "merchant" is a technical term and its
meaning as contemplated by the drafters of Article 2
arguably is vastly different from the narrow and
stereotypical concepts used by the courts. Official
Comment 2 to § 2-104 on the letter of confirmation
exception to the statute of frauds points out that
letters of confirmation and the like rest upon normal
business practices, such as answering mail, which are
familiar to any person in business. Therefore, under
the merchant language of § 2-104, "almost every
person in the business would . . . be deemed to be a
merchant . . .." This does not mean that a farmer is
a merchant as a matter of law, but an argument can
be made that answering mail -- responding to a
confirmation memorandum -- is a "non-specialized
business practice" that ought to be typical of and
familiar to anyone in business, including farmers.

The jury instruction in Colorado-Kansas Grain v.
Reifschneider (Colo.Ct.App.1991) is representative:

> In reaching its determination, a trier of fact
> should consider the following as well as any
> other relevant factors: (1) the length of time
> the farmer has been engaged in the practice
> of selling his product to the marketers of his
> product; (2) the degree of business acumen
> shown by the farmer in his dealing with
> other parties; (3) the farmer's awareness of

the operation and existence of farm markets; and (4) the farmer's past experience with or knowledge of the customs and practices which are unique to the particular marketing of the product which he sells. (citations omitted). *Id.* at 817 P.2d p. 640.

Even in cases holding farmers not to be merchants, the doctrine of estoppel sometimes protects buyers. In Decatur Coop. Ass'n v. Urban (Kan. 1976), the court noted: "the statute of frauds was enacted to prevent fraud and injustice, not to foster or encourage it, and a court of equity will not ordinarily permit its use as a shield to protect fraud or to enable one to take advantage of his own wrong." 547 P.2d at 329. To win, the grain dealer must prove that it changed its position in reliance upon the farmer's conduct, that the farmer knew or reasonably should have known that the dealer would sell forward what it had contracted to buy from the farmer, and that nonperformance by the farmer was based solely upon the farmer's desire to profit in a rising market. However, many courts do not allow estoppel as an exception to the statute of frauds. See, e.g., Cox. v. Cox, (Ala.1974); Farmland Service Coop. v. Klein (Neb.1976). This reluctance may result in part because of the need to use merchant like elements in the estoppel analysis in cases where the court would hold the farmer not to be a merchant under the UCC.

There are times when a farmer might find it beneficial to affirmatively claim merchant status. Suppose Feedlot orally agrees on August 20 to buy 5000 bushels of corn from Farmer at $3 a bushel for delivery on or before October 1. Three days later

Farmer sends a letter to Feedlot confirming the deal. One month later when harvest is underway, the cash price of corn drops to $2 a bushel. Feedlot purchases the 5000 bushels of corn from another supplier and does not accept delivery of and refuses to pay for Farmer's corn. If the farmer can claim merchant status, the protection of UCC § 2-201(2), which dispenses with the need for a signed writing from feedlot, will govern as both parties are merchants.

b. Price Increases

Forward contracts specifying a price that turns out to be much lower than the spot price at delivery time are generally enforceable and not unconscionable under UCC § 2-302. This section provides that any clause that is unconscionable at the time a contract is made is unenforceable. The UCC does not define the term, but the general rule is that unforeseen and unexpected price increases do not raise the specter of unconscionability. Rather, the test is "whether, in light of the general commercial background and the commercial needs of the particular trade or case, the clauses involved are so one-sided as to be unconscionable under the circumstances existing at the time of the making of the contract." Bradford v. Plains Cotton Coop. Ass'n (10th Cir.1976).

c. Casualty to Crop

Another enforcement issue arises when a farmer has forward contracted to deliver a specific quantity of goods, but cannot perform because his or her crops have been destroyed by casualty caused by hail, wind, insects, or drought. Two sections of the UCC, §§ 2-613, 2-615, may excuse the farmer's performance.

Under § 2-613 a casualty to the goods specified in a contract may excuse performance if the casualty is not caused by the negligence or wilful fault of the seller. When the contract describes the land on which the sold commodity is to be grown, drought, excess rain and the like can cause casualty that excuses performance. Dunavant Enterprises, Inc. v. Ford, (Miss.1974). Conversely, when a contract identifies the commodity only by kind and amount, weather problems causing crop shortfalls do not excuse performance unless the contract specifically so provides. Bunge Corp. v. Recker (8th Cir.1975). Generally, buyers do not make contracts to buy commodities which are to be produced on specifically described fields.

Failure to deliver will be excused under UCC § 2-615(a) if performance is "made impracticable by the occurrence of a contingency the non-occurrence of which was a basic assumption on which the contract was made . . ." and seller seasonably notifies the buyer that it will receive less product than expected. Under this section, the intervening condition preventing performance must not have been contemplated by the parties. In Alimenta (U.S.A.), Inc. v. Cargill, Inc. (11th Cir.1988) Cargill contracted to deliver peanuts to Alimenta, but due to a drought was unable to buy a sufficient supply from producers to perform. Cargill was excused under the impracticability test of § 2-615. The drought was considered to have been unforeseeable in part because there were no facts to indicate that it was likely to occur and cause a production shortfall. Also, for the preceding 20 years there had been surplus production of peanuts.

The foreseeability issue can arise in other contexts. In Jenson v. Haynes (Mo.Ct.App.1982) a farm tenant's cash rent payment was not excused, even though the farm flooded. Natural disasters were held to be risks assumed by the tenant as evidenced in part by the fact that tenant had taken out crop insurance. Usually, disagreements about foreseeability involve questions of fact.

B. Commodity Futures Trading

1. Commodity Exchanges

Standardized contracts for delivery of a variety of commodities are traded on a number of exchanges located in North America. 17 CFR § 1.3(e)(1994). Boards of Trade (futures markets), like stock exchanges, have members with trading privileges. Members are typically engaged in marketing or processing commodities, or are futures commission merchants (FCMs) whose principal activity is to clear trades for non-members. A farmer who wants to trade will use a FCM or its agent.

North American exchanges important to agriculture include the Chicago Board of Trade (trades grain -- wheat, oats, corn, soybeans, soybean meal and oil; iced broilers; and plywood); Chicago Mercantile Exchange (trades the meat complex -- pork bellies, feeder cattle, live cattle, live hogs, turkeys, imported boneless beef; eggs; Idaho potatoes; lumber; and butter); Kansas City Board of Trade (trades winter wheat); Minneapolis Grain Exchange (trades wheat; oats; and sunflowers); and New York Cotton Exchange (trades cotton; frozen orange juice concentrate; crude oil; and propane). The Mid-American Commodity Exchange trades smaller contracts than do most others -- 1000 rather than 5000 bushel contracts for corn, oats, soybeans and wheat.

All exchanges have rules about the type and amount of a commodity covered by a contract, and about minimum and maximum price fluctuations. The quality of a traded commodity is controlled by the exchange and all contracts for a particular commodity are identical, e.g. No. 1 hard red wheat. Futures contracts are confined to specific months. The months "for future delivery" (e.g., Sept., Dec., March, May, and July) correspond generally with months associated with planting, harvesting and exporting the commodity. Federal regulatory authority over futures markets is vested in the Commodity Futures Trading Commission (CFTC) by the Commodity Exchange Act (CEA). 7 USCA §§ 1-25.

2. The Futures Contract

A futures contract is a standardized agreement used by the particular exchange for a set amount (e.g. 5,000 bu. of wheat of a particular class and grade; 30,000 lbs. of broilers; 50,000 lbs. of cotton). A trader enters the market as a seller by making promises that fill in the "two blanks" in the standardized contract -- *to make future delivery* of the commodity on a specific date and to be paid a stated price (per bu. or other unit). A trader enters the market as a buyer by making promises that fill in the same "two blanks" -- agreeing *to take future delivery* on a specified date and to pay a stated price. Note that the price is set when the trader enters the market, not when trading closes, and not at the delivery date. A contract for September delivery is often called a "September futures". The trader who sells is described as "long" while the trader who buys is "short." While two trades are essential, they do not result in a contract between a particular seller and buyer. Futures contracts do not represent the commodity as such, but rather the right to obtain ownership or the duty to make delivery in the future. Title to the commodity is not locked in a futures contract as it is in a negotiable warehouse receipt.

Although a futures contract involves a promise to make or accept physical delivery at a future date, the holder of a contract typically liquidates his or her position before "deliver time." The liquidation, or offset, involves the trader doing the opposite of the original transaction. Thus, to get out of the market, a trader who bought one July 1995 Kansas City Board of Trade wheat contract will sell one July 1995 Kansas City wheat contract before trading is closed on July 1995 contracts. This eliminates the need to accept delivery of the commodity. Note that a trader has independent movement in and out of the market -- no need to transact business with another trader. However, there must be an opposite trans-action by a trader who sold one July 1995 contract and who then buys one contract to exit the market.

A trader who sells a contract does run some risk of not being able to exit the market by an offsetting transaction. Sometimes a trader who is "long" wants the actual commodity -- e.g. a processor who will pay less by pursuing the transaction in the futures market to physical delivery, rather than buying on the spot market. A trader who sold can wait until too close to delivery time and be unable to exit the market because there can be no opposite transaction. Sellers who get caught must deliver the actual commodity either by transporting same to the terminal elevator (Chicago for CBT), or by endorsing over a negotiable warehouse receipt issued by the terminal warehouse.

3. Who Trades in Futures and Why?

Two broad categories of traders are active in futures markets: speculators and hedgers. Speculators voluntarily risk capital with the expectation of making profits. They seek to buy contracts when the market is low and to sell when it is high, regardless of the order of their transactions. Speculators are essential if there is to be hedging.

Hedging is a protective procedure designed to minimize losses from adverse price movements. Only persons who actually produce or buy the commodity can hedge. To enter a true hedge, one takes a position in the futures market that will offset losses, should they occur in the actual sale or purchase of that commodity. Essential to hedging transactions are speculators, who risk capital with the expectation of making profits. An assumption underlying hedging is that the futures and the cash prices will move up or down roughly parallel to one another.

Hedging strategy varies depending on whether the hedger expects to sell or to buy the actual commodity in regular markets. A "short" hedge involves selling one or more futures contracts to reduce the risk of possible decline in market value of a like amount of the actual commodity already owned or growing. This hedger could be a grain dealer or a farmer. Conversely, a "long" hedge involves the purchase of one or more future contracts to reduce loss should there be an escalation in the cost of the actual commodity required by the hedger for feeding or processing. We focus on the short hedge.

Example: *Farmer with crop in field phones dealer in Sept. and agrees to sell 5,000 bu. at $2.70 with delivery and payment in 3 months in December (Dec.). The $2.70 is not the current Sept. spot price - rather the dealer checks the Dec. futures price on the pertinent Board of Trade (BT), $3.30 per bu., and subtracts its basis of 60¢ to get $2.70. The short hedge is then entered in September, with 1 contract (K) equal to 5,000 bu.:*

Grain Dealer sells 1 Dec. futures K at $3.30   *Speculator buys 1 Dec. futures K at $3.30*

Three months later in Dec. the BT price is $3.10 and the local spot price is $2.50. $3.10 - .60 = $2.50.

Grain Dealer buys 1 Dec. futures K at $3.10   *Speculator sells 1 Dec. futures K at $3.10*

The speculator loses 20¢ a bu. ($1,000) and the dealer makes 20¢ a bu. ($1,000) on the futures transaction - a zero sum game. To profit you buy low and sell high, or sell high and buy low. [Brokers fees not reflected here.]

What are the implications of this example? The farmer makers physical delivery of the commodity to the grain dealer in December as agreed. The farmer gets $2.70 per bu. under the cash forward contract even though the spot price at December delivery is $2.50. Thereafter, the dealer in Dec. sells the commodity purchased from the farmer to the terminal market at $3.10 per bu. and makes 40¢ per bu., 20¢ less than originally anticipated. However, with the 20¢ profit from the hedge in the futures market the dealer has recovered its basis of 60¢ -- its goal. Without the hedge the dealer would have had, from its perspective, a 20¢ per bu. loss from the transaction with the farmer. Observe again that the speculator lost in this example -- buying high at $3.30 a bu. and selling low at $3.10 a bu. *Now, rework the example with the same cash forward contract price, the same futures contract price as of Sept., but a $3.50 futures contract price in Dec.* Do you see why the farmer and the grain dealer come out the same financially? Note that the speculator now "wins".

Example: *Farmer could have forgone the cash forward contract, entered a short hedge in Sept., sold the commodity at the spot price of $2.50 in Dec. and have come out with $2.70, given the gain of 20¢ in the futures market. This is illustrated by inserting farmer for dealer in the above example.*

For the speculator the strategy is always the same, whether it is a buy on the other side of a short hedge, or a sell on the other side of a long hedge. That strategy is to buy low and sell high, regardless of the order of the transactions.

4. Hedging Risks

A farmer who hedges a high percentage of an anticipated crop risks financial loss if yields are low or the crop is lost. This is because losses from the short position in the futures market will not be offset by gains in the sale of the actual commodity. The farmer becomes a speculator as to the shortage.

There are further risks. A trader in futures does not have to put up the face value of the contract(s). But, if the contract moves against the trader -- as it did for the speculator in our example at p. 149 -- the trader will have to add to her deposit, a margin call. Thus, whether it is a farmer or a grain dealer doing the hedge, financing for a margin call must be arranged in advance. Otherwise, the trader may be forced out of the market at an inopportune time. In our example, the market movement caused the speculator to lose $1,000.

Another risk for the hedger is that the basis will widen. In our example, the basis set by the local grain dealer was 60¢. If the farmer (not the grain dealer) had not forward contracted, but had entered the short hedge, he would have made 20¢ in the futures market. And, having sold at a spot price of $2.50, he would have realized $2.70 per bu. Had the local grain dealer decided in Nov. to widen its basis from 60¢ to 70¢ the local price in Dec. would have been $2.40 and the farmer would have realized only $2.60 per bu.

Because of the large size of each contract on most exchanges and the risks just noted, relatively few farmers hedge. But many farmers benefit from hedges routinely entered by others -- as in our example at p. 149. Without the hedge, our hypothetical grain dealer would have been unlikely to tinker with financial suicide by contracting three months in advance to a cash price of $2.70.

CHAPTER FIVE

CROP AND LIVESTOCK FINANCING
I. INTRODUCTION

Farm debt is commonly divided into two categories: real estate (see Ch. 2) and non-real estate. Non-real estate farm debt is usually secured by collateral such as crops, livestock and farm equipment. Questions about a lender's ability to realize on non-real estate collateral are governed for the most part by Article 9 of the Uniform Commercial Code (UCC).

II. SECURED TRANSACTIONS

In all states, security interests in personal property are governed by Article 9 of the UCC. Do note that state legislatures have modified many sections of Article 9 and have thus undermined its uniformity.

Article 9 has a language of its own. The person granting credit may become a "secured party" by contracting for a "security interest" in property called "collateral," which secures the obligation of the debtor. The contract is a "security agreement." Security interest is "an interest in personal property or fixtures which secures payment or performance of an obligation." UCC § 1-201(37). Consider this illustration. Suppose F wants to borrow $10,000 from B to buy hybrid seed. B requires that the anticipated crop secure the loan. In Article 9 language, B is the secured party, F is the debtor, the planted crop is the collateral, B's interest in the crop to secure payment is a security interest, and the agreement creating the security interest is the security agreement. UCC §§ 1-201, 9-105.

The creation of an enforceable security interest requires more than a well-drafted security agreement. The secured party must give value and the debtor must have rights in the collateral. Once these three requirements are satisfied "attachment" has occurred, i.e. the security interest has attached to the property described in the security agreement. Unlike an unsecured general creditor who must win a civil judgment, obtain a writ of execution and have the sheriff levy execution upon available non-exempt property, the secured party has the right, upon default, to repossess or replevy collateral. The remedies under Article 9 usually are less costly and less time consuming than the civil judgment process. To achieve maximum protection, the secured party must "perfect" its security interest. In most cases this requires some step beyond attachment such as filing a financing statement or taking physical possession of the collateral. The perfected secured party usually prevails against the debtor's trustee in bankruptcy, and other creditors.

III. SCOPE OF ARTICLE 9

A. Generally

Before discussing cases where Article 9 has clear application, we consider situations where there has been dispute over the scope of its application. While real estate transactions are not governed by Article 9, a question does arise about its application when the flow of payments under an installment land contract is assigned by the seller to a lender as collateral. Scope issues also arise when standing crops are on land subjected to contract forfeiture or real estate mortgage foreclosure. Section 9-102 provides:

(1) Except as otherwise provided in . . . section 9-104 on excluded transactions, this Article applies (a) to any transaction (regardless of its form) which is intended to create a security interest in personal property or fixtures including goods, documents, instruments, general intangibles, chattel papers or accounts.

(3) The application of this Article to a security interest in a secured obligation is not affected by the fact that the obligation is itself secured by a transaction or interest to which this Article does not apply.

Section 9-104(j) states:

This Article does not apply . . . except to the extent that provision is made for fixtures in Section 9-313, to the creation or transfer of an interest in or lien on real estate, including a lease or rents thereunder.

Article 9 applies to any voluntary transaction, regardless of form, which is intended to create a security interest in personal property or fixtures. Personal property includes goods, documents of title such as warehouse receipts, instruments such as promissory notes, accounts receivable, and general intangibles such as contract rights.

B. Land Contract Payments

A scope issue arises when a contract seller of real estate under an installment land contract borrows money and assigns as collateral future contract payments. Clearly, the collateral in this secured transaction is not the real estate. Rather, it is the contract seller's right to receive a flow of payments.

This right to receive payments is personal property and when assigned to the lender does not involve transfer of any interest in the real estate. UCC § 9-102(3), Comment 4. Thus, the attachment, perfection and priority rules of Article 9 apply. Attachment can be established by the written assignment of the flow of contract payments. Perfection must be achieved by filing a financing statement inasmuch as the payments are either general intangibles or accounts receivable. In addition to filing a financing statement describing the flow of payments, the prudent lender will take possession of the installment land contract should it be found to be a negotiable instrument. Security interests in instruments can be perfected only by possession. UCC §§ 9-304(1), 9-105(1)(i). A prudent lender will also take an enforceable interest under state real estate law in the seller's residual interest in the underlying real estate -- protection should the buyer default on the land contract.

C. Standing Crops

Under real property rules a buyer of real estate acquires growing crops unless there is an agreement to the contrary. Standing crops are part of the realty and pass to the purchaser. Given the advent of Article 9, questions have arisen in several situations as to whether real estate law continues to apply or whether the UCC now governs: seller of land on contract repossesses land with growing crops subject to a perfected security interest of another; mortgagee forecloses real estate mortgage and claims growing crops that are subject to the perfected security interest of another; and, mortgagee claims an interest in growing crops when the farmer debtor files a bankruptcy petition. Pre-Article 9 cases hold that crops unharvested at the time of a real estate foreclosure are part of the real estate and pass with the land at foreclosure. Today, it seems clear that a real estate lender wanting an interest in growing crops must comply with Article 9. This is true in all of the situations just set out.

Section 9-102(1)(a)) states that Article 9 applies "to any transaction which is intended to create a security interest in personal property . . . including goods . . .." The definition of "goods" at UCC § 9-105 includes growing crops. Also, a reference to growing crops is found in UCC § 9-203 which governs attachment and enforceability of security interests. As to harvested crops, the secured party need not file in real estate records. Thus, it is clear that the drafters intended growing crops to be treated as personal property for collateral purposes.

Consider U.S. v. Newcomb (8th Cir.1982), where in May 1978, N sold land to R on a contract for deed. The contract made no reference to crops. In the same month, R granted to the former Farmers Home Administration (FmHA) a security interest in soybeans to be grown on the land. A financing statement was properly filed. In July 1978, R was evicted from the land for failure to make contract payments. At the time of the eviction, the soybeans described in FmHA's security agreement were growing on the land. N harvested the crop and refused to pay anything to FmHA. The government sued N to recover the proceeds of the beans. Concluding that Article 9 applied because the growing crops were personal property rather than part of the real estate, the court held for FmHA. N should have perfected an Article

9 interest in growing and harvested crops to secure payments due under the land contract.

Article 9 does not, however, deal with all conflicts between holders of security interests in crops and third parties. For example, it does resolve the priority status of holders of certain statutory crop liens. UCC §§ 9-102(2); 9-104(j). See pp. 203-04 *infra*.

D. Leases of Equipment and Livestock

Leasing of farm equipment and dairy cows sometimes raises Article 9 scope issues. The interest of a "true lessor" in the cows or equipment is not an Article 9 security interest. However, if a transaction clothed in lease terminology is not a lease but in reality an installment sale -- with the "lessor" in effect retaining "title" to secure the obligation of the "lessee"-- Article 9 governs. UCC § 9-102 (1)(a). The "label" placed on the transaction by the parties is not determinative. Prior to 1987, the definition of a security interest in UCC § 1-201(37) provided little guidance as to what transactions were true leases and what were secured transactions. When Article 2A, governing true leases, was added to the UCC in 1987, the definition of security interest at § 1-201(37) was amended. The revised definition, adopted in more than 25 states, sets forth much clearer tests for determining whether a transaction is a true lease or a disguised secured transaction.

When a "lease" proves to be a secured transaction, Article 9 rules about attachment, perfection and priority apply. Often, perfection will not have been accomplished by a befuddled "lessor." This problem can be obviated if the "lessor" files a financing statement pursuant to UCC § 9-408. Such a filing will not be a factor in a dispute over the substance of the transaction, but if the "lease" is found to be a secured transaction, the interest of the "lessor"/seller will be perfected.

IV. FARM PRODUCTS AS COLLATERAL

Article 9 contemplates several classes of collateral. We first consider the class called goods, which breaks down into four types, one of which is farm products. UCC § 9-109(3). The other three types of goods are consumer goods, equipment, and inventory. UCC § 9-109(1),(2),(4). It is essential to know the type of goods involved when describing collateral in a security agreement or financing statement, when perfecting, and when assessing the status of a buyer of the collateral vis-a-vis the secured party. In some jurisdictions the rules governing attachment and perfection of a security interest in farm products are not the same as those for other goods. And, special rules govern conflicts between secured parties and buyers of collateral, when the collateral is farm products.

The Code definition of farm products at § 9-109(3) has three elements, all of which must be present: (1) the goods must be "crops or livestock or supplies used or produced in farming operations or . . . products of crops or livestock in their unmanufactured states" . . . (2) in the possession of a debtor (3) who must be "engaged in raising, fattening, grazing, or other farming operations." Some states have amended the definition to include fish grown for sale on any fish farm. The UCC does not define the terms crops, livestock, possession, or farming operations. If crops or livestock are not farm products they generally will be inventory for Article 9 purposes. UCC § 9-109(4).

The first criterion presents little difficulty. Crops include such commodities as feed grains (corn, grain sorghum, and oats), soybeans, rice, cotton, wheat, hay, vegetables, nuts and fruits. Crops can be growing crops or crops to be grown. It is not clear, however, whether harvested crops are products of crops, or whether the term "crops" is sufficiently broad to include them. The term livestock includes all types of domestic animals -- e.g. cattle, swine, sheep and chickens -- as well as their unborn young. It is reasonable to argue that domestic fish should be classed as livestock in those states that have not amended UCC § 9-109(3) to that effect.

The possession test can be more difficult to apply. Possession issues arise when a debtor-farmer stores grain in a public warehouse, places cattle in a commercial feedlot for fattening, or consigns live-stock to a selling agent. The Code does not define possession and the intent of the drafters is not clear. If possession means physical possession by the farmer-debtor, the goods in the examples just given would be inventory, not farm products. But, the absence of the word "physical" in UCC § 9-103(3) suggests a broader interpretation, as do other UCC sections. For example, § 9-305 reads: "[i]f such collateral other than goods covered by a negotiable document is held by a bailee, the secured party is deemed to have possession from the time the bailee receives notification of the secured party's interest."

In the public warehouse and commercial feedlot examples, bailor/bailee relationships exist. The farmer, upon storing grain in a warehouse, usually receives a warehouse receipt. The stored grain is owned by the farmer who pays storage fees and decides when to sell. In the feedlot case, the debtor normally owns the animals, decides when to sell, bears the risk of animal loss, and pays the feedlot for services and feed consumed. In both examples there is a strong case for constructive possession.

Because possession is not defined in the Code, UCC § 1-103 makes relevant the state common law. Courts recognize and distinguish actual possession, constructive possession, and custody. Some cases hold that an owner may relinquish physical custody, but retain legal possession. Jacobson v. Aetna Casualty & Surety Co. (Minn.1951). Some courts have declined to limit the definition to "physical possession." In re Roberts (Bankr.Kan.1984); Oxford PCA v. Dye (Miss.1979). *Contra*, In re Walkington (Bankr.W.D.Mich.1986).

With regard to the possession issue, Comment 4 to UCC § 9-109(3) states:

> When crops or livestock or their products come into the possession of a person not engaged in farming operations they cease to be "farm products". If they come into the possession of a marketing agency for sale or distribution or of a manufacturer or processor as raw materials, they become inventory.

One of the architects of Article 9 states that "goods cease to be 'farm products' when they are subjected to any manufacturing operation . . . or when they move from the possession **and** ownership of a farmer to that of a non-farmer." I. Gilmore p. 374 (1965) [emphasis added]. Consistent with Gilmore, the court in First National Bank in Lenox v. Lamoni Livestock Sales Co. (Iowa 1987) held that livestock remain farm products when they are transferred physically by a farmer to a marketing agency for sale because the possession of a marketing agency interpretation in Comment 4 is not pertinent when the agency does not itself take ownership.

Courts have defined "farming operations" in various ways. Some have construed the term narrowly to mean a conventional farm and not farm-related or farm-like activities. In re Collins (Bankr.D.S.C. 1980). Other courts have construed the term quite broadly. In re K.L. Smith Enterprises, Ltd. (Bankr. D.Colo.1980). Some opinions do not define the term and apparently apply the principle that "I know it when I see it." See, e.g., Oxford PCA. v. Dye (Miss.1979). In the ordinary case, when the debtor lives on the land and is engaged in the production of crops or the raising or fattening of cattle for slaughter, the "farming operation" is obvious. All cases, however, are not so clear. In some instances, the goods produced are not associated with traditional farming, such as the raising and marketing of catfish. Arguably, such fish are livestock, and the debtor's purpose is raising or fattening livestock. Accordingly, a court should hold the fish to be farm products. Some states have amended UCC § 9-109(3) specifically to so provide. See, e.g., Ark. Code Ann. 4-9-109(3). Contrast the pet shop that buys fish for immediate resale. Such fish are the inventory of the pet shop.

Mechanized agricultural operations can present a farming operations issue even when the collateral is animals and commodities usually associated with production agriculture. The court in In re K.L. Smith Enterprises, Ltd., p. 161 *supra,* had to determine whether layer hens and eggs were farm products, given the facts. The court reasoned that the hens were "livestock" and the eggs were "products of livestock." It was also determined that the debtor was engaged in "farming operations." In so holding, the court rejected the bank's argument that the eggs lost their characterization as farm products because the debtor's sole business was the sophisticated, mechanized production of eggs, and because no one was living where the egg production units were located. The bank argued that the debtor's business was not a traditional farming operation and that the collateral was inventory. The court rejected a definition restricted to "traditional farms" and referred to cattle feeding operations and tree nurseries as illustrations of modern farming operations, Consequently, describing the eggs as "inventory" and the chickens as "equipment" was wrong and the security agreement failed to describe any collateral. Attachment, therefore, did not occur.

Cattle feedlots and similar operations raise the farm products versus inventory issue. Clearly, cattle in the possession of one whose sole business is livestock feeding are farm products. Cattle in the hands of a cattle trader whose sole business is marketing are inventory. What is unclear is the type of livestock collateral held by a debtor who not only fattens animals, but also trades or markets them. Arguably, the issue is whether *particular* animals are inventory and the principal test is whether they are held for immediate sale. When the debtor holds certain animals past sale opportunities and its profit depends on fattening and sale, or the production and sale of progeny, a farming operation exists and the animals are farm products.   In sharp contrast is the court that, upon finding the debtor to be a marketing agency, considers *all* animals in debtor's possession to be inventory even though some of them are being fattened.   Farmers State Bank v. Webel (Ill.1983).

V. ATTACHMENT

Under UCC § 9-203, attachment occurs when value is given, the debtor has rights in the collateral, and the debtor signs a security agreement creating a security interest in properly described collateral.

A. Value

Value is defined at UCC § 1-201(44):

> . . . a person gives "value" for rights if he acquires them (a) in return for a binding commitment to extend credit or for the extension of immediately available credit . . . ; or (b) as security for or in total or partial satisfaction of a pre-existing claim; . . . or (d) generally, in return for any consideration sufficient to support a simple contract.

B. Rights in the Collateral

Because the UCC does not clearly define "rights in the collateral", this requirement is a source of problems.   An owner has rights in property, while a thief who has mere possession does not.   Yet, a UCC debtor does not have to be an owner to create an enforceable security interest. UCC § 9-112. So, it is not clear what relationships with collateral on the continuum between actual ownership and mere possession establish rights sufficient to allow debtors to create security interests. The power can be statutory as in UCC § 2-403(1)(b). It can reside in rules of agency, fraud, and estoppel as well as other common law rules. Section 1-103 says that, unless displaced by specific UCC provisions, principles of law and equity may supplement its provisions.

Assume that the debtor farms one tract on a crop-share lease and another on a cash lease. The debtor clearly has rights in all of the crop growing on cash rented land, as well as to that portion of the crop to which the debtor is entitled under the share lease. As to the landlord's share of the crop, modern cases in some states hold title to the *entire* crop to be in tenant subject to the duty to deliver postharvest to the landlord in payment of rent. In such jurisdictions Pedersen argues that landlord should take a security interest to secure payment of rent, even if share landlord is expressly protected by a state statutory landlord's lien. See p. 204 *infra.* Meyer believes such tenant to lack rights in the collateral and that the only sensible interpretation under Article 9 is that landlord can grant a security interest in her share of the growing crop. Case law in some states does hold that share landlord has sufficient rights to grant a security interest. See, e.g., Colorado Nat'l Bank-Longmont v. Fegan (Kan.Ct.App.1992)(share landlord has ownership interest in growing crop).

A practical problem as to rights in collateral arises when the debtor is a commercial feedlot operator. Often some of the cattle in the lot are not owned by the operator, but by persons who have hired the operator to fatten them. Generally, a debtor cannot grant a security interest in animals it does not own, but holds only as bailee for the limited purpose of fattening. National Livestock Credit Corp. v. First State Bank of Harrah (Okla.Ct.App.1972); UCC § 1-103. However, if the operator is authorized to sell the animals without consulting the owner and if the animals are not specifically identified, the operator/debtor probably has the power to create a security interest in animals, even thought they are owned by another. And, the owner probably is estopped to deny the creation of such security interest. Here the amount of control exercised by the feetlot operator appears to be determinative.

Another example arises when a farmer sells grain to an elevator and receives a bad check. A lender with a perfected security interest in the elevator's inventory will argue that this grain has become part thereof. Under UCC § 2-403(1)(b) the elevator has voidable title and the power to transfer good title to a good faith purchaser for value. Given this power, the elevator can create the security interest in question. Samuels & Co. v. Mahon (5th Cir.1976).

C. Description of Collateral

1. *Generally*

An adequate collateral description in a security agreement is critical if there is to be attachment. Courts generally are unwilling to second guess ambiguous descriptions by examining the conduct of the parties. Under UCC § 9-110 a description is adequate if it reasonably identifies the collateral. The UCC does not require that an agreement include statutory terminology. For example, in K.L. Smith

Enterprises, Ltd., pp. 161-62 *supra,* the Bank could
have avoided the attachment problem had it described the collateral in non-code terms --"all hens and
eggs presently owned or hereafter acquired", instead
of "all equipment and inventory." While the use of
the term "farm products" is not required, this does
not mean that the drafter of documents for a secured
transaction can be oblivious to the proper classification of collateral. Classification mistakes can lead to
filing errors and to misapprehension of the rights of
buyers of the collateral.

2. *Livestock Descriptions*

Unless the parties intend to limit the reach of a
security interest, the description should be inclusive
and might read "all livestock of whatever type or
kind wherever located" or "all currently owned
livestock including but not limited to cows, breeding
stock, steers, unborn, bulls and any replacements or
livestock obtained in the future." If a more specific
description is used, the lender must be very familiar
with the debtor's operation. Unlike crop security
agreements, no real estate description is required.

Livestock descriptions have been the source of
much litigation. The 5th Circuit was confronted with
a security agreement describing the collateral as "all
livestock . . . now owned or hereafter acquired by
Debtor, together with all increases, replacements,
substitutions, and additions thereto." The court
liberally construed the language and held that it
reasonably identified hogs owned by the farmer-
debtor at the time the security agreement was entered
into and those that he acquired thereafter, whether
by purchase, procreation or otherwise. U.S. v. South-

east Mississippi Livestock Farmers Ass'n (5th Cir. 1980). In another case, a security agreement describing the collateral as "twenty-four head of Holstein heifers with increase" was sufficient in the abstract. Since additional Holstein heifers were owned by the debtor, a substantial burden fell on the secured party to identify cattle in which its priority existed. U.S. v. Mid-States Sales Co., Inc. (D.Neb. 1971).

Must a livestock description refer to brands, tag numbers, and other identifying marks? A security agreement and a financing statement described the collateral as cattle owned by debtor and branded "W on their right ribs, with an orange ear tag on right ear." In litigation it was concluded that the lender had a perfected security interest in livestock bearing the W brand alone, insinuating that ear tags are not permanent. American Indian Agricultural Credit Consortium v. Ft. Pierre Livestock, Inc. (S.D.1985).

3. *Crop Descriptions*

When a crop description is intended to be all encompassing, it should cover all crops growing or to be grown, all harvested crops wherever stored, and any warehouse receipts (documents of title) or other documents representing storage obligations such as scale or weight tickets. The word "crops" alone will not necessarily be construed to encompass harvested crops, crops to be grown, and documents of title. The same problem exists when the collateral is described only as "farm products."

When growing or future crops are the collateral, the security agreement must include a description of the pertinent real estate. UCC § 9-203(1). The UCC does not require a legal meets and bounds or U.S.

government survey description -- the description need only reasonably identify the land. UCC § 9-110. Typical descriptions that courts have found adequate give the name of the owner of the land, the number of acres, the county, popular name if any -- e.g., Old Stone Place", and the approximate distance from a named town or well-known landmark. See, e.g., U.S. v. Oakley (E.D.Ark.1980); In re Volker (Iowa 1977). But, to avoid problems most lenders use legal descriptions. Caveat: if the legal description is inaccurate, it might not reasonably identify the land and the security interest will not attach. An erroneous section number was held to be fatal. First National Bank in Creston v. Francis (Iowa 1984).

The failure to include a real estate description was not fatal for the secured party in In re Roberts (Bankr.Kan.1984). The court held that crops severed upon harvest become farm products of a type other than growing crops. The real estate description requirement for growing crops is then irrelevant. Because this security agreement covered farm products generally, the lender's security interest attached at harvest. Accord U.S. v. Smith (2d Cir. 1987). Roberts and Smith did not discuss the bankruptcy issue that arises when crops are severed within 90 days of bankruptcy. Because attachment then occurs within that period, the trustee will attack a Roberts type interest as a preferential transfer. 11 USCA § 547 (b), (e)(2)(B).

4. *Proceeds*

Section 9-203(3) states that "[u]nless otherwise agreed a security agreement gives the secured party the rights to proceeds provided by Section 9-306."

The latter reads in part:

> (1) "Proceeds" includes whatever is received upon the sale, exchange, collection or other disposition of collateral or proceeds. Insurance payable by reason of loss or damage to the collateral is proceeds, except to the extent that it is payable to a person other than a party to the security agreement. Money, checks, deposit accounts, and the like are "cash proceeds". All other proceeds are "non-cash proceeds".
>
> (2) Except where this Article otherwise provides, a security interest continues . . . in any *identifiable proceeds* including collections received by the debtor. [Emphasis supplied.]

Proceeds usually do not need to be mentioned in a security agreement, but they must be identifiable. In special situations proceeds should be described in the security agreement as when it is agreed that they are to be deposited by the debtor in a separate bank account reserved for proceeds. Another instance is when the farmer will receive payments for services or products. See, e.g., Fairview State Bank v. Edwards (Okla.1987) (payment for embryos from debtor's cows). The following clause is typical:

> All payments of whatever kind and all rights to payment, including but not limited to payment of money or payment in kind, whether due or to become due and whether or not earned by performance including, but not limited to, accounts, contract rights, revolving fund credits, patronage dividends,

chattel paper, leases, conditional sales contracts, documents, warehouse receipts, weight or scale tickets, instruments, and rights under any government or other loan, reserve, disaster, diversion, deficiency, soil conservation or other production control, conservation, or price or income support program.

Also, it is usual to include a clause describing as collateral the proceeds of insurance on collateral as well as unearned premiums. See UCC § 9-203(3). Caveat: proceeds of federal crop insurance will not be paid to a secured party unless an official FCIC assignment form is filed at the proper USDA office.

D. GOVERNMENT PAYMENTS

To be eligible to receive federal farm program payments, the farmer must meet program requirements and sign a contract wherein the government agrees to make the payments. Depending upon the nature of the farmer's operation and the programs opted for, the farmer will receive deficiency, disaster, diversion, CRP or other payments. See Ch. 1 *supra.* How the payments will be classified under the UCC depends upon whether it is the contract or the payments thereunder which are the collateral. A producer's right to a payment under a government contract, whether earned or unearned, is a general intangible. Actual payments could be proceeds of crops, proceeds of a general intangible, rents or an instrument. Clearly, after the contract is signed, but before any payment is made, the collateral is a general intangible (contract right). UCC § 9-106. Today, under certain federal farm programs the producer sometimes receives part of a payment in cash (check) and the balance in Commodity Credit Corporation (CCC) generic commodity certificates. We first consider cash payments.

If cash payments are considered proceeds, a security agreement need not make specific reference to them. UCC § 9-203(3). And, in most instances a new financing statement will not have to be filed pursuant to UCC § 9-306(3). Careful lenders, however, describe in the security agreement all anticipated government program payments.

Some courts have held that deficiency, disaster and diversion cash payments are proceeds. In In re Munger (9th Cir.1974), the security agreement description of "all crops . . . [and their] proceeds" was sufficient to describe federal farm subsidy payments. *Contra,* In re Kingsley (8th Cir.1989).

Even if the security agreement properly describes government payments, the proceeds must be "identifiable", a concept not defined in the Code. Problems can arise when a producer receives a single payee government check and deposits it in a bank account containing monies from other sources. When a producer bankruptcy occurs, the secured party is entitled only to proceeds deposited in the commingled account within 10 days before the bankruptcy petition is filed. UCC § 9-306(4)(d). This problem is avoided as to cash payments for conservation programs, CRP, feed grains, rice, cotton, wheat and related programs, wool and mohair programs, and feed assistance if the farmer properly assigns the government payments to the secured party who will then receive them directly. 7 CFR pt.

1404 (1994). Form CCC-36 must be completed, signed by lender and producer, and filed in the county ASCS office **prior** to the time the County Committee approves the making of the payment covered by the assignment. Form CCC-36 is essential in addition to a security agreement and financing statement. The assignment is subject to setoff for debts owned by the producer to the federal government, including FmHA. 7 CFR § 1404.6 (1994).

The security agreement and the financing statement must describe both the right to receive government payments and the actual payments. Between the time the farmer signs up for a program and actual receipt of payments, the collateral is a general intangible or an account and must be perfected accordingly. UCC §§ 9-303, 9-203, 9-401-02.

Difficult issues have arisen with the commodity specific certificates used in the 1983 PIK program and the generic commodity certificates sometimes used to make payments under current farm programs. The 1983 certificates allowed farmers and persons who bought the certificates from them to access government stores of the particular commodity. A split of authority exists as to the type of collateral created by 1983 PIK certificates. In re Schmaling (7th Cir.1986)(not proceeds); Osteroos v. Norwest Bank Minot, N.A.(D.N.D.1984) (proceeds).

The generic certificates in use since Feb. 1, 1986 present other problems. They are sometimes used by USDA to make partial non-cash payments to producers who participate in commodity programs and CRP. These certificates, not being commodity specific, state a monetary amount that is due the owner. Processors and exporters often buy the certificates from farmers and redeem them by taking physical delivery of conveniently located CCC commodities. Certificates must be redeemed for commodities or cash by a certain date. The level of use of certificates varies. As of 1992 few were being issued and those were for the cotton programs.

A major issue is whether an enforceable security interest can be taken in generic commodity certificates. On the face of each certificate, paragraph 3 states:

> This certificate shall not be subject to any State law or regulation including but not limited to State statutory and regulatory provisions with respect to commercial paper, security interests, and negotiable instruments. This certificate shall not be encumbered by any lien or other claim, except that of an agency of the United States.

Courts are split as to the validity of this provision. Some hold that Congress intended to preempt state law, but others find no clear evidence of such an intent. 15 USCA § 714b(g); 7 USCA § 1445b-4(b); In re Halls (Bankr.Iowa 1987) (valid); In re George (D.Kan.1990) (invalid). Commodity certificate and payment-in-kind regulations are at 7 CFR §§ 1470.4, .5 (1994). They state that CCC can make payments by the issuance of certificates which may be transferred, exchanged for the inventory of CCC or exchanged for cash - but such certificates cannot be assigned to creditors. Any person may transfer a commodity to any other person. 7 CFR § 1470.4(c) (1994). So, a producer can sell his certificate to A, who can sell it to B. However, the transfer must be for the full amount of the certificate and must be by restrictive endorsement signed by the transferor showing the name of the transferee and the date of the transfer. CCC will not honor any certificate transferred in a manner contrary to these regulations. And, a lender cannot obtain a security interest in a generic certificate -- if the regulations are valid. But, nothing prohibits a lender from requiring a farmer-debtor to personally transfer the actual certificates to the bank whereupon the bank could sell same and apply the proceeds to the farmer's loan.

Even if a security interest could be created in a generic certificate, it is not clear what category of collateral is involved. Possibilities might be a general intangible, a negotiable instrument (UCC § 3-104), or a negotiable document of title (UCC § 7-104). Even though a certificate is for a specific dollar amount, but an obligation payable in something other than money (e.g. grain) is not a negotiable instrument under UCC § 3-104.

VI. PERFECTION

Attachment makes a security interest enforceable against the debtor and allows the secured party to repossess or replevy the collateral. Perfection, however, is required to protect a secured party against competing third parties such as the trustee in the debtor's bankruptcy, other creditors, and purchasers. Perfection occurs when both attachment and any required steps for perfection have been completed. In general, perfection will be achieved in one of these ways: 1) attachment alone in the case of a purchase money security interest in consumer goods; 2) secured creditor taking possession of the collateral; or 3) proper filing of a financing statement (Form UCC-1). Filing usually is the only practical way to perfect when the debtor is a farmer. The key to determining in which office(s) to file is the correct classification of the collateral. Three classifications are encountered when dealing with crops and livestock -- farm products, inventory, and documents of title.

A. Farm Products

Filing rules for farm products vary from state to state and fall into three general categories. In many states, the secured party must file a financing statement in the county in which the debtor resides, so-called local filing. If growing crops or crops to be grown are the collateral and the land is located in a county other than that of debtor's residence, the secured party must file a second financing statement in the county in which the land is located. The secured party may also have to double file if the debtor is incorporated and the land upon which crops are or will be growing is located in a county other than the corporation's place of business. Some states have central filing, i.e., all financing statements are filed in one office. A few states use a combination of local and central filing.

Even if a state has central filing for all farm products and inventory, a secured party is unperfected if it files a financing statement which describes the collateral only as farm products, when it is in fact inventory -- and *vice versa*. Although the financing statement has been filed in the proper office, the description is defective. UCC § 9-402(1).

B. Documents of Title

Documents of title include warehouse receipts. UCC §§ 1-201(15), 9-105. A warehouse receipt will be either negotiable or nonnegotiable. Perfection of a security interest in a nonnegotiable receipt is accomplished in one of three ways: 1) issuance of a receipt in the name of the secured party; 2) warehouse or other bailee's receipt of notification of secured party's interest; 3) filing as to the goods. UCC § 9-304(3). Caveat: because crops stored off the farm might be considered inventory it is prudent to perfect both as farm products and as inventory.

A security interest in a negotiable document of title may be perfected either by filing or by the secured party taking possession of the document. Taking possession of the document clearly is the safest way to perfect. See p. 197 *infra*.

In some instances, a farmer delivering grain for storage will receive only a scale or weight ticket and a settlement sheet to document ownership. Arguably, scale tickets and settlement sheets are documents of title. Section § 1-201(15) which defines documents of title to include warehouse receipts and "any other document which in the regular course of business or financing is treated as adequately evidencing that the person in possession of it is entitled to receive, hold and dispose of the document and the goods it covers." If this argument is accepted, scale tickets and settlement sheets will be treated as nonnegotiable documents of title. See p. 129 *supra*. Because a nonnegotiable document of title does not have title to the good wrapped up in it, perfection of a security interest in the goods would still be essential.

C. General Intangibles, Accounts and Negotiable Instruments

The right to receive government payments is a general intangible and thus the financing statement in most states is to be filed centrally. As long as the collateral is described as the right to receive government payments, no perfection problems will arise. Should a commodity certificate be classified as a negotiable instrument, perfection can occur only if the secured party takes it into possession.

D. Financing Statement

A financing statement is a written document (Form UCC-1) containing the names and addresses of the debtor and secured party, indicating the types or describing the items of collateral, and including the signature of the debtor. Some states require a social security or a federal tax number. Filing is effective for five years. UCC §§ 9-402, 9-403. A filed financing statement provides public notice to other creditors that some or all of the debtor's personal property may be subject to a security interest. The description of the property in the financing statement need not be as detailed as in the security agreement -- mere indication of types of collateral is sufficient. But, controversies can be eliminated if the language in the two documents is the same.

VII. PRIORITIES UNDER ARTICLE 9

A. Generally

Competing parties often claim the same item of collateral. The principal classes of competitors are: 1) perfected secured parties; 2) unperfected secured parties; 3) lien creditors; 4) purchasers or buyers in the ordinary course of business; and 5) the debtor's trustee in bankruptcy. Once the competing parties are identified in a particular case, the points of departure are UCC § 9-201: "[e]xcept as otherwise provided by this Act a security agreement is effective according to its terms between the parties, against purchasers of the collateral and against creditors", *and* § 9-306(2): "[e]xcept where this Article otherwise provides, a security interest continues in collateral notwithstanding sale . . . and also continues in any identifiable proceeds . . . received by the debtor." Exceptions to these rules are commonly applied and appear at UCC § 9-301 (contests between unperfected secured parties and others and rights of lien creditors); UCC §§ 9-307, 9-308, 9-309 (contests between secured parties and certain purchasers of collateral); UCC § 9-310 (contests between perfected secured parties and holders of statutory liens); UCC § 9-312 (contests between/among secured parties claiming same collateral); and UCC § 9-306 (certain priorities as to proceeds).

B. Federal Agency Lenders

In U.S. v. Kimball Foods, Inc. (U.S.Sup.Ct.1979), consideration was given to whether contractual liens arising from certain federal loan programs (FmHA now CFSA, CCC, and SBA) take precedence over private liens. The Court held that federal law controls the government's priority rights, but absent federal legislation, state law that does not discriminate against the federal interest will be used. Thus, the same priority rules apply to private as well as to federal agency security interests. Should a state modify a UCC provision and seek to treat the U.S. less favorably than state or nationally chartered banks, it is unlikely that a court would apply the discriminatory provision of state law against the U.S. See, e.g., the former Arkansas version of § 9-312(2) at Ark. Code Ann. § 4-9-312(2) (1987, Supp. 1987). The discriminatory language as to FmHA was removed in 1989.

C. Federal Farm Products Rule

1. An Historical Perspective

Section 9-301(1)(c) of the UCC gives a buyer of farm products in the ordinary course of business (UCC § 1-201(9)) priority over a holder of an unperfected security interest when the buyer gives value and receives delivery without knowledge of the interest and before it is perfected. There is nothing particularly controversial about this rule. Rather, it was the treatment of holders of perfected security interests in farm products vis-a-vis buyers of such commodities that raised hackles and led Congress in 1985 to take the extraordinary step of preempting UCC § 9-307(1). That section states:

> A buyer in the ordinary course of business . . . other than a person buying farm products from a person engaged in farming operations takes free of a [perfected] security interest created by his seller. . ..

A buyer in the ordinary course is a "person who in good faith and without knowledge that the sale to him is in violation of . . . [a] security interest of a third party in the goods buys in the ordinary course from a person in the business of selling goods of that kind . . .." UCC § 1-201(9). When a farmer buys a combine from an implement dealer or a television from an appliance dealer, the sale to the farmer severs the security interest of the bank that is financing the inventory of combines or televisions.

Under UCC § 9-307(1), a buyer in the ordinary course did not take free of a prior perfected security interest when farm products were bought from a seller engaged in farming operations, who had created the security interest. Thus, when farmers failed to settle with their secured parties, buyers of farm products sometimes had to pay twice -- unless the buyers could show that UCC § 9-306(2) had been satisfied. This section states that "[a] security interest continues in collateral notwithstanding sale . . . unless the disposition was authorized by the secured party in the security agreement or otherwise, and also continues in any identifiable proceeds . . ." Security agreements rarely authorized the sale of farm product collateral free of the security interest. Thus, the crucial words in § 9-306(2) were "or otherwise." Neither the text of the UCC nor the Comments define them and courts generally see the issue to be whether the secured party had in any way authorized the sale. Some courts used common law concepts of waiver or estoppel to find consent. If a sale is "authorized", the secured party cannot seek redress from the buyer on a conversion theory.

The special treatment of sales of collateralized farm products by UCC § 9-307(1) was justified in several ways. Because farmers market farm products through agents or sell to financially sophisticated buyers, it was said to be reasonable to expect these parties to understand the need to check filed financing statements -- a not too difficult task. And, it is generally known that farm lenders expect pay-ment when farm products are marketed given the reality that most farm operations are cyclical and do not generate regular cash flow. Farm lenders, it is well known, commonly have all of their expectations focused on a single sale of a collateralized crop. Another justification related to problems caused by the rule that for proceeds to remain identifiable, the secured party must prevent the farmer from commingling them with other funds. This is difficult for lenders if farmers are paid by a check that is quickly deposited in a general checking account. Under UCC § 9-306(4)(d), the secured party is entitled only to proceeds from the sale of collateral which have been deposited in such an account within 10 days of insolvency proceedings. In re Gibson Products of Arizona (9th Cir.1976).

Buyers and agents argued that the liability imposed under § 9-307(1) could not be justified. Auctioneers and sales barns agreed as they risked exposure for conversion when livestock subject to a perfected security interest were sold without the consent of the lender. The farm products rule, these parties argued, effectively shifted the risk of non-payment to the buyer with a resulting unreasonable interruption of the flow of commerce. While buyers and others could have protected themselves by checking public UCC records, they argued that it was costly and impractical to do so on a transaction by transaction basis. And, farmers typically do not contact buyers in advance of sale dates and thus there was little opportunity to check records. The problem was particularly serious for packers, many of whom buy in multistate markets and were then and continue to be required to pay either immediately or within 24 hours.

2. Federal Preemption

The UCC farm products rule generated much litigation and a variety of legislative responses at the state level. California eliminated the rule. More than 20 states adopted intermediate measures designed to soften, but not to eliminate the rule. Litigation, problems created by increasing non-uniformity of state law, and ongoing buyer dissatisfaction with the situation prompted Congress to enact a federal farm products rule, effective Dec. 23, 1986.

Section 1324 of the Food Security Act of 1985 preempts the farm products rule of UCC § 9-307(1) and related state law governing priority conflicts between secured parties and buyers of farm products and between secured parties and commission or marketing agents. Section 1324 is codified at 7 USCA § 1631. The purpose of § 1631 is to afford protection to parties who buy or sell farm products that are subject to perfected security interests. The federal law does not change UCC attachment and perfection requirements and they continue to be governed by the pertinent state law.

Section 1631 might be called a strict priority rule. It is replete with Code terminology, but in some instances the definitions vary radically from those in the UCC. The definition of farm products is close to that of the UCC and accordingly the discussion at pp. 158-63 *supra* is relevant. However, if a state's definition of farm products deviates from that in § 1631's, the federal definition will control as to the sales of farm products, *but not* as to questions concerning attachment and perfection. Section 1631 and the UCC vary significantly in their definitions of buyer in the ordinary course of business. The UCC requirement that the buyer act in good faith and have no actual knowledge that the sale is in violation of the security interest in question is eliminated in the application of § 1631. Thus, as will be explained, actual knowledge of a security interest will not alone adversely affect a buyer, agent or commission merchant under the federal rule.

The general rule of § 1631 is at subsection (d). It provides that, except as provided in subsection (e), a buyer of farm products takes free of a perfected security interest created by his seller even though the buyer knows of its existence and state law provides otherwise.

Under subsection (e), a buyer of farm products will still take subject to a security interest created by the seller if the buyer receives adequate and timely direct notice of the security interest from the lender or seller, *or*, if the state has a "central filing system," and the buyer is charged with notice of the security interest thereunder. The federal law as to commission merchants and selling agents is found at § 1631 (g)(1), with the exception set out at (g)(2). The analysis mirrors that just set out with regard to rights of buyers. Congress has the power to legislate in this area pursuant to the Commerce Clause. Because Congress made clear its intent to preempt state law, states cannot legislate more extensive protection for buyers or for lenders as to issues covered by § 1631.

There is a question as to whether the state or federal courts, or both, will interpret § 1631. Under the federal statute, few matters are left to the states: choice of either the direct notice or central filing programs developed in the federal statute; defining what constitutes *receipt* of direct notice; and in the case of central filing systems determining what constitutes *regular* distribution of master lists. Congress specifically directed the Secretary of Agriculture to promulgate regulations governing and to certify central filing systems. Thus, an argument can be made that all actions relating to § 1631 should be brought in a federal court.

3. Direct Notice to Buyers

At this writing 31 states have opted for direct notice to lenders. Under this system, if within one year before the sale of farm products the buyer *receives* a proper written notice from the lender or seller and the buyer fails to comply with payment instructions therein, the buyer takes subject to the perfected security interest created by the seller. If the buyer has not received such notice, the secured party has no right to sue the buyer. This is the law even if the buyer had actual knowledge that the sale of the farm products was in violation of the security agreement given by the seller.

While federal law creates no official form for giving direct notice, the required content of the document is detailed in § 1631. The notice must: l) be written; 2) be organized according to farm products; 3) be an original or reproduced copy; 4) contain the names and addresses of the debtor and the secured party; 5) contain the debtor's social security or tax identification number; 6) contain a description of the farm products "including the amount of such products where applicable, crop year, county or parish, and a reasonable description of the property"; and 7) state any payment obligations imposed on the buyer as a condition to the release of the security interest.

Uncertainties exist about these statutory requirements for the direct notice document. Crop year could mean the year of harvest or the year of planting. Crop years for animals is a puzzle. It is not clear whether each farm product must be named or whether it is it acceptable to say "all crops." The reasonable description of the property (real estate) requirement is not clear, although it appears that less than a full legal description can suffice. See pp. 167-68 *supra.* Neither is it clear whether the real estate description requirement applies to livestock as well as to crops. Also, there is no apparent restriction on the nature of the terms of the payment obligation giving lenders tremendous flexibility. Arguably, they can require two-party checks or demand direct payment of a percentage of the proceeds.

Lenders will require some guidance as to whom direct notices should be sent. Under § 1631(h), the secured party may require the debtor to provide a list of potential buyers. Many lenders expressly incorporate this duty into the security agreement - with a new list to be provided annually. If a list of buyers is given and the debtor sells to an unlisted buyer, the debtor is subject to criminal prosecution unless he notifies the lender seven days before the sale or remits the proceeds within 10 days thereafter. Upon conviction the farmer may be fined $5000 or 15% of the value of the farm products, whichever is greater. Whether this law will deter financially strapped farmers from selling to unlisted buyers and disposing of the proceeds remains to be seen.

If a farmer sells to a buyer who has not received timely and proper direct notice, the lender becomes unsecured as to the goods and also unsecured as to the proceeds when they become beyond reach. Unless there is additional collateral, the creditor's only remedy will be to sue the farmer, who will probably be judgment-proof. Accordingly, there is some potential that bank examiners could classify loans secured solely by farm products as unsecured. However, as of this writing, regulators are not automatically considering such loans to be unsecured, even if the bank has not prenotified potential purchasers.

If the lender is willing to incur the administrative burden and costs, a high level of protection could be obtained by sending notices to all potential buyers, commission merchants and agents in the state and in adjoining direct notice states. Such action does not appear to be prohibited by § 1631. The statute refers to buyers, commission merchants and selling agents without geographic restriction. But, blanket notices may irritate debtors, and raise an invasion of privacy issue. If blanket notices are to be sent, the lender should obtain borrower consent. As the following discussion reveals, sending direct notices to buyers in a neighboring central filing state will be of no legal effect. See p. 190 *infra*.

What constitutes receipt of direct notice is left to state law. Note that the UCC does not define the terms "received" or "receipt." Cautious lenders will want to make sure they can prove that buyers in fact received their written notices, which may mean that some form of "receipt requested" mail will become the norm -- another expense that the borrower will have to pay. Note once again that the buyer's actual knowledge of the security interest will not protect the lender. Buyer's receipt of proper written direct notice is the critical requirement and such notices are effective only for one year. New notices have to be sent every year.

4. USDA Certified "Central Filing System"

The second option available to states is to create what Congress calls a "certified central filing system." Congress did not intend that this filing system be used to perfect security interests. Rather, it is relevant only to priority battles between perfected secured parties and buyers, commission merchants or agents. As of June, 1994, 19 states had a USDA certified central filing system: Alabama, Colorado, Idaho, Louisiana, Maine, Mississippi, Minnesota, Montana, Nebraska, New Hampshire, New Mexico, North Dakota, Oklahoma, Oregon, South Dakota, Utah, Vermont, West Virginia, and Wyoming. Uncertainties exist as to the operation and legal effect of these central filing systems. USDA regulations and interpretive opinions at 9 CFR pt. 205 (1994) answer some, but not all questions.

The term "central filing system" is defined in § 1631(c)(2) as a USDA certified system for filing effective financing statements (EFSs) on a statewide basis. The EFS is a document distinct from the UCC financing statement (Form UCC-1). An EFS is an original or copy of a statement that contains the names, addresses, and signatures of the secured party and the debtor; the debtor's social security or tax-payer identification number (TIN); and, a description of farm products. While a direct notice is good only if received by the buyer within one year before sale, a filed EFS is good for five years, and can be continued for another five years by refiling within six months of expiration.

Upon the filing of an EFS with the Secretary of State, the Secretary's staff must put the new data into the data base so that it will be included when the next master list or supplement is issued. Master lists must be prepared, maintained, updated and distributed to registered buyers. It must be possible to produce lists by farm product, by county or parish, and by crop year. For example, the Secretary's office must be able to generate from its data base master lists for corn, county by county (or parish by parish). Each such corn list will have the names of individual debtors in alphabetical order by last name (first word in the case of names of business entities) and will repeat that data organized by the debtor's social security number or TIN. Names of creditors need not be presented in alphabetical order or by TIN. Rather, this information is part of the entry for each debtor.

The Secretary also must maintain a list of buyers of farm products, commission merchants and selling agents who have registered with her office by filing the required form and paying the annual registration fee. The registration form will require name and address of the registrant; reason for its interest in receiving lists of filed EFSs; the farm products of interest to the registrant; and the counties for which lists are sought. The Secretary must distribute to each registered party on a regular basis written notice (master lists and supplements) for the farm products and counties requested. The meaning of "regular" is left to each state to define. Under the federal law registered buyers cannot be required to accept lists transmitted by E mail, fiche or other unwritten method. Buyers can elect to accept fiche or computer transmissions should these options be made available.

It is not contemplated that EFSs or master lists will include instructions to buyers as to how to remit payment to or otherwise deal with the secured creditor. This is in contrast with the direct notice alternative where the written notice will include "any description of the payment obligations imposed on the buyer by the secured party as conditions for waiver or release of the security interest." In a "central filing system" state the buyer will need to contact each lender to obtain instructions.

Buyers of farm products become subject to security interests only when they have received a master list or supplement thereto that includes information about the security interest in question. 9 CFR § 205.208(c)(1994). This direct notification policy is to be contrasted with the system under the UCC where time of filing establishes priority between secured parties. Under § 1631(e)(3), a buyer who has registered and received a list reflecting the information on the pertinent filed EFS, will take subject to the security interest if the buyer does not secure a waiver or release from the secured party or make payment as directed by the secured party.

Inevitably there will be a gap between the time an EFS is filed and the time a registered buyer receives the information on a master list or supplement thereto. If a farmer debtor sell listed farm products collateral during the gap, the secured party loses to the buyer. Recall that actual knowledge of the security interest by the buyer is immaterial. Lenders are experimenting with ways to deal with the gap period risk. First, some lenders will not enter into a secured transaction with a borrower close to the time when marketing of the farm products collateral will normally take place. Second, while the legal effect of the practice is doubtful, lenders in an EFS state could send direct notices to buyers as they would in a direct notice state. Colorado, an EFS state, has gone so far as to provide by statute that direct written notice can be used, but that it is valid as to registered buyers only during the gap and a 10 day period after the next ensuing master list is mailed. Colo. Stat. 4-9-307(1)(b)(II). Given the scheme of the federal statute, a court might hold that notice received in such manner in a central filing state is of no more legal effect than notice received by gossip.

Unregistered buyers, commission merchants and selling agents are charged by statute with notice of all filed effective financing statements, even those not yet reflected in distributed master lists. Section 1631(e)(2) provides that in a state with a "central filing system" a buyer takes subject to a perfected security interest if the buyer does not register and the secured party has filed an EFS describing the farm products in question. An unregistered buyer can reduce this risk by making oral inquiry of the Secretary of State on a transaction by transaction basis. Oral confirmation of the existence of a pertinent EFS must be given by the Secretary within 24 hours, and is to be followed by written confirmation. When information from a pertinent EFS is thus received, the buyer should seek payment instructions from the secured party.

Caveat: A few states have combined the EFS form and Form UCC-1 into one form. This is practical only in states with central filing for perfection of all security interests in farm products. When one form is used, rules as to perfection continue to be those in state law and rules as to EFSs and the rights of buyers are those in the federal statute.

5. Multiple-Payee Checks and CCC

Some buyers issue checks payable to multiple payees - the seller and his or her creditors. While most secured creditors will have complied with the notice requirements of § 1631, some will not have done so. Creditors in the latter group who refuse to endorse checks unless they receive "their" share, may be guilty of conversion.

In an attempt to deal with the problem created by multiple-payee checks, the CCC in October, 1992 issued Notice LP-1489 to ASCS offices. Under this directive, buyers of grain subject to a CCC perfected security interest must agree to issue a check with the CCC as the sole payee before the CCC will sign a lien waiver form. This means that the grain dealer must ignore other creditor notices under § 1631. The CCC agrees to indemnify a buyer if a creditor holding a superior interest to the CCC sues said buyer. But, CCC will indemnify only for the amount of grain specified in Form CCC-681-1 which must be signed by the producer and sent to the buyer.

CCC points out that as a standard practice before making a price support loan, county ASCS (now CFSA) offices conduct lien searches and get lien waivers from other filed lienholders on the quantity of commodity to serve as collateral for its loan. Thus, CCC gains priority over conflicting claims to the collateral. Should the search fail to reveal all lienholders with priority over CCC, it will pay them. To not permit the practice of allowing the grain dealer to ignore other creditor notices, CCC argues would require the producer or the ASCS (now CFSA) to do the same task twice, i.e. search the records at sale and obtain lien waivers and subordinations a second time. Finally, if a buyer in its dealings with CCC makes a mistake twice -- e.g. fails to issue a single payee check or to provide proof the grain was delivered -- CCC for one year will not permit the buyer to buy commodities that are subject to a CCC perfected security interest. CCC will comply with § 1631, but will not waive its security interest.

D. Priority Between Secured Parties

We now leave § 1631 and return to priority conflicts that must be resolved under the UCC and other pertinent state law. When one secured party is perfected and another is unperfected, the perfected secured creditor prevails as to the collateral. UCC §§ 9-301(1) and 9-312(5) (negative inference). A conflict between unperfected secured parties who claim the same collateral is resolved by determining whose security interest first attached. UCC § 9-312(5)(b). Competition between perfected secured parties claiming interests in goods is governed by the first to perfect rule of UCC § 9-312(5), effectively a first-to-file rule. In agriculture, however, this rule is subject to the production supplier's priority -- considered next. We do not consider farm equipment purchase money security interests.

E. Production Supplier's Priority

A priority over prior perfected secured parties is given to crop production suppliers by UCC § 9-312(2). To qualify for this priority, these conditions must be met: the production crop lender must give value; the value given must enable the debtor to produce new crops during the current production season; the value must be given not more than three months before the crops become growing crops; and the obligation owing to the earlier perfected secured party must have been due more than six months before the new crops were planted.

The principal issue is the meaning of the requirement that the previous obligation be due more than six months before the crops were planted. Most courts interpret this to require that payments be six months in default. This gives very limited protection to production lenders. Prior secured parties can easily schedule payments to fall due within the six month period.

Suppliers of fertilizer, seed, and chemicals want a super-priority in crops and livestock produced with their inputs. In most cases, unless UCC § 9-312(2) applies, a supplier obtains priority over a prior perfected crop lender only if the supplier persuades the prior secured party to sign a subordination agreement. UCC § 9-316. Most suppliers, however, do not even obtain a perfected security interest,

Suppliers have sought the amendment of UCC § 9-312(2) to allow a priority claim similar to that granted to purchase money security interest holders under UCC § 9-312(4). This change could have serious repercussions. First, all crop production suppliers would have to comply with the basic requirements of Article 9. Although farm suppliers commonly grant credit on open account, few are accustomed or equipped to handle the documentation required by Article 9. Second, crop production suppliers usually are not equipped to do necessary credit screening and cash flow projections. Third, an adverse impact on the availability of credit to farmers could result if traditional farm lenders seek to shift all crop production financing responsibility to input suppliers. Certainly, lenders would be reluctant to rely on crops or livestock as collateral if farmers could give priority to suppliers subsequent to a bank loan decision based in part on the results of a search showing no filed financing statements. Arguably, the expeditious and safe route for suppliers is to leave the credit business to the banks. The supplier could then enter into an advance arrangement with the debtor's lender to ensure payment for supplies. This could be done by the establishment of a line of credit in the supplier's name or by a bank guaranteeing payment up to a set amount.

F. Documents of Title

1. Generally

Many farmers store grain in public warehouses. Depositors usually receive weight or scale tickets upon delivery. See p. 126 *supra*. Some warehouses subsequently issue negotiable or non-negotiable warehouse receipts. However, if this does not occur a weight or scale ticket might be treated as a nonnegotiable warehouse receipt. In re Durand Milling Co., Inc. (Bankr.E.D.Mich.1981). The nature of ownership documentation can have an important impact when crops are sold or subjected to a security interest.

When a negotiable warehouse receipt is issued, title to the goods is "locked up" in the document. UCC § 7-104 provides: "(1) a warehouse receipt . . . or other document of title is negotiable (a) if by its terms the goods are to be delivered to bearer or to the order of a named person . . .. (2) Any other document is non-negotiable." A bailee-warehouseman who issues a negotiable document of title will deliver goods only to the holder of the document. UCC §§ 7-403(4), 1-201(20). Possession of a negotiable document is particularly important to secured parties because it is the functional equivalent of possession of the goods. See UCC §§ 7-502, 7-403, 9-304(2). Conflicts involving documents of title can involve a secured party with a security interest in crops, a secured party with a security interest in a warehouse receipt, a purchaser of stored grain, and a purchaser of warehouse receipts. Problems are magnified if the warehouse receipts are negotiable. Articles 2, 7 and 9 all are relevant when analyzing priority conflicts involving warehouse receipts.

2. Non-Negotiable Documents

The most common priority conflicts are between a secured creditor who has perfected a security interest in all of debtor's crops and a subsequent secured creditor who either has possession of a non-negotiable warehouse receipt issued in the name of the farmer or issued in its own name. In either case, the prior perfected secured creditor should win.

When a non-negotiable document of title is involved, title to the crops is not "locked up" in the document. Section 9-304(3) provides: "[a] security interest in goods in the possession of a bailee other than one who has issued a negotiable document therefore is perfected by issuance of a document in the name of the secured party or by the bailee's receipt of notification of the secured party's interest or by filing as to the goods." Consequently, the key to winning a priority battle is perfection as to the goods. Consider this example. On Jan. 2, Bank A obtains and perfects a security interest in all of F's crops. On July 1, F deposits grain subject to Bank A's security interest in elevator. On July 2, F grants Bank B a security interest in the stored grain and has a non-negotiable warehouse receipt issued in the name of Bank B. Bank B does not file as to the goods. F defaults and both Banks claim the stored grain. Assuming Bank A has not waived its rights in the grain, it will win under the first to file rule of UCC § 9-312(5)(a). This result is not unduly harsh in that Bank B could have protected itself by checking the filed financing statements and asking the warehouse about § 1631 notices.

Assume the same facts as above, except that the nonnegotiable warehouse receipt is issued in the name of F, and that Bank B takes possession of the receipt but does not file as to the goods or notify the warehouse of its interest. If Bank A's documentation is in order it is a perfected secured creditor and will defeat Bank B, an unperfected secured creditor. UCC § 9-304(3). Even if the grain was determined to be inventory and Bank A had treated it as farm products and filed in the wrong office, Bank A would still win because when two unperfected secured creditors claim the same collateral, the first to attach wins. UCC § 9-312(5)(b). See pp. 158-59 *supra*.

In summary, the theory of Article 9 is that the security interest is not in the nonnegotiable document, but in the goods. Thus, perfection as to the goods is the key, with priority determined by first perfection.

3. Negotiable Warehouse Receipts

When a farmer is in financial trouble and is tempted to do some double dealing, the issuance of a negotiable warehouse receipt by a bailee of crops can precipitate serious problems for a prior crop lender. Consider this hypothetical. On Jan. 2, farmer (F) borrows $20,000 from Bank A which perfects a security interest in F's growing wheat crop. On July 25, the wheat is harvested and F stores it in a local elevator, which issues a negotiable warehouse receipt for 10,000 bushels of wheat. Without permission from Bank A, F pledges the warehouse receipt to Bank B as security for a new $15,000 loan. F defaults on both loans and both banks claim the wheat. To resolve this priority conflict, we must examine both Articles 9 and 7.

The first relevant section is UCC § 9-304(2), which provides: "[d]uring the period that goods are in the possession of the issuer of a negotiable document therefor, a security interest in the goods is perfected by perfecting a security interest in the document, and any security interest in the goods otherwise perfected during such period is subject thereto." Does the storage and issuance of the negotiable document of title to F render Bank A's perfection in the wheat meaningless? Bank A will argue that UCC § 9-304(2) applies only to interests perfected in goods while the negotiable warehouse receipt is outstanding. This is the negative inference from the last sentence of § 9-304(2). Since Bank A was perfected prior to the issuance of the negotiable receipt, it will assert that it is not affected by this section and that it should win. This result would be consistent with the "notice filing" system of the UCC since Bank B would have found Bank A's interest if it had checked the records. This is the familiar first-to-file rule of UCC § 9-312(5).

Bank B will respond by arguing that it does not have to rely on UCC § 9-304 or § 9-312 because UCC § 9-309 controls. It provides:

> Nothing in this Article limits the rights of a holder in due course of a negotiable instrument (Section 3-302) or a holder to whom a negotiable document of title has been duly negotiated (7-501) or a bona fide purchaser of a security (Section 8-302) and the holders or purchasers take priority over an earlier security interest even though perfected. Filing under this Article does not constitute notice of the security interest to such holders or purchasers.

Bank B is a holder. Section 1-201(20)(1990) defines a holder as "the person in possession if goods are delivered to bearer or to the order of the person in possession." Thus, Bank B will argue that as a holder of a duly negotiated document of title, it should be given priority over Bank A.

Bank A will respond by arguing that UCC § 7-503 takes precedence over UCC § 9-309. The argument that UCC § 7-503 controls is twofold. Article 7 is specifically designed to govern document of title problems and if there is any conflict with Article 9, Article 7 should control. The second point is that UCC § 9-309 states: "[n]othing in this Article limits the rights of a holder . . .." This hints that the drafters recognized that because other UCC articles apply to holders, they might be subject to restrictions. If this interpretation is accepted, would UCC § 9-309 be rendered meaningless? It is a basic rule of statutory construction to construe statutes so that they will have meaning.

It may be that UCC § 9-309 was intended to apply only to a case where the conflict is between two creditors claiming the document of title as opposed to the case where one creditor is relying on a perfected security interest in the goods and another creditor is trying to get at the goods based on a perfected security interest in a document of title. It has also been suggested that UCC § 9-309 and § 7-503 could be read as having separate meaning if § 9-309 is read to apply only to security interests arising after the issuance of the document of title or contemporaneously with it. While the drafters of the Code could have been more explicit as to their intent, we believe that UCC § 7-503 controls.

Under UCC § 7-502 the holder of a duly negotiated document of title gets title to the receipt as well as the goods. Exceptions to this rule are found at UCC § 7-503 which provides in part :

> (1) A document of title confers no right in goods against a person who before issuance of the document had a legal

interest or a perfected security interest in them and who neither (a) delivered or entrusted them or any document of title covering them to the bailor or his nominee with actual or apparent authority to ship, store or sell or with power to obtain delivery under this Article (Section 7-403) or with power of disposition under this Act (Section 2-403 and 9-307) or other statute or rule of law; nor (b) acquiesced in the procurement by the bailor or his nominee of any document of title.

Relying on this provision, Bank A will assert that it will win, even though Bank B is a qualified holder. Bank A had a perfected security interest in the wheat when the negotiable warehouse receipt was issued to F and it has not acquiesced in the F's procurement of the negotiable warehouse receipt. If Bank A has neither acquiesced nor given the farmer the authority to store the grain and obtain a negotiable warehouse receipt, it will win. The acquiescence issue, however, can be a major problem for Bank A. Comment 1 to UCC § 7-503 suggests that knowledge of the likelihood of storage with no objection is acquiescence and will result in Bank A losing to Bank B if the latter took by due negotiation. UCC § 7-501(4). As a precaution, Bank A's security agreement should have stated that F is not to arrange for the issuance of a negotiable warehouse receipt.

VIII. ASSIGNMENTS OF SALE PROCEEDS

In certain sectors of American agriculture it is common for the farmer to be contractually bound to sell agricultural commodities to a particular buyer at a price or under a price formula determined in advance. In these instances the farmer's financier, while holding a perfected security interest in the crops, will want to make sure that it will receive its share of the proceeds upon harvest and sale. Rather than relying solely upon the perfected security interest in identifiable proceeds obtained when the collateral is sold, UCC §§ 9-203(3), 9-306(1)-(3), many lenders require the producer to sign a separate document assigning the proceeds of the sale. This document will be sent to the buyer and will usually contain three features: an assignment of proceeds signed by the debtor-producer; a notice of the assignment; and an "Acceptance of Assignment" that is to be signed by the buyer and returned to the lender with a copy of the whole document. Often, the buyer will sign, but make the acceptance subject to certain conditions. Problems can arise with these assignments if the buyer does not adhere to the agreement. See Producers Cotton Oil Co. v. Amstar Corp. (Cal.Ct.App.1988).

IX.   STATUTORY AGRICULTURAL LIENS

Statutory liens are common in the agricultural setting. In a typical jurisdiction, one might find, *inter alia,* a harvester's lien, a lien for feed and care of livestock, an agister's lien (pasture use), a labor's lien, and a farm landlord's lien. Such liens can be possessory or nonpossessory.

A.   Possessory Liens and UCC § 9-310

Section 9-310 of the Uniform Commercial Code gives the holders of certain statutory or common law liens priority over some perfected security interests. The rule applies only if the person furnishing the services or materials does so in the ordinary course of business, if the resulting lien arises by statute or rule of law, and the goods remain in possession of the person providing the materials or services. Caveat: the rule does not apply if the lien is statutory and the statute is contrary to § 9-310 as to priority.

Section 9-310 usually is not a problem for crop financiers because the possession requirement is not often met.   One exception is the warehouseman's lien for unpaid storage. A warehouse providing storage services in the ordinary course of its business has possession of the crop, and under UCC § 7-209 has a statutory lien thereon "for all lawful charges for storage and preservation of the grain . . .." Thus, under § 9-310 the warehouseman will be entitled to be paid storage fees before the prior perfected crop financier can realize on its security interest.

Thresher's liens sometimes meet the requirements of UCC § 9-310. Normally, custom harvesters will not be able to satisfy the possession requirement because harvested grain will come under the control of the grower prior to time for payment. However, a wary harvester who is not paid before harvest might decide to deposit at the local elevator in her name enough grain to cover harvesting charges. It would appear that the lien claim would then fit within § 9-310. Caveat: the manner in which the harvester obtained possession of the grain might constitute conversion. At least one state, Wisconsin, gives a statutory self-help remedy to threshers. Wis. Stat. Ann. § 779.50.

More typically, an unpaid custom harvester will not have possession of grain, but will nevertheless have a statutory lien. A priority conflict could then arise between the security interest of a prior perfected secured party and the nonpossessory lien of the custom harvester, both of whom claim the same crops. Article 9 does not resolve this conflict because UCC § 9-104(c) excludes from Article 9 coverage the status of statutory liens other than those falling under UCC § 9-310. While these conflicts usually are resolved by common law principles, some states have enacted statutes giving nonpossessory liens priority over prior security interests or other encumbrances.

B. Nonpossessory Liens

Many states have created by statute a farm landlord's lien on crops for unpaid rent, whether the lease is crop-share or cash rent. Section 9-104(b) specifically excludes landlord's liens from the operation of Article 9. Thus, any priority battle between a prior perfected secured party and a farm landlord is determined outside of the UCC. In most states, landlord liens prevail over prior perfected security interests.

While most agricultural states have landlord's liens, farm landlords should obtain and perfect a security interest in growing crops whether rent is to be paid in cash or in crop-share. There are important reasons for this advice. First, the statutory landlord's lien is unenforceable in bankruptcy under 11 USCA § 545. Second, UCC Article 9 is simpler, clearer, quicker and less expensive to use than are statutory lien enforcement procedures. In many states it is not clear at what point a landlord's lien arises or how one proceeds with enforcement. Third, an Article 9 security interest can have priority over buyers of crops if there is compliance with the federal farm products rule. 7 USCA § 1631. In many states, a buyer will take free of a landlord's lien unless it has been recorded or the buyer has actual knowledge of the lien or knowledge of facts that would cause a reasonable person to inquire as to the rights of the seller of the crop. Caveat: When rent is to be paid in crop share this advice might not be pertinent if state law provides that the landlord attains rights in his share of the crop when it is planted or when it matures.

The priority rules of Article 9 can cause problems for an unsuspecting farm landlord. The basic rule of UCC § 9-312(5)(a) is that the first to file prevails This can be a problem for a landlord who first obtains a security interest in crops after the tenant has been farming the ground. If the tenant has given a security interest to a crop lender covering future crops to be grown on the leased land, the landlord will lose if the crop lender is prior perfected. The secured party's priority dates from the filing of its financing statement. UCC §§ 9-402(1), 9-312(5)(a). A subordination agreement is a solution for the landlord, if the secured party is willing to sign. UCC § 9-316.

A farm landlord who takes a security interest in crops ought not to be precluded from asserting the state's statutory landlord's lien. By making it clear in the security agreement that there is no intent to waive the statutory lien, the landlord should be able to preserve an election of remedies. See, e.g., Mousel v. Daringer (Neb.1973).

C. Statutory Liens and § 1631

Unless compliance with direct notice or "central filing system" rules prevents such result, the general rule at § 1631(d) is that notwithstanding any other provision of federal, state or local law, a buyer in the ordinary course of business who buys farm products from a seller engaged in farming operations takes free of any security interest *created by the seller.* Many states have statutory liens on farm products -- e.g., landlord's liens and laborer's liens -- that are not necessarily cut off by their sale.

Kansas Stat. Ann. § 58-2526 provides: "[t]he person entitled to the rent may recover from the purchaser of the crop, or any party thereof, with notice of the lien the value of the crop purchased, to the extent of the rent due and damages." Does § 1631 preempt such a law? Arguably, § 1631 is a comprehensive scheme and preempts all state law governing the sale of farm products. Yet, the literal language of § 1631 does not seem to cover interests in farm products created involuntarily. Section 1631(d) applies to security interests *created by the seller.* Security interest is defined in § 1631(c)(7) to be "an interest in farm products that secures payment or performance of an obligation." This definition may be broad enough to cover involuntary interests in farm products such as statutory or judicial liens. However, "security interest" is a term of art in the UCC and encompasses only consensual interests in property created to secure payments or obligations. Moreover, the focus of § 1631 and of its legislative history is on consensual security interests. Finally, even if the federal definition of "security interest" is deemed broad enough to cover statutory and judicial liens, such liens arguably are not "created" by the seller.   See, e.g., Jenkins v. Missouri Farmers Ass'n, Inc. (Mo.Ct.App.1993).

One state, Minnesota, now has a state priority rule dealing with the sale of farm products subject to a statutory lien -- other than a landlord's lien.   Under the rule, statutory liens are treated in the same way as are security interests under § 1631. Minn. Stat. Ann. § 514.952, Subd. 6.

CHAPTER SIX

INSOLVENT WAREHOUSES AND BUYERS
I. INTRODUCTION

Virtually all public agricultural warehouses buy and sell the same commodities that they accept for storage. Such a facility is thus best described as a warehouse (storage function) *and* as a grain dealer (buy and sell transactions). Sometimes the term "elevator" is used to denote the entire warehouse and grain dealer operation.

While only a small percentage of agricultural elevators have gone bankrupt, each such event can have catastrophic consequences for farmer patrons. Factors contributing to such failures include: mishandling of commodities (e.g., deterioration of bailed grain); inadequate bookkeeping; lax credit policies; diverting of funds to support personal ventures; falsified records; commodity futures speculation; and cash flow shortages resulting from poor crop yields. Small country warehouses with storage capacities of less than 300,000 bushels are the most likely to fail. Similar problems have in some instances contributed to the failure of milk processors and feedlots.

This chapter deals in part on problems associated with elevator failures. In such cases rights of bailors, sellers, buyers and secured parties come into play. Attention also is given to failures of packers. Here rights of sellers and secured parties are the focus, but not bailment issues as there are no storage transactions comparable with those entered into with grain warehouses.

II. SHORTAGES OF COMMINGLED GRAIN
A. Status of Producer Bailors

A farmer who delivers grain to an elevator will either sell or store it. If the farmer sells and is not paid, the farmer is an unsecured creditor. If the commodity is stored, a bailment relationship is created between the warehouse and the farmer. The fact that grain is fungible and commingled in the warehouse in a common mass does not negate the bailment relationship. UCC § 7-207.

Upon delivery of a commodity to an elevator the farmer receives a scale ticket which states the gross weight of the grain delivered. Often the ticket does not indicate the exact number of bushels delivered or whether the commodity is sold or stored. Once a warehouse receipt has been issued in the farmer's name, it is clear that a bailment relationship exists. Even if a warehouse receipt is not issued, a producer holding a scale ticket that represents a storage obligation will normally be treated as a bailor-owner. See pp. 126-130 *supra*. Section 7-102(1)(a) states: "'Bailee' means the person who by a warehouse receipt, bill of lading or other document of title acknowledges possession of goods and contracts to deliver them." Bankruptcy Rule 3001(g) is also relevant. See p. 128 *supra*. The underlying issue is whether the parties intend a sale or a bailment.

A negotiable warehouse receipt is a document of title representing title to goods it describes. When a warehouse fails, a farmer, whether holding a negotiable or a nonnegotiable warehouse receipt or a scale ticket evidencing a storage transaction, is an owner of grain, not a creditor of the elevator. See pp. 126-29 *supra.* When a warehouse receipt is negotiable, title to the goods is "locked up" in the receipt. Transfer by sale or by grant of a security interest is possible only by proper transfer of the negotiable receipt. The commodity as such is not the subject of the transaction. See p. 195 *supra.*

When farmers store grain that is commingled, they become tenants in common in the whole. Section 7-207(2) provides in part: "[f]ungible goods so commingled are owned in common by the persons entitled thereto and the warehouseman is severally liable to each owner for that owner's share."

When an elevator fails a shortage of commingled grain can be expected. As stated in UCC § 7-207(2), the tenants in common share pro rata in what grain remains. Consider this simplified example:

> The maximum capacity of the warehouse is 100 bushels. Farmer A stores 5 bushels, Farmer B stores 20 bushels, and the CCC stores 75 bushels. When the elevator fails there are 50 bushels on hand. A pro rata distribution requires that each depositor receive 50 percent of the amount delivered for storage. A will get 2.5 bushels, B 10 bushels, and CCC 37.5.

This reflects the current, as well as the pre-Code rule. The court in U.S. v. Luther (10th Cir.1955) held that "each claimant . . . was entitled to share in the grain on hand in the proportion that the grain stored by it bore to the total of grain stored by the storage claimants." *Id.* at 505.

> Assume the same facts as above, except that just prior to failure the CCC withdrew 25

bushels with actual knowledge that the warehouse had a shortage. When the warehouse fails it has but 25 bushels on hand.

This situation was considered in Luther and the court proceeded as through the 25 bushels withdrawn by the CCC remained in storage at failure. Thus, 50 bushels are assumed available when calculating pro rata distribution. The distribution remains the same -- A will receive 2.5 bushels, B 10 bushels, and the CCC 37.5 bushels. The 25 bushels previously withdrawn by the CCC are part of the 37.5 awarded to it by the court.

Had CCC been without actual knowledge of the condition of the warehouse when it made its withdrawal of 25 bushels, the prorata distribution of the 25 bushels left on hand would have been calculated on the basis of claims of 5, 20 and 50 bushels -- 1.66 bu. to A, 6.66 bu. to B and 16.66 bu. to CCC. CCC actually ends up with 41.66 bu.

Assume the same facts as above, except that just prior to failure, the CCC withdrew 50 bushels with actual knowledge that the warehouse had a shortage. This cleaned out the warehouse

Courts apparently will not force CCC to replace the grain. Rather, CCC is subject to a conversion action brought by A and B for money damages as in Preston v. U.S. (7th Cir.1985).

B. Status of Bailors Other Than Producers

Persons other than producers who store commodities in a warehouse can be treated as tenants in common owning a pro rata share in commingled grain. We have already seen the example of the CCC.

At least two more possibilities exist: 1) millers or other processors who purchase commodities from a warehouse may not need immediate delivery and have warehouse receipts issued in their names; and 2) elevators issue warehouse receipts in their own names to evidence ownership of quantities of company owned grain. If at the time the receipts are issued there are sufficient commodities to satisfy all outstanding receipts, the miller and the elevator as warehouse receipt holders will be treated as tenants in common and share pro rata in any distributions. An exception is noted at p. 213 *infra.* Difficulties arises when receipts are issued for commodities that do not exist.

C. Overissue Warehouse Receipts

There are pre-UCC and post-UCC cases that indicate that warehouse receipts issued in the name of the elevator or to a purchaser of grain are null and void if issued when there is insufficient grain to satisfy outstanding producer receipts. U.S. v. Haddix & Sons, Inc. (6th Cir.1969); State ex. rel. Public Service Commission v. Gunkelman & Sons, (N.D. 1974). Some states have a warehouse statute in addition to Article 7 which, *inter alia* declares overissue receipts invalid. This sets up a direct conflict with UCC § 7-207(2).

1. § UCC 7-207(2)

The last sentence of § 7-207(2) states: "[w]here because of overissue a mass of fungible goods is insufficient to meet all the receipts which the warehouseman has issued against it, the persons entitled includes all holders to whom overissued receipts have been duly negotiated." The plain meaning is that holders who obtain negotiable warehouse receipts through due negotiation are entitled to share pro rata with farmer bailors in the grain on hand even if there was not enough grain to cover their receipts when issued. The drafters of the UCC apparently wanted to foster the free flow of commerce by protecting purchasers of negotiable documents that appear valid on their face. The effect is to give the same type of rights to holders in due course of a negotiable documents of title as are given to holders in due course of negotiable instruments. A secured party can also be a holder in due course of an overissue receipt, adding an additional complicating factor in some cases. The key is whether the holder of an overissue receipt has obtained it through due negotiation. The application of UCC § 7-207(2) to purchasers, secured parties and elevators that hold overissue receipts merits further examination.

2. *Receipts for Fungible Goods*

Overissue warehouse receipts can convey rights in goods. Section 7-402 provides that: "[n]either a duplicate nor any other document of title purporting to cover goods already represented by an outstanding document of the same issuer confers any right in the goods, except as provided in the case of . . . overissue of documents for fungible goods . . . ." Section 1-201(17) defines fungible goods to mean " goods . . . of which any unit is, by nature or usage of trade, the equivalent of any other like unit." Our focus is on overissue receipts covering fungible goods.

3. Holder by Due Negotiation

Any person claiming the benefit of UCC § 7-207(2) must be a holder. "'Holder' with respect to a document of title means the person in possession if the goods are deliverable to bearer or to the order of the person in possession." UCC § 1-201(20)(1990). Holder includes a lender who has taken possession of a warehouse receipt as collateral.

Due negotiation occurs when a negotiable document of title comes into the hands of a holder "who purchases it in good faith without notice of any defense against or claim to it on the part of any person and for value." UCC § 7-501(4) To be a negotiable document a warehouse receipt must meet the requirements of UCC § 7-104 where it says that a document of title is negotiable "if by its terms the goods are to be delivered to the bearer or to the order of a named person." Overissue *non*negotiable warehouse receipts do not give the possessor rights of ownership in common under UCC § 7-207(2). Documents of title are covered at pp. 128-29 *supra*.

4. Purchaser in Good Faith

Purchaser is a term of art under the UCC. Even a bank that is a perfected secured party can be treated as a purchaser. This is so because of language at UCC §§ 1-201(32) and 1-201(33): "'Purchase' includes taking by sale, discount, negotiation, mortgage, pledge, lien, issue or reissue, gift or any other voluntary transaction creating an interest in property. 'Purchaser' means a person who takes by purchase." Clearly, our grain buyer who received a negotiable warehouse receipt also is a purchaser under this definition.

Purchasers must have acted in good faith when their overissued warehouse receipts were obtained. "Good faith" is defined in three places in the 1990 UCC: §§ 1-201(19), 2-103(1)(b) and 3-103(a)(4). Section 1-201(19) provides: "'Good faith' means honesty in fact in the conduct or transaction concerned." This definition applies unless the relevant article has another definition. Article 2, which applies to sales of goods, has its own definition. Section 2-103(1)(b) reads: "'Good faith' in the case of a merchant means honesty in fact and the observance of reasonable commercial standards of fair dealing in the trade."

Because Article 9 has no special definition of "good faith", the honesty in fact standard of § 1-201(19) is applied. This is a subjective test focused only on the state of the holder's mind when the warehouse receipt is obtained. In our examples, lack of good faith results if the bank as secured party or the purchasers from the warehouse knew that the warehouse receipt was invalid when they took it. Some courts go further and hold that parties cannot intentionally keep themselves ignorant of facts, which if known, would defeat their rights in a negotiable document. One court wrote that the UCC is not designed to allow those dealing in commercial circles to obtain rights by lack of inquiry in circumstances amounting to an intentional closing of eyes and mind to defects in defenses to the transaction. Branch Banking & Trust Co. v. Gill (N.C.1977).

5. *Without Notice of Claim or Defense*

The party asserting due negotiation must also take the warehouse receipt "without notice of any defense against or claim to it on the part of any person." UCC § 7-501(4). Notice is defined in UCC § 1-201(25): "A person has 'notice' of a fact when (a) he has actual knowledge of it . . . or (c) from all the facts and circumstances known to him at the time in question he has reason to know that it exists." Usually a lender will not accept a negotiable document as collateral until it has examined it. So, if state law requires that a warehouse receipt issued in the name of an elevator satisfy special requirements as to content, a person taking a non-complying receipt would have notice of a defect on the face of the document.

If a warehouse receipt appears to be valid on its face, the holder could still have notice that it was fraudulently issued. The crucial question is whether the secured party and the buyers, from all the facts and circumstances known to them at the time they took possession of receipts, had reason to know that the warehouse did not have sufficient grain on hand to satisfy all outstanding warehouse receipts. For example, a bank would probably have notice of a shortage of grain when pledged warehouse receipts involve a significant percentage of the facility's storage capacity. Prudent elevator operations do not keep inventories of company owned grain on hand for long periods. There is a substantial price risk, i.e., if the market price goes down, it loses money. The bank arguably has a duty to inquire about storage capacity and to be concerned about proffered receipts that total a large percentage of that capacity. Consider this illustration:

> Bank has been financing T Elevator for 10
> years. It has a storage capacity of 1 million

bushels. As collateral for its loans, Bank has received from T a perfected security interest in all company-owned grain and negotiable warehouse receipts representing that grain. Bank always takes possession of endorsed, negotiable warehouse receipts issued in the name of T Elevator. On Oct. 1, T Elevator is declared to be insolvent.

Farmers hold warehouse receipts showing ownership of 950,000 bushels and Bank holds receipts totaling 400,000 bushels. All of the receipts held by Bank were issued when no company-owned grain existed. The elevator had only 500,000 bushels on hand when declared insolvent. Bank claims it can share pro rata with the farmers.

Farmers would argue that at the very least the Bank had a duty to inquire as to the storage capacity of the elevator and the number of outstanding receipts when it took as collateral warehouse receipts representing 40% of the facility's capacity. Unless the elevator protected itself by forward contracting or by using the futures market to hedge its position, it is at great risk if prices fall. See hedging discussion at pp. 148-151 *supra*. Because holding so much grain is an unlikely strategy, Bank arguably is on notice that the elevator might not have as much company owned grain as it claims.

Courts have had difficulty with the good faith and notice requirements. While very few cases deal with warehouse receipts, there are many reported cases where courts have dealt with the same good faith and notice requirements when assessing holder in due course claims in the context of UCC § 3-302. See, e.g., Branch Banking & Trust Co. v. Gill (N.C. 1977). These cases are relevant here.

6. *Value*

Purchasers must give value. A person who bought commodities and stored them has given value as has the lender who loaned money. Value is defined in UCC § 1-201(44). See p. 163 *supra.*

III. REMEDIES FOR SHORTED BAILORS

In many cases the most significant strategy for the shorted farmer bailor is to seek to limit the number of parties who can claim against whatever remains of the commingled mass in the failed elevator. The discussion at II *supra* sets forth most of the pertinent law. Consider also the case where negotiable warehouse receipts were issued by the now defunct elevator to itself when there was ample company owned grain on hand. The court in Preston v. U.S. (7th Cir.1985) held that if the elevator is responsible through its fault or negligence for later shortages, then it will not be entitled to share prorata in what remain following the loss. The same should be true for the elevator's trustee in bankruptcy.

Persons entitled to bailed grain who do not receive full redelivery or equivalent value, will have a claim against the bond of the warehouse. Given low statutory minimums, these bonds usually do not cover all of the losses. Accordingly, producers have sought other types of protection. Private insurance covering loss due to warehouse failure is one alternative. This option has not been popular and is not available in many areas.

Legislatures in a number of states have responded to this problem, some by tightening laws regulating state licensed warehouses. Others have authorized indemnity funds. See, e.g., Iowa Code §§ 543A.1 - .7; Okla. Stat. tit. 2, §§ 9-44-47.1 to 9-47. The typical indemnity program is funded by assessing a fraction of a cent on each bushel of grain moved into an elevator. When the fund reaches a set level assessments stop but will renew if claims are paid. Critics argue that indemnity funds stifle competition by equalizing warehouse operations regardless of the soundness of their management. However, not all indemnity programs cover 100% of bailor losses.

In 1984, Congress passed grain warehouse amendments to the Bankruptcy Code. 11 USCA §§ 507(a), 546(c), 557. These amendments were touted as providing significant protection to farmers, but are of minor significance. Bailors not receiving complete satisfaction have a fifth-level priority up to $4000 in the distribution of the bankrupt estate. Code § 507(a)(5)(as amended 1994). For the balance of their claims, shorted bailors remain general unsecured creditors in the warehouse bankruptcy. Other proposed federal legislative relief has been rejected: authorizing USDA to pay with cash or CCC -owned surplus commodities all farmer losses when a federally or comparable state licensed elevator fails; establishing a Grain Elevator Insurance Corporation, to give farmers protection similar to that provided by the Federal Deposit Insurance Corporation.

In states without indemnity funds, shorted farmer bailors have made unsuccessful efforts to obtain satisfaction from buyers who bought grain from the elevator at a time when there was no company owned grain. Section 7-205 provides that "[a] buyer in the ordinary course of business of fungible goods sold and delivered by a warehouseman who is also in the business of buying and selling such goods takes free of any claim under a warehouse receipt even though it has been duly negotiated." Buyer in the ordinary course is discussed at p. 179 *supra*. In addition, UCC § 2-403(2) provides that a merchant who has been entrusted with goods can transfer all the entrustor's rights to a buyer in the ordinary course. See pp. 222-24 *infra*. Thus, a farmer or lender holding a negotiable warehouse receipt duly negotiated to it, will not be able to obtain recourse from a buyer in the ordinary course from the elevator who has taken delivery of fungible goods. Recall that a good faith purchaser who has *not* taken delivery will share with others entitled to a pro rata share if such purchaser claims under a duly negotiated warehouse receipt.

Farmers in several states have urged legislatures to revamp UCC §§ 7-205 and 2-403(2) to limit in some measure the protection of buyers. Proponents often fail to realize the negative aspects of their proposal. States that limit buyer protection could suffer economically if buyers shift business to states that have not changed the law. Moreover, such legislation could lead buyers to patronize only larger, established warehouses and grain dealers, which in turn could force smaller elevators to raise prices paid and to lower selling prices, thus cutting into profit margins. Many small country elevators already face considerable economic pressure because of deregulation of freight rates and reduced rail service. See Staggers Rail Act of 1980 and 49 USCA § 10713.

Suits in conversion against the elevator manager or other employees actually engaged in wrongful conduct can be considered if such persons have assets worth pursuing. However, when bailed grain is converted the general rule is that members of the elevator's board of directors are not personally liable by reason of their office for torts committed by the manager or some other officer. Rather, director liability results from participation, knowledge amounting to acquiescence, or negligence in the management and supervision of corporate affairs -- if such behavior causes or contributes to the injury. Smith v. Great Basin Grain Co. (Idaho 1977).

Other parties such as a major creditor of an elevator may have liability exposure if the operation fails. For example, Cargill, having assumed control of a North Dakota elevator's business, was held liable for the wrongful acts committed by the elevator as it bought, sold and stored grain. A. Gay Jenson Farms Co. v. Cargill, Inc. (Minn.1981).

Suits by shorted bailors against private financial record and physical stock auditors for negligence or fraud can be considered if the evidence is adequate. Suits against careless or incompetent federal and state warehouse inspectors are hampered by discretionary functions immunity. But see Appley Brothers v. U.S. (8th Cir.1993)(no immunity for negligent inspection where duty to inspect exists). Immunity might not extend to an official who took bribes to issue false reports or otherwise engaged in malicious or criminal activity.

IV. REMEDIES FOR UNPAID SELLERS

A. Sales to Grain Dealers

Our focus now shifts away from the storage transactions to the grain dealer function. When a grain dealer fails farmers can be caught as unpaid, un-secured creditors. Some may have sold grain and received a bad check. Other farmers may have sold grain on a deferred payment contract or a price-later contract and not have been paid. Still others will have made a spot sale one or two days before the bankruptcy and will not have received their checks as usual. In these situations, farmers have physically delivered their grain and have transferred title to the grain dealer.

Assuming no valid reclamation claim under Bank-ruptcy Code § 546 (Code), the trustee in bankruptcy can defeat producer-seller claims to grain owned by the grain dealer. These farmer sellers are unsecured creditors, not bailors. They sold grain and expected to receive cash payment -- typically by check.

The trustee is given specific avoidance powers that can defeat certain types of creditors. One of these is found in 11 USCA § 544(a)(1) where the trustee is given the status of a hypothetical lien creditor at the date the bankruptcy petition is filed. Because unsecured creditors lose to such a lien creditor under state law, this is the result in the bankruptcy of a grain dealer. UCC § 9-301(1)(b),(3), and Code § 544(a)(1).

When a spot sale or a recent deferred payment or price-later contract is involved, the farmer might be able to reclaim the goods under UCC § 2-702(2). An unpaid seller has a right to reclaim if: 1) a credit sale was involved; and 2) buyer was insolvent when the goods were received; and 3) the demand for reclamation is made orally or in writing within 10 days of the buyer's receipt of the goods or within three months of written misrepresentation by buyer of solvency.

Reclamation is controlled in bankruptcy by Code § 546(c) & (d). The 1984 amendments to the Bankruptcy Code added § 546(d), dealing with sellers of grain or fish. Section 546(d) does not create a right of reclamation but determines the effect bankruptcy has on the right of reclamation created under UCC § 2-702. A seller who can satisfy these requirements cannot be defeated by the trustee under Code §§ 544(a)(1), 545, 547, and 549:

1) seller has a right of reclamation under non-bankruptcy law;

2) sale was in the ordinary course of the seller's business;

3) buyer received the goods while insolvent;

4) seller makes written demand within 20 days of buyer's receipt of the goods -- 10 days prior to 1994 amendment of § 546(c)(i).

In contrast with UCC § 2-702, note that Code § 546 requires that the reclamation demand always be in writing. Also, § 546(c) does not have a three month provision. The reclamation remedy is lost if the farmer is unaware of the need to make timely demand.

Even if the farmer makes a timely reclamation demand, the claim will fail if the grain has been sold by the grain dealer to a buyer in the ordinary course. This is so irrespective of the farmer's ability to trace the grain to the buyer. Section 2-702(3) of the UCC provides: "[the] seller's right to reclaim under subsection (2) is subject to the rights of a buyer in ordinary course or other good faith purchaser under this article (UCC § 2-403)." To be protected the buyer from the grain dealer must act in accordance with reasonable commercial standards of fair dealing and "without knowledge that the sale to him is in violation of the ownership rights . . . of a third party." UCC § 1-201(9).

The reclamation scenario is different if Farmer sells grain to a grain dealer and receives a bad check. Even though a sale in return for a check is not a credit sale, the unpaid seller has a right of reclamation. UCC §§ 2-507(2); 2-511(3); Szabo v. Vinton Motors (1st Cir.1980). No specific time limit is imposed on the cash seller to exercise reclamation. However, the right will be defeated by delay causing prejudice to a buyer. Comment 3 to UCC § 2-507(2)(1991 version)

Assume Farmer sells grain to a grain dealer and gets a bad check. In turn the grain dealer sells the grain to ADM. When payment is due on delivery, Official Comment 3 to UCC § 2-507(2) states that the unpaid cash seller's ability to reclaim is subject to Article 2 rules about bona fide purchasers. Section 2-403(1)(b) provides that when goods have been delivered under a transaction of purchase, the purchaser has the power of one with voidable title even though the delivery was in exchange for a check later dishonored. A person with voidable title (grain dealer) has power to transfer a good title to a good faith purchaser for value (ADM).

Voidable title is not specifically defined in the UCC. But see UCC § 2-403(1)(apparent examples of when voidable title is created). The key is that the seller of the goods (grain dealer) must have obtained possession by purchase as opposed to gift or involuntary taking (e.g. theft). In the ADM example, the grain dealer has voidable title because UCC § 2-403(1)(b) applies. The bad check does not alter the fact of a transaction of purchase. Thus, the grain dealer has the power to convey good title to a good faith purchaser. ADM, in seeking to be protected from Farmer's claim, will assert that it is a good faith purchaser for value under the standard is at UCC § 2-103(1)(b). See p. 214 *supra*. If ADM had prior knowledge that it was grain dealer's only large buyer and that dealer had issued bad checks to sellers in the past, ADM probably has a duty to inquire and to seek payment instructions if direct payment to the dealer is found by that inquiry to be inappropriate.

An unsecured unpaid seller of grain should file a claim in the grain dealer bankruptcy. The fifth-level priority up to $4,000 in distribution of assets of the bankrupt estate, discussed at p. 218 *supra,* is not just for grain conversion claims, but also extends to unpaid sellers of grain.

A few states have experimented with legislation designed to give unpaid sellers of grain statutory liens on the commingled mass. But such efforts offer little as these liens would be effective only on amounts remaining after bailment claims have been fully satisfied. Even then, such liens will be undone in the grain dealer's bankruptcy if they become effective upon insolvency (disguised priority) or are not good against bona fide purchasers under state law at the date of the petition. Code § 545(1), (2).

In states where licensing of grain dealers is required there is likely to a bonding requirement.

While the protection may not be extensive, the claim of the unpaid seller against such a bond should not be overlooked. Several states have created statutory indemnity fund programs, a few of which protect unpaid sellers as well as shorted bailors. See p. 218 *supra*. Finally, suits against creditors who have taken control of the debtor, and culpable auditors and inspectors can be explored. See p. 220 *supra.*

A prophylactic approach in the case of deferred payment contracts might be to require a grain dealer, at the seller's request, to obtain an irrevocable standby letter of credit in favor of such seller. Of course, only the strongest and most conservative of grain dealers are likely to be in a position to open such a credit with a financial institution.

The legal situation is quite different when the farmer has not delivered on a forward contract by the time the grain dealer becomes a bankrupt. Consider this example: On December 1, Farmer who has all of his grain stored on the farm, sells 5,000 bushels of corn to grain dealer to be delivered and paid for on February 1. The grain dealer is cast into bankruptcy on January 15. Under UCC § 2-702(1) the farmer can refuse to deliver the grain except for cash. But, the grain dealer's trustee may decide not to buy the grain. The trustee can reject or accept the contract under Code § 365 which deals with executory contracts. In making this decision the trustee must act in the best interests of unsecured creditors.

B. Unpaid Sellers and Secured Parties

The discussion now expands to include unpaid sellers of livestock, poultry and perishable agricultural commodities. In common with sellers of grain, these parties encounter problems when they are unpaid but find that the farm products they have sold are characterized as part of the inventory of their buyer. A number of courts have considered whether an unpaid seller can reclaim goods that are claimed as collateral by a perfected secured party of the buyer.

In re Western Farmers Ass'n (Bankr.W.D.Wash. 1980), is a case where the seller sold and delivered grain, meat, feed, and other fungible commodities to an insolvent buyer, Western Farmers Association. The seller made a written demand for reclamation within 10 days. Bank, the financier of Western Farmers, had a perfected security interest in all of Western's present and after-acquired property. Bank claimed its security interest attached to the seller's goods upon their delivery to Western. The court agreed and held secured party's security interest to be superior to the seller's right of reclamation. The reasoning is that under UCC § 2-702(3), the seller's right to reclaim is invalid against a good faith purchaser, here the secured party. See pp. 222-23 *supra*.

A meat packer in In re Samuels & Co. (5th Cir. 1976) purchased cattle from ranchers on a "grade and yield basis," as was the custom in the industry. About two days after delivery, the purchase price was set and checks were issued by Samuels to the sellers. Samuels filed a bankruptcy petition and ranchers' checks were dishonored. Ranchers sought reclamation under UCC § 2-702(2). This was contested by C.I.T., which financed Samuels and had a perfected security interest in all of Samuels' inventory, including after-acquired inventory, and proceeds.

The Samuels court held for C.I.T., using two theories to justify the result. Under both, C.I.T. obtained rights in the cattle once they had come into the possession of Samuels and became part of its inventory. Analyzing UCC §§ 2-702(3), 2-507, and 2-511, the court recognized that the seller's right of reclamation is subject to the good faith purchaser rule of UCC § 2-403(1)(b). While Samuels gave rancher-sellers bad checks, C.I.T., the secured party, was nevertheless a purchaser under the UCC. The court determined that C.I.T. was a good faith purchaser, having satisfied the standard of UCC § 2-103(1)(b). See p. 214 *supra*. The other justification used an assumption that the reclamation rights of the farmer-sellers were really security interests -- unperfected and subject to C.I.T.'s perfected security interest. Note that most courts reject the suggestion that an unpaid seller's right to reclaim is a security interest.

In Samuels, the court pointed out that the sellers were aware of the risk that when cattle were delivered, timely payment might not be forthcoming. They could have protected themselves under UCC § 9-312(3) by obtaining a perfected security interest. The court failed to note that it is unrealistic to assume that buyers of live cattle are going to consent to granting security interests to sellers so that they might be protected for one or two days -- the normal amount of time that elapses before payment. It is also unrealistic to think that a rancher in the normal course of sales transactions is personally or through legal counsel going to attempt compliance with UCC § 9-312(3). This would require a security agreement and a financing statement bearing the debtor's (packer's) signature and the filing of such financing statement before the packer obtains possession. The rancher (secured party) would also need to give written notice to other secured parties having perfected security interests in buyer's inventory. This would require a search of UCC filings to determine the identify of any such prior filed secured creditors. In addition to satisfying the requirements of UCC § 9-312(3),

In 1976 in the wake of Samuels, livestock sellers were given protection when Congress amended the Packers and Stockyard Act by adding 7 USCA § 196(b). This section requires packers to hold in trust for unpaid livestock sellers all proceeds from cash sales of livestock as well as the inventory of carcasses as such. This change effectively reverses the outcome in the Samuels type case. See pp. 249-52 *infra*. When the trust is in effect, the security interest of a financier such as C.I.T. cannot attach to its corpus.

Today, unpaid sellers of poultry and perishable agricultural commodities are also protected by federal statutory trusts. See pp. 266-67 *infra*. Unpaid sellers of grain and dairy products are not similarly protected by federal statute. At least one state, Oklahoma, has created for dairy producers a statutory trust similar to those at the federal level for sellers of livestock, perishable agricultural commodities and poultry. Okla. Stat. tit. 2, § 751-56.

CHAPTER SEVEN

ANIMALS

This chapter explores selected legal issues pertinent to animal agriculture. First, private relationships are considered -- rights and duties associated with membership in breed associations, and issues associated with the identification and private sale of animals. Thereafter, the focus of this chapter shifts to government regulation of packers and stockyards, communicable diseases of livestock, and animal patents

I. BREED ASSOCIATIONS

A. Basics

The purpose of a breed association is to promote and develop a particular animal breed. To accomplish this, the association establishes standards of quality and purity of blood strain. Just one association exists for a particular breed and it has a complete monopoly. An animal will not be considered purebred unless it is registered with the appropriate breed association. Refusal to register may result if the animal is the progeny of other than purebred animals, or for reasons such as inappropriate color-markings. The difference in value between a pure-bred and non-purebred animal is significant. For example, a registered quarter horse colt can be worth 10 times more than if not registered.

Registration is usually a straight forward process. An application is submitted by the owner together with a breeder's certificate detailing the animal's pedigree, a registration fee, and, if relevant, description of color markings. In most cases a photograph is required. Physical inspection of the animal is often mandatory.

In addition to registration rules, associations have rules governing member conduct. Because members can be suspended or excluded for violation of these rules, breed associations can literally put a particular breeder out of business.

B. Due Process Issues

Most lawsuits against purebred associations follow upon a refusal to register or the revocation of the registration of an animal, or the suspension or exclusion of a member. Because state action is not involved, there is no basis for the application of constitutionally rooted equal protection and due process requirements. But, requirements such as right to notice and fair hearing must be satisfied when a private association adjudicates matters of a legal nature. Exercise of its power to deny registration or to expel or suspend a member, triggers application of these "traditional" principles of due process. Hatley v. American Quarter Horse Ass'n (5th Cir.1977); Adams v. American Quarter Horse Ass'n (Tex.Ct.App.1979).

Courts are reluctant to get involved in the internal affairs of voluntary organizations. When due process violations are asserted, two questions must be resolved: do the association's rules comport with minimum due process by providing for notice of charges and an opportunity to prepare and present a defense; and, were the rules applied in a fair and reasonable manner. Terrell v. Palomino Horse Breeders of America (PHBA)(Ind.Ct.App.1980). In Terrell, the PHBA rules were deemed sufficient because they required at least 15 days notice of the time and place of the hearing and an opportunity to present evidence and to be heard, either in person or by counsel. And, the accused was allowed to hear and refute evidence offered to prove violations.

The court in Terrell had an additional issue to resolve. In an earlier proceeding on the same matter, the association gave the member neither notice nor a hearing. Although the original suspension was tainted by the denial of due process, Terrell held that the association could retry the member. Contrast Hatley where the court held that the association's offer of a hearing after the institution of court proceedings was not sufficient because "[t]he adamantine position of the litigants makes it unlikely that a hearing could be conducted in a neutral and detached fashion."

C. Antitrust Issues

Antitrust issues are raised when a purebred animal association excludes a member, refuses to accept new members or refuses to register an animal. Typically, an aggrieved party will allege the action to be a group boycott or a refusal to deal in violation of the Sherman Antitrust Act, 15 USCA §§ 1 & 2. The complainant must show that the association's actions were a "contract, combination . . . or conspiracy to restrain commerce" which amounts to an unreasonable restraint on trade or commerce. The bylaws of the association are sufficient to establish the agreement. If the action of the organization has a "pernicious effect on competition" and "lacks any redeeming virtue," the action can be considered unreasonable "per se," and the plaintiff's difficult task of proving unreasonableness is obviated.

The court in McReery Angus Farms v. American Angus Ass'n (S.D.Ill.1974) held that the association's actions in indefinitely suspending a member without notice, hearing or opportunity to confront the accuser was unreasonable "per se." The court stressed the fact that the association had no rules to provide even the most basic elements of a fair hearing. In Hatley, p. 230 *supra*, a similar charge grew out of the association's refusal to register a colt. The 5th Circuit held that there was no "per se" violation of the Sherman Act, and that the Association's rules and procedures for denial of registration did not constitute an unreasonable restraint on commerce, even though no hearing was afforded the aggrieved member. The rules governing denial of registration were seen as a legitimate tool to improve the breed. If the cases are to be reconciled it will be because in Hatley the association followed legitimate prescribed rules, while in McCreery the association had no rules and did not give the member a hearing.

II. BRANDING LAWS

A. In General

Several methods have been devised to identify farm and ranch animals as property of a particular individual. Where brand registration is used, the owner is entitled to its exclusive use during the effective time period after recording. New Mexico has entered some 30,000 registered brands in its computer data-base, thus facilitating the identification of the person who registered a particular brand.

At least 30 states have enacted branding laws. While such laws vary, all are designed to provide a way of identification of ownership, and concomitantly to prevent theft. In many western states, hot iron branding is required. Where permitted, animals can be marked for identification by tattooing the lip, ear-notching, ear tagging or freeze branding.

In most states branding of cattle is not optional. The same is usually true for horses, mules and asses. Sheep are included under some state laws. Most statutes contain exceptions for registered purebred animals and unweaned calves standing with the branded mother. Branding laws commonly require that the seller of an animal provide to the purchaser a written bill of sale stating the date of transfer, sex of the animal, the carrying brand on the animal -- including the symbol and location, the name and address of the seller, and of the buyer.

State laws requiring branding and/or inspection of brand prior to sale have been held to be legitimate exercises of the police power -- including criminalization of noncompliance. U.S. v. Christiansen (D. Nev.1980); Black Hills Packing Co. v. South Dakota Stockgrowers Ass'n (D.S.Dak.1975). Some states create brand districts and allow each to decide whether or not to require brand inspection. In South Dakota inspection is required only in counties west of the Missouri River. Because equal protection does not have to do with geographical areas, a constitutional problem is not presented. State v. Smith (S.Dak. 1974). If a district opts for inspection, the brand must be inspected before a valid written bill of sale can be issued.

Brand laws also proscribe activities such as use of an unrecorded brand, branding animals belonging to another, or tampering with a brand. Violators may be subject to penalties, including criminal sanctions.

B. Brands as Evidence of Ownership

The primary purpose of branding laws is to provide an effective means of establishing ownership of livestock. Because brands are unique, the brand constitutes prima facie evidence of ownership when it is shown that the person claiming ownership is the recorded owner of the brand on the livestock. But, a person in possession of an animal purchased from another, but bearing the possessor's recorded brand, can still have problems proving ownership if a bill of sale from the seller cannot be produced. Consider this situation: X purchases from A cattle which bore the brand of Y, without requiring A to produce a bill of sale or other evidence of ownership. X then places his own brand over Y's. Under most branding laws, in a replevin action brought by Y, X will bear the burden of proof to show that he has rightful ownership and failing that will lose the cattle. Coomes v. Drinkwalter (Neb.1967).

This result is consistent with the common law doctrine that a person can receive no better title to property than was held by his transferor, and that a thief can acquire no title to stolen property. Hence, the purchaser of stolen property has no defense in an action brought by the true owner.

In the above example. suppose that X purchases cattle bearing Y's brand from a sale barn that had unknowingly accepted the cattle on consignment from a thief. Can Y now replevy the cattle bearing the Y brand from X? Absent a contrary statute, the UCC would apply and X would lose to Y, the true owner, unless Y is somehow at fault. UCC § 2-403.

The general rule of UCC § 2-403 is that a purchaser of goods gets no better title than that of the seller. In our problem, unless X can fit within one of the exceptions at § 2-403(1), (2), X gets no better title than that of the seller -- and that was no title at all. The sale barn did not have voidable title. Section 2-403(2) does not help X even though the sale barn is undoubtedly a merchant under UCC § 2-104. The cattle were entrusted to the sale barn, but a merchant can transfer only the *rights* of the entrustor. UCC § 2-403(2),(3). Because the thief had no title, X loses even if he is a buyer in the ordinary course. However, the sale barn likely will be the ultimate loser because X can sue it for breach of implied warranty of good title -- if the sale barn is the agent of the seller and impliedly warrants good title. See UCC §§ 2-312 and 2-714(2).

C. Bill of Sale Requirement & the UCC

Many states require by statute that purchasers of branded livestock obtain from the owner a written bill of sale granting the purchaser the right to possession, together with a properly issued brand inspection certificate showing the brands involved and the number of cattle purchased with each brand. Typically, the bill of sale and brand inspection certificate will be included in a single document. Failure to obtain these documents may leave the purchaser open to charges of theft or wrongful possession. See, e.g., Cugnini v. Reynolds Cattle Co. (Colo.1984).

III. SALES OF ANIMALS

A. Generally

Sales of animals can give rise to problems not present in other sale transactions. Animals may be afflicted with disease, often latent, and those purchased for breeding purposes may be infertile. Many states have tailored their commercial laws to accommodate animal sales, particularly warranty law.

A purchaser of diseased animals, in addition to rejecting or revoking acceptance, may have damage claims for breach of contract Actual damages may involve the replacement of the diseased animals at a higher price, and consequential damages may flow from the spread of disease to other animals on the purchase's farm. The purchaser may consider suit based upon UCC Article 2 (breach of contract and warranty law), tort claims of fraud, deceit or negligent misrepresentation, simple negligence, or strict liability. Our focus is on warranties and the UCC.

B. Warranties

In general, a warranty is a seller's agreement or representation, express or implied, about the goods, their description, basic attributes or special suitability. For example, when the seller (S) says to buyer (B), "This bull is in sound condition" or "this bull is a particularly good breeder," S is making representations about conditions that may or may not be true and over which he has little or no control. If the sale is completed and the bull has a disease or is not a good breeder, B will claim that S's representations became part of S's legal obligation to B and that the non-conformity entitles B to pursue remedies for breach of warranty. Whether such representations become part of seller's obligation is an often litigated matter. Comment 4 to UCC § 2-314 states that the "whole purpose of the law of warranty is to determine what it is that the seller has in essence agreed to sell."

The UCC recognizes three types of warranties: express, § 2-313; implied warranty of merchantability, § 2-314; and implied warranty of fitness for a particular purposes, § 2-315. The UCC also contemplates that warranties may be disclaimed or limited by agreement. § 2-316. In case of seller breach, one or more remedies may be available to the buyer under Article 2. As the following examples show, the later the defect is discovered, the less flexibility there is as to remedies. For example, if B discovers the defect before acceptance, the animals may be rejected under § 2-601 and the remedies for rightful rejection under § 2-711(1) become available. After the animals are accepted, the burden is on B to establish breach with respect to the accepted goods. § 2-607(4). Unless B can revoke acceptance under § 2-608, B is liable for the price of the animals. § 2-607(1),(2). If B can justifiably revoke acceptance, the remedies under § 2-711 are available. Even if B has accepted defective goods and is unable or unwilling to revoke acceptance, a remedy still exists if "within a reasonable time after he discovers or should have discovered any breach" he notifies S of the breach. § 2-607(3)(a). Section 2-714 sets out the measure of damages and established damages may be deducted from the contract price. Also, B may claim incidental damages under § 2-715(1) (damages for inspection, care of rightfully rejected goods or expenses in effecting cover) and under § 2-715(2) consequential damages resulting from the breach (e.g., injury caused to property).

1. Express Warranties

An express warranty arises when S does something affirmative to create buyer expectations about the characteristics or performance of goods. Under UCC § 2-313, S can create an express warranty three ways: 1) by any affirmations of fact or promise relating to the goods made to B; 2) by a description of goods; or 3) by displaying a sample or model of the "whole" of the goods. The affirmation, the description, or the sample must be shown to be "part of the basis of the bargain." It is not necessary for B to prove that she relied upon the affirmation, promise, description, or sample; the assumption being that they become part of the basis of buyer's bargain unless S produces "clear affirmative proof" to the contrary. Yet, many courts indicate that the nature of B's reliance is not as irrelevant as the Code appears to make it. See, e.g., Price Brothers Co. v. Philadelphia Gear Corp. (6th Cir.1981). Also, "an affirmation merely of the value of the goods or a statement purporting to be merely S's opinion or commendation of the goods does not create a warranty." UCC § 2-313(2). A classic example of puffing or opinions not amounting to warranties is: "[t]his bull calf will 'put the buyer on the map' and 'his father was the greatest living dairy bull'." Frederickson v. Hackney (Minn.1924).

Consider two examples of express warranties. An oral statement by S to B that these cows are "clean" and this herd is a "good reputable herd" is a warranty that the herd is free from disease. Young & Cooper v. Vestring (Kan.1974). An oral statement made by S to B that this bull is a sound healthy bull, perfect in all parts, a one-hundred percent breeder - a sure calf getter, is an express warranty that the bull is capable of breeding. Adrian v. Elmer (Kan.1955). The line between puffing and warranting is often difficult to draw, but the more specific the statement the more likely it is a warranty. Downie v. Abex Corp. (10th Cir.1984).

The creation of express warranties is not limited to language in sales contracts or statements made in sales negotiations. An advertisement, catalogue, or brochure can create an express warranty if it is part of the basis of the bargain. The general rule is that B must have at least read " . . . the catalogue, advertisement or brochure." Interco, Inc. v. Randustrial Corp. (Mo.Ct.App.1976). See also Torstenson v. Melcher (Neb.1976)(express warranty created by catalog ad seeking buyers for registered bulls).

If an express warranty is made, the risk of the quality of the goods is placed on S even though S was unaware of and had no control over the actual condition of the goods. Generally, as S seeks to induce the sale, the more S says about the goods, in a setting where S speaks as if he has actual knowledge, the more likely it is that the representations will become part of the basis of the buyer's bargain. On the other hand, the more general the statements made in a context of equal ignorance or where B has a better opportunity to determine quality, the greater the probability that the statements will not be considered express warranties. It is a question of fact to be determined on a case by case basis, as in this example:

> S, a rancher, and B, a breeder, discussed a sale of a purebred Hereford cow. S stated that the cow is "with calf." B, after examining the cow and consulting a veterinary, agreed. The written contract specified that S agreed to sell a purebred Hereford cow with calf and B agreed to pay $10,000. After delivery, it was discovered that the cow was barren and worth only $3000.

Was there an express warranty? On these facts it does not appears that S's statement and the contract description became part of the basis of the buyer's bargain. B had equal information, had equal to or greater than experience than the seller and may have relied upon the veterinarian's judgment. However, assuming both parties were mistaken, B may be able to avoid the contract on grounds of mutual mistake the under common law. See UCC § 1-103.

Once an express warranty is given, it is almost impossible to disclaim it. UCC § 2-316(1). In states that have eliminated or restricted implied warranties as to animal health, express warranties from sellers take on a particular importance.

2. Implied Warranties

In many sales transactions, no express warranties are made. Yet, the UCC gives buyer (B) the benefit of one or more implied warranties. They are made part of the contract by operation of law and generally must be construed liberally in B's favor. The UCC specifically provides for implied warranties of merchantability at § 2-314, and fitness for a particular purpose at § 2-315. While not called an implied warranty, § 2-312 states that unless otherwise provided, all contracts for the sale of goods contain a warranty that the seller has good title, the transfer is rightful, and the goods delivered will be free of any security interest or other lien or encumbrance. S need not be a merchant, and it is irrelevant whether S has knowledge of the title's defect. If B can show the breach and no presale knowledge of the defect, he is entitled to damages which can include "the difference between the value of the goods accepted and the value they would have had if they had been as warranted" as well as incidental and consequential damages, if demonstrated. UCC § 2-714.

Section 2-314(1) of the UCC governs **implied warranties of merchantability** and provides in part: " . . . unless excluded or modified (§ 2-316), a warranty that the goods shall be merchantable is implied in the contract for their sale if the seller is a merchant with respect to goods of that kind." For an implied warranty of merchantability to be breached, several conditions must be met. 1) S must be a "merchant with respect to goods of that kind." UCC § 2-314. Some courts hold that certain farmers are not merchants. See pp. 140-42 *supra*. 2) There must be a contract for the sale of the particular goods and no effective clause excluding or disclaiming the implied warranty. 3) The goods must be unmerchantable under UCC § 2-314(2). The warranty is implied from the nature and descriptions of the goods and "circumstances" in which they are sold and used. This warranty establishes what some call a "bottom line" of quality which a buyer who pays a fair price can reasonably expect. Breach of such warranty is a question of fact. 4) The damage must be proximately caused from the defect in the goods. Comment 13 to § 2-314. 5) Notice of the breach of warranty must be given to the seller within a reasonable time after B discovers or should have discovered the breach. UCC § 2-607(3).

The implied warranty of merchantability may be excluded or disclaimed by: 1) a waiver in the contract; 2) buyer's examination of the goods; or 3) "course of dealing or course of performance or usage of trade." UCC § 2-316. As to waivers in the contract, an implied warranty of merchantability can be negated if it is provided that the goods are sold "as is" or "with all faults" or similar language. UCC § 2-316(3)(a). If a written contract is to effectively disclaim the implied warranty of merchantability, the "language must mention merchantability and in the case of a writing must be conspicuous." UCC § 2-316(2).

Issues concerning the creation and waiver of implied warranties of merchantability have been litigated frequently. Many of the cases deal with protection of buyers of animals. For example, in Vlases v. Montgomery Ward & Co., Inc. (3rd Cir. 1967), a seller of chicks was held liable for a breach of a warranty of merchantability because the chicks were infected with a disease that impaired egg production and eventually lead to the death or destruction of the entire flock. A defense could not be predicated on the theory that there was no human skill, knowledge or foresight which would have enabled the supplier of the chicks to prevent, detect, or to treat the disease.

The implied **warranty of fitness** for a particular purpose is more difficult to establish. The seller must have reason when the contract is formed to know the particular purpose for which the goods are being acquired, and that the buyer is relying on the seller's skill and judgment to select or furnish suitable goods. It is also necessary the buyer in fact so relies. With these elements the warranty is established unless waived or modified under UCC § 2-316. For example, a breeder who sells hogs for breeding, knowing that the buyer is relying on his judgment, gives an implied warranty that they are fit for that purpose. If the hogs turn out to be infected with a disease that renders them useless as breeders, the hogs are not fit for the purpose intended and there is a breach of the implied warranty for which the seller is liable. Paullus v. Liedkie (Idaho 1968).

The rules for establishing waiver of an implied warranty of fitness are basically the same as the implied warranty of merchantability. One difference is in the language of the disclaimer. Section 2-316(2) of the UCC provides that to "exclude or modify any implied warranty of fitness the exclusion or waiver must be by a writing and conspicuous." The waiver need not specifically refer to fitness. It is sufficient if it states, for example, that "[t]here are no warranties which extend beyond the description on the face hereof." UCC § 2-316(2). To effect waiver of an implied warranty of merchantability the word merchantability must be mentioned.

Special rules for animal warranties exist in some jurisdictions. At least 24 states (Arkansas, Florida, Georgia, Illinois, Indiana, Iowa, Kansas, Kentucky, Michigan, Mississippi, Missouri, Montana, Nebraska,

North Dakota, Ohio, Oklahoma, Oregon, South
Dakota, Tennessee, Texas, Utah, Washington,
Wisconsin, and Wyoming) have amended one or
both of the UCC implied warranty provisions as they
apply to livestock sales. Most of these statutory
changes do not apply to poultry sales.

The statutory changes fall roughly into three
categories. One approach completely eliminates
implied warranties in the sale of livestock. See, e.g.,
Mo. Rev. Stat. § 400.2-316(5); and Texas Bus. &
Comm. Code § 2-316(f). In these states, buyers who
have not been given an express warranty will, in
essence, contend with the *caveat emptor* rule. These
changes shifted the risk of loss to the buyer and
were heavily lobbied for by persons in livestock
marketing, particularly auctioneers. In at least 11
states the implied warranties are revived when state
and federal health regulations are violated.

In some states the changes have been made
applicable only to certain types or species of
livestock. For example, Florida exempts cattle and
hogs from implied warranties, but the statute says
nothing about other species such as sheep, horses,
and poultry. Oklahoma dropped implied warranties
as to livestock and their unborn young, but
specifically preserves their application to sales of
horses. Most states that enumerate species in their
statutes have eliminated implied warranties only as to
cattle, hogs and sheep.

Some states, Kansas and Ohio as examples, do not
exempt livestock sold for immediate slaughter from
implied warranties. It is not clear why this has been
done inasmuch as a packer would normally be in a

better position than an individual producer to absorb losses. One explanation is that because the bulk of the cattle slaughtered today are fattened in feedlots, packers need protection when an unscrupulous operator sells livestock that are unfit for human consumption -- e.g., animals that have been fed prohibited growth hormones or antibiotics. Going its own way, California has eliminated the implied warranties only when livestock is sold for slaughter. Cal. Food and Agric. Code §§ 18501-18502.

Some exceptions are very limited. Under Georgia Code 11-2-316(3)(d), only licensed cattle, sheep and hog livestock auctions and agents are excluded from the imposition of implied warranties, and even they lose the benefit of the exclusion if within one month after sale animals react positively to brucellosis tests conducted by the state. Under Kentucky law, it will be necessary to ascertain whether the animals were sick when sold and if the seller knew they were sick. Because the change is in the UCC, the § 1-201(25) definition of knowledge as actual knowledge appears to apply. Thus, if a buyer could show that the seller had actual knowledge of disease or sickness, she could rely upon implied warranties.

IV.　PACKERS AND STOCKYARDS ACT

A.　Introduction

The Packers and Stockyards Act of 1921 (PSA) was originally designed to regulate five large packing concerns - Swift, Armour, Morris, Cudahy, and Wilson. It was thought that these packers were manipulating markets, restricting the flow of foods, controlling the price of dressed meat, defrauding producers and consumers of food, and crushing competition. Many livestock producers are concerned about the existing concentration of power in the big three, ConAgra, IBP, and Excel, which together have 60 percent of beef-packing sales.

PSA provides a broad multi-purpose regulatory program reaching packers, stockyards dealers, marketing agents and live poultry dealers. 7 USCA §§ 181-229. In general, its goal is to assure the integrity of livestock, meat and poultry markets. The Act prohibits unfair, deceptive, discriminatory and monopolistic practices. Its anti-competitive provisions are broader than the those of the Sherman Antitrust Act and than § 5 of the Federal Trade Commission Act (FTC). This is so because PSA proscribes affirmative anticompetitive acts as well as refusals to buy. Swift & Co. v. U.S. (7th Cir.1968).

The PSA is administered by the Packers and Stockyards Administration, a part of USDA. Most cases arising under PSA will be heard initially by a USDA administrative law judge. Appeals of administrative decisions are to the USDA Judicial Officer (JO) who has the authority to issue final decisions for the Secretary of Agriculture. Because the JO is not controlled by USDA's general counsel, agency heads or assistant secretaries, it has been concluded that fair adjudicatory proceedings can be conducted. In re DeGraaf Dairies, Inc., (Agric.Dec.1982).

B. Packers

1. Activities Regulated

A packer is defined at 7 USCA § 191 as:

> . . . any person engaged in the business (a) of buying livestock in commerce for purposes of slaughter, or (b) of manufactur-

ing or preparing meats or meat food
products for sale or shipment in commerce,
or (c) of marketing meats, meat food
products, or livestock products in an unmanufactured form acting as a wholesale
broker, dealer, or distributor in commerce.
[Livestock defined to include "cattle, sheep,
swine, horses, mules or goats." § 182(4)]

This broad definition not only encompasses the
big slaughterhouses and meat packers, but reaches
businesses that purchase processed meat for resale in
quantities suitable for hospitals, schools, restaurants,
and hotels. U.S. v. Jay Freeman Co., Inc., (E.D.Ark.
1979). Nationwide supermarket chains that have
central facilities where they cut up carcasses, grind
meat, make corn beef, and cut and wrap meat also
have been held to be packers. Safeway Stores, Inc.
v. Freeman (D.C.Cir.1966). Similarly, packers can be
freezer plant operators who cut up sides of beef into
consumer cuts and who freeze prepared meat for
ultimate sale to consumers. Bruhn's Freezer Meats
of Chicago, Inc. v. USDA (8th Cir.1971). However,
retail sales of meat, meat food products and poultry
products in unmanufactured form are the primary
responsibility of the Federal Trade Commission.
PSA § 182(7), § 227. The jurisdiction of USDA
over poultry products is limited to enforcement of
the unpaid poultry sellers trust fund at PSA § 197(b)
and the prompt payment rules at PSA § 228b-1.

Packers, on the other hand, are subject to broad
control. For example, PSA § 192 prohibits packers
from engaging in: any type of unjustly discriminatory or deceptive practice; any practice restraining, or
any agreement with another to restrain, commerce or

creating a monopoly; or any activity either designed to, or which does manipulate or control prices. These statutory prohibitions have been construed in cases that involved commercial bribery by sellers, price refunds, price discounts, agreements on prices, and conspiracy to set terms of sale.

Regulations expand the statutory rules by forbidding such activities as circulation of misleading reports on market conditions or price; use of false weights when livestock are sold on a weight basis; and exchange of information among packers for the purpose of limiting competition. See, e.g., 9 CFR §§ 201.53, 201.55-.56, 201.61, 201.67-.70, 201.82 (1994). Other problems arise when a packer fails to pay the full price or to accept delivery, asserting that seller has not complied with the contract. Such disputes normally concern condition, grade, weight or shipping instructions. 9 CFR § 203.7(1994).

Packers with annual purchases greater than $500,000 who purchase cattle through an affiliate or wholly-owned subsidiary must file a bond with USDA. However, packer buyers registered as dealers to purchase livestock for slaughter only are not required to maintain a bond. 9 CFR § 201.29(1994).

If the Secretary has reason to believe that a packer is engaged in PSA § 192 prohibited practices, he or his delegate will file a complaint. The charged party is entitled to a hearing. Upon finding of a violation, the Secretary may assess a civil penalty of not more than $10,000 and issue cease and desist orders. Judicial review is the Court of Appeals for the Circuit in which the packer has its principal place of business. Violation of a final order of the Secretary

-- e.g., a cease and desist order -- is punishable by fine, imprisonment, or both. PSA §§ 193-95.

2. *Statutory Trust For Unpaid Cash Sellers*

In an effort to assure livestock producers of full and prompt payment, Congress in 1976 amended PSA by adding §§ 196 and 228b. Prior to 1976, a packer's secured creditor, with a perfected security interest in packer's inventories, accounts receivable and proceeds, had priority over the unpaid unsecured producer's claim to the sold livestock or proceeds thereof. In re Samuels & Co., Inc. (5th Cir.1976). As unsecured creditors, producers usually receive little if anything in a packer bankruptcy. See In re Gotham Provision Co., Inc. (5th Cir.1982).

Section 196(b) requires that a packer with annual purchases exceeding $500,000 establish a trust fund for the benefit of all unpaid cash sellers of livestock until full payment has been received by said sellers. Livestock is defined to be cattle, sheep, swine, horses, mules of goats. PSA § 182(4). Unpaid sellers of poultry are not protected under § 196. However, in 1987 a poultry trust was added at PSA § 197. See pp. 266-67 *infra*. While these trust statutes are not identical, the basic concepts are the same. Section 196's cash sale and timely notice rules merit special attention.

The trust corpus is made up of livestock and all proceeds of livestock from cash sellers, paid and unpaid. In re Harmon (Bankr.N.D.Tex.1980). Livestock, proceeds and receivables generated from credit sales are not part of the trust, but remain general assets of the packer subject to the claims of all creditors. However, when funds from credit sales are commingled with funds from cash sales, the combined assets have been classed as trust funds by USDA.

Section 196(c) of the PSA defines a cash sale as one where the seller does not expressly extend credit to the buyer. Under 9 CFR § 201.200(1994), a credit sale cannot be established unless prior to the sale the seller signs and receives a copy of an acknowledgement stating that the seller will have no claim to the assets of the trust fund under § 196. The packer retains a copy which is attached to any documents setting out the agreed upon credit terms. In re Arbogast and Bastian, Inc. (Bankr.D.Pa.1984).

To preserve a valid claim against the trust, the unpaid seller must give written notice of nonpayment to the packer and file such notice with the Secretary within 30 calendar days of the final date for making payment under PSA § 228b, or within 15 business days of being notified that the payment of a promptly presented check was dishonored. PSA § 196(b). The last day of the 30 day period cannot be a Saturday or Sunday. In re Gotham Provision Co., Inc. (5th Cir.1982).

Section 196(b) does not indicate how the time periods can be satisfied, nor do the PSA regulations. Taken literally, the statute suggests that a written notice must be physically delivered to the Secretary's office. However, acceptance and the stamping of "received by the Packers and Stockyard Administration Office" should be sufficient. Physical delivery is crucial in that depositing of the notice in the mail is not to be considered "filing."

Recall that it is a written notice that "must" be given to the packer before the running of the pertinent time period. In re Marvin Properties, Inc. (9th Cir.1988), holds that neither oral notice nor actual notice is sufficient for purposes of preserving rights under the Perishable Agricultural Commodity Trust Fund. Because the PACA trust is modeled in large part on the Packer trust, cases such as Marvin Properties can be relevant to our discussion. At 9 CFR § 203.15(a) (1994) one of the ways to satisfy the notice requirement "is to make certain that notice is given to the packer . . . within the pre-scribed time by letter, mailgram, or telegram . . .." It appears that a fax or other electronic transmission, would be satisfactory. The copy must be filed either with the Packers and Stockyards Administration area office, or with the Administration's national office in Washington, D.C.

Questions can arise as to whether a notice timely given is adequate as to content. Compare In re D.K.M.B., Inc. (Bankr.D.Colo.1989)(strict compli-ance with regulations on contents of notice) with In re Richmond Produce Co. (Bankr.N.D.Cal.1990) (substantial rather than strict compliance). The rule on notice content was relaxed in 1989 to require "any written notice which informs [of failure] . . . to pay is sufficient . . .." 9 CFR § 203.15(b) (1994).

If a packer does not pay, the unpaid seller has a contract action under state law and a federal private right of action under § 196 to enforce the statutory trust. Section 196(b) provides that the livestock and its proceeds shall be held in trust "until full payment has been received . . .." Full payment includes the purchase price, prejudgment interest from the time the packer accepted delivery, and costs incurred by producers to enforce their rights. See, e.g., Pennsylvania Agricultural Coop. Marketing Ass'n v. Ezra Martin Co.(D.M.D.Pa.1980)

3. *Prompt Payment Rule*

Section 228b of the PSA provides that packers, marketing agents or dealers purchasing livestock must deliver to the seller or its duly authorized agent full payment before the close of the next business day following the purchase, unless the parties agree otherwise in writing before the purchase, or the sale is on a grade and yield basis. In the latter case, the payment must be made by the close of the next business day following the determination of the price. 9 CFR § 201.99 (1994). Often the producer will not be present at the point of transfer of possession of the livestock and wants the check mailed. The packer must either wire transfer funds or place a check in the U.S. mail within the time limit. Notice to the packer in advance of the sale that the check is to be sent directly to the producer is not an extension of credit and does give the packer having more time pay. 9 CFR § 203.16(a) (1994).

Any delay or attempt to delay payment is an "unfair practice" under PSA § 228b(c). An example of delay is found in Beef Nebraska, Inc. v. U.S. (8th Cir.1986), where a packer used a "country bank" 125 miles from its sole processing plant. The resulting delay of payment by one day was considered a violation. Yet, the Secretary does not have specific statutory authority to issue cease and desist orders or assess civil penalties for the failure to pay promptly. Section 193 deals with packers and prescribes remedies when they commit violations of "this subchapter" which includes only §§ 192, 196 and 197. Section 213 does provide for penalties when unfair practices are committed, but only as to stockyard owners, market agencies and dealers.

In 1987 Congress amended PSA by adding § 228b-1 which made live poultry dealers subject to the prompt payment rule. Failure of live poultry dealers to pay promptly is now an unfair practice. The Secretary is authorized to issue cease and desist orders as well as assess civil penalties up to $20,000.

There is no reason to believe that Congress intended that packers be treated any differently. So, USDA currently treats the failure to pay as an unfair practice under § 192(b) and in case of a violation pursues the remedies of § 193 in spite of the fact that specific statutory authority does not exist.

4. Packer and Feedlot Operations

Historically, unlike the poultry industry, the livestock industry has not been vertically integrated. Indeed, there has been steadfast and vigorous opposition to allowing the large packers to take over the industry. Prior to 1984, packers were prohibited from owning, financing, controlling and managing feedlots. But a packer was able to hire the services of a feedlot or to have its own livestock fed for slaughter. 9 CFR § 201.70a (1983). However, since September 1984, packer ownership or control of a feedlot is not a per se violation of the PSA. 9 CFR § 203.18 (1994). But, the new regulation reflects a concern about possible anticompetitive practices if a packer owned feedlot feeds cattle owned by others. There is a potential conflict of interest in that a packer as buyer wants to pay the lowest price possible, while the feedlot's obligation is to get the highest price for its customer. The new regulation requires the feedlot operator to advise the customer of these risks. Because dealers and buyers purchase livestock for resale or to fill orders for others than packers, a potential conflict of interest arises when the packer -- who is also buying livestock for its own needs -- is a dealer. See 9 CFR § 203.19 (1994).

C. Stockyards, Market Agencies and Dealers

The production and sale of livestock and poultry is a major part of the farm economy in many areas. Sales of live animals to slaughter houses is but one part of an industry that is characterized by the sale of live animals at various stages of their development. For example, a slaughter steer may be sold at least three times. A cow-calf operator may sell to a "backgrounder," one who typically buys calves at 300-400 lbs. and sells them as "feeders" at 600-800 lbs. A feeder in turn usually sells the live finished product, a market weight steer, to a packer or slaughter house. Variations of this theme are possible.

Livestock marketing occurs in public markets at big city stockyards, at auction stockyards in rural areas, or in direct transactions. While big stockyards like those of Chicago, Kansas City, and Omaha are dying, many auction stockyards continue to operate in smaller cities, towns and rural locations. And, market agents and dealers still play vital roles in livestock marketing.

1. Stockyards

Stockyards, market agencies and dealers are governed by PSA §§ 201-228b. Essential terms are defined in § 201(a) and (b):

(a)   The term "stockyard owner" means any person engaged in the business of conducting or operating a stockyard;

(b)   The term "stockyard services" means services or facilities furnished at a stockyard in connection with the receiving, buying or selling on a commission basis or otherwise, marketing, feeding, watering, holding, delivery, shipment, weighing, or handling in commerce, of livestock.

Section 202(a) defines stockyard as:

. . . any place, establishment, or facility commonly known as stockyards, conducted, operated or managed for profit or nonprofit as a public market for livestock producers, feeders, market agencies, and buyers, consisting of pens, or other enclosures, and their appurtenances, in which live cattle, sheep, swine, horses, mules or goats are received, held, or kept for sale or shipment in commerce.

Once the Secretary has decided that an operation is within the definition, the yard must be "posted," i.e. the Secretary has posted in three places in the stockyard a public notice stating that it is covered by the Act. PSA § 203; 9 CFR §§ 201.5, .6, .10 (1994). Upon "posting" the operator and all market agencies and dealers doing business at the stockyard must register and file schedules of rates and charges. PSA §§ 203, 207, 209. Bonds are required for most market agencies and dealers under PSA § 204.

Stockyard and marketing agencies must refrain from charging unreasonable rates, must respond to a reasonable request for services, should operate in a reasonable and nondiscriminatory manner, supply annual reports, and keep appropriate records. PSA §§ 201-217a; 9 CFR pts 201-204 (1994). Failure to comply with the requirements of the PSA or engaging in prohibited activities can result in the issuance of orders, fines, activity suspensions, and rate changes. See PSA §§ 204, 207(G),(E), 209, 210(e),(f), 211, 215, and 217. Any order issued by the Secretary other than for payment of money, may be enforced in federal district court. PSA § 216.

2. Market Agencies and Dealers

A market agency is defined in PSA § 201(c) to be "any person engaged in the business of (1) buying or selling in commerce livestock on a commission basis or (2) furnishing stockyard services." A dealer is "any person, not a market agency, engaged in the business of buying or selling in commerce livestock, either on his own account or as the employee or agent of the vendor or purchaser." PSA § 201(d). A person who sells or buys livestock for another without charging a fee can be a dealer, but not a market agency. It is also clear that the "Act does not require that a dealer in order to come under the Act be engaged in the sole business of buying and selling of livestock in commerce." Kelly v. U.S. (10th Cir.1953). A rancher who buys livestock for himself and for resale can be a dealer. See, e.g., U.S. v. Rauch (8th Cir.1983) (held to be dealer -- bought cattle for resale, not for increasing herd).

An important issue is whether feedlots are subject to PSA. To be subject, feedlots must be market agencies or dealers. If they are covered, they would need to register, be bonded, make reports, keep records, and pay promptly. Violators would be subject to PSA sanctions.

In Solomon Valley Feedlot, Inc. v. Butz (10th Cir. 1977), Solomon fed cattle raised or purchased by its customers. Solomon gave advice as to the purchases. When the cattle reached the appropriate weight, they were sold directly to a packer who paid the customer-owner, *not* the feedlot. Solomon assisted the customer in the sale transaction but received no specific fee for this service. Because Solomon made its money solely from feeding cattle, the court held that the evidence did not establish that it was acting as an agent or employee of customers The 10th Circuit concluded that Congress did not intend to class as dealers feedlots that received no specific fee for buying and selling services and that handled no money of customers.

A different result was had in In re Sterling Colorado Beef Co. (Agric.Dec.1980). The Judicial Officer (JO) held that the feedlot (Sterling) was a dealer and thus subject to PSA. Sterling, in addition to charging a fee for feeding cattle, charged a processing fee for handling purchases and sales. It also received payments from the packer on behalf of its customers. The JO held that the feedlot was an agent of its customers. This is so, the JO wrote, because a feedlot that is buying and selling animals on behalf of a patron is a dealer. The fact that the feedlot charges a specific fee for its services is irrelevant. The JO explains that the ultimate question is the intent of Congress as to the scope of the definition of dealer.

3. Unlawful Practices

At 7 USCA § 213(a) PSA deals with unfair and discriminatory acts:

> It shall be unlawful for any stockyard owner, market agency, or dealer to engage in or use any unfair, unjustly discriminatory, or deceptive practice or device in connection with determining whether persons should be authorized to operate at the stockyards, or with the receiving, marketing, buying or selling on a commission basis or otherwise, feeding, watering, holding, delivery, shipment, weighing, or handling of livestock.

If a violation is found after a due process hearing, the Secretary can issue a cease and desist order, assess a civil penalty of not more than $10,000 for each offense, and suspend registration. The violator is also liable to the person injured for the full amount of damages sustained. PSA § 209. A stockyard owner, market agent or dealer, who knowingly fails to follow a USDA order under § 213, must pay $500 for each failure. Each day of a continuing violation is a separate offense. PSA § 215.

Activities prohibited by PSA § 213 include false weighing, gratuities to truckers, paying higher prices to shareholders than to non-shareholders, bribery, charging for services not rendered, refusals to sell higher grade animals separately from other consignments, boycotts, market agency financing of a dealer, price discounts to selected purchasers, the "turn system" where livestock dealers flip a coin to determine the order in which each would bid on livestock, and market agency misuse of custodial accounts. The bulk of the cases arising under § 213 have involved false weighing, misuse of custodial accounts, and marketing systems.

Stockyards, market agencies, dealers, packers and live poultry dealers are subject to regulations about false weighing. 9 CFR §§ 201.71-.82; 201.108-1 (1994). Persons subject to the Act must install and operate accurate scales with a device for stamping the weight on a scale ticket. Scale tickets must be serially numbered and include specific information. The scales must be operated by trained, qualified persons and the scale's balance must be checked every day before weighing begins and after every 15 minutes or 15 drafts, whichever occurs first. 9 CFR § 201.73-1(a) (1994). Scales must be checked for accuracy by a qualified person at least twice a year at intervals of about six months. Warning letters are sent when the evidence indicates inaccurate, but not deliberate false weights. If deliberate false weighing is found, administrative action is instituted. A suspension or civil penalty will not be overturned in court unless it is "unwarranted in law or . . . without justification in fact." Butz v. Glover Livestock Commission Co. (U.S.Sup.Ct.1973).

Market agencies that sell livestock belonging to others are required to establish and maintain separate custodial accounts for the consignor's proceeds. The account must clearly indicate that it is a trust account and that the marketing agency is acting in a fiduciary capacity as to funds deposited therein. Each payment the marketing agency receives from the sale of livestock owned by another is a trust fund and must be deposited in the custodial account by the close of the business day following the sale. 9

CFR § 201.42(a) (1994). However, the statutory trust fund for packers under PSA § 196 and live poultry dealers in § 197 does not apply. Thus, if the agent does not deposit the funds in the trust account and goes bankrupt, there is no special protection for the unpaid owner other than a claim against the bonding company.

Section 213 prohibits marketing systems that are not just and reasonable. A just and reasonable system is one that is likely to produce the best price for the seller. The "turn system" or any other system which limits the number of buyers is prohibited. Berigan v. U.S. (8th Cir.1958). Such a system restrains competition and depresses the market. See also 9 CFR § 201.56 (1994).

4. Reparation by Private Persons

One of Congress' objectives in enacting the Packers and Stockyards Act was to provide for farmers and other shippers of livestock a fair and quick procedure to present claims for damages caused by violations of the PSA. Section 210 authorizes an administrative reparation proceeding that can be initiated by any person who complains that a stockyard owner, dealer or marketing agency violated any provisions of subchapter III of the PSA, §§ 203-217a. Violations include the failure of a stockyard company to provide reasonable stockyard services for the care of cattle; failure of a dealer to promptly pay the full purchase price of livestock; failure of marketing agency to use reasonable care in handling livestock; failure of a market agency to give the owner of cattle the net proceeds from the sale; misrepresentation of livestock; and the failure of a dealer, market agency or stockyard to abide by an order of the Secretary.

To institute a reparation proceeding, the aggrieved party, within 90 days after the cause of action occurs, must file with the Secretary a complaint that briefly states the facts upon which the action is based. The complaint is served upon the respondent who is required to satisfy the complainant or respond in writing within the time set by the Secretary. If the respondent makes reparation he is relieved of liability to the complainant for the violation. If reparation is not made and the Secretary determines there is a reasonable ground for investigation, the Secretary will so proceed. If after a hearing the Secretary determines the complainant is entitled to damages, an order will be issued directing the defendant to pay by a certain date. If the order is not satisfied, an action to enforce it may be filed in federal district court. If complainant wins in court, she can recover attorney fees from the defendant. Rules of practice governing reparation proceedings are found in 9 CFR §§ 202.101-.123 (1994).

Caveat: persons harmed by PSA violations by packers or live poultry dealers are not able to use the quick and relatively easy reparation process. Such persons must file actions in federal court.

D. Live Poultry Dealers

The Poultry Producers Financial Protection Act of 1987, (PPFP Act) made substantial changes in the PSA's regulation of poultry, poultry products and live poultry dealers and handlers. The key changes are: 1) redefinition of certain terms; 2) creation of a statutory trust; 3) prompt payment requirements;

and 4) new enforcement powers for the Secretary when poultry dealers fail to keep appropriate records or fail to pay promptly. The PPFP Act makes clear that the Federal Trade Commission has primary jurisdiction over poultry products. However, the USDA has jurisdiction over poultry products when it is necessary to use the trust fund of PSA § 197(b) and to enforce the prompt payment rules of PSA § 228b-1.

1. Terminology

Poultry is defined to include all domestic fowl, and poultry product means "any product or by-product of the business of slaughtering poultry and processing poultry after slaughter," PSA §§ 182(6), (7). The old term "live poultry handler" is eliminated. Sections 182(9) and (10) now define poultry growing arrangement and poultry grower:

(8) The term "poultry grower" means any person engaged in the business of r a i s i n g and caring for live poultry for slaughter by another, whether the poultry is owned by such person or by another, but not an employee of the owner of such poultry;

(9) The term "poultry growing arrangement" means any growout contract, marketing agreement, or other arrangement under which a poultry grower raises and cares for live poultry for delivery, in accord with another's instructions, for slaughter.

The new definition of live poultry dealer in § 182(10) is very broad and provides:

The term "live poultry dealer" means any person engaged in the business of obtaining live poultry by purchase or under a poultry growing arrangement for the purpose of either slaughtering it or selling it for slaughter by another, if poultry is obtained by such person in commerce, or if poultry obtained by such person is sold or shipped in commerce, or if poultry products from poultry obtained by such person are sold or shipped in commerce.

The USDA's position is that any sale of live poultry in interstate commerce makes the seller a dealer. This position is based on the broad definition and the fact that it does not require a threshold amount of sales for the seller to be a dealer. Contrast the $100,000 of sales needed to trigger the statutory trust. See U.S. v. Perdue Farms Inc. (2nd Cir.1982).

2. Unlawful Practices

Regulation of practices of live poultry dealers under PSA began in 1935. PSA § 192 enumerates unlawful practices for packers and for live poultry dealers. The 1987 Act changed § 192(c) to make clear that any sale or transfer from one packer or live poultry dealer to another packer or dealer "for the purpose or with the effect of apportioning the supply between any such persons" is an unlawful act. The prior version provided it to unlawful "if such apportionment has a tendency or effect of restraining commerce or creating a monopoly."

Prior to 1987, the live poultry dealer who violated PSA § 192, was not subject to the same penalties meted out to packers because the penalty provisions of §§ 193-95 referred only to packers. Courts held that the USDA did not have the power to file administrative complaints, hold administrative hearings or issue cease and desist orders when poultry dealers violated § 192 and attendant regulations. Davis v. U.S. (5th Cir.1970); Arkansas Valley Industries, Inc. v. Freemand (8th Cir.1969). Yet, federal regulations subject live poultry dealers to the same weighing requirements as packers. See 9 CFR § 201.49, .71 (1994) (weighing). But PSA § 213, which prohibits stockyards, marketing agencies and dealers from committing certain unfair and deceptive practices, does not apply to live poultry dealers. Thus, as to these matters cease and desist orders and monetary penalties for violations cannot be imposed on live poultry dealers.

The 1987 Act did *not* amend PSA §§ 193-195 or 213 to extend their application to live poultry dealers. However, § 209(a) was amended to make it applicable to live poultry dealers. Now, if a live poultry dealer violates any applicable provision of the PSA, it is liable to the person(s) adversely affected for the full amount of damages caused by the violation. With the reparations process unavailable, the only way the injured party can pursue damages is to file an action in U.S. District Court.

The Secretary does have authority to go to court and seek a restraining order or temporary injunction under PSA § 228(a), if the Secretary has reason to believe that any person subject to the PSA: 1) has failed to pay or is unable to pay for livestock or poultry, or failed to pay a grower what is due under a grower contract; or 2) operated while insolvent or in a manner which violated the PSA and could be reasonably expected to cause irreparable damage; or 3) does not have the required bond; **and** it would be in the public interest either to enjoin the person from operating or subject it to conditions that would assure that consignors of commodities or sellers are protected. Also, a dealer could be subjected to court imposed cease and desist orders under PSA § 224 which provides in part: "[t]he Secretary may report any violation . . . to the Attorney General . . . who shall cause appropriate proceedings to be commenced and prosecuted in the proper courts of the United States without delay."

Injunctions provide the sole method for closing down a live poultry dealer because such dealers, like packers, are not required to register with the USDA as a prerequisite to doing business. Accordingly, there is no power to suspend operations by revoking registration. Cf. 7 USCA § 203; 9 CFR §§ 201.10-.11 (1994).

3. Prompt Payment Rule

Since 1987 when 7 USCA § 228b-1 was enacted, live poultry dealers have been subject to prompt payment rules similar to those made applicable to packers in 1976. When a dealer buys live poultry for cash (seller does not expressly extend credit), the dealer must deliver the full payment to the seller before the close of the next business day following the purchase. When live poultry is obtained under a poultry growing arrangement, the dealer must pay before the close of the 15th day following the week in which the poultry is slaughtered. Credit cannot be extended under a growing arrangement. To delay, attempt to delay payment, or to attempt or cause an extension of the normal pay period is an unfair practice under PSA § 228b-1(b).

If the Secretary believes the dealer is violating the prompt payment rule, the Administrative discipline process can be initiated and a written complaint will be served on the dealer. If after a hearing, it is determined the live poultry dealer has violated this rule, the USDA may issue a cease and desist order and assess a civil penalty up to $20,000 for each violation, but in no event "can the penalty assessed by the Secretary take priority over or impede the ability of the live poultry dealer to pay any unpaid cash seller or poultry grower." The disciplinary determination is final unless an appeal is filed with the federal court of appeals for the circuit in which the live poultry dealer's principal place of business is located. Finally, 7 USCA § 228a now authorizes the Secretary to ask the Attorney General to seek a temporary restraining order if the live poultry dealer does not pay or is unable to pay for live poultry.

4. Statutory Trust For Unpaid Sellers

Since 1987, statutory trust provisions have been applicable to live poultry dealers with average annual sales of live poultry over $100,00, or with an "average annual value of live poultry obtained by purchase or by poultry growing arrangement, in excess of $100,000." PSA § 197. Assets of the trust consist of the poultry obtained by cash or grower arrangement and "all inventories of, or receivables or proceeds from such poultry or poultry products derived therefrom." As with the packer trust fund, the idea is to protect unpaid sellers from the dealer's secured creditors and dealer's trustee in bankruptcy.

The protection of the trust is triggered when the seller or grower receives no payment at all or is paid with an instrument that is dishonored. The protection of the trust is lost, however, if the seller or grower does not give written notice to the dealer and file such notice with the USDA: 1) within 30 days of the final date for the dealer's payment under the prompt payment rules; or 2) within 15 business days of seller's or grower's notice of dishonor of a promptly presented check. Because the poultry trust fund is so similar to the fund authorized at § 196, the discussion at pp. 249-52 *supra* is relevant. See also 9 CFR § 203.15 (1994) as to trust benefits for both packers and live poultry dealers.

5. Records Kept and Furnished

Live poultry dealers, like packers, stockyard owners, market agencies, and dealers must keep records that fully and correctly disclose all relevant business transactions. The Secretary may prescribe the form and manner in which the records must be kept and a violation is punishable upon conviction by a $5,000 fine or three years in prison or both.

Every live poultry dealer, packer, stockyard owner, and market agency, when requested, must submit annual reports containing information relevant to enforcement of the PSA. 9 CFR § 201.94 (1994). Live poultry dealers are also required to supply poultry growers and sellers with information relevant to sales of inputs and the growing contracts as such. The grower is also entitled to a true and accurate settlement sheet (final accounting) which must contain sufficient information to compute the payment due the grower. See generally 9 CFR § 201.100 (1994). As with PSA § 192 violations, Congress did not empower USDA to file administrative complaints or to issue cease and desist orders. However, 7 USCA § 221, which provides that live poultry dealers can be fined $5000 or imprisoned for three years or both for failure to keep and maintain appropriate records, appears to be relevant.

V. COMMUNICABLE ANIMAL DISEASES

Many federal and state statutes and regulations thereunder are designed to prevent the introduction and the spread within the U.S. of communicable animal diseases. At the federal level there is no comprehensive statute governing the regulation of diseased animals. More than 17 regulatory programs are found in USCA Titles 19 and 21 and in 9 CFR pts. 49-147(1994). Related laws include: Federal Meat Inspection Act, 21 USCA §§ 601-95; Poultry Products Inspection Act, 21 USCA §§ 451-70; Egg Production Inspection Act, 21 USCA § 1031 et. seq.

Responsibility for implementing the federal statutes and regulations is vested primarily in the Veterinary Services subdivision of the Animal and Plant Health Inspection Services (APHIS), a part of the USDA. The broad powers granted to the USDA are typified by 21 USCA § 134a(a). It says that the Secretary, to guard against the introduction or spread of communicable diseases of livestock or poultry, may in a reasonable manner seize, quarantine, and dispose of animals which he finds moved or handled in interstate or foreign commerce contrary to any federal law or regulation on the subject.

Moreover, the USDA has the power to regulate: 1) importation of certain animals such as cattle, sheep, horses, mules, and poultry; 2) importation of certain animal products such as carcasses of poultry, frozen meats, and milk and milk products; 3) interstate movement of diseased animals; 4) interstate movement of animals to prevent the spread of certain enumerated diseases such as Texas (splenetic) fever in cattle; scabies in cattle; scabies in sheep; communicable diseases in horses, asses, ponies, mules and zebras; hog cholera and other diseases in swine; tuberculosis in cattle; brucellosis in cattle, bison, and swine; scrapie in sheep; paratuberculosis in domestic animals; certain common poultry diseases; exotic poultry diseases like New Castle disease; and pseudo-rabies. 9 CFR pts. 72-82, 85 (1994).

While Congress has the power to act to control the spread of animal diseases in the United States, it has not completely preempted the field. Consequently, states, are free to regulate in nonpreempted areas. Clearly both levels of government are anxious to control highly contagious diseases and strive to work together harmoniously. 9 CFR pts. 49-56 (1994).

One method employed by states to control and eradicate infectious or contagious diseases in farm animals is quarantine. Quarantined areas may be single ranches or farms or regions of a state. In addition, most states authorize condemnation and destruction of diseased animals with appropriate compensation allowed to the owners, except to the extent federal indemnity payments are available. See, e.g., Colo. Rev. Stat. §§ 35-50-110 -111. A third method used by states is to limit the importation of certain animals and by requiring that animals have an official health certificate showing that they are free from contagious or infection diseases. See, e.g., Colo. Rev. Stat. § 35-50-102. While most states have criminal penalties for failure to comply with such controls, a few also provide a private statutory remedy for damages resulting from such violations.

The power of the state is immense. For example, once the state has reason to believe brucellosis exists in a given area, it has the power to require owners to assemble their cattle for testing without notice or a hearing. If cattle test positive, the animals are branded and must be disposed of immediately. Usually, all animals in the herd must be destroyed, even those that do not test positive. This forced disposal is not considered a taking of private property without due process. While the owner is not given notice and a hearing concerning his animals, notice and hearing opportunities were provided when legislation dealing with brucellosis was developed by the legislature. Burt v. Arkansas Livestock and Poultry Commission (Ark.1983). Also, because brucellosis can sometimes be transmitted to humans as undulant fever, state action is needed to protect the public. Thus, statutes controlling the spread of brucellosis are a valid exercise of the state's police power. The fact that the value of animals is reduced by the condemnation is not controlling because in these circumstances individual rights must yield to the protection of the health and welfare of the public. See Hadacheck v. Sebastian (U.S.Sup.Ct.1915). There is no absolute right to indemnity even if there is a reduction in value of the animals in a forced sale.

The standard of compensation for federally required destruction of animals and poultry is found in 7 USCA § 134(d) which provides in part:

> [T]he Secretary shall compensate the owner
> of any animal, carcass, product, or article

> destroyed pursuant to the provisions of this
> section. Such compensation shall be based
> upon the fair market value as determined by
> the Secretary . . . at the time of the
> destruction thereof. Compensation paid any
> owner under this subsection shall not exceed
> the difference between any compensation
> received by such owner from a State or
> other source and such fair market value of
> the animal, carcass, product, or article.

Owners can also be compensated for materials destroyed and for the expenses incurred for destruction and disposition of animals as well as for disinfection of premises, conveyances, and vehicles. See, e.g., 9 CFR pts. 53, 71 (1994).

Animals and poultry normally must be appraised by a USDA Veterinary Services employee. Fair market value is determined at the time of destruction and does not include post-destruction profits. Julius Goldman's Egg City v. U.S. (Fed.Cir.1983). Fair market value is based on the meat, egg production, dairy or breeding value of the animals. Purebred status will affect value. The USDA's computation is subject to judicial review but will not be changed unless the owner establishes that it was arbitrary, capricious, an abuse of discretion or contrary to law.

An outbreak of avian influenza in Virginia resulted in a USDA imposed quarantine in certain areas of the state. Caught in the quarantine area was a farmer with a healthy flock of 3,000 turkey breeder hens. Unable to market hatching eggs or the turkeys in or outside Virginia, farmer sold the flock for meat and filed a claim with USDA for a

$63,556. indemnity. Because there was no provision in the program for payment to farmers with undiseased birds, no payment was made. Farmer sued and a taking was found by the Claims Court and on review. Yancey v. U.S. (Fed.Cir.1990). Using Penn Central Transportation Co. v. City of New York (U.S.Sup.Ct.1978), it was determined that the economic impact was severe (value of flock fell from $91,616 to $20,887) with no meaningful way to mitigate; that investment backed expectations were interfered with in an unexpected way; and that the losses resulted from government action. Cf. Empire Kosher Poultry, Inc. v. Hallowell (3rd Cir.1987) (no taking because healthy chickens could still be used in the quarantine area for original purpose).

In an attempt to control the spread of salmonella enteritidis the USDA on Feb. 15, 1990, announced the establishment of a mandatory testing program for breeder hens that produce table eggs. In addition, a "trace back" system is to be developed so that the USDA could trace infected eggs back to the farm on which they wee produced. As part of this plan, egg distributors will be required to keep records indicating the source of eggs they distribute.

VI ANIMAL PATENTS

Prior to 1980, plants were the only living organ - isms for which the Patent and Trademark Office (PTO) would grant a patent. The PTO maintained that living organisms were not within the statutory definition of patentable subject matter. 35 USCA § 101 (1982). Plants were the sole exception to this policy pursuant to the Plant Protection Act of 1930. This changed with the decision in Diamond v.

Chakrabarty (U.S.Sup.Ct.1980) upholding granting of a patent for a genetically engineered bacterium that could be used to clean up oil spills. The court held that any nonnaturally occurring organism with utility to man could be patented. After Chakrabarty, PTO granted patents on single celled organisms, but still refused to patent multicellular animals. This policy changed following Ex Parte Allen (Bd.Pat. App.1987)(patent of nonnaturally occurring polyploid oysters allowed). PTO by official notice on April 7, 1987 reiterated that multicellular organisms, other than genetically altered humans, are per se patentable. Subsequently a patent issued for a mouse genetically engineered to be susceptible to cancer.

No one knows what impact animal patents could have on an already fragile agricultural economy. Proponents argue that the increased efficiency of genetically engineered animals could benefit all farmers through decreased production costs and help meet the food need of a growing world population. Critics fear that large agribusiness enterprises will be the beneficiaries with family farmers facing the dilemma of paying ruinous patent royalties or raising genetically inferior livestock. While Congress has not acted, it could limit patent infringement by statute to sale of germ cells, semen or embryos of the patented animal. This would allow a farmer to breed a patented animal, use it in his operation, and sell it or its offspring without infringing the patent.

A related policy area focuses on regulation of genetic engineering. As yet, there are no laws forbidding genetic alternation of animals.

CHAPTER EIGHT

AGRICULTURAL COOPERATIVES
I. INTRODUCTION

It is rare that business transacted by one farmer or rancher can have a downward impact on prices paid for inputs or an upward impact on prices received upon sale of farm products. Founders of agricultural cooperatives hoped to move farmers and ranchers away from this status of price takers. Today, such cooperatives fall into three primary classes. Supply cooperatives make economical large scale purchases of needed inputs such as fuel, pesticides, and fertilizers which are then sold to members and other patrons. Marketing cooperatives allow producers to work together to sell their output in larger volume and to better time sale transactions. Service cooperatives offer specialized help in areas such as dairy herd improvement, services that otherwise might not be affordable in the particular area.

Principles essential to the cooperative movement in American agriculture evolved out of the efforts of the Rochdale Society of Equitable Pioneers, a group of textile workers who established a cooperative in London in 1844. In the United States important roles in the development of cooperative principles were played by the National Grange (Patrons of Husbandry) following the Civil War and the International Cooperative Alliance (ICA), established in 1930.

274

Modern cooperatives usually follow at least the following principles: 1) democratic ownership and control by users; 2) limited returns to capital; 3) return of benefits or margins to users on the basis of use; 4) the obligation of user-owner financing. The first principle translates into one member, one vote regardless of the magnitude of a particular member's patronage or stock purchases. Many state cooperative statutes continue to require observance of this principle. Where permitted by pertinent state law, some cooperatives base voting in part upon volume marketed or some other measure of business done with the cooperative. Such statutes usually limit the power of a single member by allowing no one member to cast more than a small percentage of total qualified votes, 3%, for example.

The principle requiring limits on the return on investment capital has been codified in most state cooperative statutes. Typically, 8% is the maximum. The Capper-Volstead Act, discussed hereinafter, sets a maximum dividend rate on capital stock of 8%. 7 USCA § 291(as an alternative to the one man, one vote requirement). See pp. 301-02 *infra*. And, limits on dividends on capital stock appear in certain federal tax statutes. See pp. 293 *infra*. The underlying principle is that agricultural cooperatives are not deemed to be vehicles for investment for profit. Rather, the emphasis is on members cooperating to achieve common business goals.

The next principle is that monies accumulated in excess of net operating costs -- savings or margins as they are often called -- be refunded to members in accordance with patronage, which is measured by the amount of a patrons business with the cooperative.

In other words, the goal of a cooperative is to maximize the interests of its members as it transacts its business. To accomplish this cooperatives will market the commodities of patrons at the highest possible prices and will buy quality inputs at lowest possible prices. Operating costs will be minimized, but not at the sacrifice of best business practices. The resulting savings or margins -- cooperatives prefer not to call them profits -- belong to the patrons and are refunded to them at least annually, though not necessarily all in cash. How retained patronage savings or margins can be used by cooperatives to help finance ongoing operations is discussed at pp. 278-83 *infra*.

II. FORMATION OF COOPERATIVES

The steps for forming an agricultural cooperative resemble those for forming a regular business corporation. Articles of incorporation will be prepared, in most states pursuant to a statute governing the formation of such cooperatives. The state's business corporation statute may be incorporated by reference into the cooperative statute to fill in gaps. However, in the formation of a cooperative there are unique factors to consider.

Membership in an agricultural cooperative usually is limited to "agricultural producers." They join by purchasing a share of stock or a membership certificate, depending on whether it is a stock or nonstock cooperative. The objective for producers is to take advantage of the benefits of cooperative membership, rather than to seek return on investment. The cost of a share or a certificate is usually nominal. Membership certificates and stock are usually not classed as securities. See pp. 296-99 *infra.*

Bylaws are adopted and in the case of a marketing cooperative may require members to patronize the cooperative. In some marketing cooperatives, the commitment by a member to market through the cooperative is set out in a marketing agreement, the legal effect of which may be governed by statute.

Members of the cooperative elect directors, who in turn hire the manager or chief executive officer. In most states directors must be members of the cooperative. As is the case for noncooperative companies, directors of cooperatives who violate statutory or common law duties, or who violate rules set forth in the governing documents of the cooperative, can incur personal liability.

Agricultural cooperatives are affected by an array of statutes that do not apply to regular business corporations. In addition to state statutes governing incorporation, attention must be given to provisions of the Internal Revenue Code (IRC) governing taxation of cooperatives, to the status of cooperative financial instruments under state and federal securities laws, to the special treatment of agricultural cooperatives under antitrust laws, and to statutory provisions governing eligibility to borrow from those Farm Credit System banks that serve cooperatives. These and other statutes are pertinent not only at the formation of an agricultural cooperative, but in its ongoing operations.

III. FINANCIAL STRUCTURE

A fertilizer supply cooperative might need financing for plant construction, to meet payroll during months of limited cash flow, to buy inputs, and to cover extensions of credit to producer-members. Similarly, a grain marketing cooperative may need financing for warehouse construction, to meet payroll during months of limited cash flow, to cover other operating expenses, and to purchase commodities from members. Since agricultural cooperatives are associations whose farmer members typically have limited liquidity, and since the return on funds invested in cooperatives is usually not attractive to outsiders, cooperatives must use unique methods to raise capital and monies for operations.

A. Stock and Membership Purchases

Members help finance cooperatives by purchasing common stock or membership certificates, preferred stock, bonds, promissory notes, or debentures. Note the mix of equity and debt financing. The purchase of a share of common stock or a membership certificate will be a prerequisite to voting membership. Since the purchase price is almost always minimal, common stock and membership certificate sales usually do not constitute major sources of capital for agricultural cooperatives. Absent a specific contractual or statutory right, a member cannot require a cooperative to redeem or repurchase membership stock.

B. Patronage Based Financing

Patronage based financing is the most important source of equity financing for most agricultural cooperatives. This financing is generated in two principal ways -- through the issuance by the cooperative of either per-unit retain certificates *or* written notices of allocation of patronage refunds.

The less widely used of the two methods, the per-unit retain, is particularly suited to certain marketing cooperatives. Pursuant to bylaws or an agreement with each member, the cooperative deducts and retains a set amount per unit marketed from the payment due the member. The unit will vary depending on the commodity -- e.g., x cents per bushel or x cents per hundred weight. The net earnings of the cooperative are not used in the calculating the retain. To the extent that per-unit retains are not paid out annually in cash to patrons, the cooperative will be authorized to make payment to patrons in the form of per-unit retain certificates. The effect is to capitalize the cooperative while giving patrons documented equity interests. If certain rules in the Internal Revenue Code are followed, per-unit retains, whether paid in cash or certificate form, must be treated as income by patrons and are not taxed as income to the cooperative. See pp. 291-92 *infra*.

The more common method of equity financing is tied directly to the net earnings of the cooperative. These net earnings belong to the members and are refunded at least annually on the basis of patronage which is usually calculated on the basis of dollar volume of business done. Absent an agreement to the contrary, cooperative structure requires that the net earnings -- savings or margins -- be refunded to members at least annually. When patronage refunds are not paid in full in cash, the cooperative is generally authorized to make refunds to patrons in the form of written notices of allocation. Since it is common for members to grant to their cooperative the power to do this, a large percentage of a cooperatives net earnings can be retained for equity funding. As with per-unit retains, patronage refunds are not in fact kept or retained. Understand that they have been paid to members in written notices of allocation -- evidence of each member's equity in the cooperative. As with per-unit retains, patronage refunds are taxed as income to the patron recipients, but not to the cooperative if IRC rules are observed. See p. 291 *infra*.

To take advantage of the federal tax strategy just described, the annual refund to each member must be paid at least 20% in cash and the remaining percentage in qualified patronage retain certificates or qualified written notices of allocation. The objective is to pass 100% of patronage earnings and patronage retains to patrons so that they, rather than the cooperative, will be subject to income tax on such amounts.

There is no law prohibiting capitalization of a cooperative by issuing nonqualified written notices of allocation. Patronage refunded in the form of written notices exceeding 80% would fall into this category as would refunds not based entirely on patronage. For example, a cooperative might issue nonqualified allocations in a year when its other taxable income is low and then redeem in a later tax year when other income is high. This strategy can be used only if patrons consent. Amounts represented by the 80% plus notices will be included in the cooperative's taxable income in the year of issuance, there being no pass through to patrons. Of course, when nonqualified notices are redeemed in a subsequent tax year, the member has taxable income while the cooperative takes a deduction.

Over time, the equity interest of a farmer in a cooperative can grow to tens of thousands of dollars. While it might seem appropriate to revolve out equity when a member ceases active farming, or upon a member's death, some cooperatives do not have liquid assets sufficient to make such disbursements. Put another way, some cooperatives may not have sufficient stability of equity. Generally, cooperative directors have discretion as to revolving out patronage retains upon a member's retirement or death. Unless there has been an abuse of that discretion, courts support decisions of directors not to repurchase stock or redeem patronage certificates, even if the request is made by the estate of a deceased member. Evanenko v. Farmers Union Elevator (N.D.1971); Georgia Turkey Farms, Inc. v. Hardigree (Ga.App.1988).

Abuse of discretion by directors can occur in certain circumstances if they do not revolve back equity. Fact patterns that can be particularly treacherous include those where inactive members and the estates of deceased members are in effect financing the cooperative for the benefit of newer members; excess reserves have accumulated; there is inconsistency in treatment of repurchase and redemption requests; or where the cooperative could borrow the necessary funds without jeopardizing its financial well-being. In Lake Region Packing Ass'n, Inc. v. Furze (Fla.1976), the court stated that while the facts of the case at bar did not merit intervention, remedial action would be available in future cases "if the directors refusal to pay constituted an abuse of discretion, a breach of trust, or was based on fraud, illegality or inequity." See also Mitchellville

Cooperative v. Indian Creek Corp. (Iowa 1991)(fiduciary duty exists as to administration of redemption rights, but not breached under facts).

Generally, third parties such as a member's creditors, a member's trustee in bankruptcy, or a member's divorced spouse cannot compel a cooperative to take action that the member could not compel. In bankruptcy, for example, the member's interest may vest in the trustee, but the cooperative will not be required by bankruptcy law to make immediate payment. In re Cosner (Bankr.D.Or. 1980). But, where the debtor, during the pendency of the bankruptcy, receives cash payments from the cooperative based on pre-petition farming operations, said payments will be property of the bankrupt estate. In re Bennett (Bankr.N.D.Tex.1991). When the bankrupt farmer member is a corporation, the trustee in the bankruptcy will argue that bylaws or current practices requiring payment upon the death of an individual patron should also apply in cases of corporate "death." In re Great Plains Royalty Corp. (8th Cir.1973).

Termination of membership, withdrawal, or expulsion rarely work forfeiture of a member's equity. However, such termination rarely triggers immediate redemption. Provisions of the bylaws, unless overridden by state statute, will still govern as they do for continuing members. See, e.g., Sanchez v. Grain Growers Ass'n of California (Cal.1981). Where the bylaws are silent on treatment of former members, provisions in the statutes of some states may afford such persons more immediate redemption rights than those of continuing members. See, e.g., Code of Georgia Ann. § 2-10-86(b)(12)(disbursement in cash required within one year after termination).

C. Borrowed Capital

Eligible agricultural cooperatives have access to certain Farm Credit System (FCS) banks for long term capital improvement loans and short term operating loans. The Agricultural Credit Act of 1987 continued the international lending authority of FCS banks, and, subject to certain conditions, gave new authority to finance cooperative partnerships, joint ventures and subsidiaries.

Prior to its reorganization in the late 1980s, the FCS included 12 district banks for cooperatives and the Denver-based Central Bank for Cooperatives. Pursuant to the Agricultural Credit Act of 1987, votes by stockholders resulted in the merger of 10 of the 12 district banks with the Central Bank for Cooperatives to form the National Bank for Cooperatives (CoBank). This merger became effective on January 1, 1989. The St. Paul Bank for Cooperatives and the Springfield Bank for Cooperatives chose to remain independent. Each of the three banks is authorized to make loans anywhere in the United States. CoBank operates regional service centers throughout the United States.

To be eligible to borrow from a bank for cooperatives a cooperative must do at least 50% of its business with members. And, 80% of the voting control of an eligible cooperative must be held by "farmers, producers or harvesters of aquatic products, or eligible cooperative associations." 12 USCA § 2129(a)(4). This percentage is reduced to 60% for certain service cooperatives, as well as for certain farm supply cooperatives. Finally, an eligible cooperative must do one of the following: observe the one-member one-vote rule, *or* set and hold dividends on stock or membership capital at or below a rate of return currently approved by the Farm Credit Administration.

While cooperatives borrow from FCS banks and other lenders, interest rates are generally lower for Commodity Credit Corporation (CCC) price support loans. See pp. 10-11 *supra*. For certain commodities, CCC loans can be made to approved cooperatives, the members of which have placed their commodities in a marketing pool with title in the cooperative. The cooperative can hold the commodities until prices improve, but pass through to members at once a part of CCC loan proceeds. To the extent that some of the loan money stays temporarily with the cooperative, the need for the cooperative to borrow short term at more expensive rates may be obviated. A challenge by private grain dealers, who claimed injury because of an alleged unfair competitive advantage for cooperatives, was rejected in Hiatt Grain and Feed Inc. v. Bergland (D.C.Kan.1979).

IV. MARKETING CONTRACTS

Marketing contracts are important to the ongoing operations of marketing cooperatives. The specified quantity that a member must deliver is usually expressed in one of three forms: full production; defined volume; or set acreage. The risk to the cooperative in using the set acreage requirement is noted at p. 144 *supra*. State statutes governing cooperative marketing contracts sometimes authorize

contract terms that might not be enforced in a noncooperative commercial setting. But, in most cases,
general rules of contract law and the UCC govern.

Performance by members of marketing agreements often constitutes the life-blood of a marketing
cooperative. For this reason, courts are sometimes
willing to order specific performance or to enjoin
breach even though the contract is for the sale of a
fungible commodity. This is true even when money
damages can be ascertained, or the contract includes
a liquidated damages clause favorable to the cooperative. To permit breaching members to respond in
money damages could threaten the marketing
system of the cooperative to the detriment of all
patrons. The physical movement of commodities
through the cooperative can be essential if it is to
maintain its credibility with "downstream" buyers.

This favorable view of contract enforcement is
further illustrated by the following cases. Where
members market in violation of their marketing
agreement, the cooperative may seek to enforce a
liquidated damages clause even though the resulting
award is greater than the actual damages. Fisher-
man's Marketing Ass'n. Inc. v. Wilson (Or.1977). It
has been held that a court acts improperly if it
enjoins a cooperative from enforcing marketing
contracts that prohibit members from selling directly
to dealers. Goshen County Cooperative Beet Ass'n.
v. Pearson (Wyo.1985), Specific performance of
cooperative marketing contracts has been compelled
even in the face of an unprecedented rise in price. In
reliance on cash forward marketing contracts wherein members agreed to sell at 30¢ per pound, a
cooperative forward marketed cotton to a manufac-

turer. At delivery time the spot market price available to farmers had increased to almost 90¢ per pound. The court ordered specific performance even though the contracts contained liquidated damage clauses. Carolinas Cotton Growers Ass'n, Inc. v. Arnette (D.S.C.1974).

Usually, marketing contracts are either exclusive sales contracts or agency contracts. In an exclusive sales contract it might be agreed that title to commodities produced by a member will pass to the cooperative prior to physical delivery. If such a contract is poorly drafted there may be questions as to whether title is intended to pass at planting, germination, harvest, delivery or some other point. Once title passes from member to cooperative under an exclusive sales contract, there are legal ramifications: a creditor of the farmer who levies on the commodities under a writ of execution will be a converter; the farmer will no longer have rights in the collateral and cannot give a valid security interest; and, a sale by a member to a third party will be an act of conversion. Clearly, difficult problems await parties dealing with a farmer if the existence of such a contract is not revealed. Wisconsin provides for public filing of these contracts. Wis. Stat. Ann § 185.42. Such filing constitutes notice to all persons of the cooperative's rights under the contract.

Occasionally, marketing contracts blur the agency/sales distinction. For example, a marketing contract that expressly creates an agency relationship may also empower the cooperative to commingle the member's goods. In an agency type contract it is not uncommon to see a provision stating that the member is no longer liable for losses after delivery of the crop. In effect, the risk of loss has passed to the cooperative though title technically remains with the member.

There is a legal distinction between efforts by a third party to induce an anticipatory breach of a marketing contract, and efforts to induce a member to exercise a contractual right to cancel. The latter effort can be safely pursued by a competitor, so long as improper means are not employed. Physical violence, fraud, misrepresentation, threat of civil suit or criminal prosecution are examples of improper means. Pure Milk Products v. National Farmers Organization (Wis.1974, 1979, 1981)

According to the 10th Circuit, bargaining cooperatives have considerable power to enforce their contracts with members. In Holly Sugar Corp. v. Goshen County Coop. Beet Growers Ass'n (10th Cir.1984), the exclusive marketing contracts of a cooperative were enforced even though the cooperative's negotiations on behalf of members with processor buyers had broken down.

V. TAXATION

A. Generally

The Internal Revenue Code (IRC) at Subchapter T allows cooperatives "operating on a cooperative basis" to exclude certain items from gross income through a series of "deductions." IRC §§ 1381-1388. This special tax status reflects the view of Congress that cooperatives are designed to operate at cost and that "profits" belong to members. Under IRC § 521, further exclusions from gross income are available to farmer cooperatives that elect to meet additional requirements.

A farmer cooperative that meets the requirements of Subchapter T does not include in its gross income patronage refunds and per-unit retains paid in money, other qualified property, or by qualified written notices of allocation, qualified per-unit retain certificates or qualified written notices of allocation. IRC § 1382(b)(1),(3). Patrons are taxed on such distributions, including those amounts paid in the form of equity in the cooperative. Pass through tax treatment is not available as to amounts paid to patrons in the form of nonqualified written certificates or allocations. Such treatment does become available for the tax year of redemption.

If a farmer cooperative aspires to even more favorable tax treatment, it may make a § 521 election and manage its affairs in accordance with the additional requirements of that Code section. A farmer cooperative granted § 521 status is referred to as a "tax exempt" association, although this is something of a misnomer. The gist of § 521 is that the electing cooperative can take advantage of certain exclusions from gross income in addition to those available under Subchapter T. Specifically, amounts paid during the taxable year as dividends on capital stock are excluded. The same is true for certain distributions of earnings from business with the United States or nonpatronage sources. IRC § 1382(c)(2)(A). With these additional exclusions, a § 521 cooperative is likely to have little, if any, taxable income. Such a cooperative, as a practical matter, is "exempt" from the federal income tax. However, from a legal perspective it important not to lose sight of the fact that a cooperative is subject to the corporate income tax.

We have omitted discussion of the complex tax issues that arise in cases of dual function cooperatives, i.e. marketing and supply. Such cooperatives can be either nonexempt or exempt.

B. Non-Exempt Cooperatives

For a farmer cooperative to have the basic benefits of Subchapter T, it must be "operating on a cooperative basis." The Internal Revenue Code does not define this critical phrase. The position of the IRS is that the question of whether an association is operating on a cooperative basis under IRC § 1381(a)(2) is to be determined from all of the facts and circumstances and by application of principles found in Puget Sound Plywood, Inc. v. CIR (Tax Ct.1965): limit on financial return paid on contributed capital; democratic control; excess of revenues over costs returned at least annually to patrons in proportion to the value or volume of business done with the cooperative. Revenue Ruling 93-21, 1993-1 C.B. 188. Other courts may see Puget Sound as a guide, but not necessarily the embodiment of the definitive test for this critical determination.

If the principles in Puget Sound Plywood are satisfied, it is still essential to look at all of the facts and circumstances. Revenue Rulings and reported cases draw a distinction between organizations performing functions consistent with a corporation-shareholder relationship and those organizations offering a true cooperative-patron relationship. Consider a fertilizer cooperative established by a group of farmers to supply their needs. The fact that the cooperative purchases raw products, blends them, and sells fertilizer to members for use in their farming operations clearly points to an association operating on a cooperative basis.

Now, assume that non-farm investors purchase the capital stock of a for-profit fertilizer corporation and thus enjoy the classic corporation-shareholder relationship. The corporation does not sell fertilizer to farmers. Rather, it sells sacked lots to each shareholder and then markets same to farmers on behalf of those shareholders. The nonessential transaction is obvious. While it might be argued that the corporation exists to supply shareholder "members," the IRS and courts have refused to recognize such a scheme as consistent with operating on a cooperative basis. However, in CF Industries, Inc. v. CIR (7th Cir.1993) it was held that a central cooperative can be operating on a cooperative basis when it sells fertilizer to member regional cooperatives which then sell to their farmer patrons.

In Revenue Ruling 72-602, 1972-2 C.B. 510, the IRS took the position that a cooperative could not be operating on a cooperative basis if it did less than 50% in value of its business with its members. The 8th Circuit in Conway County Farmers Ass'n v. U.S. (1978) refused to follow the 1972 ruling, labeling it unworkable. It took until 1993 for the IRS to recant and do away with the 50% rule. Revenue Ruling 93-21, 1993-1 C.B. 188. As a result, a cooperative that operates on a for-profit nonpatronage basis with nonmembers will no longer be automatically precluded from being found to be operating on a cooperative basis for federal income tax purposes. Nevertheless, the breakdown of member versus nonmember business will still be one factor examined in making the determination as to eligibility for Subchapter T treatment.

Finally, Subchapter T requires that amounts refunded to patrons (members and nonmembers) be paid pursuant to valid, preexisting obligations requiring the cooperative to pay each patron from the net earnings of the cooperative's patronage business. Dividends on capital stock are to be paid out before the net is determined.

Cooperatives operating on a cooperative basis, whether nonexempt or § 521 "exempt," may exclude from gross income for tax purposes patronage dividends or refunds paid in money, other property, per unit retains and qualified written notices of allocation. Qualified written notices of allocation must reveal how much of the patronage refund is being retained by the cooperative for capital accumulation purposes. If all of the technical requirements of Subchapter T are met and at least 20% of patronage dividends for the tax year are paid to patrons in cash, the cooperative can properly exclude from its income the total patronage refund. This assumes that the patron has consented to the inclusion in his or her income of the entire amount. This consent may be given in a written agreement, by a member becoming subject to pertinent bylaws, or by endorsement when the patron cashes a qualified check for the 20% or larger percentage being paid out in cash.

Per-unit retain allocations are deductible by cooperatives operating on a cooperative basis when distributed to patrons in the form of qualified per-unit retain certificates. Like patronage refunds, the patron must consent to the arrangement which creates tax liability for the patron where no cash is received, as when qualified per-unit retain certificates are issued. Unlike patronage refunds, no cash payment has to accompany issuance of per-unit retain certificates to be qualified.

Generally, interest and rental income of a cooperative are not considered patronage sourced by the IRS. Courts, however, have found such income to be patronage sourced when generated by activities integrally related to bona fide cooperative functions and not merely gain from incidental for profit ventures. Both interest on temporary investment of excess funds and rent from temporary leasing out of vacant warehouse space have been held to be patronage-sourced income. Cotter and Co. v. U.S (Fed.Cir.1985)(leasing of excess space); CF Industries v.CIR (7th Cir.1993)(rejecting theory that only interest on funds invested for 30 days or less could be deemed patronage sourced).

C. "Exempt" Cooperatives

A farmer cooperative that meets the requirements of IRC § 521 may request and receive a "letter of exemption." The advantage of § 521 status is the availability to the cooperative of two additional deductions from gross income: dividends paid on capital stock paid to patrons; and distributions of non-patronage income allocated to patrons based on patronage with the cooperative. As to the latter, it is clear that a § 521 cooperative can exclude from gross income rents and interest passed on to patrons on the basis of patronage whether or not the rents and interest are patronage sourced.

The requirements for a § 521 election for marketing and supply cooperatives are these: a) it must be a farmer, fruit grower or like association organized and operated on a cooperative basis to market farm products or to purchase inputs for members and other patrons; b) the annual dividend rate on capital shares must not exceed the greater of 8% or the legal rate of interest in the state of incorporation; c) financial reserves are restricted to amounts required by state laws or amounts reason- able and necessary, and reserves must be allocated to patrons unless the cooperative includes them in computing its taxable income; d) business with non-members shall not exceed 50% of the cooperative's total business; e) purchasing for persons who are neither members or producers may not exceed 15% of the cooperative's total purchasing; f) non-members are to be treated the same as members in pricing, pooling, payment of sales proceeds, pricing of supplies and equipment, fees charged for services, and allocation of patronage refunds to patrons; g) records of patronage and equity interests of members and non-members must be kept; h) the legal structure of the organization must be cooperative in character and the association must be so operated; and, i) *substantially all* of its stock (other than preferred non-voting stock) must be owned by producers who market products or purchase supplies through it, if the cooperative is organized on a capital stock basis.

Now we examine selected issues that have arisen under § 521. Must substantially all of the stockholders of a marketing cooperative be current patrons as well as producers if the cooperative is to elect and maintain § 521 status? In Cooperative Grain &

Supply Co. v. C.I.R. (1969), the 8th Circuit answered yes, noting that Congress did not intend exempt status to be granted if the producers market their products or purchase their supplies through the cooperative only at such times as they find expedient.

Because "substantially all" had been interpreted to mean 85% or more, the slippage of a few, perhaps even just one farmer member from active to inactive status could be fatal to continued qualification for § 521 treatment. Until 1990, the IRS took the position that one is not a current or active patron unless one does 50% or more of pertinent farm business with the cooperative. This was an unworkable rule for most cooperatives as they had no way of knowing how a particular patron was dividing up business at any given time. In 1990 the IRS revoked earlier rulings and announced that a member doing less than 50% of pertinent business with a cooperative will be counted when the "substantially all" test of IRC § 521(b)(2) is applied. Rev. Proc. 90-29, 1990-1 C.B. 533. Caveat: members who stored grain in a cooperative's warehouse, but who did not market or purchase through it were considered inactive in West Central Co-op v. U.S. (8th Cir.1985). The holding is flawed if one considers storage for a fee to be a service offered to patrons by the cooperative.

In the case of supply cooperatives, § 521 requires that purchasing for persons who are neither members nor producers must not exceed 15% of the cooperative's total purchasing. Thus, the use of even a few profit-taking retail middlemen to facilitate distribution could lead to a violation of the 15% rule. The argument that the such a middleman is an agent of the cooperative and that the ultimate consumers are patrons entitled to patronage dividends should not be taken to be persuasive. Land O'Lakes, Inc. v. U.S (8th Cir.1975).

Farmer cooperatives sometimes join together to form a federated cooperative to increase marketing efficiency or to increase bulk purchasing capability. A federated cooperative is an association the membership of which includes farmers' cooperative associations. It is possible for a federated cooperative to have § 521 status. Because a federated serves the interests of the patrons of its member cooperatives, it is necessary to "look through" to the patrons of such member cooperatives when determining whether or not the federated meets the requirements of § 521. In this context, the federated is considered to be dealing directly with the patrons of its member cooperatives. In determining who controls the federated, it is necessary to examine the composition of the membership of each of its member cooperatives. Revenue Ruling 69-651, 1969-2 C.B. 135.

A practical problem arises when a federated cooperative seeks to exclude from its gross income patronage refunds. It must trace net margins and patronage refunds back to the farmers who actually dealt with one of the federated's local member cooperatives. By the time net margins and savings find their way back to the local in two or three years, its farmer membership may have changed. The IRS position is that tracing to those who actually patronized the cooperative is mandatory, but the practical problems associated with this position can be insurmountable. A solution was approved in Kingfisher Cooperative Elevator Ass'n v. CIR (Tax

Ct.1985) where allocations were based on patronage in the year refunds were actually received from the federated cooperative. There is also an issue as to how long income can be deferred in the federated setting. If it takes two or three years for net margins to pass back from the central through the regional to the local cooperative, the farmers involved may not be reporting income until several years after the actual transaction with the local. The IRS would like to impose a two year limit on deferral.

VI. SECURITIES

Generally, equity and debt instruments issued by cooperatives are not considered "securities" for purposes of federal and state securities laws. A key case is United Housing Foundation v. Forman (U.S.Sup.Ct.1975), where it was held that common stock issued by a housing cooperative to its members did not fall under the federal definition of "securities" because the stock was not purchased by members in expectation of realizing profit through appreciation in value or payment of dividends. Other factors for not classing cooperative stock as securities are these: shares typically can be transferred only with board approval; and, the one vote per member rule regardless of number of shares owned.

Is it unlikely that equity certificates issued to patrons by agricultural cooperatives will be deemed to be securities. The Securities and Exchange Commission, in a no action letter, stated that it would not recommend enforcement with respect to per-unit retain certificates and patronage refund allocation certificates issued by Mid-America Dairymen. In re

Mid-America Dairymen, Inc. (SEC 1977). The court in B. Rosenberg & Sons, Inc. v. St. James Sugar Coop, Inc. (E.D.La. 1976), found membership stock not to be a security or an investment contract. And, per-unit retain certificates and written notices of allocation will not be deemed to be securities if these instruments are issued as a result of the patronage process. It is the means and purpose of the issuance that is controlling.

Some financial instruments issued by cooperatives will be classed as securities under federal law. When cooperatives sell interest bearing notes and debentures to investors who have reasonable expectations of profit, the issuance of securities may well be involved. Uncollateralized demand notes issued by a cooperative were found to be securities under § 3(a)(10) of the Securities Exchange Act of 1934 (1934 Act) in Reves v. Ernst & Young (U.S.Sup.Ct. 1990). The Court held that the "investment contract" test of SEC v. W.J. Howey Co.(U.S.Sup.Ct. 1946) is *not* to be used in ascertaining whether notes are securities. Instead, the Court adopts the "family resemblance" test which uses a presumption that every note is a security. The presumption is rebuttable and some notes, those generated in routine consumer, mortgage and business financing, are quickly disposed of as not being securities. In less obvious cases the courts sets out four factors to consider in determining whether particular notes bear a "family resemblance" to those not considered to be securities. In Reves the notes issued by the cooperatives failed the "family resemblance" test and the presumption was not rebutted. 1) The notes in Reves were not issued to deal with some immediate transaction or cash-flow problem, but rather to raise money generally and they were bought by persons primarily interested in making a profit. 2) There was a plan of distribution of the notes that involved promotion and an invitation to investment. 3) The public perception was of an investment and not of the type of lending transaction where repayment ability and other factors would normally be checked. 4) There was no other regulatory program (e.g., FDIC as to bank CDs) to serve a risk-reducing factor. The fact that the notes in Reves were bought by nonpatrons as well as patrons was not a determinative factor. Note that the definition of security is the same under the 1933 and 1934 Acts.

A cooperative that makes a public offering of a security must file a registration statement under the Securities Act of 1933 (1933 Act), unless exempt status can be claimed. Section 3(a)(5) of the 1933 Act exempts from the registration requirement those relatively few cooperatives that have "exempt" status under § 521 of the Internal Revenue Code.

The 1934 Act regulates the trading of securities in secondary markets. Registration is required as is periodic reporting, filing of proxy statements and compliance with insider trading rules. The 1934 Act at 15 USCA § 78l(g)(2)(E) contains an exemption from these requirements for an issuer of securities which is a "cooperative association" as defined in the Agricultural Marketing Act of 1929. 12 USCA §§ 1141j(a).

Cooperatives that can claim the above exemptions are not excused from compliance with the antifraud provisions of the 1933 and 1934 Acts, if securities are in fact issued. Directors, officers, accountants and attorneys can incur liability when securities laws are violated. Robertson v. White (W.D. Ark.1986).

Finally, issues can arise under state Blue Sky Laws (securities laws) as to whether cooperative-issued membership stock, per-unit retain certificates, written notices of allocation, notes, debentures and other financial instruments are securities. If securities, registration exemptions that might potentially apply to cooperatives are not clear in some jurisdictions. Even if a registration exemption applies, the anti-fraud provisions of the state's Blue Sky Law could be applicable if securities have in fact been issued.

VII. ANTITRUST LAWS

The treatment afforded agricultural cooperatives under the antitrust laws of the United States has had an impact on their organization and operation. While this discussion focuses exclusively on federal anti-trust law, a number of states regulate trade and marketing practices.

A. Sherman Act

In 1890, Congress passed the Sherman Antitrust Act, 15 USCA §§ 1-11. Section 1 of the Act prohibits combinations or conspiracies that work unreasonable restraints of trade or commerce, and § 2 of the Act makes it unlawful to monopolize or attempt to monopolize. The Congress, when considering the Sherman Act, rejected an amendment designed to exempt "arrangements, agreements, associations, or combinations among persons engaged in horticulture or agriculture made with a view of enhancing the price of their own agricultural or horticultural products." 21 Cong. Rec. 2726 (1890).

B. Clayton Act

The Clayton Act was enacted in 1914. 15 USCA §§ 12-17. It makes unlawful certain price fixing, price discrimination and related activities. Also, the Clayton Act introduces a treble damages remedy for any person injured in his or her business or property by reason of anything forbidden in the antitrust laws.

Of particular significance to agriculture, Section 6 of the Clayton Act was designed to give nonstock agricultural associations limited immunity under the antitrust laws. 15 USCA § 17 provides:

> The labor of a human being is not a commodity or article of commerce. Nothing contained in the antitrust laws shall be construed to forbid the existence and operation of labor, agricultural, or horticultural organizations, instituted for the purposes of mutual help, and not having capital stock or conducted for profit, or to forbid or restrain individual members of such organizations from lawfully carrying out the legitimate objects thereof; nor shall such organizations or the members thereof, be held or construed to be illegal combinations or conspiracies in restraint of trade, under the antitrust laws.

Many agricultural cooperatives had been formed with capital stock, although they were not conducted for the purpose of generating corporate profits and payment of dividends. Cooperatives with capital stock did not receive protection under § 6 of the Clayton Act. Also, even for nonstock agricultural associations, the Clayton Act was hard to apply because it did not enumerate the types of activities in which a cooperative could lawfully engage. To address these problems, Congress in 1922 enacted the Capper-Volstead Act.

C. Capper-Volstead Act

1. Generally

The Capper-Volstead Act, 7 USCA §§ 291-292, while not totally immunizing agricultural cooperatives from the reach of federal antitrust laws, allows such associations, formed with or without capital stock, to carry on a limited range of activities that would otherwise be prohibited. Section 1 of the Capper-Volstead Act provides:

> Persons engaged in the production of agricultural products as farmers, planters, ranchmen, dairymen, nut or fruit growers may act together in associations, corporate or otherwise, with or without capital stock, in collectively processing, preparing for market, handling, and marketing in interstate and foreign commerce, such products of persons so engaged. Such associations may have marketing agencies in common; and such associations and their members may make the necessary contracts and agreements to effect such purposes: *Provided, however,* that such associations are operated for the mutual benefit of the members thereof, as such producers, and conform to one or both of the following requirements: *First.* That no member of the association is allowed more than one vote because of the amount of stock or membership capital he may own therein,

or, *Second.* That the association does not pay dividends on stock or membership capital in excess of 8 per centum per annum. And in any case to the following: *Third.* That the association shall not deal in the products of nonmembers to an amount greater in value than such as are handled by it for members.

Without these special provisions, agricultural marketing cooperatives probably could not exist. The member farmers likely would be engaged in prohibited price fixing.

2. Cooperative Membership Structure

For farmers to have the protection of Section 1 of the Capper-Volstead Act, their cooperative must be an association of farmers, planters, ranchmen, dairymen, nut or fruit growers -- i.e. agricultural producers. The association cannot deal in the products of non-members to an amount greater in value than those handled for members. It must be operated for the mutual benefit of producers. Further, the association must meet one of the following tests: no member of the association shall be allowed more than one vote regardless of the amount of membership capital or stock owned; or, the association shall not pay dividends on stock or membership capital in excess of 8% per annum. Most cooperatives comply with both requirements as a matter of practice or because their state statute requires both.

Sunkist Growers, Inc., owner of the trade name Sunkist, found it necessary to go through a major reorganization in the late 1960s in order to qualify for Capper-Volstead protection. Sunkist controlled approximately 70% of the oranges grown in California and Arizona, and approximately 67% of the oranges used in canned or concentrated juice. It was charged with violations of §§ 1 and 2 of the Sherman Act. The threshold issue was whether Sunkist was an association of "[p]ersons engaged in the production of agricultural products as . . . fruit growers" within the meaning of § 1 of the Capper-Volstead Act. The U.S. Supreme Court in Case-Swayne Co., Inc. v. Sunkist Growers, Inc. (1967) held that the presence of commercial packing houses in the membership of Sunkist disqualified it from Capper-Volstead protection.

Sunkist had two classes of members, district exchanges and local associations. At the base of the organizational pyramid were some 12,000 growers, organized into some 160 local associations, each of which operated a packinghouse. In turn, the local associations were members of district exchanges which numbered about 60. Representatives of the district exchanges selected the board of directors of Sunkist. About 15% by number of the local associations were non-producer commercial pack-inghouses. The fact that they were private corpora-tions and partnerships was not the issue. The problem was that these commercial packinghouses dealt with growers not by cooperative marketing agreements, but by packing contracts. The U.S. Supreme Court concluded that Congress did not intend to extend Capper-Volstead protection to organizations which included nonproducer interests. It was the intent of Congress to assist actual farmers rather than non-producer associations operated for corporate profit. Restructuring eliminated non-producer packinghouses' membership in Sunkist. It was not necessary, however, to make changes with respect to the 5% or so of Sunkist's members who were corporate growers with their own packing-houses. The new membership structure was approved as being within Capper-Volstead.

3. Vertically Integrated Cooperatives

Vertical integration, as well as other structural innovations within agriculture, are likely to continue to generate Capper-Volstead litigation. In National Broiler Marketing Ass'n (NBMA) v. U.S. (U.S.Sup. Ct.1978), the availability of Capper-Volstead protection to the integrated poultry industry was tested. The majority of the court indicated that for NBMA to enjoy the exemption and to thus avoid liability under federal antitrust laws for certain of its collective activities, all of its members must be qualified as agricultural producers. The majority found that not all of the NBMA members were farmers, planters, ranchmen, dairymen, nut or fruit growers. NBMA had argued that Capper-Volstead was meant to protect all who must bear the costs and risks of a fluctuating agricultural economy. The majority concluded that the intent was to aid only those whose economic position rendered them comparatively helpless. The court found fault with 9 of the approximately 75 NBMA members not owning or controlling a breeder flock or hatchery, but purchased chicks for placement with contract growers. The majority opinion reads in part:

> We, therefore conclude that any member of NBMA that owns neither a breeder flock nor a hatchery, and that maintains no grow-out

facility at which the flock to which it holds title are raised, is not among those Congress intended to protect by the Capper-Volstead Act. The economic role of such a member in the production of broiler chickens is indistinguishable from that of the processor that enters into a preplanting contract with its supplier, or from that of a packer that assists its supplier in the financing of his crops. Their participation involves only the kind of investment that Congress clearly did not intend to protect. We hold that such members are not "farmers," as that term is used in the Act, and that a cooperative organization that includes them -- or even one of them -- as members is not entitled to the limited protection of the Capper-Volstead Act. 436 U.S. at 827-829.

4. Activities of Capper-Volstead Cooperatives

Activities allowed by Capper-Volstead include agricultural producers acting together in associations to collectively process, prepare for market, handle and market products. Producers in one association can agree on marketing practices with producers of another association by informal means, by use of a common marketing agent, or via a federation.

In Northern California Supermarkets, Inc. v. Central California Lettuce Producers Cooperative (N.D.Cal.1976) it was held that a cooperative, through its producer-members, could legally set the prices at which the members would sell their produce -- given the provisions of § 6 of the Clayton Act and § 1 of the Capper-Volstead Act. The lettuce association was nothing more than a meeting ground for member producers to agree upon pricing. The association did not handle or sell lettuce. Section 1 of the Sherman Act, which makes illegal per se combinations formed to raise the price of a commodity, does not apply to Capper-Volstead cooperatives -- so long as they do not engage in predatory pricing.

In Treasure Valley Potato Bargaining Ass'n v. Ore-Ida Foods, Inc. (9th Cir.1974), the court approved the collective activity of two cooperative bargaining associations. Neither association handled or actually sold potatoes, but bargained collectively on behalf of their respective members as to prices and other terms. The court read the term "marketing" in § 1 of Capper-Volstead to be sufficiently broad to encompass exchange of market information.

Capper-Volstead cooperatives are not totally exempt from the scope of the antitrust laws. A Capper-Volstead cooperative may lose its limited antitrust exemption if it conspires or combines with persons who are not producers of agricultural products. For example, a dairy cooperative combined with labor officials, municipal officers and other non-producers to seek to control the supply of fluid milk in the Chicago area by paying to producers artificially high non-competitive prices. Any immunity that the dairy cooperative might have had under § 6 of the Clayton Act or under § 1 of the Capper-Volstead Act was lost. U.S. v. Borden Co. (U.S.Sup.Ct.1939).

In Fairdale Farms, Inc. v. Yankee Milk, Inc. (2nd Cir.1983), the court held that Capper-Volstead prevents the full application to agricultural cooperatives of the Sherman Act monopolization test, as developed in U.S. v. Grinnell Corp. (U.S.Sup.Ct. 1966). The test has two parts: 1) possession of monopoly power in the relevant market, and 2) willful acquisition or maintenance of that power as distinguished from natural growth as a consequence of superior product, business acumen, or historic accident. Conceivably, a Capper-Volstead cooperative could safely acquire 100% of a particular market so long as this results from growth of membership. However, an agricultural cooperative is not given a license by Capper-Volstead to acquire or exercise monopoly power by harassment, coercion, uneconomic pricing, boycotts, discriminatory pricing, or other predatory practices. Capper-Volstead cooperatives are also not privileged to engage in predatory practices, even in dealing with other cooperatives. Maryland & Virginia Milk Producers Ass'n v. U.S. (U.S.Sup.Ct.1960).

Section 2 of the Capper-Volstead Act does not protect cooperatives that unduly enhance prices of agricultural products. While the Secretary of Agriculture can enforce § 2 by investigating complaints of undue price enhancement, there has not yet been a case where the evidence has been deemed sufficient to go to a hearing. Rules governing potential § 2 cease and desist orders are at 7 CFR §§ 1.160 - 1.175 (1994). The U.S. Department of Justice, the Federal Trade Commission, and private parties may bring actions against a cooperative when the alleged conduct is not protected by Capper-Volstead or in the first instance when the cooperative failed to meet the Capper-Volstead organizational requirements.

D. Other Federal Statutes

Four years after the passage of the Capper-Volstead Act, Congress enacted the Cooperative Marketing Act of 1926, 7 USCA §§ 451-457, which provides that agricultural producers and their associations can legally acquire and exchange past, present and prospective data on pricing, production and marketing. Also, the Agricultural Marketing Agreement Act of 1937 provides that the making of any marketing order shall not be held to be in violation of any of the antitrust laws and generally shall not be deemed unlawful.   7 USCA § 608b.

Another statutory exception for cooperatives appears in the Robinson-Patman Act, 15 USCA §§ 13, 13a, 13b, 21a. The Act, which became law in 1936, focuses on price discrimination between purchasers. It provides that cooperative patronage refunds will not be characterized as illegal rebates.

The Agricultural Fair Practices Act of 1967 (AFPA) became effective in April, 1968. 7 USCA §§ 2301-2306. Because the marketing and bargaining positions of individual farmers may be adversely affected if they are unable to freely join together in cooperative organizations, AFPA forbids any coercive practices by handlers who receive farm products that would interfere with the exercise of such right by farmers. AFPA does not prohibit other discriminatory practices by handlers, nor does it require them to deal with or bargain in good faith with a cooperative. AFPA preempts certain provisions of state agricultural marketing and bargaining laws. Michigan Canners & Freezers Ass'n Inc. v. Agric. Marketing and Bargaining Bd. (U.S.Sup.Ct.1984).

CHAPTER NINE

AGRICULTURAL EMPLOYMENT LAW
I. BACKGROUND

Production agriculture in the United States uses a labor force made up of farm operators, paid and unpaid family members, permanent employees, seasonal and migrant workers, and documented and undocumented aliens. While the number of farm operators and unpaid family members continues to fall, the hired farm labor force is estimated to have stabilized at about 2.5 million. However, only about 900,000 to 1.7 million are in the work force at any given time. For example, a July, 1990 USDA survey found 1,106,000 hired farm workers then currently employed. As to seasonal farmworkers, the Report of the Commission on Agricultural Workers (Nov. 1992) reports 70% to be of Latin origin. Other minorities are represented, but tend to be concentrated in particular localities.

We first explore longstanding agricultural exemptions in laws governing wages, hours, child labor, Social Security, unemployment compensation, and workers' compensation. Constitutional issued raised by these exemptions are discussed. The focus then turns to federal law governing the recruiting and hiring of agricultural workers, and their treatment while employed: Wagner-Peyser Act (job placement services); Migrant and Seasonal Agricultural Worker Protection Act (sweeping 1983 law); Immigration Reform and Control Act of 1986 (SAWs and H-2A programs). After a look at occupational safety and health and agriculture, we conclude with an overview of agricultural labor-management relations law.

II. WAGE AND HOUR LAWS

A. The Agricultural Minimum Wage

The federal Fair Labor Standards Act (FLSA), 29 USCA §§ 201-219, requires that certain agricultural employers pay an agricultural minimum wage, pegged since January 1, 1978 at the same rate as the general minimum wage. FLSA § 206(a)(5). Specifically, an agricultural employer who uses 500 mandays of agricultural labor in any calendar quarter of a particular year must pay the agricultural minimum wage to certain agricultural employees in the following calendar year. Man-days are those days during which an employee performs any agricultural labor for not less than one hour. The man-days of all agricultural employees count in the 500 man-days test, except those generated by members of an unincorporated employer's immediate family. FLSA § 203(e)(3).

An agricultural employer who is required to pay the agricultural minimum wage must pay it to all agricultural employees except: 1) members of his or her immediate family, unless the farm is incorporated; 2) local hand-harvest piece-rate workers who come to the farm from their permanent residences each day, but only if such workers were employed less than 13 weeks in agriculture in the preceding year; 3) children, age 16 and under whose parents are migrant workers, and who are employed as hand-harvest piece-rate workers on the same farm as their parents, provided that they receive the same piece-rate as other workers; and 4) employees engaged in range production of livestock. FLSA § 203(a)(6). Where the agricultural minimum wage must be paid to piece-rate employees, the rate of pay for piece-rate work must be sufficient to allow a worker reasonably to generate that rate of hourly income.

When the minimum wage must be paid, FLSA § 203(m) allows the employer to include as part of the compensation paid, the reasonable cost of meals, housing and other perquisites actually provided, if they are customarily furnished by the employer to his or her employees. However, in Soler v. G & U, Inc. (S.D.N.Y.1991), the housing deduction was disallowed for a period during which the labor camp was overcrowded in violation of a state permit.

B. Employment and Joint-Employment Issues

It is not uncommon for farm labor contractors (FLCs) to supply labor intensive farms with needed crews. Farm labor contractors are also referred to as crew leaders, crew bosses, or *contratistas*. It is not always clear whether a FLC stands in an employment or in an independent contractor relationship with a particular farmer. If the FLC is an employee of the farmer, it follows that the crew members are employees of the farmer as well. On the other hand, if the FLC is an independent contractor he may or may not be the sole employer of the crew. Under the FLSA joint-employment doctrine, the farmer in some instances will be a joint-employer and thus responsible with the FLC for compliance with FLSA.

In Castillo v. Givens (5th Cir.1983) the court was faced with the question of whether a particular crew leader was an independent contractor or an employee of the farmer. While other factors can be relevant, the ultimate test of a crew leader's status is whether he is in a position of economic dependency vis-a-vis the farmer. Here the crew leader was a registered farm labor contractor who recruited and transported an unskilled crew, supervised rote cotton chopping, kept minimal records and dispersed the crew's pay. Yet, he was characterized as an employee of the farmer rather than an independent contractor as he supplied crews to no other farmer, had no business of his own, did not set crew wages, had no meaningful investment in his "business", and was dependent economically on the farmer's operation. For FLSA purposes, crew members were considered to be employees of the farmer, not of the crew leader.

Where the FLC is an independent contractor, the FLSA joint-employment doctrine might nevertheless apply with the result that both the FLC and the farmer are treated as employers of the crew members for compliance purposes. Beliz v. W.H. McLeod & Sons Packing Co. (5th Cir.1985). Whether a farmer will be classed as joint-employer with an independent contractor crew leader requires an examination of the level of certain of the farmers activities: the nature and degree of control of the workers; the degree of direct or indirect supervision of the work; the power to determine pay rates or methods of payment to the workers; the right, directly or indirectly, to hire, fire or modify employment conditions; and preparation of payroll and payment of wages. As noted in Real v. Driscoll Strawberry Associates, Inc. (9th Cir.1979), no one factor is determinative and ultimately the focus in these cases must be on the economic realities of the total circumstances.

C. Agriculture Defined

Only employment in agriculture can be counted to reach the FLSA 500 man-days threshold and to trigger FLSA coverage -- subject to the specific agricultural exemptions. The 1949 decision in Farmers Reservoir & Irrigation Co. v. McComb (U.S. Sup.Ct.) includes this analysis of FLSA § 203(f), the Act's definition of agriculture:

> First, there is the primary meaning. Agriculture includes farming in all its branches. Certain specific practices such as cultivation and tillage of the soil, dairying, etc., are listed as being included in this primary meaning. Second, there is the broader meaning. Agriculture is defined to include things other than farming as so illustrated ["the raising of livestock, bees, fur-bearing animals, or poultry"]. It includes any practices, whether or not themselves farming practices, which are performed either by a farmer or on a farm, incidently to or in conjunction with "such" farming operations. 337 U.S. at 762-3.

In Farmers Reservoir, a cooperative that owned an irrigation system assigned its employees to tend the ditches and gates. The duties of the employees did not require their physical presence on the farms served by the system. The court noted that while water is essential to agricultural operations, the operation of an irrigation system as a distinct business is not farming or a specific farming practice. Thus, the "primary meaning" of agriculture could not be invoked. The court also found no secondary agriculture. The work was not per-formed on a farm, nor was it performed by a farmer.

The FLSA definition continues to generate litigation, particularly with respect to categorizing employment at different levels of vertically inte-grated agricultural operations. Generally, a vertical integrator is an enterprise that owns or controls all aspects of putting a commodity into the retail market place -- from on farm production to processing and sales to retailers. See p. 43 *supra*. A line of cases distinct from FLSA reported cases exists because Congress used the FLSA definition of agriculture to define the scope of the agricultural exemption in the National Labor Relations Act. Results in NLRA cases are sometimes at variance with those in FLSA cases because of the policy of judicial deference to the administrative determinations of the National Labor Relations Board (NLRB).

FLSA cases, like the NLRA cases, focus on the business of the integrator rather than that of the contract farmer when determining the status of the integrator's employees. In deciding Coleman v. Sanderson Farms, Inc. (5th Cir.1980) the court found a poultry integrator's loader operators and live haul drivers to be agricultural employees for FLSA purposes. These workers traveled to contract farms, caught and cooped grown out broilers and hauled them to a subsidiary of the integrator for processing. While this was not primary agriculture, the court did find secondary agriculture since the workers were deemed to be employed by a farmer -- the integrator -- in activities incident to a farming operation. The fact that chicks owned by the integrator were placed temporarily with a contract grower did not work a termination of the integrator's status as a farmer. This outcome is inconsistent with the decision of the Supreme Court in Bayside Enterprises, *infra*, but Coleman makes it clear that in a FLSA case, deference will not be given to NLRB interpretations.

The facts in Bayside Enterprises, Inc. v. NLRB (U.S.Sup.Ct.1977) involved a vertical integrator, Bayside, that contracted with individual farmers to raise it's chicks to a certain stage. A subsidiary of Bayside operated a feedmill and employees of the mill trucked feed to contract farms. In deciding whether the truck drivers were employed as an incident to or in conjunction with Bayside's farming operations, the outcome turned on whether Bayside was or was not a farmer. The court indicated that it was the character of Bayside's activities as employer that were to be examined, not the activities of the 119 contract farmers. The operation of the feedmill was held to be sufficiently divorced from Bayside's agricultural operations, so as to constitute a non-agricultural activity. Deference was given to NLRB findings that a poultry integrator is not a farmer as to operations subsequent to delivery of chicks to farmers who contract to "grow them out." This is so even though title to the chicks remains in the integrator. Thus, the feed truck drivers were not employed by a farmer and could not be classed as agricultural employees. But, Bayside was "clearly" a farmer in its operation of its own farms for breeding hens, producing eggs and hatching same.

An employee who usually works only in primary agriculture will nevertheless be characterized as engaged in non-agriculture employment for FLSA purposes for a particular week if during that week the employee does both exempt (agricultural) and non-exempt (non-agricultural) work. For example, if an employer raises livestock and assigns associated duties to an employee, the latter is working in primary agriculture. However, as determined in Hodgson v. Wittenburg (5th Cir.1972), time spent caring for livestock bought by the employer for immediate resale involves duties that are not incident to the agricultural operation.

D. Overtime Pay

The FLSA requires payment of an enhanced rate for work over 40 hours in a week. But, a sweeping FLSA exemption denies persons employed in agriculture the benefit of mandatory overtime payment. FLSA § 213(b)(12). The 500 man-days test is irrelevant in this context. Also, there are specific FLSA hour exemptions for certain employment that is not within the FLSA definition of agriculture. For example, while the ditch tenders in Farmers Reservoir, p. 313 *supra*, were not engaged in agricultural employment and were thus entitled to minimum wage protection, a special exemption relieved their employer from being required to pay at an enhanced rate for hours over 40 in a week. *Id.*

E. Remedies

FLSA authorizes three causes of action: 1) an employee may sue his employer for unpaid overtime, unpaid minimum wages, and, subject to the discretion of the court, up to an additional equal amount in liquidated damages; 2) the Secretary may sue on behalf of employees to recover such amounts; 3) the Secretary may sue to enjoin violations of FLSA. FLSA § 216. Criminal penalties are provided for cases of wilful or repeat offenses. *Id.* Caveat: state laws that extend minimum wage or overtime protection to workers not covered under FLSA are not preempted by federal law and must be observed. Further, states can enact and enforce wage and hour benefits for agricultural workers at levels more favorable than under federal law. FLSA § 218

III. CHILD LABOR LAWS

At the federal level, FLSA makes it unlawful to employ oppressive child labor. FLSA § 212. Unless an exemption applies, oppressive child labor exists when anyone, other than the child's parent, employs a child under age 16. Employ is broadly defined to include letting a child help out without pay -- "suffering or permitting to work" -- as well as hiring with pay. 29 CFR § 570.70(c)(2)(iii)(1993).

Exceptions in federal law allow the employment of children under age 16 in agriculture -- albeit with certain qualifications. The FLSA definitions of agriculture and employer govern. Under federal law a child age 14 or 15 may be employed in agriculture; a child 12 or 13 may be so employed but only with parental consent; and a child under age 12 may with parental consent be so employed, but only on farms not required to pay the agricultural minimum wage to any employee. FLSA § 213(c)(1).

At 29 CFR § 570.71(1993) appears a lengthy list of particularly hazardous tasks that may not be assigned to an agricultural employee under age 16. They range from the operation of most tractors and farm machines to working around female animals caring for newborn offspring. But, children age 14 or 15 can be assigned certain of these forbidden tasks if they have completed a pertinent 4-H or other approved training program.

At the behest of strawberry and potato growers, Congress in 1977 added the "strawberry" amendment to the FLSA. It allows an agricultural employer who is required to pay the federal agricultural minimum wage to apply for an administrative waiver permitting the employment of children of others, ages 10 and 11, outside of school hours and for not more than eight weeks in the calendar year. FLSA § 213(c)(4). Applicants for the waiver must submit objective data showing a crop with a short harvesting season, unavailability of employees ages 12 and above, a past tradition of employing younger children, and the potential of severe economic disruption if this work force is not available.

Also, the applicant must demonstrate that the level and type of pesticides and other chemicals used will not have an adverse effect on the health or well-being of the individuals to whom the waiver would apply. Compliance with adult field worker standards will not necessarily satisfy this requirement. The issue is whether the federal statute requires the application of an absolute safety (zero risk) test or whether the intended test is reasonable assurance of safety based on best available evidence. While the zero risk test might effectively cancel the waiver scheme, there is doubt that reasonable assurances of safety were intended by Congress to be adequate to protect children working in chemically treated fields. National Ass'n of Farmworkers Organizations v. Marshall (D.D.C.1980). The new EPA fieldworkers standards do not speak to this issue. See p. 344 *infra.*

The assigning of actual handling of most agricultural chemicals to children under age 16 is prohibited by federal law, except where the employer is the parent. 29 CFR § 570.71(9)(1993). Unless an FLSA exemption applies, children must be paid the agricultural minimum wage. See p. 310 *supra*. This is so even where children are employed illegally.

If state child labor laws are more stringent than the federal, they must be observed. FLSA § 218(a). Such laws can absolutely prohibit employment of children under an age such as 12 or 14, rule out employment during certain hours of the day, and limit the number of hours a child may work during a set period of time. State school attendance laws also apply, even when the parent is the employer.

IV. SOCIAL SECURITY

Three pieces of legislation define the operation of OASDHI (Old-age, Survivors, Disability, and Health Insurance): the Social Security Act of 1935, 42 USCA § 401 et seq (benefit programs); the Self-Employment Contributions Act, IRC § 1401 et seq (contributions by the self-employed to fund programs); and the Federal Insurance Contributions Act (FICA), IRC § 3101 et seq (contributions by employee and employer). Entitlement to benefits does not result just because taxes have been paid on wages. Each program has eligibility requirements.

The 1935 Act excluded from coverage individuals employed in agriculture. In 1951 some 710,000 regularly employed agricultural laborers were brought into covered employment, with that number jumping significantly in 1955 as a result of the elimination of the regularly employed requirement and the substitution of a wage threshold. From 1957 through 1988 the law focused on the earnings of the particular agricultural employee. An agricultural laborer had FICA wages from agricultural employment if in a calendar year the employee generated $150 or more in cash wages, or had 20 days or more of employment on other than a piece rate. The focus was on an agricultural worker's employment with a single employer and there was no cumulative effect if the worker moved from job to job. Once either threshold was met all cash wages from the particular employe were subject to the employer FICA tax and to the withholding tax. Today, the 20 days test is no longer in the law.

Beginning in 1989, wages paid are subject to FICA tax for any year in which the employer has an annual payroll for agricultural labor of $2,500 or more. This is true even as to an employee whose wages for FICA purposes do not exceed $150. However, the annual payroll test does not apply to hand harvest agricultural laborers employed on a piece-rate basis in a customary piece-rate operation who commute to the farm from their residences each day and who worked less than 13 weeks in agriculture in the preceding calendar year. These employees, along with those who work on farms with an annual payroll for agricultural labor of less than $2,500, must individually meet the $150 test. Accumulation of cash wages from job to job is still not permitted. IRC § 3121(a)(8)(B).

IRC § 3121(o) provides that a crew leader/FLC can be the sole employer of crew members for FICA purposes if the crew leader handles the payroll (even when it is the farmer's funds passing through), so long as the crew leader has not entered into a written agreement with the farmer wherein the crew leader is designated as the employee of the farmer. When a crew leader is the employer for FICA purposes, a crew member has a better chance of meeting the $150 threshold than when the determination is made anew as the worker moves from farm to farm.

Only cash wages count in the threshold test and only cash wages are potentially subject to FICA tax. IRC § 3121(a)(8)(A). Included are payments by check or other monetary media of exchange. Perquisites such as lodging, food, clothing, transportation, farm products, or other goods do not count as cash wages. But, payment by a commodity storage receipt that can be immediately converted to cash is treated as cash wages. Rev. Rul. 79-207, 1979-2 C.B. 351. Contrast the treatment of perquisites at p. 311 *supra*.

The FICA has its own definition of agricultural labor. IRC § 3121(g). Certain nonagricultural employment under FLSA is included as agricultural labor in the Social Security definition, and vice-versa. For example, the irrigation workers in the Farmers Reservoir case, p. 313 *supra*, fell outside the FLSA definition of agriculture, but clearly fall within the current FICA definition of agricultural labor. When construing the Social Security definition, FLSA cases have no application. Instead, guidance comes in Revenue Rulings and Treasury Regulations.

IRC §3121(b)(16) treats as independent contractors certain share farmers (**not** lessees) who would be classed as employees under common law rules. This occurs when the share farmer, pursuant to an agreement with the owner of land, "undertakes to produce" and harvest commodities on a specific tract, divides what is produced or the proceeds with the owner, and thus shares the risk of production. This triggers application of the self-employment tax as to the share farmers and leaves the owner without obligation under FICA.

V. UNEMPLOYMENT COMPENSATION

The first permanent extension of federal unemployment law to agricultural employees became effective Jan. 1, 1978. Covered employment was redefined to add employment in agriculture where the employer has 10 or more hired workers during 20 weeks of the current or preceding calendar year, or a cash payroll of $20,000 or more in any calendar quarter of the current or preceding year. 26 USCA § 3306(a)(2), (c)(1). In certain instances the crew leader (FLC) will be the employer. § 3306(c)(1,2,3). Since the unemployment system is managed at the state level, states moved quickly to bring their laws in line with the federal law on employment in agriculture so as to preserve federal funding and the employer credit against federal unemployment tax which equals a substantial percentage of the employer's contribution to the state fund.

Certain states define covered employment in agriculture less restrictively than does federal law. Thus, there is a greater chance for agricultural workers to earn sufficient credits to qualify for benefits. For example, California puts agricultural employment on a par with other covered employment - using a test of one or more employees in any calendar quarter of the current or preceding calendar year and a payroll of over $100 for such services.

The definition of agricultural labor in the Federal Unemployment Tax Act (FUTA) and in most related state statutes, follows the Social Security definition at IRC § 3121(g) -- with one modification.   26 USCA § 3306(k).   This modification moves certain work in handling, planting, drying, packing, processing, freezing, grading, storing or delivering unmanufactured agricultural or horticultural commodities from the nonagricultural into the agricultural sphere.

Wages for FUTA purposes include payments that count as cash wages for FICA purposes.   Nonexempt wages up to $7,000 per employee are used to calculate the federal tax due from the employer under FUTA.   People do not qualify for unemployment benefits simply because they have been employed in covered employment. Benefits are paid only to unemployed persons who have accumulated sufficient credit weeks, wage credits, or both.

VI. WORKERS' COMPENSATION

All states have workers compensation laws designed to provide benefits to workers and their families in the event of job related accident, illness, disease or death.   Negligence of the employer need not be demonstrated.   Income protection benefits are provided, subject to statutory limits; medical bills are paid, in some states without upper limits; and survivor benefits are provided, subject to various cutoff points. Employers, unless exempt by statute, are required to carry private insurance, to be self-insured, or in some states to contribute to a state compensation fund.

Where an employer has failed to obtain required coverage, an injured employee will be paid benefits from a special state fund, if one exists. The state may then seek full reimbursement for the employer, although such claims are often compromised if a first "offense" and the employer did not willfully disregard the workers' compensation law.

While some 17 jurisdictions continue to maintain agricultural exemptions, many state legislatures have moved to eliminate them. In some states coverage of agricultural employees becomes mandatory when the employer has attained a statutory threshold tied to amount of payroll, number of employees or some other factor. Where workers compensation coverage does not exist, a worker injured on the job may find the only recourse to be in a negligence suit against the employer for breach of common law duties such as failure to furnish a safe place to work, to warn of known dangers, to provide safe tools, or to provide competent fellow workers. Traditional defenses may be available to the employer: i.e. contributory negligence or assumption of risk by the employee, the fellow-servant doctrine, and pure accident.

In each state where an agricultural exemption persists, a definition of agricultural employment is required. Definitions vary and the line between agricultural and non-agricultural employment is not necessarily the same from one state to the next. In some states exempt employees can be brought under coverage if their employer so elects and buys appropriate coverage. Family members may qualify as employees in some states, particularly if a family farm corporation is the employer. If not considered employees, some states permit elective coverage.

Traditionally, where an employee is able to recover under a workers' compensation program, no further recovery is permitted against the employer. Exceptions to this rule of exclusive remedy have been rare. But, under Adams Fruit Co., Inc. v. Barrett (U.S.Sup.Ct.1990) migrant and seasonal farmworkers who are injured on the job may -- even in the face of an exclusivity provision in the state workers' compensation law -- pursue a statutory private right of action for money damages against the employer for violations of the Migrant and Seasonal Agricultural Workers Protection Act (MSPA) growing out of the same event. State law cannot alter or preempt the MSPA remedial scheme. Congress later amended MSPA to rule out recovery of actual, but not statutory damages in such cases. See p. 335 *infra*.

VII. CONSTITUTIONAL ISSUES

Virtually every federal and state exemption discussed above has been the subject of equal protection challenges brought by excluded farmworkers. Courts have discerned discrimination, but have consistently found no denial of fundamental rights. Thus, the burden has been on the challengers to demonstrate that there is no rational basis for the discrimination. Even today, courts routinely find the required rational basis, citing factors such as: relieving farmers of administrative burdens; saving "small" agricultural employers from undue economic burdens; indirect subsidizing of "beneficent" agricultural enterprises; recognition of the political compromise needed to enact social and labor legislation; and, in the case of unemployment laws, the need to keep an allegedly "deficit" industry out of the system. Doe v. Hodgson (2d Cir.1973); Romero v. Hodgson (U.S.Sup.Ct.1971); Otto v. Hahn (Neb.1981); Baskin v. State ex rel. Worker's Comp. (Wyo.1986); Collins v. Day (Ind.Ct.App.1992).

Critics will say that these courts have passed up chances to apply the principle that a classification -- reasonable at the time of enactment -- can become arbitrary given societal changes occurring over time. The singular decision in Gutierrez v. Glaser Crandall Co. (Mich.1972) holding that discrimination against agricultural employees in that state's workers' compensation law could no longer be justified by traditional arguments, failed to spark a trend even in Michigan where Gutierrez was overruled by Eastway v. Eisenga (Mich.1984).

VIII. JOB SERVICES

The Wagner-Peyser Act, 29 USCA §§ 49-49*l*-1 directs the United States Employment Service (USES) to aid states in providing employment services. This is accomplished through federally funded state Job Services offices. 20 CFR pt. 652 (1994). When a farm employer files a job order with a local Job Services office, that office will seek to place local workers. If locals are not available the office will use the interstate clearance system to recruit through offices in other states. 20 CFR pt. 653, subpt. B (1994). Workers recruited through the system, whether locals or migrants, are protected by Employment and Training Administration (ETA) regulations governing minimum working conditions, housing standards, transportation and subsistence from the place of recruitment to the place of employment and back, a guarantee of work during a certain percentage of the days covered by the agreement, workers compensation insurance, and three meals a day. 20 CFR pt. 653, subpt. F (agricultural clearance order activity); pt. 654, subpt. E (housing of agricultural workers) (1994). A family farm that uses Job Services has no special status and must comply with ETA regulations. There are no statutory civil or criminal penalties for Wagner-Peyser violations. An employer or crew leader who abuses the system can, however, be denied further services.

Employers who violate Wagner-Peyser regulations arguably can be sued for money damages on a federal implied private cause of action theory. Gomez v. Florida State Employment Service (5th Cir.1969). In the post-Cort v. Ash (U.S.Sup.Ct.1975) environment, doubt was cast on the availability of such an implied cause of action. De La Fuente v. Stokely-Van Camp, Inc. (7th Cir.1983). The issue is academic because the facts of most Wagner-Peyser violations will give rise to an express statutory cause of action for damages under the Migrant and Seasonal Agricultural Worker Protection Act. Donaldson v. USDOL (4th Cir. 1991). See p. 334 *infra.*

IX. MIGRANT & SEASONAL AGRIC. WORKER PROTECTION ACT

A. Overview

The Migrant and Seasonal Agricultural Worker Protection Act (MSPA herein, AWPA or MSAWPA in some other sources), 29 USCA §§ 1801-1872, became effective April 14, 1983. MSPA repealed the Farm Labor Contractor Registration Act of 1963

(FLCRA), as amended in 1974. State laws regulating farm labor contractors are not preempted by MSPA.

MSPA creates three principal classes of regulated persons: agricultural employers; farm labor contractors; and agricultural associations. These persons achieve regulated status by engaging in certain pre-season recruitment and in-season employment activities involving protected workers. There are two classes of protected workers, migrant agricultural workers and seasonal agricultural workers. The classes are afforded slightly different protection.

Regulated parties must observe affirmative worker protection requirements found in MSPA and the regulations promulgated thereunder. However, only farm labor contractors and their employees are required to register with the U.S. Department of Labor. The basic thrust of MSPA is to provide wide application of worker protection requirements, but to require only non-fixed situs employers to register, thus resolving certain objections to the FLCRA.

B. Regulated Persons

An **agricultural employer** is any person who owns or operates a farm, ranch, processing establishment, cannery, gin, packing shed or nursery, or who produces or conditions seed, *and* who either recruits, solicits, hires, employs, furnishes, or transports any migrant or season agricultural worker. The term "operates" is undefined and has produced litigation. MSPA § 1802(2). An **agricultural association** is a nonprofit or cooperative association of farmers, growers, or ranchers, incorporated or qualified under applicable state law, which engages in any of the activities listed in the preceding sentence.

MSPA § 1802(1). A **farm labor contractor** is any person, other than an agricultural employer or association, or an employee of either, who, for a fee, performs any farm labor contracting activity. The focus is on itinerant middlemen who move about the country supplying crews for agricultural operations. MSPA § 1802(7).

Certain MSPA requirements apply only to **farm labor contractors** and their employees. Mandatory registration with USDOL is an important example. MSPA § 1811. If a registered person desires to provide transportation, drive a vehicle, or provide housing, such activities must be specially authorized and noted on his or her Certificate of Registration in addition to the basic authorization to recruit, furnish, hire and employ. The MSPA provision making it illegal for farm labor contractors but not others to hire undocumented aliens was repealed in 1986 and supplanted by a general ban on hiring illegal aliens in the Immigration Reform and Control Act of 1986.

C. Protected Individuals

For hired agricultural workers to enjoy the protection afforded by MSPA, they must fall within one of two protected classes. Not all do. The first class -- **migrant agricultural workers** -- encompasses individuals engaged in agricultural employment of a seasonal or other temporary nature and who are required to be away overnight from their permanent residences. MSPA § 1802(8)(A). In Bracamontes v. Weyerhaeuser Co. (5th.Cir 1988) MSPA protection was found for planters of pine seedlings on a tree farm. Specifically excluded from the definition of migrant agricultural workers are family members of the employer or labor contractor, and temporary nonimmigrant alien workers admitted under the H-2A program. 29 USCA § 1802(8)(B).

The other protected class -- **seasonal agricultural workers** -- encompasses individuals employed in specific agricultural employment of a seasonal or other temporary nature that does not require them to be absent from home overnight. These workers are divided into two subclasses: 1) those employed on a farm or ranch performing field work related to planting, cultivating, or harvesting, regardless of how they travel to and from work; 2) those employed in canning, packing, ginning, seed conditioning or related research, or processing operations, but only if transported to or from the place of employment via a day-haul operation. 29 USCA § 1802(10)(A). Not included within the definition are migrant agricultural workers, immediate members of the family of the agricultural employer or farm labor contractor, and aliens admitted temporarily under the H-2A program (see p. 336 *infra.*). MSPA § 1802(10)(B).

D. Worker Protection Requirements

While worker protection requirements for migrant and for seasonal agricultural workers are largely the same, certain differences will be noted. MSPA §§ 1821-1823 (migrant); MSPA §§ 1831-1832 (seasonal). Observe that there are distinct pre-season and in-season requirements.

Certain disclosures are to be made in writing by regulated parties to migrant agricultural workers at the time of their recruitment. These disclosures must include: place of employment; wage or piece rate; work assignments; period of employment; benefits such as transportation and cost to employee; workers compensation and unemployment insurance; existence of a labor dispute; commissions charged; and as to migrant workers only, housing arrangements.

The same disclosures are to be made to seasonal agricultural workers when they are recruited for canning and other specified operations by a day-haul operation. As to other seasonal workers, the disclosures are to be made in writing at the time of an offer of employment, but only if requested.

In-season requirements include a provision that regulated persons who employ migrant and seasonal agricultural workers display a USDOL prescribed poster listing workers' rights. Wages are to be paid on time and at intervals of no more than two weeks or semi-monthly and must be accompanied by an itemized statement. Detailed rules exist as to contents and preservation of payroll records.

Persons who are required to comply with the housing provisions of MSPA must comply with existing state and federal standards. MSPA § 1823. This includes OSHA standards and, in cases where still applicable, standards promulgated by the federal Employment and Training Administration (ETA). See p. 326 *supra*. Whether the regulated provider would have been required to comply with such standards absent MSPA appears to be irrelevant. A satisfactory inspection certificate is required prior to occupancy, but failure of authorities to inspect does not excuse compliance with housing standards. Posting of terms and conditions of occupancy is required. Subject to an exclusion for certain commercial innkeepers, a supplier of housing to any migrant agricultural worker is regulated by MSPA even if the supplier does not fit into any of the classes of regulated persons noted at p. 328 *supra*.

Vehicles used or caused to be used by a regulated person to transport one or more migrant or seasonal agricultural workers are subject to MSPA safety and insurance requirements. MSPA § 1841. Limited exclusions exist for transport on certain farm machinery when used in a field, and for some car pools.

E. Joint Employment Doctrine

The FLSA joint-employment doctrine, discussed at pp. 311-12 *supra*, is specifically incorporated into MSPA at § 1802(5). As a result, a protected worker engaged in a single job may have more than one employer with responsibilities under MSPA. Beliz v. W.H. McLeod & Sons Packing Co. (5th Cir.1985); Aviles v. Kunkle (S.D.Tex.1991). A farm labor contractor who supplied a crew and the farmer on whose farm the work is being performed, have the potential of being joint-employers. Certain of the worker protection requirements found in MSPA are triggered at the point a protected worker is employed. In a case of joint employment, both employers are responsible for observing worker protection requirements. For this reason, the MSPA legislative history declares the joint-employment doctrine to be the "central foundation" of the Act. H.R. Rep. 97-885 at 6.

The joint-employment doctrine will not be relevant as to those requirements triggered solely by recruiting, providing housing, use of a motor vehicle, and the like. But, more than one person may be subject to regulation in such cases quite apart from the joint-employment doctrine. For example, when a farmer owns farm worker housing that is controlled by a farm labor contractor, both are regulated.

F. Exemptions

One series of MSPA exemptions extends to migrant and seasonal agricultural employment activities of the following individuals and entities: common carriers; certain labor organizations; certain nonprofit charitable and educational institutions; persons engaged in any farm labor contracting activities solely within a 25 mile intrastate radius of their permanent residences and for not more than 13 weeks per year; certain custom operations such as hay harvesting, sheep shearing and combining; and certain poultry, tobacco and seed production operations. MSPA § 1803(a)(3)(A)-(I). Employees of any of the exempt parties just described also are exempt when performing farm labor contracting activities within the scope of their employer's exemption and exclusively for such employer.

Pursuant to the family business exemption at MSPA § 1803(a)(1), an individual is exempt from MSPA requirements when engaging in a farm labor contracting activity on behalf of an operation owned or operated exclusively by such individual or an immediate family member, even if the business is incorporated. This assumes that the activities are performed exclusively by such individual or a family member and only for the family business. Immediate family includes only spouses, children, parents, and brothers and sisters. Permitting existing employees who are not family members to recruit new workers for the farm will result in the loss of this exemption, even if the actual hiring is done by a family member. Bueno v. Mattner, (6th Cir.1987). In Calderon v. Witvoet (C.D.Ill.1991), the exemption was lost because a non-family member transported workers. But, in Flores v. Rios (6th Cir.1994), the use by a family farmer of Job Services referrals to obtain farm workers was held not to invalidate the exemption. Contra, Martinez v. Hauch (W.D.Mich1993)

At MSPA § 1803(a)(2) appears a distinct small business exemption extending to any person, other than a farm labor contractor, who enjoys the FLSA 500 man-days exemption. See p. 310 *supra*, This exemption does not have a restriction limiting recruiting, hiring and transporting to family members.

G. Determination of Contractor Registration

A person who cannot claim an MSPA exemption is not to engage the services of a farm labor contractor without first taking reasonable steps to determine that the contractor possesses a valid certificate of registration which authorizes the activity for which the contractor is to be utilized. MSPA § 1843. Reasonable steps include reliance upon a Certificate of Registration which appears to be valid on its face, or contact with the central registry maintained by USDOL.

H. MSPA Penalties and Remedies

Noncompliance with MSPA can result in criminal and civil sanctions. In addition, aggrieved workers have a statutory cause of action for money damages against a noncomplying regulated party. MSPA § 1854. No limit is placed on actual damages. Statutory damages of "up to" $500 per plaintiff per violation are authorized by MSPA. A limit is placed on total awards in class actions -- the lesser of $500 per plaintiff or $500,000. In 1992, § 1854 was amended to provide that when an employee's workers' compensation recovery is the exclusive remedy under state law, recovery under the same facts for a MSPA violation is limited to statutory damages or an injunction. This is in response to the Adams Fruit case, discussed at p. 325 *supra*.

An employer may be ordered to hire, rehire or reinstate with back pay a migrant or seasonal agricultural worker where it is determined that the worker was discharged or otherwise discriminated against because of the filing of a MSPA complaint or engaging in activities such as testifying or planning to testify in MSPA proceedings. Also, MSPA § 1862(c) makes it a violation for any person to "unlawfully" resist, oppose, impede, intimidate or interfere with an official charged with enforcement of MSPA. Warrantless entry by inspectors into open fields and quasi-public or common areas of migrant labor camps has been held constitutional. And, workers can "invite" inspectors as "visitors". McLaughlin v. Elsberry, Inc. (11th Cir.1988).

X. ALIEN FARMWORKERS

There are several categories of aliens working in U.S. agriculture: commuters, H-2A workers, permanent resident aliens, and undocumented workers. Commuters are persons from Canada and Mexico who have obtained immigrant visas. Most of these "green carders," an appellation derived from the original color of the Alien Registration Receipt Card, do not actually reside in the U.S. but freely enter to work, in some cases in agriculture. From a legal perspective it is essential to use an "amiable fiction" that the commuter's place of employment in the U.S. coincides with an unrelinquished lawful U.S. residence. A challenge to this interpretation was rejected in Saxbe v. Bustos (U.S.Sup.Ct.1974).

Each year several thousand non-immigrant foreign workers are issued visas to enter the United States to perform agricultural services or labor of a temporary or seasonal nature under the auspices of the **H-2A program.** The program derives its name from the number of the pertinent federal statute, 8 USCA § 1101(a)(15)(**H**)(**ii**)(**a**). Agricultural employers can make application to use H-2A workers, but there must follow a finding that domestic workers are unavailable. The greatest interest in the program has come from the fruit, vegetable and horticulture sectors. H-2A workers must be paid at an administratively established adverse effect wage rate (AEWR) which must be at least the prevailing wage rate for similarly employed domestic workers. Domestic workers are to be offered funds to cover travel and subsistence costs to the place of employment if the employer offers this to potential H-2A workers and bears risk of loss for no-shows and early departures in both instances. If a foreign government advances such funds with no risk to the U.S. employer, the offer of travel and subsistence support does not have to be extended to domestic workers. Orengo Caraballo v. Reich (D.C.Cir.1993).

Some agricultural employers are said to prefer H-2A workers to domestic workers because there are no family groups to contend with, no unions, no Social Security tax (26 USCA § 3121(B), no federal unemployment tax (26 USCA § 3306(c)), and no involvement with MSPA. See p. 330 *supra.* The only standard employee benefit that an employer must extend to an H-2A worker is workers' compensation coverage, or its equivalent if not required by the state. H-2A workers are protected, however, by mandatory terms and conditions of employment in 20 CFR pt. 655, subpt. B (1994). Growers who use H-2A workers say that they are responding to a lack of a reliable source of domestic labor.

Prior to November 6, 1986, the only federal legislation that made the employment of **illegal aliens** unlawful was the MSPA provision that prohibited farm labor contractors from recruiting, employing, or utilizing "with knowledge," such workers. The few state laws on the subject have generally not been enforced.

The Immigration Reform and Control Act of 1986, codified in various sections of Title 8 (IRCA), contains a number of provisions of special interest to production agriculture. IRCA makes it unlawful for any person to recruit, to hire, or to refer for employment an alien "knowing" the alien to be unauthorized. Use of a labor contractor to "knowingly" obtain the services of an illegal alien is also unlawful. At the same time, persons lawfully in the United States are protected from arbitrary denial of employment based on their "foreign" appearance, speech patterns, or national origin.

Employers, including farmers, must comply with the **IRCA Employment Verification System.** This system requires that at hiring, certain documents be presented by the employee at the request of the employer. A verification form must be completed by the employer which attests that the documents appear on their face to be genuine and that they demonstrate citizenship or other lawful presence in the U.S. for employment purposes. The employee also must attest in writing that he or she is a citizen or national of the United States, or an alien lawfully admitted for permanent residence, or an alien authorized to work in the U.S. Civil and criminal penalties can be imposed for paperwork violations.

IRCA contains special concessions to agriculture, more specifically to the labor intensive perishable commodities sector. The program, in its first phase, contemplated qualifying as **special agricultural workers** (SAWs), certain undocumented aliens who, among other requirements, had performed qualifying seasonal agricultural services in the United States for at least 90 days during the 12-month period ending May 1, 1986. 8 USCA § 1160(a)(1). Seasonal agricultural service is defined to mean the performance of field work relating to planting, cultural practices, cultivating, growing and harvesting of fruits and vegetables and other perishable agricultural commodities. While individual administrative determinations as to eligibility for SAW status were not subject to judicial review, a general pattern of unfair and superficial conduct in Immigration & Naturalization Service fact finding interviews was rectified in McNary v. Haitian Refugee Center, Inc. (U.S.Sup.Ct.1991). Persons admitted into the U.S. under the SAWs program are not limited to agriculture as they seek work. Eventually, SAWs can become permanent residents. 8 USCA § 1160(a)(1).

If a shortage of SAWs had developed, the second phase of the IRCA program contemplated the admission of a limited number of **replenishment agricultural workers** (RAWs) to fill the needs of producers of perishable agricultural commodities. The RAWs program was never implemented and has expired. 58 Fed. Reg. 64695 (1993).

XI. OCCUPATIONAL SAFETY & HEALTH

A. Generally

Federal jurisdiction over safety and health issues important to agricultural employees is divided between the Environmental Protection Agency (EPA) and the Occupational Safety and Health Administration (OSHA), an agency within USDOL. Our first focus is on the Williams-Steiger Occupation Safety and Health Act of 1970 (Act), 29 USCA §§ 651-678, which brought federal regulation of safety and health conditions at the workplace to American agriculture, as well as to industry generally. However, the Act and the standards promulgated by OSHA through the rulemaking process do not apply to all agricultural workplaces.

The Act requires two basic things of regulated employers. The first is to furnish employment and a place of employment free of recognized hazards that are causing or are likely to cause death or serious physical harm to employees. This is the gist of the so-called general duty clause. Act § 654(a)(1). Second, at § 654(a)(2) the Act requires employers to be in compliance with pertinent OSHA standards governing workplace conditions.

"Agricultural operations" with employees are regulated, albeit at a limited level compared with most other industries. The operative provision making certain of the OSHA standards applicable to "agricultural operations" is 29 CFR pt. 1928 (1994). "Farming operations" enjoy a statutory exemption. The terms "farming operations" and "agricultural operations" are not used interchangeably in OSHA standards. Members of the immediate family of an agricultural employer are not employees under the Act or OSHA standards.

B. Agricultural and Farming Operations

Little guidance exists as to the definition of agricultural operations, a term introduced in OSHA standards. The Occupational Safety and Health Review Commission in Secretary v. Darragh Company (OSHRC 1980), indicates that the key is not whether the employer is an agricultural employer, but whether the task in question, and thus the workplace, is part of or integrally related to an agricultural operation. This begs the question as to what constitutes an agricultural operation. However, the Review Commission appears to look to the activities classed as agricultural production in the Standard Industrial Classification Manual, chicken and egg production as an example.

In the Darragh case, employees of a vertically integrated poultry operation delivered grain to feed bins on contract farms. Given language in the grow-out contracts, the vertical integrator was said to control the workplace, including ladders on the farmer's feed bins which were not up to OSHA standards. The Review Commission refused to be guided by Bayside Enterprises Inc. v. NLRB (U.S. Sup.Ct.1977), p. 315 *supra*, and concluded that regardless of the status of the employer, the violation for which the employer -- here the vertical integrator, not the contract farmer -- was cited was integrally related to the contract farmers' agricultural operations. Thus, the task and workplace involved agricultural operations. This meant that the OSHA ladder standards, which are not set out in 29 CFR pt. 1928, nor incorporated therein by reference, had no application and could not be the basis of an OSHA citation.

If in Darragh violation of the general duty clause had been alleged, the integrator would have attempted to rely on the statutory farming operation exemption. Each year since 1977, Congress has inserted language in USDOL appropriations bills prohibiting the enforcement of the general duty clause and all of the OSHA standards in cases involving farming operations. Three tests must be met to qualify: 1) no farm labor camp; 2) 10 or fewer employees; and 3) a farming operation. OSHA Instruction CPL 2.51G provides:

> A "farming operation" is defined as any operation involved in the growing or harvesting of crops or raising of livestock or poultry, or related activities conducted by a farmer on sites such as farms, ranches, orchards, dairy farms or similar farming establishment.

Accordingly, farming operations are a subcategory of agricultural operations. This means that an agricultural operation can claim exemption from the general duty clause and all OSHA standards and regulations by showing that it is a farming operation. But, again, not all agricultural operations are farming operations.

C. OSHA Standards - Agricultural Operations

While agricultural operations with employees are subject to the general duty clause, few of the OSHA workplace standards are made applicable. The only OSHA standards that apply to agricultural operations are those printed full text in 29 CFR pt. 1928 (1993) and those general industrial standards from pt. 1910 specifically incorporated by reference into pt. 1928. Standards printed full text in pt. 1928 are those governing tractor rollover protective structures (ROPS); farm machinery safety devices; field sanitation; and exposure to cadmium (metallic element used, e.g., in welding). Cotton dust standards for ginning operations once appeared in pt. 1928, but have been deleted. Five sets of general industrial standards are incorporated by reference into pt. 1928 and thus apply to agricultural operations: temporary labor camp standards at § 1910.142; certain of the anhydrous ammonia standards at § 1910.111(a),(b); pulpwood logging standards at § 1910.266; slow-moving vehicle emblem standard at § 1910.145; and the hazard communication standard at § 1910.1200. The violation of a standard in pt. 1910 that does not apply to agricultural operations, might indirectly support a charge that the agricultural employer has violated the general duty clause.

The OSHA hazard communication standard requires disclosure of risks to employees. Information needed by employers comes on labels and in material safety data sheets (MSDSs) provided by the manufacturer. The theory is that upon disclosure, employees can decide if the risks of the particular employment outweigh the benefits. The standard was extended to agriculture in August, 1987. Also, at least

20 states have enacted right-to-know laws. While some exempt agricultural, transmittal of information about hazardous chemicals to agricultural workers does appear to be required in at least 10 states.

D. Housing Conditions - OSHA

Conditions at the workplace are regulated by Williams-Steiger, but farm labor housing is not necessarily a part of the workplace. The 11th Circuit uses the condition of employment test under which housing is classed as part of the workplace only if it is company policy that employees live in it or practical necessity forces at least one employee to do so. Frank Diehl Farms v. Secretary (11th Cir.1983). The Review Commission, on the other hand, has rejected the condition of employment test and has applied the less restrictive direct relationship to employment test. This test requires a showing that the employer owns, controls or provides the housing, and maintains the housing on its premises to ensure an adequate supply of labor.

E. Grain Warehouses - OSHA

Public grain warehouses are not agricultural operations and thus are subject to the general duty clause, and the full array of OSHA industrial standards. This includes housekeeping rules on grain dust accumulations. 29 CFR § 1910.272 (1993); National Grain & Feed Assoc., Inc. v. OSHA (5th Cir.1990).

F. EPA Fieldworker Standard

In 1973, OSHA used its emergency rule-making power to promulgate standards to protect fieldworkers from exposure to certain pesticides. But, the 5th Circuit in Florida Peach Growers Ass'n, Inc. v. U.S. (1974), struck down the regulations on the theory that there was no grave danger. Then, EPA, using rule-making power under FIFRA, 7 USCA §§ 135-136y, promulgated regulations that preempted OSHA from acting further. Organized Migrants in Community Action v. Brennan (D.C.Cir.1975).

The longstanding and much criticized EPA fieldworker protection standards at 40 CFR pt. 170 were replaced "on the books" by new EPA standards. 57 Fed. Reg. 38,102 (1992)(codified at 40 CFR pts. 156, 170). Compliance was to have been phased in at various intervals over two years, but by special Act of Congress implementation of certain of these standards begins in 1995. These standards impact operational practices and costs for enterprises that employ fieldworkers in the production of fruits, vegetables, nuts, herbs, and turfgrass. They also protect employees working in forests, nurseries and greenhouses.

Since April, 1993 all containers of regulated pesticides must be labeled so as to inform growers of the new standards. 40 CFR pt. 156 (1993). Some of these requirements must be articulated and other are merely referenced on the label. The fieldworker standards printed on the label require action on the part of employers in 1994 and may include: giving of warnings (oral and written) in advance of pesticide applications; observance of restricted entry intervals (REIs) after application -- from 12 to 72 hours depending on the particular chemical; and furnishing personal protective equipment (PPE) to workers who must reenter a field before the REI has run. By Pub. L. 103-231 compliance was deferred to Jan. 1, 1995 as to requirements that do not appear directly on the label such as providing of soap, water and a place to change clothes (decontamination sites); training employees about dangers and safe practices; providing emergency transportation and identifying the encountered pesticide to medical professionals; posting of warning signs and giving verbal warnings identifying treated areas. 40 CFR pt. 170 (1993).

Additional points about the EPA standard include these. There is no farming operations or small farm exemption from compliance with the EPA rules. Certain of the new standards require protection of employees who mix, load and apply selected pesticides. Those who repair application equipment are also protected. And, there are special provisions for employees who work in treated areas where there are still surfaces with pesticide residues, foliage as an example, but not if the surfaces are livestock or harvested portions of plants. There is nothing in these regulations suggesting that their observance is sufficient when the employees are children, rather than adults. Farmers and their immediate families are not protected agricultural employees.

Workers who are harmed by exposure to pesticides might consider suits against the applicator, the manufacturer of the chemical, and the farmer employer. If the state workers' compensation law bars recovery of money damages against the farmer personally, injunctive relief could still be sought to compel warnings and safety practices consistent with and perhaps beyond those in EPA regulations. Consider also suit under MSPA as suggested in Adams Fruit Co., Inc. v. Barrett. See p. 325 *supra* (inadequate disclosure of work assignment).

XII. FARMWORKER UNIONS

It is lawful for farmworkers to form labor organizations and to engage in collective bargaining. However, because agricultural laborers are excluded from the National Labor Relations Act (NLRA), their unions have not enjoyed the leverage and protection provided therein. 29 USCA § 152(3). Congress has determined that the FLSA definition of agriculture will determine the scope of the NLRA exclusion. However, because deference is given to National Labor Relations Board (NLRB) interpretations, the definition often takes on a meaning different from that used in FLSA cases. See pp. 314-15 *supra.*

Most states do not have labor-management relations laws applicable to agriculture. Efforts have been made in Ohio, Michigan and Iowa to create private vehicles to resolve agricultural labor-management disputes. Arizona in 1972, Kansas in 1974 and California in 1975 enacted agricultural labor-management relations laws. Ariz. Rev. Stat. Ann §§ 23-1381 to -1395; Kan. Stat. Ann. §§ 44-818 - 44-830; Cal. Labor Code §§ 1140-66. The Kansas statute has seen little use.

An examination of the NLRA and the Arizona California and Kansas Acts reveals different views on how to achieve a proper balance between agricultural labor and management. The Kansas Act is a "meet and confer" statute and must be distinguished from the other Acts as it does not require parties who have negotiated an agreement to proceed in good faith to enter into a binding contract. This stands in contrast with the collective bargaining statutes in Arizona and California. The California Act is modeled in large part on the NLRA and adopts NLRA precedents where applicable. Where the California Act departs from the NLRA, it is to better accommodate the agricultural sector. The Arizona Act departs from NLRA in many areas, but with a management tilt.

Agricultural labor management relations statutes can be expected to deal with many things, including: creation of and grant of powers to an agricultural labor board; make-up of membership of worker bargaining units; petitioning for elections to select bargaining representatives; eligibility to vote in elections; conduct of elections and runoffs; appeals of alleged irregularities; certification of bargaining representatives; conduct of collective bargaining; enforcement of resulting contracts; delineation of union and employer unfair labor practices; procedures for identifying such practices; remedial measures; limits on strikes, particularly at harvest and marketing; limits on secondary activities; and, rules as to whether one must join a union when hired by an employer whose workers have organized.

Access rights for union representatives are important to organizing efforts, particularly where employees are housed on the farm. While the California Act is silent, regulations delineate access rules. Under the Arizona Act a farmer is not required to provide materials, information, time or facilities, to facilitate union organizers.

In California, all agricultural employees of an agricultural employer constitute the bargaining unit. In Arizona the unit consists of all temporary agricultural employees, or all permanent agricultural employees, or both, depending on the circumstances.

The Arizona Agricultural Labor Relations Board determines bargaining unit questions.

In agriculture, timing can have an impact on who votes in an election to certify a bargaining representative. If the statute allows the passage of several weeks or months from the filing of the petition for an election to the date it takes place, seasonal worker-petitioners might no longer be on the payroll and thus not entitled to vote. In California, the statute requires an election within seven days of filing, with that time cut to 48 hours where a majority of the petitioning employees are on strike. In contrast, the Arizona Act requires steps that can take two or more months from petition to election.

If the vote is for certification of a particular union, election challenges can delay the actual certification. Once certification occurs, collective bargaining can go forward. Subjects about which the employer must bargain in good faith may be listed in the statute. The California Act speaks of "wages, hours, and other terms and conditions of employment." One issue is whether "other terms and conditions" includes proposed mechanization by the employer.

Given the importance of product picketing in the history of farm worker unions, it is not surprising to find efforts to regulate such picketing. The Arizona Act, while authorizing product picketing, forbids the use of generic product names that might include the products of an employer with whom the union has no dispute. The California Act authorizes picketing that not only follows a struck product, but that asks consumers to totally withdraw their patronage from retailers selling the struck product. In recent times, however, farmworker unions, in efforts to remedy flagging support, have turned their focus to the dangers of agricultural pesticides and health risks to field workers and consumers alike.

A buyer of a farm who is a successor employer, has a statutory duty to bargain with the previously certified bargaining representative. The successorship test in California is whether there is continuity of operation of the farm. Successor status clearly exists if a going farm is run by a new owner virtually unchanged and with employees kept in their jobs.

When a California agricultural employer commits an unfair labor practice by refusing to bargain, not only will a cease and desist order issue, but the employer can be ordered to reinstate employees and to make them whole if they have suffered loss of pay as a result of the employer's refusal to bargain. Cal. Lab Code § 1160.3. While make-whole relief is to be used sparingly, its application is not limited to cases of blatant refusal to bargain. Sometimes complex issues of law can make the employer's duty uncertain. If the employer refuses to bargain in such circumstances, make-whole relief can be ordered. The theory is that the economic burden resulting from litigation delays should be shared by employer and employees and not be cast totally on employees. Make-whole relief is not provided in the Arizona Act and is not mentioned in NLRA.

CHAPTER TEN

FARMLAND PRESERVATION LAW
I. A FARMLAND CONVERSION CRISIS?

Some observers believe that American farmland is being permanently and indiscriminately converted to nonagricultural uses at a rate sufficient to jeopardize the nation's long range ability to supply food, fiber and energy. They call for the use of incentives to keep farms in place, as well as for close regulation of farmland conversion. Others argue that the "crisis" is more myth than fact, a specter created by the use of faulty data. These observers express confidence that an unfettered free market will put land to its best use.

The National Agricultural Lands Study (NALS 1981) reported that each year almost three million acres of privately held agricultural lands were being converted to nonagricultural uses such as residential subdivisions, shopping malls, industrial parks, highways, recreational facilities, and dams. At this rate, the nation would be eliminating between two and three percent of its agricultural land per decade. Critics, in addition to challenging this data, argue that conversion for such uses as interstate highways and dams and lakes has been largely a passing phenomenon. In the early 1990s the annual rate of conversion, including forest lands, is estimated to have been about one million acres.

350

The national debate over farmland preservation has generated relatively little federal legislation. Most legislative efforts have been at the state and local level, where the debate has tended to be provincial. Rather than lofty discussions about the future of American agriculture in the 21st century, the concerns have been about the survival of local agriculture and with it local businesses, schools, hospitals and other institutions. Even more significant in many localities has been the concern of urban dwellers about open space and scenic vistas. Recently, increased attention has been paid to the preservation of historic farms. The policy debate aside, it is a fact that in recent decades state and local governments throughout the United States have put into effect a wide array of laws to preserve farmland.

II. STATE AND LOCAL LAWS

A. Property Tax Relief

1. The Basics

When non-agricultural development occurs in rural areas, owners of agricultural land can be faced with rapidly escalating real property taxes. These are ad valorem taxes -- tied to the market value of real estate. Scattered residential and commercial development in rural areas tends to make neighboring agricultural lands prime targets for developers and speculators. In most instances the market value of such farmland ceases to be related to its value for agricultural use, but turns on its potential as a subdivision, shopping center, industrial park, or other urban use. Even in areas outside the urban-rural fringe, the coming of a freeway exchange, an airport, or an amusement park can have a considerable impact on the market value of nearby agricultural land. Without relief, owners of such land may find that an extra several thousand dollars in real estate taxes cuts deeply into annual net farm income. Thus, farmers who might otherwise resist selling to developers may consider such transactions. Such sales can contribute to real estate valuation increases over yet another tier of nearby agricultural lands.

All states have taken steps to require that real property taxes on agricultural land be based on its value for agricultural uses. Most states have enacted one of three types of *differential assessment* laws. Under *preferential assessment* eligible lands are assessed at their agricultural use value. Upon the conversion of such land to nonagricultural uses, no penalty or recovery of tax savings is imposed.

Under *deferred taxation* an agricultural use valuation is applied, but upon conversion of the land to a non-agricultural use, some or all of the tax savings must be paid. These payments are called rollback taxes. In some states interest is charged on the amount required to be repaid.

A few states limit agricultural use value assessment to cases where the owner of eligible agricultural land and the state enter into a *long-term contract* that puts the land in protected status as an agricultural district or preserve. See pp. 369-73 *infra*. During the term of the contract removal of the land from protected status is prohibited or made difficult.

Wisconsin and Michigan have taken a different approach. Rather than differential assessment relief, an owner of eligible agricultural land takes farm real estate taxes as a tax credit for state income tax purposes. This is called "circuit breaker" tax relief.

2. Constitutional Issues

Differential assessment programs have been challenged as violating uniformity clauses in state constitutions. Such clauses require that real estate taxes be levied uniformly based on the fair market value of the land. In about one-half of the states, constitutional amendments have been approved to provide clear authorization for differential assessment programs. For example, Neb. Const., Art. VIII, § 1, was so amended in the aftermath of Kearney Convention Center v. Buffalo Co. Bd. of Equalization (Neb.1984)(differential assessment invalid).

In Illinois, a distinct constitutional issue was presented when the state's deferred taxation program was challenged on equal protection grounds. Neighboring tracts of agricultural land located in the path of development ended up being taxed at different rates though both were in agricultural use during the three year period in question. The rate categories were: a) valuation at agricultural value for the tract that remained in agricultural use after the three years in question, and b) valuation at development value for the tract that was converted to nonagricultural use with recapture of tax savings for the same three year period. The court found a rational basis for the different treatment -- the state's effort to discourage the conversion of farmland to other uses. Hoffman v. Clark (Ill.1977).

3. Who Benefits? Who Loses?

Some states limit eligibility for tax relief to active family farms or closely-held family farm corporations. Under such statutes other categories of owners may benefit only if they have been in possession of the land for a requisite number of years during which agricultural uses have prevailed.

Other states do not limit the categories of owners who may apply for and obtain property tax relief. Instead, rollback provisions are relied upon to discourage developers and speculators from accumulating inventories of agricultural land for future conversion, Critics argue that developers and speculators may view rollback taxes as a minor cost falling due at conversion when construction money is available. Viewed another way, the reduced real estate taxes might help a developer maintain an inventory of agricultural land for future development. To have tax relief during the holding period the developer usually will need to rent the land to a farmer who uses it in agricultural operations.

School districts and units of local government have struggled with the adverse financial impact of differential assessment. See, e.g., Bd. of Education v. Bd. of Revision of Lake Co. (Ohio 1979). Residential development can require more funds for services than the revenue it generates. If taxes on farmland are not based on actual market value, subvention payments from the state might be needed to compensate school districts and units of local government for lost revenues. The circuit breaker approach used in Wisconsin and Michigan leaves local property tax assessments and collections intact. Relief for owners of eligible agricultural lands is provided by an income tax credit, the cost of which is absorbed by taxpayers state-wide.

B. Special Assessment Relief

Special assessments for local improvements become liens against benefitted lands. Assessments imposed by a drainage district or a rural water district are likely to include farms located in the project area. However, in the rural-urban fringe special assessments often are for storm and sanitary sewers, local streets, water mains and other infrastructure. Assessments may be levied against all benefitted lands, agricultural and nonagricultural. While such improvements are rarely of benefit to farming operations, the land can be benefitted if the improvements increase its value for nonagricultural uses. Assessment payments, though spread over a number of years, may be substantial. Farms may need protection against levies for improvements not benefiting agriculture.

Some states have coupled their property tax relief programs with relief from such special assessments. Under a statutory deferred payment program the assessment and interest thereon need not be paid until the land is converted to nonagricultural use. A second approach involves a legislative determination that no benefit can accrue to agricultural land from specified "improvements." This prevents levying of special assessments. When development does occur significant hook up and access fees will be charged. See, e.g., Minn. Stat. Ann. § 473H.11. These relief programs present financial problems for local governments as they cannot shift to nonagricultural lands assessments that are not consistent with the level of benefits to such lands. Yet, local governments need sufficient cash flow to meet annual payments on bonds issued to finance improvement projects. Subvention payments from state government can ease the problem.

C. Right-to-Farm Statutes

1. The Basics

When nonagricultural development takes place in agricultural areas, significant alterations in the character of the countryside are to be expected. Inhabitants of residential subdivisions and commercial establishments adjoining agricultural operations sometimes find the normal spill-over effects of agriculture to be offensive. Common complaints are about dust, flies, odors, noise, chemical drift, and pollution of streams and lakes. It follows that agricultural operations can become defendants in nuisance suits.

While courts may approach nuisance analysis in varying ways, it is not uncommon for the initial task to be the ascertainment of the boundaries of the geographical "district" in question. The agricultural operation may now find itself within a predominantly rural residential or rural-urban district. Pendoley v. Ferreira (Ma.1963). If damage to neighbors results from the spill-over effects of the agricultural operation, the issue is whether the agricultural uses are reasonable given the current character of the particular district. It may be difficult to sustain an argument that concentrated poultry operations, hog confinement facilities, feedlots, and certain other types of agricultural operations are reasonable uses within a rural residential or rural-urban district. The agricultural operation may be found to be a nuisance, and in the absence of a common law coming to the nuisance defense, its continued operation could be enjoined. Money damages could be assessed.

At least 42 states have responded by enacting right-to-farm statutes. An exercise of the state's inherent police power, these statutes are designed to protect existing agricultural operations from certain nuisance suits and to encourage their improvement for the production of food and fiber.

A variety of statutory approaches have been utilized by these states. A common approach is to provide that an agricultural operation or facility shall not be deemed to be a nuisance as a result of "changed conditions" around it if the agricultural operation or facility was established first and had been in operation for one year or more before non-agricultural development changed the character of the locality. Some other right-to-farm laws create a rebuttable presumption that an agricultural operation is not a nuisance if it is operated in conformity with accepted farming practices and in compliance with environmental regulations. Under either of these approaches the agricultural operation or facility is not protected if it was a nuisance before the coming of changed conditions. Shatto v. McNulty (Ind.Ct. App.1987)(hog farm protected); Laux v. Chopin Land Associates Inc. (Ind.Ct.App.1990)(hog farm not protected).

Typically, right-to-farm statutes invalidate local ordinances that have the effect of characterizing certain agricultural operations as nuisances. But, most of these statutes specifically do not protect agricultural operations that pollute streams and lakes or cause overflow of water upon neighboring lands.

2. Construction of Right-to-Farm Statutes

While there have been few reported cases thus far, right-to-farm laws invite litigation over issues of statutory construction. Defendant owners of agricultural land in Georgia argued in Herrin v. Opatut (Ga.1981) that the nonagricultural plaintiffs should lose because they had waited for more than one year after conditions had changed to bring their nuisance suit. This argument focused on Georgia Code Ann. § 72-107: "[n]o agricultural or farming operation . . . shall be or shall become a nuisance . . . as a result of changed conditions in or around the locality of such . . . operation . . . if such agricultural or farming operation . . . has been in operation for one year or more." The Georgia court found this "statute of limitation" construction to be erroneous. The issue, according to the court, was whether the agricultural operation was there first and had been in operation for one year or more before conditions had changed. If so, the plaintiff nonagricultural neighbors could not prevail. While never widely accepted, some courts used to hold that the right to continue a nuisance could ripen by prescription -- if maintained adversely, openly and continuously for the statutory period, 20 years in many states.

The term "changed conditions," if left undefined in a right-to-farm statute, has the potential of varied interpretation. A progression of events will occur as a tract is developed and at some point in the process this critical statutory event occurs. But when? In the case of residential development the event probably will be one of these: change of zoning from agricultural to residential by map amendment; subdivision platting of the rezoned land; issuance of building permits; beginning (or completion) of construction; or, occupancy of homes by buyers or renters. In the absence of a statutory definition, newer agricultural operations may have to litigate this issue when it is crucial to a demonstration that the agricultural operation was up and running for one year before conditions changed.

Expansion of a protected agricultural operation or its adoption of new technology might raise more issues. Unless the applicable right-to-farm statute permits expansion, the protected aspect of the agricultural operation probably will be restricted to its original size and characteristics. Contrast the Arkansas right-to-farm statute which provides that the benefits of "[t]his Act shall *not* apply to an agricultural facility which *materially* changes its character of operation or *materially* increases the size of its physical plant [emphasis added]." Ark. Stat. Ann. § 2-4-104. This language signals a legislative intent to permit some expansion, sufficient perhaps to accommodate new technology or a revised economy of scale.

Right-to-farm protection is typically extended only to "agricultural or farming operations." Thus, it may be difficult for agricultural processing plants and other industrial branches of agriculture to qualify for protection. But, some right-to-farm laws protect agricultural "plants" and "facilities" and list processing as an agricultural activity. The scope of these protected activities awaits judicial definition.

Right-to-farm statutes focus on nuisance cases and do not appear to provide a defense when a farmer is sued in trespass for invading neighboring land with chemical or dust particles, or sounds or odors. Also, right-to-farm statutes do not afford farmers a defense when sued by neighbors in negligence or on a strict liability theory.

D. Agricultural Zoning

1. Introduction

Zoning involves the exercise of the police power to regulate the use of privately owned land. While the police power is inherent in each state, land use typically is regulated by local units of government pursuant to authority granted by a home rule provision in the state's constitution, or by state enabling legislation. As an exercise of the police power, land use regulations must bear a reasonable relation to the promotion of the public health, safety and general welfare. In recent decades, courts in zoning cases have taken an expanded view of what falls within the scope of the general welfare. This has allowed land use regulation to extend beyond the simple dividing of a town into districts for different uses, to encompass zoning that fosters the preservation of open space and agricultural uses.

Zoning necessarily contemplates a plan for land use in the city, county or township. Traditionally, this plan was manifested within the zoning ordinance and map as such. In recent times, land use plans -- many mandated by state law -- have been formulated as distinct documents apart from zoning ordinances. These comprehensive or master plans represent efforts to set long-term goals for land use management within the boundaries of the particular unit of government. An important legal issue is whether an approved plan is merely advisory or whether zoning ordinances and other implementing devices must by law be consistent with it. Other implementing devices are subdivision and planned unit development regulations, official maps, building codes and the like. In certain jurisdictions even the advisory plans have taken on legal significance when courts have consulted them in determining whether challenged land use regulations are reasonable.

Initially, zoning is a legislative process and involves the adoption by the unit of local government of the text of a zoning ordinance. In a simple zoning ordinance the classifications might be: A-1 agricultural uses; A-2 agricultural and rural residential uses; R-1 single family residences; R-2 single family and duplex residences; M multi-family and apartment uses; C commercial uses; I industrial uses. The text of the ordinance will list uses permitted in each of the seven districts, and those additional uses which may be carried on in each district upon the issuance of special (conditional) use permits.

Once the text is adopted, a zoning map will be approved by the local unit of government. This map divides the area governed into districts, assigning a zoning classification to each district. Preexisting uses that do not fit within a particular district will be allowed to continue as nonconforming uses, though not necessarily permanently. Once zoning is in place, efforts to makes changes can be anticipated.

2. Mutability of Agricultural Zoning

A well-conceived agricultural zoning plan, once implemented, will not necessarily withstand political and economic pressures for change. Landowners

may press for a text amendment that will add
development uses to the list of permitted uses for
any tract zoned A1 agricultural. Map amendments
may be sought to rezone a particular tract of land
from A1 agricultural to another classification where
the desired development is a permitted use. If zoning
or rezoning of the particular tract must by law
conform to an existing comprehensive plan, some
map or text amendments will need to be preceded by
amendment of that plan, often an elaborate -- even
daunting process.

Variances can be granted administratively by the
local unit of government to permit a particular
landowner to deviate from the zoning applicable to a
particular tract of land. Zoning authorities are not
permitted by most zoning laws to issue variances
simply to authorize new uses or to alleviate a
personal hardship of the owner. Variances are the
safety valve of zoning law, a way to grant relief to
the owner of that odd piece of land, which because
of its size, shape or geological character cannot
readily be used for any of the permitted or
conditional uses in its particular district. The proper
granting of a variance can head off a regulatory
takings challenge -- a claim that the zoning deprives
the owner of reasonable economic use of the tract
because its unique characteristics make it incompati-
ble with any permitted or conditional use. But, the
process of granting variances can get a bit "loose"
in the face of political and economic pressure for
development or in response to an owner's personal
financial crisis. Courts generally make it clear that
variances, when granted, must be justified by the
peculiarities of the particular lot or tract as such.

See, e.g., Appeal of Buckingham Developers, Inc. (Pa.Cmwlth 1981).

Special use permits -- sometimes referred to as conditional use permits or zoning exceptions -- allow a landowner to use land for purposes listed as special or conditional uses in the text of the zoning ordinance. However, before proceeding, the owner must apply for a special use permit and it may or may not be issued, To obtain issuance, the landowner must demonstrate that standards set out in the text have been met and that the granting of the permit will not have an adverse impact on the public health, safety and general welfare. In the case of an agricultural district, it might be that operating a stone quarry or a gravel pit will be listed as a special or conditional use. However, the permit might be denied if the quarry or pit operation would be adjacent to a rural elementary school

3. Constitutional Issues

Constitutional challenges to zoning are not uncommon. Two principal legal theories emerge. Under the first, landowners may mount a facial challenge, arguing that the text of the zoning ordinance, or a part thereof, violates the guarantee of substantive due process under the 14th Amendment of the U.S. Constitution or a similar state constitutional provision. For example, a rural zoning program in Pennsylvania allowed the development of no more than five single family residences on any tract of agricultural land, regardless of the size of the tract. The court found that this zoning gave comparatively greater development opportunities to small as opposed to large farms, with no rational connection of the five residence limit and the achievement of the avowed goal of farmland preservation. Hopewell Township Bd. of Supervisors v. Golla (Pa.Cmwlth 1982). Subsequently, and with specific reference to substantive due process analysis, an ordinance using a sliding-scale of number of dwellings permitted on farms survived facial attack -- 1 dwelling on 0-5 acres; 2 on 5-15; 3 on 15-30; 4 on 30-60; 5 on 60-90; 6 on 90-120; 7 on 120-150; 8 over 150 acres (with 1 for each additional 30 acres). The sliding scale system was found to relate to a legitimate government purpose and to use a method rationally related to such public purpose. So, the scales tipped in favor of the system -- balancing of public interest versus private loss. The lack of a perfect linear relationship of dwellings to acres was justified by the greater importance of bigger farms in the larger preservation effort. Boundary Drive Associates v. Shrewsbury Township Bd. of Supervisors (Pa.1985).

The second type of attack is the tract specific challenge, focusing on zoning as it is applies to a particular piece of land, and raising the possibility that a "taking" without just compensation has occurred. Suppose a zoning authority demands an exaction of a public recreational easement (hiking and bike path) across a farm to a river in return for granting a change in zoning to accommodate the construction of a "speculative" house. Because the exaction is unrelated to public needs generated by the new house, it will work a physical taking. See Nollan v. California Coastal Commission (U.S.Sup. Ct.1987); Dolan v. City of Tigard (U.S.Sup.Ct. 1994). However, as to agricultural zoning, allegations of regulatory takings are more likely -- cases where government regulation works no physical invasion, but allegedly eliminates all reasonable economic use of the land or interferes with reasonable investment backed-expectations. See pp. 366-67 *infra*.

Area wide districting -- the placing by a township, county or city of tracts of land in the various use district of the zoning ordinance -- is constitutionally proper given general reciprocity of advantage and disadvantage. Isolated lots not suited to any use within their district could be deemed "taken" if a variance or special use permit is unavailable or denied. In determining whether a regulatory taking has occurred, some courts ask whether the zoning classification deprives the owner of the land of all reasonable economic use, while other courts may apply a balancing test asking whether the hardship on the owner is excessive given the benefit to the public. Suppose that it is determined that the benefit to the public interest in preserving a specific tract of marginal farmland is minimal compared to the loss sustained by the owner because of a refusal to rezone. In some states, courts engage in this type of cost-benefit analysis and given these facts would be quite likely to find that the presumption of validity of the zoning map legislation is overcome. See, e.g., Wilson v. County of McHenry (Ill.Ct.App.1981)

In Thurston v. Cache County (Utah 1981), the court was faced with claims by nonagricultural parties that an ordinance forcing them to obtain special use permits violated their equal protection rights. The ordinance had two provisions as to development on rural lands. On land being used in agriculture, the owners could -- without a special use permit -- construct secondary dwellings. However, owners of rural lands who were not engaged in agriculture needed a special use permit before proceeding with construction. The ordinance as applied did discriminate. Yet, there was no classification by race or other suspect class, nor was some fundamental right being infringed. Applying the rational basis test the court found that it was reasonable to allow an operating farm business to add a residence -- perhaps for family members or employees -- without having to deal with county government. Land use practices in derogation of agricultural operations were thought to be unlikely to occur. However, as to nonagricultural interests, it was held to be rational to conclude that county government had an interest in how such owners used rural land and to deal with that concern by requiring special use permits.

The use of the police power to stop all development -- even agricultural -- on wetlands, beachfronts and other environmentally sensitive lands was dealt a blow in Lucas v. South Carolina Coastal Council (U.S.Sup.Ct.1992). In effect, the Court ruled that even where there is no environmentally sound use to which the property can be put, restrictions that allow no economic use cannot be constitutionally sanctioned as to undeveloped tracts acquired by the owner with reasonable investment backed expectations and before the challenged land use regulation was adopted. An exception in Lucas allows the enforcement without compensation of a challenged regulation if it mirrors preexisting restrictions in effect under the common law of the state. The scope and application of this exception is one of a number of unknowns in the contemporary law of regulatory takings.

It is possible that the widely noted decision in Just v. Marinette County (Wis.1972) might today be decided in favor of the landowner because he had acquired the shoreland and wetlands in question in their natural state prior to imposition of zoning allowing only natural uses. To prevail, however, the landowner would need to prove interference with investment backed expectations -- e.g., contemplated sales of lakefront lots -- and denial of all economic use. Also, it would have to be determined whether the public trust doctrine, as applied in Wisconsin, is within the Lucas exception. See p. 366 *supra*. Wisconsin is conceived to be trustee of its navigable waters, not to secure a public benefit from private parties, but to eradicate and prevent pollution so as to maintain the quality of the natural environment. In contrast with the Just case, there seems to be no prospect that Lucas would impact a case such as Chokecherry Hills Estates, Inc. v. Deuel County (S. Dak.1980). Lakeshore land was acquired as part of an operating farm with development objectives in mind. But, the zoning existing at purchase placed the land in a limited use Natural Resources District.

Traditionally, when a regulatory taking was found, the land use regulation was voided as to the particular parcel and, depending on the applicable state law, the local unit of government might or might not have had an immediate opportunity to adopt valid regulations to govern its development. Until recently, money damages were not awarded to parties damaged by a regulatory taking of land. Recent cases have established money damages as an available remedy for losses sustained during the time, temporary though it may be, that a land use regulation takes all economic use of the property. First English Evangelical Lutheran Church of Glendale v. County of Los Angeles (U.S.Sup.Ct.1987). In addition, there now is doubt whether the government, upon losing a takings case, has any option but to pay for the imposition of the regulation -- absent a negotiated settlement. Preseault v. ICC (U.S.Sup. Ct.1990).

4. Agricultural Zoning Techniques

A survey of the agricultural zoning experience in the United States reveals the following creative efforts, among others. *Sliding scale zoning* has been discussed at pp. 363-64 *supra*. *Quarter/quarter zoning* first emerged in rural Minnesota and divides the countryside into 40 acre grids that mesh with the United States Government Survey. Development is severely restricted in all quarter/quarters, thus ruling out large scale subdivisions and other forms of intensive development. *Large lot zoning* also is used to limit development in agricultural areas, a method that had been upheld by courts in most instances. Construction of residences is permitted in an agricultural zone, but only on lots of 10 or 20 acres or some other large size.

Each of these devices permits some development on what will presumably remain an active farm. The thinking is that agricultural zoning will be less likely to be challenged if farmers are allowed to realize a part of the development value of their farms.

In some states, zoning designed to eliminate agriculture as a permitted use is ruled out if the land is in an agricultural district or preserve. A more general restriction on local zoning results if the state's enabling act withholds from counties and townships the power to zone out agricultural uses in unincorporated areas. County of Lake v. Cushman (Ill.Ct.App. 1976); Helmke v. Board of Adjustment, City of Ruthven (Iowa 1988). Restrictions on annexation of farmland by incorporated areas may also be needed.

E. Agricultural Districts

1. The Concept

Preservation of agricultural land from indiscriminate conversion to nonagricultural uses may require more than some combination of the programs already discussed. Thus, a number of states have experimented with agricultural districting statutes, or, as in the case of Minnesota, a set of agricultural preserve statutes. In Pennsylvania the term in use is agricultural security area.

Essentially, agricultural districting statutes offer qualified landowners the opportunity to voluntarily place their eligible farmland into district status in return for specific benefits. While current state programs vary in detail, they do share the voluntary participation feature and, except in Pennsylvania, the concept of creating districts on a farm by farm basis. Thus, the countryside might be comprised of both district and nondistrict lands with the ratio varying depending on local interest in the program.

Qualified owners of agricultural land enroll land in district status by entering into written contracts with the state wherein they covenant to keep the land in agricultural use for a set number of years or until a prescribed period has passed following the giving of notice of withdrawal. By statute these covenants run with the land and are binding on all heirs and assigns until district status is properly terminated. In return, the landowner receives benefits which vary from state to state. Some districting laws limit the identity of owners who can qualify to place agricultural land in district status. For example, a state law may deny districting benefits to speculators and to corporations other than statutorily defined family-farm corporations.

2. Selected Issues

An agricultural districting statute must offer incentives to encourage owners of eligible agricultural lands to participate. Since these statutes are so varied, the exact mix of benefits and duties in a particular state can be determined only by an examination of the pertinent statute and administrative regulations.

Differential assessment, deferral of special assessments, some measure of protection from eminent domain, insulation from annexation, and protection from local anti-agriculture ordinances are popular devices. Ohio has elected to offer a somewhat different set of incentives by providing right-to-farm protection, but not relief from real estate taxes. In Ohio relief from such taxes is available for all eligible agricultural land regardless of district or non-district status. Since relief from real property taxes may be an important, if not the major attraction of an agricultural district, it is appropriate to ask whether failure to limit that relief to lands placed in district status will undercut the statutory purpose. Where tax relief is offered, increases in agricultural tax rates may cause participation to fall off as has been the case recently in Minnesota,

Depending on the particular statute, not all agricultural land will be eligible for district status. Parcels under a set number of acres may be ineligible because of concerns about administrative efficiency or because the legislature concludes that small parcels are not critical to the overall goal of farmland preservation. In some states, land zoned for other than agricultural use is not eligible for district status even if currently in agricultural use. In Pennsylvania, at least 500 acres of farmland must be in the petition for a security area.

Under some statutes, land placed in district status receives limited protection from eminent domain. Before district lands can be taken for utility lines, pipelines or other public uses, consideration of alternative corridors may be required, along with review by the state environmental quality board. In some states, district statutes allow suspension of eminent domain proceedings for up to one year if feasible alternatives have been identified. This may discourage implementation of a project, or as a practical matter, force the condemning authority to select an alternative parcel or route.

Many districting statutes prohibit local governments from enforcing ordinances that unreasonably restrict normal agricultural practices. An example might be an ordinance that applies residential building codes or electrical codes to farm structures. Ordinances that restrict the operation of heavy farm equipment during weekends, or that impose set-back requirements on the placement of hog or poultry

confinement facilities may also be made unenforceable. In addition, the power of an incorporated unit
of local government to annex unincorporated district
lands may be limited.

A state legislature that is considering enactment of
an agricultural districting statute must determine
whether to make district status available in all
counties or just in those contiguous to urban areas.
Since the pressure for conversion to nonagricultural
uses may be more intense in the latter counties,
disparate treatment of agricultural lands within the
state probably has a rational basis. However, such a
policy might have the effect of promoting undesir-
able "leapfrog" development. Minnesota began
with a 1980 statute allowing the creation of agricultural preserves only in the seven county Twin
Cities area. Minn Stat. Ann. §§ 473.01-.18 (Metropolitan Agricultural Preserves). In 1985, a parallel
statutory program was enacted to enable counties
outstate to institute preserve programs. Minn. Stat.
Ann. §§ 40A.01-.19 (Agricultural Land Preservation
Program).

Under certain of the districting statutes, owners of
agricultural land seeking district statute will be
required to do more than refrain from engaging in
nonagricultural development. Soil and water conservation management practices are prescribed, with
penalties if they are not instituted.

Existing districting statutes vary as to length of the
commitment that is required from participating
landowners. In Ohio the commitment is for a five
year term. After expiration of the term, the owner is
free to seek zoning changes and to sell or develop

the land. Minnesota and California allow withdrawal
of land from protected status only upon notice given
by the landowner. In Minnesota, preserve status
does not terminate until eight years after notice of
withdrawal. Under California's Williamson Act,
termination occurs 10 years following the giving of
notice. Emergency cancellations are allowed for
cause, but are granted only in cases of ascertained
public emergency.

F. Severing of Development Rights

The law of real property contemplates not only
severance of the mineral estate from the surface
estate, but also severance of development rights from
the surface estate. Given perceived weaknesses in
farmland preservation measures already discussed,
there has been an ongoing search for alternative
approaches that might offer more certain long-term
protection.

Programs have been instituted to compensate
owners of agricultural land who transfer development rights or conservation easements to nonprofit
corporations or to public entities dedicated to
farmland preservation. The underlying fee simple
title remains in the farm owner, with all attendant
rights to alienate. But, the farmer and his or her
successors in interest hold subject to the rights of the
public or private entity that owns the development
rights.

1. Purchase of Development Rights (PDR)

Where development pressure has been particularly
intense, state and local units of government have in
some instances implemented programs to purchase
development rights. These programs do not involve

exercise of the power of eminent domain. Instead, arms-length negotiations result in payments of money for the development rights on key agricultural tracts. To acquire development rights, the preservationist entity purchases a negative easement that prohibits nonagricultural use of the land in question. By 1985 Maryland had about 38,000 acres protected through its PDR program. PDR programs also exist in Connecticut, New Hampshire, New York, New Jersey, Pennsylvania, Rhode Island, Washington state and a few other jurisdictions. In 1985 Massachusetts enacted legislation giving local units of government a "right of first refusal" to purchase conservation easements on farmland about to be sold for development. Connecticut has legislation that authorizes the state to buy farms in fee simple for protection and resale.

Critics of PDR programs insist that governments cannot justify the expenditure of funds when the same results can be achieved through the exercise of the police power. If a unit of government receives no valid legal consideration when it pays money for development rights, the expenditure could be viewed as an unconstitutional gift. The issue was raised under the Washington state constitution in Louthan v. King County (Wash.1980), a case challenging the King County PDR program. The court found that methods such as rural zoning, tax relief and deferred special assessments had been ineffective in achieving agricultural land preservation goals. Thus, the court found no merit in the argument that a purchase of development rights resulted in a gift to the seller. Instead, the county was determined to be spending funds to accomplish public goals that could not effectively be attained by the exercise of the police power.

2. Purchase of Agricultural Conservation Easements (PACE)

Designed to replace the PDR concept, the Purchase of Agricultural Conservation Easements (PACE) program has been authorized by legislatures in 8 states, though not all are funded. In Kentucky, for example, the 1994 PACE legislation sets up a statewide board to implement and oversee the program. Localities are directed by law to identify and map agricultural lands of statewide importance. As funding becomes available, easements will be purchased with a view to preserving the state's agricultural land base which is dominated by small farms of 155 acres on the average. The other PACE states are in the mid-Atlantic and northeast.

3. Transfer of Development Rights (TDR)

Transferable development rights (TDR) programs seek to accomplish goals similar to those of PDR and PACE programs, but without the expenditure of public funds. While TDR programs originated in an urban context (e.g., historic preservation), some TDR programs have been instituted to control and direct development on rural lands.

The establishment of a rural TDR program involves a series of steps: comprehensive planning to identify lands that are of critical importance to agriculture (granting areas) and other lands that are not so suitable for agricultural uses (receiving areas); downzoning of land in both categories; areas zoned for exclusive agricultural use to be granted development rights that cannot be used on site, but that can be transferred to lands in receiving areas; lands in receiving areas to be zoned to permit moderate levels of development, but more extensive development if an owner negotiates the purchase of TDRs from owners in granting areas. Private money, therefore, is supposed to compensate farmers whose lands are restricted to agricultural uses under the program. The extensive Montgomery County, Maryland, TDR program to save open space and agricultural lands is described in West Montgomery County Citizens Ass'n v. Maryland-National Park and Planning Commission (Md.1987).

TDR programs are not without practical problems. It is difficult to construct a fully efficient program -- used by private landowners at a meaningful level. A TDR program that does not provide certainty of monetary compensation to owners of restricted lands may become the target of lobbying for legislative change or the subject of a takings challenge. A TDR program might be activated by modest public funding of a development bank where some TDRs can be sold, even though owners of receiving lands are not then in the market to buy.

Should courts in takings cases begin to focus on a specific property right such as the development rights, rather than on the entire bundle of rights attendant to fee simple ownership, dormant TDR programs might be open to successful challenge under Lucas. See pp. 366-67 *supra*. However, if the reasoning in Penn Central Transportation Co. v. City of New York (U.S.Sup.Ct.1978) continues to prevail, a TDR program that leaves owners of granting and receiving lands with reasonable economic use of their lands should withstand constitutional attack.

This analysis calls for the *ad hoc* balancing of the "character of the government action," the economic loss to the property owner, and the degree to which there has been an interference with reasonable investment-backed expectations. The typical farmland TDR program involves no physical invasion, results in mere diminution in property value, and leaves a reasonable return on investment through farming. This is not a taking under Penn Central.

4. Donative Transfers

PDR, PACE and TDR programs provide compensation to owners of development restricted agricultural lands. Programs that encourage gifts of development rights (conservation easements) to governmental units or tax qualified nonprofit charitable organizations offer the incentive of charitable deductions under federal income tax law. An accompanying reduced assessment may lower real property taxes as well. For some donors, the tax benefits are an extra incentive, with the real motivation being the assurance that the home farm will be protected into the distant future.

Conservation easements must be carefully drafted. One requirement is that covenants restricting use run with the land so as to be binding on the heirs, assigns and successors in interest of the grantor. To be tax deductible, gifts of conservation easements must be made to qualified recipients in perpetuity for conservation purposes. IRC § 170(h)(4)(A) defines conservation purposes to be:

> (i) the preservation of land areas for outdoor recreation by, or the education of the general public;

(ii) the protection of the relatively natural habitat of fish, wildlife, or plants, or similar ecosystems;

(iii) the preservation of open space (including farmland and forest land) where such preservation is (I) for the scenic enjoyment of the general public, or (II) pursuant to a clearly delineated Federal, State or local government conservation policy and will yield a significant public benefit.

See also Treas. Reg. § 1.170A-14 (1986).

The amount of the deduction from income is based on the difference between the appraised value of the land before and after imposition of the easement. In a given year, the amount deducted cannot exceed 30% of the donor's adjusted gross income. There is a five year carryover.

G. Impact of State Programs

Certain implications as to the practical impact of state farmland preservation programs can be drawn from legal developments. The court in Louthan v. King County (Wash.1980) wrote that programs of rural zoning, tax relief and deferral of special assessments had not brought about the desired preservation of important pieces of agricultural land in King County, Washington. Thus, there was just-ification for a publicly funded PDR program. These judicial findings support the observation that while such programs can be of help to farmers who wish to continue their agricultural operations, they do little to make important farms unattractive or unavailable for development.

Agricultural district, preserve and security area statutes were conceived as offering a method for interested landowners to take their farmland out of the running for development for several years. These programs are reflective of the key parcel theory -- protected status for farms of particular importance to the local economy and located in the midst of development prone areas might make unattractive development on neighboring available agricultural land. Nonagricultural uses, it is hoped, will locate elsewhere on lands less critical to agriculture. But, renewal is not mandatory and protected status is relatively short term when viewed in the historical time frame of development of many American metropolitan areas.

This has lead to a search for even more powerful farmland preservation tools, while keeping voluntary participation in such efforts. Clearly, the move to TDR, PDR, PACE and donative transfer programs has been the main response. Of course, any proposal that development rights from all farms in an area be severed is unrealistic. Rather, the goal is to put key parcels out of the reach of development interests into the distant future. Exit of lands from such programs can come only with the unlikely agreement of the nonprofit private or government entity holding the conservation easement, or in the case of TDR programs, the entity with the legislative power to alter underlying zoning. And, while some farms in an area remain available to developers, projects that seem certain to have farms as next door neighbors well into the 21st century often are unattractive.

Farms not in district status or with development rights unsevered may still enjoy some mix of the protective devices set out in A through E, *supra*. But, the preservation of key farms into the distant future is the economic mortar often needed to hold the local agricultural infrastructure together. Without local farm input and marketing businesses, farming can cease to be feasible in a given area.

III. FEDERAL INITIATIVES

A. Farmland Protection Policy Act of 1981

After debating a variety of proposals over several years, Congress enacted the Farmland Protection Policy Act of 1981 (FPPA). 7 USCA §§ 4201-4209. The purpose of FPPA is to minimize the extent to which programs of federal departments and agencies contribute to unnecessary conversion of farmland to nonagricultural uses and to insure that federal prorams, to the greatest possible extent, are compatible with state and local goals of farmland preservation.

Pursuant to the FPPA, USDA recently developed criteria to be used by federal agencies to assist in identifying and considering the adverse effects of proposed federal programs on agricultural land. This includes federal loans for housing construction. 7 CFR pt. 658 (1994), amended 59 Fed. Reg. 31110 (1994). Various site assessment criteria, (social and economic) and land evaluation criteria (soil science), weighted using a point system, are designed to facilitate decisions as to which tracts of farmland are the most suited for protection. This Land Evaluation and Site Assessment system (LESA) is also in use in some 209 state and local government programs in 31 states, though almost entirely as an advisory tool.

Prior to its amendment in 1985, FPPA did not include any substantive requirements. Nor did it confer a private right of action. However, § 1255 of the Food Security Act of 1985, 7 USCA § 4209, gives the governor of a state with a state policy or program to protect farmland standing to bring an action in federal district court to enforce the requirements of FPPA. 7 USCA § 4202.

Even after the 1985 amendment, a federal agency, after complying with the procedural requirements of FPPA, may proceed with the proposed conversion of agricultural land. FPPA merely requires prior meaningful consideration of the impact of a proposed conversion and an evaluation of alternative sites. The impact of FPPA upon agricultural land conversion remains difficult to measure. For the first time in 1994, SCS has funding to provide technical assistance to help implement FPPA.

B. Other Federal Programs

Under the Farms for the Future Act of 1990, federal guarantees and interest assistance is authorized for eligible loans to a state trust fund. Eligible uses of state trust fund monies include purchase of development rights, conservation easements, fee simple or lesser estates. A trust can also use its funds to pay transaction costs and to fund enforcement. A pilot project in Vermont is the only one funded so far. 1990 Act §§ 1465-1490 (uncodified, noted after 7 USCA § 4201); 7 CFR pt. 1980, subpt. J (1994)

The Food Security Act of 1985 allows the Farmers Home Administration (FmHA) to acquire for the U.S. conservation easements on eligible mortgaged farmland. Payment must be made through reduction of the farmer borrower's FmHA loan principal.   7 CFR § 1951.909 & Exhibit H

(1994). This function of FmHA was transferred in Oct. 1994 to the new Consolidated Farm Service Agency (CFSA) within USDA.

C. Federal Tax Policy

The Internal Revenue Code tends to give mixed public policy signals on farmland preservation. For example, the sale of appreciated farmland to a developer is facilitated by installment sale treatment for the farmer seller. Gain can be spread over several tax years. A long-term capital gain tax rate favorable to certain sellers was replaced by lowered income tax rate schedules. Developers, in turn can look to income tax benefits too numerous to mention, but which include an election not to capitalize but to deduct or amortize certain construction period taxes and interest expenses; favorable cost recovery under the Accelerated Cost Recovery System (1981-86), and the Modified Accelerated Cost Recovery System (after 1966). But, donative farmland preservation transfers can result in tax benefits. The primary example is the deduction by the donor of the value of a gift to a qualified donee of an easement that meets the requirements of IRC § 170(h)(4)(A). See pp. 377-78 *supra*.

The elections to use IRC § 2032A special use valuation and IRC § 6166 deferred installment estate tax payment are available to qualified estates of farmer decedents. The maximum reduction in the value of a taxable estate is $750,000. The lower use valuation, coupled where elected with payment of the federal estate tax over 15 years can obviate the need to sell part of the farm to raise money to pay estate taxes.

CHAPTER ELEVEN

SOIL AND WATER MANAGEMENT
I. SOIL RESOURCES LAW
A. Soil Erosion

In spite of significant state and federal legislative efforts over the past 50 years, soil erosion problems remain a major concern for American agriculture. Not surprisingly, therefore, soil conservation issues loomed large in the debate over the 1985 farm bill and significant new measures designed to fight soil erosion emerged in the Food Security Act of 1985. The Food, Agriculture, Conservation and Trade Act of 1990 (1990 farm bill), brought more measures.

Human factors often are cited as contributing to the soil erosion problem. In hard economic times farmers sometimes have reduced soil conservation expenditures and have attempted to generate added income with existing equipment by putting marginal lands into production. Speculators in the 1970s sought quick profits by converting fragile range-lands to tillable acres, raising a crop or two of wheat and then selling to investors. In certain localities, poor and uneducated farmers have not always sought out available assistance that could help correct bad soil management practices. In addition, it is alleged that tenants, particularly those who rent from absentee landholders, have little economic interest in soil conservation. This is a debatable proposition, difficult to support or disprove with available data.

Government programs, particularly those related to export crops, have been cited as encouraging fence-to-fence planting on highly erodible lands. Federal tax policy has been identified as a factor encouraging poor practices, i.e., the conversion of erosion prone acreage to irrigated agriculture in past years when both investment tax credit and rapid depreciation have been available.

Over the past 6 decades, billions of dollars in state and federal money have been spent to combat soil erosion. Eventually it became apparent that these expenditures had not been targeted to the most serious sites of resource loss. Cost sharing payments may have contributed more to upgrading well run agricultural operations than to correcting problems on farms with the most serious erosion problems.

Soil scientists usually measure soil erosion in terms of tons of soil moved per acre annually, with one ton of soil being roughly equivalent to one cubic yard. A loss of five tons per acre annually will result in the loss of 1 inch of topsoil in about 30 years. T-5 is the typical soil loss limit set by public policy, although highly erodible land will often have a lesser tolerance. T stands for loss tolerance and T-5 a loss tolerance of five tons per acre per year. Controlling the movement of water and wind over the surface of the soil is the principal way to reduce erosion.

B. Role of the States

1. As Forums for Litigation

In the history of Anglo-American jurisprudence, there has been much litigation over husbandry practices on agricultural lands. Holders of reversions and vested remainders can proceed in waste against a tenant for a term of years or for life whose practices injure the reversion or remainder. Remedies in waste include injunction, money damages, termination of an estate for years, and in some jurisdictions, termination of a life tenancy.

Actions by a landlord against a farm tenant need not be couched in terms of waste. Farm leases include an implied covenant of good husbandry, a breach of which may permit termination of the tenancy. Increasingly, however, farm landlords are incorporating detailed soil management clauses as conditions in farm leases. The object is to avoid disputes over the meaning of the implied covenant and to tailor requirements to the particular farm. Remedies also can be crafted, particularly as to the rights of the tenant to notice of violation and opportunity to correct and as to circumstances permitting landlord to terminate in the midst of a growing season. See p. 114 *supra.*

When life tenancies are created by grant or devise, there is an opportunity, often overlooked or rejected, to impose strictures on the use of the land that may be more stringent than those imposed by the law of waste. Equally rare is the inclusion of soil management conditions in the grant of the fee simple, the violation of which would make available the exercise of a power of termination or trigger a possibility of reverter. Theoretically, these devices continue to have potential value -- e.g., to control to control conversion of fragile rangelands to uses requiring cultivation until their expiration under rules of state law.

There is, as yet, no judicial recognition of an action by a "next of friend of the soil" to enjoin bad husbandry by the owner or operator of a farm. However, where the tillage practices on a farm have caused damage to an adjacent farm, the neighbor might be able to sue successfully in nuisance, trespass, or negligence.

A conservation easement with strict soil management provisions may be granted by a fee owner to a non-profit farmland preservation trust. See pp. 377-78 *supra*. Such easements will be structured to run with the land. States with programs that allow agricultural lands to be placed in protected district or preserve status, require owners to promise in writing that approved soil management practices will be employed. See pp. 369-73 *supra*.

Absent a contract or statute that delineates required soil management practices, litigation over alleged non-compliance can be difficult. An express or implied covenant of "good husbandry" requires the articulation of some standard. Reasonable farmers and experts may differ as to the efficiency of particular practices on particular terrain or soil types and under particular weather or climatic conditions. While private litigation over soil management can be of importance to the parties, it is unlikely to have a noticeable impact on county-wide soil management problems, to say nothing of regional, state or nation-wide problems.

2. *State Legislation*

In 1937, USDA developed the Standard State Soil Conservation District Law, to serve as a model for state enabling acts authorizing the creation of soil conservation districts. These units of local government have planning duties, responsibility for administering federal and state cost-sharing programs, and regulatory powers. The stringency of erosion and sediment control statutes and regulations varies markedly from state to state as does their applicability to agricultural operations. Two examples illustrate the scope of the regulatory spectrum in the 20 or so states that have statutory and regulatory programs for agriculture.

The Agricultural Sediment Pollution Abatement Rules at Chapter 1501:15-3 of the Ohio Administrative Code are characteristic of programs that encourage, rather than command, the desired behavior. Elaborate standards are set forth on sheet and rill erosion, concentrated water erosion, wind erosion, ditching and sloughing, and agricultural sediment pollution abatement cost sharing. There is a system for receiving and investigating private complaints. The non-coercive character of the Ohio program is summarized at rule §§ 1501:15-3-09(D)(5)(b):

> If . . . erosion and soil losses are not equal to or less than permissible soil loss values, the district will utilize the expertise of all appropriate agencies to provide information and education, assist the owner or operator in developing specific alternative solutions inform him of financial and technical assistance available to implement or construct certain erosion control practices, and assist him or her in achieving compliance with the rules for sediment pollution abatement.

The command and control end of the spectrum is illustrated by the Iowa Soil Conservation statute. Under this legislation, soil conservation districts are authorized to promulgate regulations, including regulations establishing soil loss limits (e.g., T-5 per acre per year). In Woodbury County Soil Conservation District v. Ortner (Iowa 1979), complaints of adjacent landowners led to a finding that two farmers were in violation of permitted soil loss limits, T-5 on these farms. Pursuant to an administrative order issued by the district, the farmers were required to remedy the situation in six months and were given the choice of either terracing the land in question or seeding it to permanent pasture. Iowa's 75% cost sharing program was triggered, rather than the 50% program available for voluntary projects. Even with 75% of the cost contributed by the state, one farmer would have had an out-of-pocket cost of $12,000 for terracing, and the other farmer $1,500. The court held that the statute was a reasonable exercise of the police power. Specifically, the Woodbury opinion noted the public interest in protecting the soil quality of agricultural land, given the fact that Iowa's most important industry is agriculture.

The Iowa Supreme Court also rejected claims that the regulatory program, when applied to the particular tracts of land in question, constituted a taking of property without just compensation. The Court applied a balancing test, and concluded that the benefit to the public outweighed any private deprivation. The Court also noted that the farmers were not deprived of all use of their property. The availability of cost sharing was probably not essential to the court's finding that no taking had occurred.

If pasturage is the only economic use of a particular tract of agricultural land, it is arguable that a farmer has not suffered a taking when the police power is used, under an Iowa-type regulatory system, to bar more profitable uses. Such regulations would be analogous to those that survived a takings challenge in State v. Dexter (Wash.1949)(regulation of private forestry practices). On the impact of Lucas v. South Carolina Coastal Council (U.S.Sup.Ct.1992), see pp. 366-67 *supra*.

C. Role of the Federal Government

1. Prior to the 1985 Farm Bill

Contemporary federal soil conservation programs have their roots in legislation enacted in the 1930s. Three major programs survive in the company of more recently added programs.

The Conservation Operations Program (COP) was first authorized in the Soil Conservation Act of 1935. 16 USCA §§ 590a-590f; 7 CFR pt. 610 (1994). Under the program, farmers may voluntarily approach the Natural Resources Conservation Service (NRCS), successor in 1994 to the Soil Conservation Service (SCS), for technical assistance in planning soil management programs. Such assistance is available through local NRCS offices and is coordinated with local soil and water conservation districts. Funding for on farm conservation measures and structures is not a part of COP.

The Agricultural Conservation Program (ACP) emerged in the Soil Conservation and Domestic Allotment Act of 1936. 16 USCA §§ 22590g et seq.; 7 CFR §§ 701.3-.26 (1994). Farmers may voluntarily enter into short and long term contracts and receive financial assistance for approved soil conservation practices. The current publication of the regulations is confusing in that the ACP program regulations are among others within 7 CFR Ch. VII, Sub.Ch. A which is oddly entitled Agricultural Conservation Program. Within Sub.Ch. A appear regulations for such programs as Experimental Rural Clean Water Program, 7 CFR pt. 700 (1994); Wetlands Reserve Program, 7 CFR pt. 703 (1994); 1986-1990 Conservation Reserve Program, 7 CFR pt. 704 (1994); and Conservation and Environmental Programs, 7 CFR pt. 701 (1994). It is in this last set of programs that we find ACP; the Emergency Conservation Program (ECP)(assistance for emergency restoration work following a draught or other natural disaster) 16 USCA § 2201 et seq.; 7 CFR §§ 701.46 -.57 (1994); and the Forestry Incentives Program (FIP)(assistance to encourage good private silviculture practices) 16 USCA § 2103 et seq.; 7 CFR §§ 701.27-.45 (1994).

The Great Plains Conservation Program (GPCP) is designed to provide cost sharing and technical assistance for certain conservation measures (e.g. shelter belts) on farms in designated counties in Kansas, Montana, Nebraska, New Mexico, North Dakota, Oklahoma, South Dakota, Texas and Wyoming.   16 USCA § 590(d); 7 CFR pt. 631 (1994). NRCS, formely SCS, administers all aspects of this voluntary program. About 556 counties are designated as subject to serious wind erosion.

As the decades passed, questions were raised as to the effectiveness of federal soil programs. Farmers with serious erosion problems did not necessarily participate and some who did eventually abandoned their efforts. Financial problems sometimes made it difficult to cover the cost of ongoing conservation practices and in other cases fence row-to-fence row farming became attractive, as during the export boom of the 1970s. In addition, these programs did little to prevent sodbusting, the practice of breaking fragile grasslands for cultivation. The same was true with swampbusting, the practice of draining wetlands and converting them to cropping operations. See pp. 405-07 *infra*. Finally, it was charged that other federal programs undermined conservation efforts by encouraging increased crop production and intensive cultivation of fragile lands. Tax incentives that encouraged installation of irrigation systems in the Nebraska Sand Hills, and price and income support programs that encouraged wheat production on Colorado rangeland are examples.

Given mounting concern about the condition of the nation's soil and water resources, Congress enacted the Soil and Water Resources Conservation Act of 1977 (RCA). 16 USCA §§ 2001-2009. The Secretary of Agriculture was instructed to appraise the national soil and water resources, and to develop priorities and a program to address problems. Extensive reports were issued in 1980. In the Food Security Act of 1985, Congress extended RCA and instructed the USDA to again assess soil and water resources in 1995 and 2005.

As a result of RCA reports and increasing concern expressed by nongovernmental groups, a number of developments took place in the early 1980s. Budget planning for the funding of existing conservation programs began to include the concept of targeting. Rather than making funds available on a first come, first served basis across the nation, specific monies were targeted to counties with the most serious soil erosion problems. The 1985 farm bill included long debated provisions to discourage "sodbusting" on highly erodible agricultural land. Conservation compliance -- the implementation of an approved plan to reduce soil erosion on highly erodible land -- is the 1985 Act's mechanism to control "sodbusting."

2. Sodbuster and Conservation Compliance

Farmers who violate the provisions of the sodbuster law risk losing eligibility for a variety of federal program payments and benefits for the year in question. Since Dec. 23, 1985, any person who produces an agricultural commodity on a field in which highly erodible land (HEL) is predominant risks sanctions including those added by the 1990 farm bill. 16 USCA §§ 3811-3813; 7 CFR § 12.4 (1994). To bring unfarmed HEL into production a farmer must implement a conservation compliance plan approved by the SCS, now NRCS. Such a plan will require compliance with SCS/NRCS technical standards designed to assure that soil loss on the newly converted HEL will not exceed a rate at which the soil is believed to regenerate itself. 16 USCA § 3812(a)(2).

An exemption allows continued farming on HEL used to produce agricultural commodities during the years 1981 through 1985. 16 USCA § 3812(a)(1); 7 CFR § 12.5(a) (1994). But, as to such "cropped HEL" the farmer must have had an approved conservation compliance plan in place by January 1, 1990, or within two years after the land had been mapped for SCS classification purposes. 7 CFR

§ 12.5(b) (1994). Compliance standards for such fields are found in the local SCS (now NRCS) office manual and are not as tough as the SCS technical standards. Farmers had until Jan. 1, 1995 to fully implement approved conservation compliance plans. For those who violate sodbuster rules, the 1990 Act provides graduated sanctions -- less than full loss of all program benefits in a given year. 7 CFR § 12.5 (a)(5) (1994). See p. 406 *infra* (benefits at risk).

3. Conservation Reserve Program

The Conservation Reserve Program (CRP), as authorized in the Food Security Act of 1985, has the goal of removing from production 40 to 45 million acres of highly erodible crop land. Under the CRP eligible farmers submit bids and offer to place HEL under a 10 year land retirement contract. Reconsideration and appeal provisions as to HEL determinations are at 7 CFR pt. 614 (1994).

Those who are awarded contracts must agree to plant HEL to grasses, trees or other acceptable vegetative cover for the contract period. Technical help is available through NRCS (successor to SCS), local conservation districts, U.S. Forest Service, state forestry departments and other offices. Farmers who enter the program may be eligible to receive a one time reimbursement for one-half of the cost of establishing vegetative cover. Severe restrictions are imposed on the use of the CRP land for grazing, hay crops, and other economic uses during the contract period. If haying and grazing are authorized under emergency conditions, the next annual rental payment will be reduced by the number of acres involved times 25% of the per acre CRP payment.

Statistics from the initial CRP sign-up periods reveal an average ASCS accepted bid per acre of $46.94, although some accepted bids have been as high as $90.00 per acre. Accordingly, a farmer who puts 100 acres in the program at $46.94 will receive a rental payment of $4,694.00 per year. There is a distinct $50,000 limit on total annual CRP payments received by one person.

The Consolidated Farm Service Agency (CFSA), successor to ASCS, is the lead agency in administering CRP. It determines if the cropland designated by the producer meets the minimum two out of the previous five years under active tillage requirement. NRCS determines if the cropland falls under the eligible land classifications, as well as the suitability of the producer's proposed vegetative cover. State forestry officials assists if the applicant proposes planting trees. CFSA is the contracting agency and is responsible for annual compliance spot checks.

Farmers who sell land which is subject to a CRP contract remain liable under the contract with CFSA. Thus, it is essential that the buyer agree to continuing compliance with program regulations. A repayment of all government costs, with interest will be demanded if the terms of the contract are breached. This is not a unique requirement, as the same has been true since conservation cost-sharing programs were first instituted in the 1930s.

When a 10 year CRP contract expires several options are open to the owner: conversion to trees and extension of contract; return to farming of previously farmed HEL (in production prior to Dec. 23, 1985) if conservation compliance plan applied; and, new cropping of other HEL if allowed under the farm's conservation plan as applied. By action of the Secretary, the first CRP contracts, expiring Sept. 30, 1995, can be extended for one year. The future of CRP will be determined in the 1995 farm bill.

4. FmHA/CFSA Conservation Easements

The 1985 farm bill added the FmHA (now CFSA) Conservation Easement Program. Certain financially stressed farmer loan program borrowers may propose granting to the U.S. a conservation easement over certain encumbered highly erodible lands. The farmer will not be paid cash for the easement, but the value thereof will be deducted from the outstanding balance due the U.S. on the farm ownership loan. 7 CFR § 1951.909 & Exhibit H (1993). See p. 77 *supra.*

5. Surface Mining Control

Surface mining on prime farmland is regulated by the Surface Mining Control and Reclamation Act of 1977 (SMCRA), 30 USCA §§ 1202-1328. Under the Act a permit for surface mining on prime farmland will be granted only if the operator can demonstrate the technical capacity to restore the strip mined area to equivalent or higher yields as measured on non-mined farmland in the surrounding area.

The Act survived constitutional attack in Hodel v. Indiana (U.S.Sup.Ct.1981), a case involving a facial challenge to "steep slopes" coal mining limitations, but not the question of taking as to a particular tract of land. However, in Whitney Benefits, Inc. v. U.S. (Fed.Cir.1991), the denial of a permit to mine an alluvial valley floor was deemed a taking in a classic Penn Central analysis. See pp. 376-77 *supra.* Peder

Kiewit Sons' Co. had acquired part of the tract in fee and as to the rest leased the mineral estate. Subsequently, SMCRA was enacted. A license could not issue thereunder if the surface mining would damage water quality or preclude future farming to a substantial extent. On balance, the regulation was held to interfere with reasonable investment backed expectations without payment of just compensation. Kiewit was not required to accept federal "coal exchange lands" as compensation. Consistent with recent cases allowing money damages for a regulatory taking, Kiewit has been awarded more than $140 million dollars including prejudgment interest compounded annually and attorney's fees. See pp. 367-68 *supra.* Note that by compelling takings cases against the federal government to be litigated in the Federal Claims Court under the Tucker Act, the Supreme Court has seemingly eliminated the opportunity for the regulator, when challenged, to choose not to enforce the regulation and to argue only temporary taking. Preseault v. ICC (U.S.Sup.Ct.1990).

II. WATER RESOURCES LAW:
AN AGRICULTURAL PERSPECTIVE
A. Water Quality
1. Generally

Agricultural operations may be the nation's foremost source of water pollution. For example, irrigation returns can be loaded with pesticides, nutrients, salts and minerals; feedlots and other animal confinement facilities can directly or indirectly discharge animal wastes; runoff from fields and pastures commonly carries sediment, nutrients, pesticides and animal wastes. Even conversion of wetlands, considered hereinafter, involves the discharge of pollutants. This recital of practices illustrates both point source and non-point source pollution, a distinction of major legal significance.

Pesticides used in agriculture are comprised of chemicals of several classes. Insecticides are used in crop production to control insects that damage or kill field or horticultural crops. They also are used in animal agriculture. Herbicides are used to control unwelcome plants (weeds) that compete for nutrients, moisture and sunlight. Some herbicides are incorporated into the soil, while others are sprayed directly on growing plants. Fungicides are used to control minute plants, known as fungi, which can be a problem in vegetable, fruit and tree nut production. Rodenticides are used to control mice and rats, and sometimes birds and wildlife.

Plant nutrients consumed from the soil by previous crops commonly are replaced artificially. Nitrogen (N) is the most significant nutrient and is applied to fields in the form of gas -- anhydrous ammonia, or in solid form -- urea. Phosphorous (P) and potassium (K) are also part of the typical fertilizer mix. Through soil testing the farmer can determine the appropriate N-P-K formula for a particular field. Even if applied with strict control, significant residues of pesticides and nutrients find their way into surface and groundwater as water flows and leaches.

2. Point Source Pollution

Under the Federal Clean Water Act, 33 USCA §§ 1251-1387, any discharge of a pollutant into the broadly defined navigable waters of the United

States is illegal, unless done pursuant to a mission limitation incorporated in a permit issued by the Environmental Protection Agency (EPA). Congress has structured the permitting program to allow states to impose more stringent standards. This has occurred in certain jurisdictions, particularly as to regulation of animal feedlots. EPA has delegated authority to administer its permit program to states that have an EPA approved program.

The Clean Water Act defines a *point source* as "any discernable, confined and discrete conveyance, including but not limited to any pipe, ditch, channel, tunnel, conduit, well, discrete fissure, container, rolling stock, concentrated animal feeding operation, or vessel or other floating craft from which pollutants are or may be discharged . . .." 33 USCA § 1362(14). While there is no statutory definition of *non-point source*, it is generally understood that any pollution other than that emanating from a point source falls into this category.

The operator of a concentrated animal feeding operation must obtain a § 402 National Pollution Discharge Elimination System (NPDES) permit and comply with its terms. The definition of "concentrated" feedlots is developed in the regulations. 40 CFR § 122.23 (1994). Where there is direct discharge of animal waste, lots *in excess of* 300 slaughter or feeder cattle, 200 dairy cows, 750 swine (over 55 lbs.), 150 horses, 3,000 sheep or lambs, 9,000 laying hens or broilers (with liquid manure system), 30,000 laying heads or broilers (with overflow watering), 16,500 turkeys, or 1,500 ducks are classified as concentrated. The same is true of a combination of over 300 animal units.

EPA, through rulemaking, has exempted from the definition of concentrated animal feeding operations those operations of less than a certain size, operations that do not discharge, and operations that discharge only in event of a 25-year, 24-hour storm event. In Carr v. Alta Verde Industries, Inc. (5th Cir. 1991) the court points out that simply constructing holding ponds so as to contain discharge except in the 25-year 24-hour event is not a way to avoid having to obtain a permit, where a permit would otherwise be required.

Certain fish farms, hatcheries and other aquatic animal production facilities may also be subject to the permit program. The same is true as to some silviculture (logging, forestry, etc.) operations.

EPA regulations promulgated in 1973 provided exemptions for discharges from a number of point sources, including irrigation return flows from areas of less than 3,000 contiguous acres or 3,000 noncontiguous acres sharing the same drainage system. This exemption was successfully challenged in Natural Resources Defense Counsel v. Costle (D.C.Cir.1977), on the theory that EPA had exceeded its authority. The court rejected agency arguments that it would be infeasible to administer a permit system which would supervise practices on thousands of irrigated farms. The court found that Congressional intent unequivocally required permits in all cases involving pollution from agricultural point sources. Western agricultural interests convinced Congress in 1977 to amend the statutory definition of point source to exclude irrigation return flows. In 1987, Congress amended the definition to exclude "agricultural storm water discharges."

3. Nonpoint Source Pollution

Agricultural water pollution from point sources is a less significant problem than agricultural water pollution from nonpoint sources such as irrigation returns and surface water runoff from fields, rangeland, pastures and woodlots. Runoff moves vast quantities of sediment, nutrients, pesticides and animal wastes. Since it is usually impossible to trace nonpoint pollutants to a particular farm or field, assigning responsibility for nonpoint source agricultural pollution is difficult.

Section 208 of the Clean Water Act requires states to engage in area-wide waste treatment management planning designed to combat water pollution not addressed by the permit system. 33 USCA § 1288(b)(F). Each § 208 plan is to focus principally on future municipal and industrial waste treatment management, and on identification and control of nonpoint sources of pollution. EPA grants will not be approved to a state for construction of waste treatment plants unless a state § 208 plan is being implemented or reasonable progress is being made toward implementation.

In addition to addressing surface water pollution, these plans must establish a process for identifying and controlling potential sources of groundwater pollution. Section 329 requires that § 208 plans identify Best Management Practices (BMPs) to control pollution from agricultural nonpoint sources and to take into account the relation of such practices to groundwater quality. BMPs are not defined in the Clean Water Act, but EPA regulations contemplate a wide variety of measures including combating soil erosion with contour farming, terracing, minimum tillage and installation of grassed waterways. BMPs also encompass measures to trap or cleanse run-off such as vegetative buffers along streams and construction of manure storage pits. States are not required, however, to compel farmers to utilize such practices. But a state that fails to submit and obtain approval of an assessment report and a management plan may lose planning funds and jeopardize the eligibility of individual farmers and ranchers for financial and technical assistance. While a plan may have been approved and implemented at the state level, actual adoption of nonpoint source pollution control practices by individual farmers is largely voluntary.

The Federal Insecticide, Fungicide and Rodenticide Act (FIFRA), 7 USCA §§ 136-136y, prohibits the sale or use of pesticides which are not registered with the EPA. While the EPA must be satisfied that a particular pesticide will not cause unreasonable adverse effects on the environment, it must take into consideration the economic, social and environmental costs and benefits associated with its use. The EPA may, under FIFRA, issue an order stopping or restricting the sale or use of a pesticide when the agency has reason to believe the statute will be violated. One of the objectives of FIFRA is to protect groundwater from pesticide pollution, but it is an open question as to how effective the Act has been in this regard. Few pesticide registrations have been canceled or suspended. Examples are DDT, aldrin, dieldrin, kepone, chlordane, and heptachlor. Amendments to strengthen FIFRA are proposed from session to session in the Congress.

The Safe Drinking Water Act (SDWA), 42 USCA §§ 300f-300j-10, in two of its programs addresses agricultural nonpoint source pollution. State and local governments may apply for grants to develop and implement demonstration projects to protect aquifers that are the sole or principal drinking water source for an area. 40 CFR pt. 149 (1993). A second program focuses on protection of surface and subsurface areas surrounding a water well or well-field supplying a public water system. States with an EPA approved wellhead protection program can seek federal grants to develop and implement such program. 40 CFR § 35.450 (1992).

4. Policy Alternatives

A variety of proposals seek to address two distinct aspects of surface and groundwater pollution. On one hand, there is the question of what to do about existing contamination -- particularly of aquifers that do not cleanse themselves over time even though pollutants are no longer introduced. Then, there is the matter of reducing or preventing further introduction of pollutants into surface and groundwater areas.

Informed policy making with respect to aquifers requires accurate information about existing water quality and probable future needs. Cleaning up contaminated aquifers will be costly and there is a sense that scarce economic resources should be used to clean up and protect water where the need is greatest. One hope is that recombinant DNA technology will develop bacteria that can economically break down existing chemical contamination. Wisconsin funds various groundwater programs by imposing license fees on pesticide formulators and applicators. Also, there is a sales tax on fertilizer and on septic tank pumping services.

A major issue is whether the standard for groundwater quality should be zero pollution or simply the avoidance of "unacceptable" levels of pollution. At present, EPA establishes maximum contaminant level goals (MCLG). The MCLG is set at zero for a chemical proved to be carcinogenic in humans or a probable carcinogenic as a result of animal studies. Enforceable standards, maximum contaminant levels (MCLs), are set by EPA as close as possible to MCLG -- but at least in a range that is considered protective of human health.

At the federal level the adequacy of funding for research is an ongoing issue. While there has been some work done on and some application of Integrated Pest Management (IPM), further research may be needed if farmers are to be convinced to use IPM on a widespread basis. The concept involves precision application of pesticides and the concurrent use of non-chemical means of control. Non-chemical means include introduction of natural predators or pathogens, the use of cropping practices that make fields less attractive for pests, and the use of resistant plant varieties.

Advances in biotechnology may allow reduction or elimination of the use of some pesticides. Genetic engineering allows the transfer of pest resistant characteristics from one strain of plant to another. And, recombinant DNA technology may allow the introduction on plants of bacteria that will deal with certain problems.

BMPs, described at pp. 400-01, are developed by states pursuant to the Clean Water Act. Compliance by individual farmers is voluntary. Use of BMPs could be made "mandatory" through a compliance scheme similar to that used in federal farm programs to enforce the implementation of soil conservation plans on highly erodible soils. See pp. 392-93 *supra.* In other words, farmers would be required to implement BMPs or risk the loss of farm program benefits. Such a program could emerge in the Clean Water Act reauthorization or the 1995 farm bill.

One of the purposes of FIFRA, p. 401 *supra,* is to protect groundwater from contamination. If FIFRA is strengthened and better funded by Congress more stringent testing of pesticides before registration and more intensive enforcement may result. There is an ongoing problem of a backlog of review of pesticides registered before adequate testing procedures were devised. More than 600 active ingredients are involved and only a small number have been reviewed and declared safe by EPA.

State and local governments may be best suited to impose site specific controls and general land use regulations. Zoning to regulate land use above aquifers or other sensitive areas is one possibility. The police power also could be used to prohibit the use of certain pesticides or fertilizers in sensitive areas where leaching into groundwater is an established fact. There is a problem, however, as the boundaries of local governments rarely coincide with the boundaries of aquifers or watersheds. Therefore, states may need to consider using existing or newly created special districts and interstate compacts.

California voters, in 1986, approved Proposition 65, the Safe Drinking Water and Toxic Enforcement Act of 1986. The Act provides that no person, in the course of doing business, may knowingly discharge or release chemicals known to the state to cause cancer or reproductive toxicity into water or onto land where such chemicals pass into any source of drinking water. Warning notice are to be given to persons who might be exposed. The Governor is required to publish annually a list of chemicals known to cause cancer or reproductive toxicity. Violations can result in court ordered cessation of the activity and fines of up to $2,500 per day. The Act defines a "person in the course of doing business" to be businesses with ten or more employees. So, some California farms are not under the Act.

B. Wetlands Preservation

Wetlands are valued because they provide habitat for wildlife and waterfowl, act as collecting basins for rainfall and consequently as natural flood control facilities, contribute to ground water recharge, and serve as natural water purification systems. Federal and state laws protecting wetlands have proliferated in recent years, and present tough questions as one seeks to coordinate the various provisions. The focus here is on federal law.

1. Swampbuster

The swampbuster law at 16 USCA §§ 3821-3823, uses two key definitions. *Wetland* - land that has a preponderance of hydric soils; that is inundated or saturated by surface or groundwater often enough to support a prevalence of hydrophytic vegetation which is typically adapted for life in saturated soil conditions; and that under normal circumstances does support a prevalence of such vegetation. 16 USCA § 3801(a)(16), 7 CFR § 12.2(a)(29)(1994). *Conversion* of a wetland results when draining, dredging, filling, leveling, or other manipulation makes it possible to produce an agricultural commodity. 7 CFR § 12.2(a)(6)(1994).

The swampbusting program applies to those conversions of wetlands begun after Dec. 23, 1985. Any person who after Dec. 23, 1985 produced an agricultural commodity on such converted wetlands was rendered ineligible for income support payments, CCC loans, federal crop insurance, federal disaster payments, as well as certain FmHA (now CFSA) loans. After the effective date of the 1990 farm bill, conversion alone constitutes a violation, even if a crop is not produced. The fact that a farmer is implementing an approved conservation plan for her farm does not give her the option to convert wetlands thereon. The sanction of withholding federal farm program benefits applies to any commodity produced by such person during that crop year and in subsequent years. The harshness of this law is softened in several ways.

Administrative exemptions are authorized where negative environmental effect would be minimal. 7 CFR § 12.5(b)(1)(iii)(1994). Swampbuster restrictions do not apply to persons who produce agricultural commodities on wetlands that have dried out as a result of drought or other natural conditions, as long as the producer does not destroy natural wetlands characteristics. Farming on *prior converted wetlands* is not a violation -- lands where conversion was commenced or completed on or before Dec. 23,

1985. 7 CFR § 12.5(b)(1)(i),(2),(3),(4),(5)(1994). Operations on *farmed wetlands* are sanctioned by government manual provisions. These are wetlands farmed prior to Dec. 23, 1985 but which still possess wetlands characteristics. But, no further drainage is permitted. Conversions subsequent to Dec. 23, 1985, but prior to effective date of the 1990 Act can be cured if the government agrees to accept mitigation -- restoration of a prior converted wetland in the same area at the landowners expense. 7 CFR § 12.5 (b)(6) (1994). An easement over such mitigation area must be granted to the U.S. The 1990 farm bill authorizes graduated penalties, rather than total loss of federal farm benefits if the farmer can show that the conversion was done in good faith, as defined in the statute. 7 CFR § 12.5(b)(7) (1994).

2. U.S. Army Corps § 404 Permits

If a particular wetland is determined to be part of or will impact the navigable waters of the United States, conversion is regulated by the Rivers and Harbors Act of 1899 and the Clean Water Act. The jurisdiction of the U.S. Army Corps of Engineers (Corps) extends over navigable waters and their tributaries, interstate waters and their tributaries, and non-navigable intrastate waters, the use or misuse of which could affect interstate commerce. Section 404 of the Clean Water Act, 33 USCA § 1344, prohibits any discharge of dredged or fill materials into waters under the Corps' jurisdiction without a permit. See pp. 397-98 *supra*.

In U.S. v. Riverside Bayview Homes, Inc. (U.S. Sup.Ct.1985), it was determined that the jurisdiction of the Corps encompasses all wetlands adjacent to navigable or interstate water, even where the source of the water held in the wetland is ground water, as opposed to flooding. However, the 7th Circuit has determined that non-adjacent or isolated wetlands are not under the Corps' jurisdiction. Hoffman Homes, Inc. v. EPA (1992). Isolated wetlands are those that are not part of an aquatic ecosystem and do not control floods or pollution in other bodies of water. Regulation by EPA would be possible if the isolated wetland could affect interstate or foreign commerce. Actual use by migratory birds that are watched, photographed or hunted by humans could satisfy this test. Hoffman has significance for farms with isolated "potholes". Note that the Corps and the EPA share responsibility for administering and enforcing the Clean Water Act.

In January of 1989 the Corps, the EPA, the Soil Conservation Service and the U.S. Fish and Wildlife Service entered into a short-lived agreement on wetlands delineation which then was published in the Federal Manual for Identifying Wetlands. At this writing, however, the 1987 Corps Wetland Delineation Manual is in use for areas other than agricultural lands. For agricultural lands the delineation process is set forth in the National Food Security Act Manual, 3rd ed. This manual is also used for a narrow category of nonagricultural lands owned by USDA program participants. See MOA, 59 Fed. Reg. 2920 (1994). There is potential for disharmonious results if the same land is delineated twice using both manuals. So, it is agreed in the MOA that if SCS has made a final written delineation, the Corps or EPA will use same in pursuing a CWA violation. But, if the SCS, now NRCS, has not made such a delineation and the Corps or EPA is pursuing a CWA violation, SCS, now NRCS, will use their determination in subsequent pursuit of a Swampbuster violation.

In the Mississippi delta states, as in some other states, owners of timbered wetlands have been known to harvest the timber crop, completely clear the land, install drainage ditches, and commence production of row crops. As illustrated by Avoyelles Sportsmen's League v. Alexander (W.D.La.1979), such activities on jurisdictional wetlands require a § 404 permit. In Avoyelles, the court found the land clearing equipment to be a point source and that the conversion involved the discharge of dredge materials from that point source. Failure to obtain the required permit may result in injunctive relief, civil penalties, and possibly criminal penalties. Citizen suits are also authorized. Note that while the Crops issues the permit, EPA promulgates the regulatory framework for permit issuance. EPA has authority to veto issuance of a permit by the Corps.

Normal farming or silviculture (tree farming) operations are exempt from the § 404 permit requirement, but courts have made it clear that this exemption applies only to established and ongoing agricultural or silvicultural operations. Thus, the exemption does not reach new land clearing operations designed to transform forest bottom land or other wetlands into cropland.

Even after Lucas, pp. 366-67 *supra,* the prospects of finding a denial of a § 404 permit to be a taking are remote since the tracts of land in question virtually always include economically usable uplands as well as wetlands. An exception is reflected in

Loveladies Harbor II (Fed.Cl.Ct.1990) where the presence of one acre of uplands on a 12.5 acre tract did not defeat the takings claim because denial of the permit to fill the 11.5 acres precluded development of the upland acre as well. The government also failed to show that there was a market for or a probability of economic use of the unfilled land for hunting, bird-watching, agricultural conservation, a marina, or a mitigation site. Permit denial resulted in a 99% diminution in value of the 12.5 acres.

Caveats. There is nothing in the Swampbuster law that suggests that its penalties are inapplicable when wetlands are converted to agricultural production pursuant to a § 404 permit. And, the mere fact that a wetland is "isolated" for § 404 permit purposes does not mean that Swampbuster or a distinct state wetlands protection program is inapplicable.

3. Wetlands Reserve Program

Created in 1990 farm bill, the Wetlands Reserve Program (WRP) is designed to enroll one million acres of eligible wetlands in long term or permanent easements by 1995. 16 USCA § 3801 et seq.; 7 CFR pt. 703(1994). The targeted wetlands are those that were converted to cropland prior to 1985. The first appropriated funds came in FY 1992 - $46 million for long term easements over as much as 50,000 acres. Such easements are for up to 30 years or the maximum duration allowed under state law. The private participant must implement a plan to restore and protect the land in WRP. Cost sharing of 50 to 75% of the restoration work is available. Under the Emergency Wetlands Reserve Program the government can purchase wetland conservation easements over lands damaged by the 1993 Midwest Floods. 16 USCA §§ 3837-3837f; 7 CFR pt. 623 (1994).

4. Other Federal Laws

Federal efforts to protect the nation's wetlands extend beyond the § 404 permitting program and WRP. Pursuant to the Migratory Bird Hunting Stamp Act, the Secretary of the Interior is authorized to acquire easements over wetlands suitable for migratory waterfowl breeding and nesting grounds. Section 3 of the Wetlands Act of 1966 provides that such easements cannot be acquired unless the acquisition has been approved by the governor or an appropriate agency of the state where the land is located. State statutes that authorize drainage of wetlands contrary to the terms of approved easements, are hostile to federal interests and are not to be applied. North Dakota v. U.S. (U.S.Sup.Ct.1983).

C. Hazardous and Toxic Substances

In 1980 Congress enacted the Comprehensive Environmental Response, Compensation and Liability Act (CERCLA). 42 USCA § 9601-9675. Remedial actions may be undertaken by the EPA with cost covered out of a "superfund." In the Superfund Amendments and Reauthorization Act of 1986 (SARA), Congress reauthorized the program for five years and set the superfund at $8.5 billion for 1986-1991. Congress again replenished superfund through Sept. 30, 1994. One of the many goals of the cleanup program is to prevent the movement of hazardous substances into groundwaters. The 103rd Congress, however, failed to refund in 1994.

As amended in 1984, RCA, p. 391 *supra,* regulates underground storage tanks used to hold certain substances, including motor fuels. States are to conduct inventories and testing is required. Leaks are to be repaired at once or owners or operators will be exposed to liability. Leak-prone tanks are to be phased out over a 10 year period. Storage tanks on farms are not exempted. The statute does not apply to sites where farmers dispose of pesticide containers, but states may act to regulate such activity.

D. Allocation of Water Resources

1. The Problem

Agriculture on irrigated land accounts annually for more than one-fourth of the value of the nation's crops. In some areas irrigation is essential to agriculture because rainfall is unreliable or insufficient. Even in places that are not arid or semi-arid, irrigation can be used to increase yield, deal with occasional drought, facilitate double cropping, or allow a farmer to introduce a crop such as rice. The 1977 National Resources Inventory revealed that 55.8 million irrigated acres of farmland are in use in the U.S. in contrast to 357.5 million dryland acres. About 83% of the irrigated acres are in the 17 western states (Arizona, California, Colorado, Idaho, Kansas, Montana, Nebraska, Nevada, New Mexico, North Dakota, Oklahoma, Oregon, South Dakota, Texas, Utah, Washington and Wyoming).

Water for irrigation comes from three principal sources: rivers and streams, aquifers, and federal reclamation projects. Often, the legal system must allocate scarce water among competing users. Conflicts between agriculture and other users have been more common than those between competing agricultural interests. Historically, water has been available to agriculture free of charge, or at low cost through government subsidized projects. There is an ongoing debate as to whether agricultural users should be compelled to pay the real cost of water.

2. Rivers and Streams

In eastern states where water supplies are generally abundant, the riparian system of water rights is prevalent. Under the riparian system, rights are acquired by virtue of ownership of land abutting a river, stream or lake. All riparian owners abutting the same body of water have equal rights to reasonable use of the water. Courts have developed various doctrines to resolve disputes. The natural flow doctrine provides that upstream owners may withdraw water only to the extent that the volume available to downstream users is not diminished. The reasonable use doctrine provides each riparian owner reasonable use of the water. The effect of applying either doctrine is similar.

Generally, riparian systems do not provide a basis for non-riparian private users to acquire rights to withdraw water from rivers, streams or lakes. As a result, some riparian states have enacted statutory permit systems to provide for non-riparian rights. These systems expand the water use constituency and give water rights a more precise definition.

In general, western states use the prior appropriation doctrine. It grants a prioritized right to divert a given quantity of water to the party who first diverts water from a stream or lake and puts it to a beneficial use. Given the first in time, first in right nature of the system, holders of lower priority claims may find themselves totally without water in times of shortage. The justification for the prior appropriation system is that it provides an incentive for the development of irrigated agricultural and other water dependent activities by offering the holders of higher priority status considerable assurance of a regular water supply in spite of the arid or semi-arid nature of the area. More particularly, it provides water rights to parties who do not own land which abuts the water source.

Today, prior appropriation rights have been formalized in western most states and are a matter of public record, typically by permit. In some states a water right is a vested property right and is transferable independently of the land. This has enabled some farmers and ranchers to sell their water rights to urban water districts for considerable sums of money. As a result, irrigated farms have been converted to dryland operations.

Certain western states have sought to combine features of the riparian and prior appropriation doctrines, but there is little uniformity in their methodologies. An interesting question is whether a state with both arid and water rich regions could use one doctrine for certain parts of the state and the other in the remainder.

3. Groundwater

Deep well irrigation is found in many areas, but is particularly evident over the Ogalala aquifer that underlies a vast area from the Nebraska-South Dakota border to the southern reaches of the Texas Panhandle. While short-term economic interests may encourage deed well irrigation to produce flourishing agriculture, the future of both the agricultural and nonagricultural users in an area may be jeopardized as a result of the unabated depletion of the underlying aquifer at a rate exceeding its ability to recharge. Even worse, such aquifer mining can withdraw the support function of the groundwater and allow the weight of the earth above to compress aquifer structures and destroy recharge capability.

Production agriculture is rarely the sole major user of water in an area of intense irrigation. Municipalities, agricultural processing plants, and industrial users may make heavy demands on water obtained from deep wells. A water-use permit system that regulates withdrawals is one method of dealing with competing demands for limited water.

Under traditional common law rules, the owner of the surface estate held a property right in the waters percolating beneath. Under the absolute ownership rule, surface owners were free to withdraw underground waters with no restrictions as to use or location of use. As knowledge of the hydrological cycle and the ecological role of underground water resources has developed, common law doctrines gradually have changed. The reasonable use rule recognizes that some use limitations are required, not as to the amount of water withdrawn as such, but as use of water on land not appurtenant to the well site, and wasteful use on the appurtenant land.

The correlative rights rule provides coequal rights of reasonable beneficial use to owners of lands that overlie a common supply of groundwater. The rule addresses shortages, requires reasonable sharing, and may provide the foundation for a requirement that the owner of a large capacity deep well divert some water to neighbors who have been left "high and dry." Such a remedy for neighbors would seem particularly appropriate if their wells are dry because the aquifer has been drawn down by a deeper, more powerful well.

In many jurisdictions, groundwater disputes are no longer resolved by common law. Statutory permit systems have been established to define the legal parameters of allocation and use. These statutes prioritize uses, with agricultural somewhere in the hierarchical scale.

In Crookston Cattle Co. v. Minnesota Department of Natural Resources (Minn.1980), the court wrote that "[l]ike zoning legislation, legislation which limits or regulates the right to use underlying water is permissible." While the state of Minnesota does not own groundwater beneath private surface estates, it does assert that such waters are subject to police power regulation for the general welfare of the state's inhabitants. Having established the theoretical basis for regulation, the state enacted a regulatory program recognizing preexisting groundwater rights, but regulating new drilling and pumping. Control is effected through a permit system that allocates water according to absolute preferences. Minn. Stat. Ann. § 105.41 puts agricultural uses third.

> First priority. Domestic water supply, excluding industrial and commercial uses of municipal water supply. Second priority. Any use of water that involves consumption of less than 10,000 gallons of water per day. For purposes of this section "consumption" shall mean water withdrawn from a

supply which is lost for immediate further use in the area. Third priority. Agricultural irrigation, involving consumption in excess of 10,000 gallons per day, and processing of agricultural products. Fourth priority. Power production, involving consumption in excess of 10,000 gallons per day. Fifth priority. Other uses, involving consumption in excess of 10,000 gallons per day.

Consider the application of such a priority system to a farm drawing water only for human consumption. With the addition of a large livestock operation or the irrigation of one or more fields, the third priority might well be triggered. It is unclear whether the term "processing" is intended to refer only to first processing of agricultural commodities. If the term is used in a more expansive sense, questions arise as to whether animal and irrigated agriculture must share the third priority with canning companies, soft drink bottling plants, and taco makers.

Consider the status of a farmer who contemplated converting to irrigated agriculture, but did not do so prior to the imposition of a permit system designed to allocate limited water? After the system is in place, the state might conclude that first and second priority needs require all of the water from the aquifer. As a result, the farmer will not get a permit. If the priority scheme is not inherently irrational, is there a taking of property requiring due process and just compensation? Since the farmer is not being deprived of an established irrigation operation, there is no taking in that sense. In addition, the farmer arguably is left with reasonable use of his land -- grazing or dryland farming. Even if a balancing test is applied, the benefits that would accrue to a farmer by irrigated rather than dryland farming might not outweigh the public benefits from the permit system.

The decision in Bamford v. Upper Republican Natural Resources District (Neb.1994) deals with the constitutional impact of limiting water to an existing irrigated operation. Groundwater control regulations in the area of the district were put in place under the Nebraska Ground Water Management and Protection Act. Neb. Rev. Stat. § 46-656. A five year allocation of 75 acre-inches per irrigated acre was assigned, an average of 15 acre-inches a year. Farmers in the district could pump as much as they wanted in a given year but could not go over the 75 acre-inch limit during the five year allocation period. Owner of nine center pivots exhausted his allocation in the fourth year and sued on various theories after failing to get a lower court to enjoin enforcement of the regulatory program. The court rejected a Lucas type takings argument. See pp. 366-67 *supra*. It held that even though the owner could not withdraw enough water to grow a corn crop, there was no deprivation of all economic use of the land. The land could be grazed for a year until the next allocation kicked in. Also, the court noted that it had been conclusively established that there was insufficient water for all users and that the state legislature could determine public policy and alter the common law regarding use of groundwater.

Proposals to transfer water from one state to another have been examined by several courts. Fearing unregulated sales and transfers by private parties, some states have moved to establish permit systems, both for surface water and groundwater. In

Sporhase v. Nebraska ex re. Douglas (U.S.Sup.Ct. 1982), it was held that a state cannot simply ban water exports across state lines, nor make export rights totally contingent upon reciprocity. However, reasonable regulations governing export are clearly permissible. For example, an export permit can be denied if there is a finding that the proposed withdrawal would damage an aquifer or make it unlikely that the domestic needs of the exporting state's citizens could be met.

In states where oil and gas production occurs, farmers and ranchers often lease extraction rights to oil and gas companies. Water management and allocation problems should be *explicitly* covered when negotiating and drafting a lease or contract between the parties. Sun Oil Co. v. Whitaker (Tex. 1972) provides an example of a problem that can arise for agriculture. Under Texas law the oil and gas lessee's estate, not the surface estate, is the dominant estate and has the benefit of an implied grant to withdraw without payment groundwater for use in the oil and gas operation. The court recognized that the ground water was to be used in a secondary recovery process -- the injection in large quantities of water into the oil and gas formation to build pressure to enhance recovery. Under Texas law, the result would not change even if it were shown that irrigated agriculture on the surface estate would have to cease.

Some argue that society will make the most efficient use of water resources if the marketplace governs their use. But an unregulated marketplace might exhaust water resources or render them unfit for human use. Viewing water resources as non-renewable, others argue for prioritized use and quality control. The oil and gas sector deals with a nonrenewable resource, but except for federal petroleum reserve areas, the market determines the rate of depletion. The distinction, arguably, is that alternative energy sources can be developed. As to water, practical, environmental, and legal barriers may not give us the option of moving vast quantities over long distances, e.g. from the Missouri River Basin or the Great Lakes to the High Plains of Texas.

4. Reclamation Projects

The Reclamation Act of 1902 encouraged the settlement and agricultural development of western states. By 1975 the Bureau of Reclamation (Bureau), through contracts with local water or irrigation districts, was delivering 26 million acre-feet of water each year to those states. Of the nine million acres receiving project water, four million received all of their water from project sources. Through the years, federal interest-free loans funded the construction of reclamation projects. The $3.62 billion spent by the Bureau for dam and canal projects is being recovered 56.7% from electricity sales, 40% from general tax revenues, and 3.3% from farmers who receive subsidized water.

Actual supplies come to farmers from irrigation or water districts, organized under state law, that have long term contracts with Bureau projects. For one California irrigation district the rate under its long term water service contract is $3.50 per acre foot. Today, an O & M rate covering the Bureau's operating and maintainance cost would be at least $6.12 per acre foot. The "full cost" rate for O & M plus debt service would be at least $38.45 per acre foot.

Under the 1902 Act the amount of land that could benefit from water from a reclamation project was limited to 160 owned acres per person. To foster the agrarian settlement objective, it was required that the owner reside on or near that land. Through the years, the Bureau did not require water districts to enforce either requirement. In the Reclamation Reform Act of 1982 (RRA) the residency rule was removed. 43 USCA § 390kk.

The basic rule under the 1982 Act is that the price of project water continues as stated in existing contracts. However, water districts were required under the "hammer clause" of RRA to opt for one of two new approaches to distribution of subsidized water and the price to be paid. 43 USCA § 390cc(b). First, existing contracts could be amended to conform to RRA so that subsidized water (O & M rate, but not full cost) could be supplied to 960 acres (whether owned or leased). As to land over 960 acres, full cost would have to be paid by the farmer. Farmers owning lands over 960 acres were required to enter into recordable contracts to sell such land within a set time at a price excluding any value associated with the existence of the reclamation project. The second option was for the water district not to amend its contract, but to limit its delivery of water at the original contract price to farms of 160 owned acres. Water delivered to additional acres would be at full cost. Farmers owning lands in excess of 160 acres were required to enter into recordable contracts to sell -- as above. The full cost aspect of this option kicked in after April 12, 1987. Because the existing contracts of water districts had nine to 15 years left to run, it was argued that the hammer clause violated the due process and takings clauses of the federal Constitution. Both arguments were rejected in Peterson v. U.S. Dept. of the Interior (9th Cir.1990)(retained sovereignty doctrine).

Allocation issues are raised by provisions in the Central Valley Project (CVP) Improvement Act of 1992 requiring CVP to honor obligations under the federal Endangered Species Act and decisions of the California State Water Resources Board. This has resulted in a 50% reduction in water service to agricultural contractors south of the Delta of the Sacramento River. Also, there is a $6 per acre foot surcharge for irrigation water for the Fish, Wildlife & Habitat Restoration Fund. Pending litigation over these changes and charges may turn in part on provisions in existing contracts with the U.S., which have several years to run.

The Bureau of Reclamation has announced that it will no longer build dams to create surface water reservoirs. It is believed that this is based on a determination by the Bureau that it is economically more efficient to mine aquifers.

E. Drainage

1. Generally

In some areas an overabundance of water creates problems for agriculture. Man made drainage allows water to subside in a controlled manner, thus reducing soil erosion and damage to roads, bridges and streams. Drainage removes excess gravitational water that interferes with plant development and opens low-lying field areas to regular production. Drainage systems have been built on 75 to 100 million acres of the nation's finest agricultural lands.

2. Common Law Drainage Principles

Surface water drainage disputes arise from a variety of fact situations. For example, one farmer may dike a field to keep water from accumulating in a low-lying area, thus flooding part of a higher field. Or, a farmer may dig a field ditch and cause surface water to concentrate on a neighbor's land.

In most jurisdictions, courts determine whether the dispute involves surface water in a natural watercourse or diffused surface water. Different rules apply depending on the categorization. Often it is difficult to determine whether water is diffused surface water -- meandering across the surface of the earth as the result of rain or melting snow -- or part of a natural watercourse. During a dry spell when there is no flow, a field inspection may be inconclusive because the watercourse is not deeply etched into the earth. In such cases, aerial photographs obtained from the NRCS or CFSA may reveal the "brightly" traced sediment deposits that highlight natural channels. If a dispute involves a natural watercourse, the common law prohibits the lower owner from blocking the flow. There is a servitude on the lower tract for the benefit of the higher.

If the case involves diffused surface waters, the law varies from jurisdiction to jurisdiction. The common enemy rule of the common law emphasizes the possessor's right to rid his land of surface water at will. This rule, in essence, allows a possessor of land an unrestricted legal privilege to discharge surface water regardless of the harm that such action causes to others. Most courts have qualified this rule to prohibit discharge of large quantities of water onto adjoining land by artificial means in a concentrated flow, except through natural drainways.

The civil law rule imposes liability upon one who interferes with the natural flow of surface water and thus invades another's interest in land. Some states have modified this rule to accommodate artificial changes in the natural flow of surface water if the change is incidental to the normal use and improvement of the land. These changes are most likely to be acceptable when the water empties into an existing natural watercourse.

An increasing number of jurisdictions, disenchanted by the increasing equivocation evident in the above-stated rules, have adopted a rule of reasonableness to give a more flexible approach to diffused surface water drainage problems. Each case is resolved as a question of fact -- i.e. whether the benefit to the actor's land outweighs the harm that results from the alteration of the flow of surface water onto neighboring lands.

Alternatives to litigation are used to resolve drainage disputes. The local NRCS office can provide free technical assistance to develop a plan of field drainage that will help both farms. Although NRCS cannot fund construction, money that the disputants might have spent on litigation can be used for drainage improvements. Care must be taken not to violate wetlands laws. See pp. 405-11 *supra.*

Often a drainage problem cannot be resolved by neighboring farmers because it is part of an areawide problem. In such situations, it was once common to institute drainage proceedings pursuant to a state drainage code.

3. Drainage Codes

State drainage codes authorize proceedings for construction, repair or improvement of agricultural drainage ditches. See, e.g., Mo. Rev. Stat. chs. 242, 243. Such systems may involve several miles of open main ditch and laterals. Ditch proceedings are *in rem* and must be conducted in strict compliance with the code. Benefitted lands are assessed for benefits received. Any taking of land for physical construction will be compensated as in eminent domain, although there will be a set off against benefits to the balance of the tract. Funding for construction typically is by sale of bonds by the ditch district or authority. Bonds are repaid with funds from special assessments against benefitted lands.

Ditch systems require maintenance. Some codes provide for funds from general revenues for minor maintenance such as cutting weeds, removing saplings, and repairing minor washouts. Major repairs are often funded in formal proceedings. Under many codes, a distinction is made between repairs and improvements. Whereas a repair seeks to restore the ditch to its original specifications, subject only to minor resloping of washouts, an improvement contemplates deepening and widening of all or parts of the ditch, installation of larger culverts, and maybe the addition of a lateral over added lands. Improvement proceedings require constitutionally mandated notice and hearing as in original proceedings.

Today, many ditch proceedings are stymied as a result of laws protecting wetlands. See pp. 405-11 *supra.* Systems that have fallen into disrepair tend to be left to deteriorate.

INDEX

Administrative Agencies

Agricultural Stabilization & Conservation Service (ASCS), iii, 8, 10, 32, 34-36, 47, 119, 172, 191-192, 394, 423

Animal and Plant Health Inspection Service (APHIS), 268, 271

Bureau of Reclamation, 3, 420-422

Commodity Futures Trading Commission (CFTC), 146

Consolidated Farm Service Agency (CFSA), iii, 8, 30, 31, 32, 34, 44, 47, 49, 51, 52, 68-73, 75-80, 82-87, 91, 119, 178, 382, 394, 395, 406, 423

Corps of Engineers, U.S. Army (Corps), 407, 408, 409

Employment and Training Administration (ETA), 326, 327

Environmental Protection Agency (EPA), 318, 343-345, 398-399, 400, 401, 402, 403, 404, 408, 409, 411

Farmers Home Administration (FmHA), 36, 44, 49, 51, 52, 68-86, 87, 88, 92, 178-179, 381-382, 395, 406

Federal Crop Insurance Corporation (FCIC), iii, 31, 170

Federal Grain Inspection Service (FGIS), 125

Federal Trade Commission (FTC), 247, 262, 307

Foreign Agricultural Service (FAS), 38

Immigration and Naturalization Service (INS), 338

National Labor Relations Board (NLRB), 314, 315, 346

Natural Resources Conservation Service (NRCS), iii, 24, 31, 389, 390, 392, 393, 394, 407-408, 423, 424

Occupational Safety and Health Administration (OSHA), 331, 339, 340-343, 344

Packers and Stockyards Administration, 246, 250, 251

Patent and Trademark Office (PTO), 2, 272, 273

Rural Housing and Community Development Service (RHCDS), iii, 68

Securities and Exchange Commission (SEC), 296

Soil Conservation Service (SCS), 24, 31, 36, 381, 389, 390, 392-393, 394, 408-409, 423, 424

U.S. Department of Labor (USDOL), 328-329, 331, 334, 339

U.S. Employment Service (USES), 326

U.S. Fish & Wildlife Service (USF&WS), 408

U.S. Forest Service (USFS), 393

Agricultural Acts
Generally, 11-14
Agricultural Act of 1949, 9, 15
Agricultural Adjustment Act of 1933, 7, 8, 40
Agricultural Adjustment Act of 1938, 7, 9, 15
Agricultural Fair Practices Act of 1967, 308
Agricultural Marketing Agreement Act of 1937 (AMAA),
        24-25, 27-28, 308
Cooperative Marketing Act of 1926, 308
Disaster Assistance Act of 1988, 30
Emergency Livestock Feed Assistance Act of 1988, 29
Farmland Protection Policy Act of 1981 (FPPA), 380-381
Farms for the Future Act of 1990, 381
Federal Crop Insurance Reform Act of 1994, 30-31
Food, Agriculture Conservation and Trade Act of 1990 (1990
        farm bill), 9, 15, 16, 21, 23, 24, 29, 37, 38, 383,
        393, 410
Food Security Act of 1985 (1985 farm bill), 9, 15, 16, 21,
        23, 24, 37, 38, 182, 381, 383, 392, 393, 395
Soil Conservation Act of 1935, 389
Soil Conservation and Domestic Allotment Act of 1936, 8,
        389
Soil and Water Resources Conservation Act of 1977 (RCA),
        391, 411

Agricultural Districts
See also **Irrigation**
Brand, 233
Farmland protection, 369-373
Groundwater protection, 404, 418
Natural resource, 418
Property tax relief, 352
Soil conservation, 386-387
Zoning, 361, 362, 365. 404

Aliens
Agricultural Foreign Investment Disclosure Act, 47
Employment of, 329-330, 335-339
Farmland ownership by, 48
USDA programs, eligibility, 48

Bankruptcy
Chapter 12 farm bankruptcies, 52, 86-95
Cooperative members in, 282
Elevators in, 217, 218, 221, 225
FmHA borrowers in, 81, 88, 91-92
Reclamation rights of sellers, 222, 226-227
Rule 3001(g), 127-128
Statutory liens, 103, 203, 224
Statutory trusts for unpaid sellers, 249, 266

Casualty to Crops, 30-31, 75-76, 143-145

Commerce Clause Issues
Animal and Plant Health Inspection Services, 268
Dairy equalization fund, 28-29
Farm products rule, federalized, 183
Hoosac Mills case, 8
U.S. Warehouse Act, 121-122
Water transfers, 418-419
Wickard v. Filburn, 9

Commodity Credit Corporation (CCC)
ASCS, administrative role, 32
Cash payments from as collateral, 171-172
CFSA, administrative role, 32
Commodity inventories held by, 14, 17, 19, 30, 32, 39, 121
Cooperatives and price support loans, 284
Creation of, 9-10
Dairy price support program, 17
Emergency programs, 29-30
Export programs, 38-40
Generic commodity certificates, use of, 19, 170-171, 172-174
National Appeals Division and, iv
Price support loans, 10-11, 12, 15, 17, 20, 22, 53, 121, 128, 133, 170-171, 406
Secured transactions with, 128, 178-179, 191-192
Storage payments, 22, 24

Commodity Futures Contracts, 145-151

Cooperatives
See also **Farm Credit System; Sherman Antitrust Act; Taxation**
Generally, iv, 50, 274-308
Capper Volstead Act, 4, 275, 301-307, 308
Clayton Act, 4, 300-301
Patronage based financing, 278-283
Securities laws, state and federal, 296-299

Corporate Farming, 45-47

Crop Insurance, iii, 30-31

Dairies
Breed associations, 229-232
Cooperatives, 306-307
Cow descriptions, 166
Cow sales, warranties, 236-245
Diseases, control of, 268-271
Exports, promotion, 39
Food assistance, 32
Herd improvement, 274
Herd termination, 24, 30
Indemnity program, federal, 29
Leases of dairy cows, 157
Milk marketing orders, 26-28, 49, 308
Pollution caused by, 398
Price supports, dairy products, 16, 17
Pricing orders, 28-29
Statutory trust for sellers, 228

Disaster Payments, 29-31, 33

Emblements, Doctrine of, 115-116

Employment, Agricultural
Aliens, 329-330, 335-339
Child labor, regulation of, 317-319
EPA, pesticides, 343-345
Exclusions, constitutionality of statutory, 325-326

Employment, Agricultural - Con't
Farm labor contractors, regulation of 327-335
FLSA, wages and hours, 310-317
FUTA, 322-323
Migrant and seasonal workers, protection, 327-335
National Labor Relations Act exclusion, 314-315, 346
OSHA, 339-343
Social Security, 319-322
Unions, state law, 346-349
Wagner-Payser Act (Job Services), 326-327, 334
Workers' compensation, 323-325

Environment, Agriculture and the
   See also **Administrative Agencies,** Environmental
          Protection Agency; **Agricultural Districts;**
          Pesticides; Soil Erosion; Water; Wetlands
CERCLA, 411
Farmland protection, 350-382
Underground storage tanks, 411-412
Water allocation, 412-422
Water quality, control of, 396-405

Equal Protection Challenges
Aliens, restrictions on land ownership, 47-48
Anti-corporate farming laws, 46-47
Brand inspection districts, 233-234
Exemptions, farm labor laws, 325-326
Differential assessment, property taxes, 353
Payment caps, treatment of women, 34
Special use permits, land use, 365-366

Experiment Stations, 3, 50

Farm Credit System
Bailout, federal, 58-59
Bankrupt borrowers, 91-92
Banks for Cooperatives, 283-284
Farm Credit Banks and Associations, 54-68
Federal Agricultural Mortgage Corporation, 60, 62
System generally, 4, 51, 52, 54-55

Farm Programs (USDA)
   Generally, 11-15
   Acreage Reduction Program, 21
   Administrative review, 34-36
   Conservation compliance plans, 23-24, 392-393
   Conservation Reserve Program (CRP), 23, 31, 33, 393-395
   Constitutionality of, 8, 9
   Decentralized administration, 8
   Deficiency payments, 13, 17-20, 31, 33, 406
   False Claims Act, 37
   Farmer-Owned-Reserves, 13, 22
   Federal Claims Court jurisdiction, 36
   Findley Amendment, 19, 33, 37-38
   Generic commodity certificates, 14, 170-174
   Government payments as collateral, 170-174
   Income supports, 13, 17-20, 33, 406
   Loan deficiency payments, 19
   Marketing loans, 17, 33
   Marketing quotas, 22-23
   Paid Land Diversion, 21-22
   Parity, 7, 11, 13
   Payments limitations, 14, 19, 23, 30, 32-36, 44-45, 49
   PIK (1983), 13-14, 172
   Price support loans, nonrecourse, 10-11, 12, 15-17, 33, 128, 133, 191-192, 284, 406
   Price support loans, recourse, 20
   Production controls, 20-23
   Program Fraud Civil Remedies Act of 1986, 37
   Set-aside program, 21
   Target price, see deficiency payments
   Tenants, rights of, 119-120
   Voluntary nature, 8
   0-85 program (feedgrain), 19-20
   50-85 program (upland cotton & rice), 20

Farm Products Rule, 179-191, 205-206

Farm Sales
Conservation contracts, subject to, 394
Development purposes, restraints, 350-382

Farm Sales - Con't
Divestitures, 46, 48
Financing
  Commercial banks, 51, 52
  Consolidated Farm Service Agency, generally, 68-86
  Farm Credit System, generally, 54-68
  Farmers Home Administration, generally, 68-86
  Life insurance companies, 51, 52
  Private parties, 51, 53, 154, 155-157
  State programs, 48-49
Liquidation plans in Chapter 11, 89
Options to purchase, 62-63, 82, 83, 104-105
Reclamation Reform Act of 1982, 421
Union contracts, successorship, 349
Water rights, 414

Farmers Home Administration
  Generally, 44, 49, 51, 52
Bankruptcies, borrowers, 88, 91
Conservation easements, 77, 381, 395
Farmer program loans, 31, 68-71, 156-157, 406
Guaranteed loans, 84-86
National Appeals Staff, 36, 83-84
Preservation loan servicing, 81-83
Primary loan servicing, 71-72, 76-81
Release of normal income security, 73-74

Feedlots
Labor, 316
Nuisance law, 358-360
Operational financing, 159-160, 161, 162, 164-165
Packers and Stockyards Act, 253-254, 256-257
Water quality, 396, 398-399

Field Crop Production & Marketing
  See also **Cooperatives; Farm Programs (USDA);
          Grain Dealers; Warehouses**
Commodity Credit Corporation practices, 191-192
Commodity exchanges, 145-146
Buyers of farm product collateral, 179-191

Field Crop Production & Marketing - Con't
Export programs, 38-40
Forward contracts, 133-145
Futures contracts, 146-148
Grain storage transactions, generally, 121-133, 207-220
Hedging, 148-151
Insolvent grain dealers, 220-228
Lease termination, harvest after, 110-113, 115-117
Marketing contracts, cooperatives, 284-287
Strategies, marketing generally, 133
U.S. Grain Standards Act, 4, 125-126
Warehouse receipts, 194-200, 208-217

Frauds, Statute of
Farm leases, 100-102
Sales by farmers under UCC, 138-143

Fruit & Vegetable Production and Marketing
Agricultural Marketing Agreement Act of 1937, 24-25, 308
Collateral, as, 159
Cooperatives, price setting, bargaining, 305-306
Crop insurance, 31
Cropper, 99
Farm programs, general inapplicability, 7, 16
Labor, generally, 309-349
Marketing contracts, 284-287
Marketing orders, 25, 28, 308
Perishable Agricultural Commodities Act, 4, 37, 251
Pesticides, types, 397
Phytosanitary issues, 4, 42
Statutory trust, 228, 251
Storage, 121
Sunkist, cooperative structure, 302-304

Grain Dealers, 121, 122, 125, 133-145, 220-225

Income Supports
See **Farm Programs (USDA)**

Insolvent Buyers of Farm Products, 220-228

International Agricultural Trade
  Generally, 12-13, 19, 37
Cooperator program, 38
Embargoes, 12-13
Export Enhancement Program (EEP), 38-39
GATT, 40-42
GSM programs, Foreign Agricultural Service, 39-40
Market Promotion Program (MPP), 38
Marketing loan program, 17, 38
NAFTA, 42
Public Law 480, 12, 40
Quotas, 40
Section 22 cases, 40
U.S./Canada Free Trade Agreement, 42
Uruguay Round agreement, 41-42

Irrigation
Districts, 54, 418, 420
Employment in, 313-314, 316
Oil and gas production, conflicts with, 419
Priorities, groundwater, 414-418, 419
Priorities, rivers and streams, 413-414
Reclamation projects, 3, 44, 49, 420-422
Return flows, 399, 400
Water quality generally, 396-405
Water transfers, 418-419, 419-410

Land Grant Colleges, 2

Leases
Alien parties, restrictions, 47-48
Corporate parties, restrictions, 45-47
Cropper contracts distinguished, 98-99
Custom farming contracts distinguished, 98-99
Farm equipment, leases of, 157-158
Farmland, generally, 96-120
Leasebacks from FCS institutions, 63
Leasebacks from FmHA, 82-83
Lien for rent, farm landlord, 103, 203-206
Livestock, leases of, 157-158

Leases - Con't
Pastures, 109
Reclamation reform and, 421
Soil erosion and, 383
Tenants' farm program rights, 119-120

Livestock Production and Marketing
  See also **Dairies; Feedlots; Poultry Production**
Bankruptcy financing, 94
Branding law, 167, 232-236
Breed associations, 229-232
Child labor in, 317
Collateral, animals as, 158-159, 160, 161, 162, 163, 164-
        165, 166-167, 185, 194
Disease control, 4, 268-272
Emergency feed programs, 29-30
Farm programs, few applicable, 7, 9, 16, 24, 29-30
FLSA, 313, 316
Grazing, 14, 21, 393
Leasing animals, 157-158
Meat imports, 40
Nuisances, 356, 357
Packers and Stockyards Act, 37, 245-261
Pasture leases, 109
Patents, animal, 272-273
Pollution caused by, 398-399, 400
Sales of, 235-236, 236-245
Unpaid sellers of, 225-228, 249-252
Vertical integration of, 45
Warranties, live animal sales, 236-245

Marketing Orders
See **Dairies; Fruit & Vegetable Production**

Payment Limitations, 14, 19, 23, 30, 32-36, 49

Pesticides
Dairy indemnity program, 29
Farmworker exposure, 318-319, 342-343, 343-345, 349
Federal Insecticide, Fungicide and Rodenticide Act (FIFRA),
        401, 404

Pesticides - Con't
Integrated pest management, 403
Labeling of containers, 342, 344-345
Lease provisions on use, 102
Nuisances, 356, 359-360
Proposition 65, 405
Water quality, 396-397, 400-405

Poultry Production
Collateral, poultry as, 162, 165-166
Disease control, 268-272
Farm programs, few applicable, 16
FLSA, 313, 314-315
OSHA, 340-341
Packers and Stockyards Act, 261-268
Pollution caused by, 398, 400
Poultry Producers Financial Protection act of 1987, 261-262
Unpaid sellers of, 225, 228, 266-267
Vertical integration of, 43, 45, 304-305, 314-315, 340-341

Price Supports
See **Commodity Credit Corporation; Farm
         Programs (USDA)**

Railroads, 2, 219

Reclamation Law, 3, 44, 49, 420-422

Regulatory Takings, Allegations of
Alluvial valley floor, 395-396
Diseased animals, destruction, 270
Erosion control measures, 388-389
FCS institution stock, 58-59
Groundwater, 417-418
Healthy animals, destruction, 271-272
Reclamation "hammer" clause, 421-422
Transferable development rights, 376-377
Wetlands and beachfronts, 366-368, 409-410
Zoning exactions, 364-365
Zoning, generally, 365

Right-to-Farm Laws, 356-360

Sherman Antitrust Act, 231-232, 246, 299, 306, 307

Secured Transactions
  Generally, 152-206
Collateral descriptions, 165-170
Farm products vs. inventory, as collateral, 158-163, 165
Farm products rule, federal, 179-191, 205-206
Farm program payments, as collateral, 170-174, 177
Farmer as a merchant, 138-143
Federal agency lenders, 178-179
Filing, for perfection, 174-175, 177
Filing, under farm products rule, 187-191
Liens, statutory and common law and, 201-206
Priorities under Article 9, 177-200
Proceeds, assignment of, 200-201
Production money security interests, 192-194
Warehouse receipts, as collateral, 176, 194-200

Soil Erosion
Agricultural Conservation Program, 389-390
Best management practices, 400-401, 404
Conservation compliance planning, 23-24, 36, 392-393
Conservation Operations Program, 389
Conservation Reserve Program, 23, 36, 172, 390, 393-395
Conserving uses, farm programs and, 14, 21
Covenant of good husbandry, 113, 385-386
Defined, 384
Depression era legislation, 8-9, 389-390
Emergency Conservation Program, 390
Farmland preservation districts, 372, 386
FmHA conservation easements, 77, 381, 395
Great Plains Conservation Program, 390
Natural Resources Conservation Service, iii, 24, 31, 389,
        390, 392, 393, 394, 407-408, 423, 424
Problem of, 7, 383-384, 390-391
Sodbuster 24, 36, 392-393
Soil Bank, 12
Soil and Water Resources Conservation Act of 1977 (RCA),
        391-392

Soil Erosion - Con't
State regulation, 386-389
Strip mining, 395-396
Water quality and, 396-405

Target Prices
See **Farm Programs (USDA)**

Taxation
Conservation easement deduction, 377-378, 382
Cooperatives, 277, 287-296
Decedents estates, 118-119, 382
FUTA, 322-323, 336
Grain sales, 136-137
Policy, environment, 382, 391
Real property, ad valorem, 351-354, 370-371
Social Security, 319-322, 336

United States Department of Agriculture
  See also **Farm Programs (USDA); Farmers Home
      Administration; Marketing Orders**
Administrative procedure, 32-37
Creation of, 2
General Counsel, 79, 246
Judicial Officer, 37, 246, 257
National Appeals Division, iii, 36, 70, 83-84

Vertical Integration
Anti-corporate farming statutes, 45
Defined, 43-44
Financing, role of, 54
Poultry industry, 262-267, 304-305, 314-315, 340-341

Warehouses
  See also **Grain Dealers**
Bailees, duty of care, 130-133
Bailor, remedies, 217-220
Bankruptcy of, 218
Conversion of commodities by, 219-220
Cooperatives, 292

Warehouses - Con't
Delivery to storage in, 123-126
Federal regulation of, 3-4, 121-122
Indemnity funds and failed, 218
Insolvencies of, 207-217
Inspectors, 220
OSHA and, 343
Scale tickets issued by, 123, 126-128, 208
State regulation, 3-4, 121-122
Terminal elevators (markets), 147, 148
U.S. Warehouse Act, 4, 122
Warehouse receipts issued by, 128-130, 194-200, 208-217

Water
See also **Irrigation, Reclamation Law, Wetlands**
Allocation, 412-422
Drainage, 422-425
Quality. 396-405

Wetlands
Development of, 366-367
Drainage of, 409, 425
Dredge and fill (§404) permits, 407-410
Emergency Wetlands Reserve Program, 410-411
Migratory waterfowl, 411
Swampbuster, 24, 36, 391, 405-407, 409, 410, 424, 425
Wetlands Reserve Program (WRP), 23, 31, 390, 410-411

Zoning
See also **Regulatory Takings, Allegations of;
Equal Protection Challenges**
Agricultural, 360-369, 372, 375-376
Groundwater protection, 404